X-TREME X-MEN

SCHISM

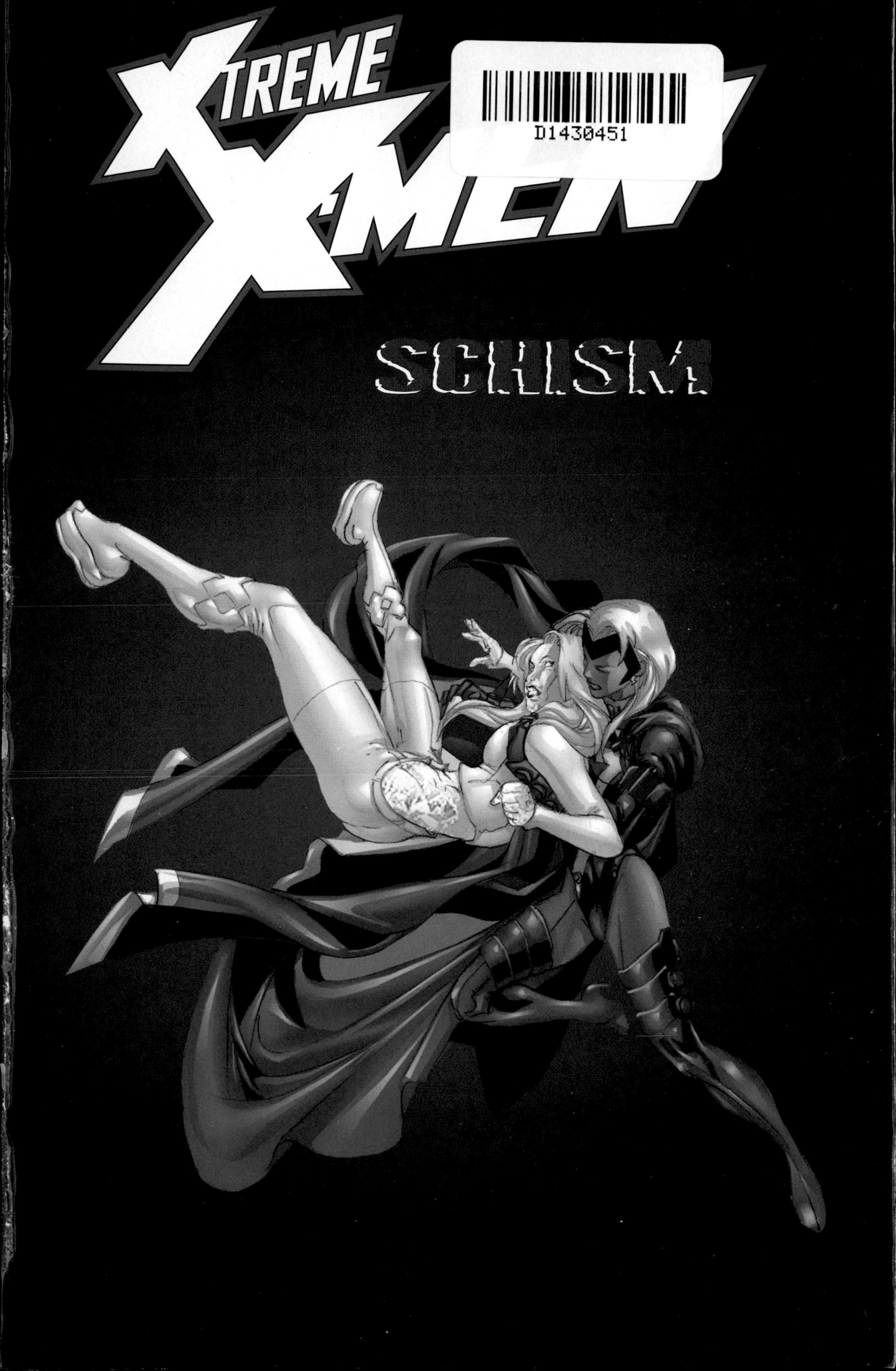

X-TREME X-MEN

SCHISM

Writer:
Chris Claremont

Artists:
Salvador Larroca and Arthur Ranson

Cover Art:
Rodolfo Migliari

Colors:
Liquid! Graphics

Letters:
Tom Orzechowski

Assistant Editors:
Lynne Yoshii and Nova Ren Suma

Editors:
Andrew Lis and Mike Raicht

Editor in Chief:
Joe Quesada

President:
Bill Jemas

X-TREME X-MEN VOL. 3: SCHISM. Contains material originally published in magazine form as X-TREME X-MEN #19-23, and X-TREME X-MEN: X-POSE #1 and #2. First printing 2003. ISBN# 0-7851-1084-4. Published by MARVEL COMICS, a division of MARVEL ENTERTAINMENT GROUP, INC. OFFICE OF PUBLICATION: 10 East 40th Street, New York, NY 10016. Copyright © 2002 and 2003 Marvel Characters, Inc. All rights reserved. $16.99 per copy in the U.S. and $27.25 in Canada (GST #R127032852); Canadian Agreement #40668537. All characters featured in this issue and the distinctive names and likenesses thereof, and all related indicia are trademarks of Marvel Characters, Inc. No similarity between any of the names, characters, persons, and/or institutions in this magazine with those of any living or dead person or institution is intended, and any such similarity which may exist is purely coincidental. **Printed in the U.S.A.** STAN LEE, Chairman Emeritus. For information regarding advertising in Marvel Comics or on Marvel.com, please contact Russell Brown, Executive Vice President, Consumer Products, Promotions and Media Sales at 212-576-8561 or rbrown@marvel.com

10 9 8 7 6 5 4 3 2 1

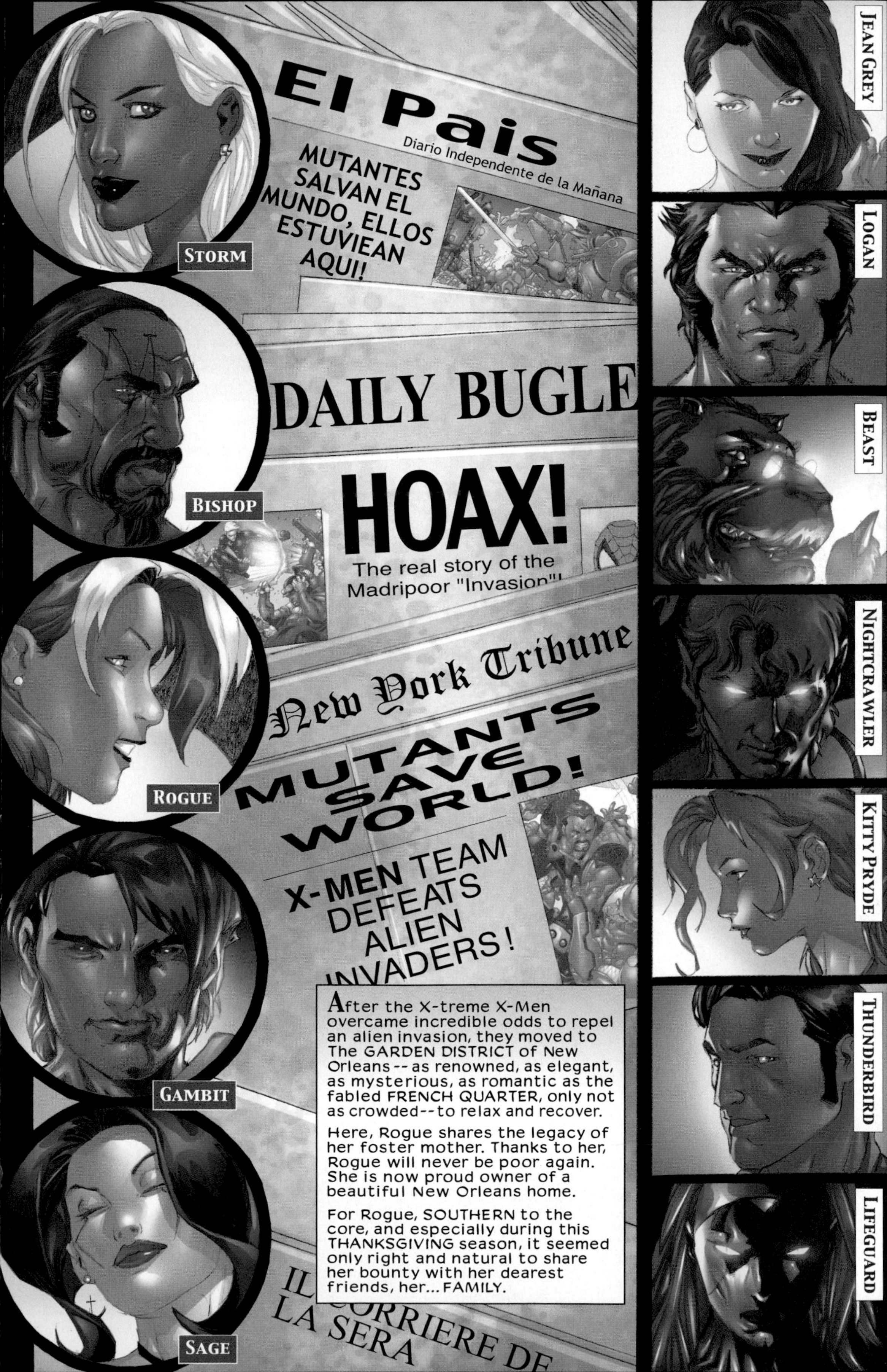

El Pais
Diario Independente de la Mañana
MUTANTES SALVAN EL MUNDO, ELLOS ESTUVIEAN AQUI!
STORM
DAILY BUGLE
HOAX!
The real story of the Madripoor "Invasion"!
BISHOP
New York Tribune
MUTANTS SAVE WORLD!
ROGUE
X-MEN TEAM DEFEATS ALIEN INVADERS!
GAMBIT
After the X-treme X-Men overcame incredible odds to repel an alien invasion, they moved to The GARDEN DISTRICT of New Orleans -- as renowned, as elegant, as mysterious, as romantic as the fabled FRENCH QUARTER, only not as crowded--to relax and recover.
Here, Rogue shares the legacy of her foster mother. Thanks to her, Rogue will never be poor again. She is now proud owner of a beautiful New Orleans home.
For Rogue, SOUTHERN to the core, and especially during this THANKSGIVING season, it seemed only right and natural to share her bounty with her dearest friends, her... FAMILY.
IL CORRIERE DE LA SERA
SAGE
JEAN GREY
LOGAN
BEAST
NIGHTCRAWLER
KITTY PRYDE
THUNDERBIRD
LIFEGUARD

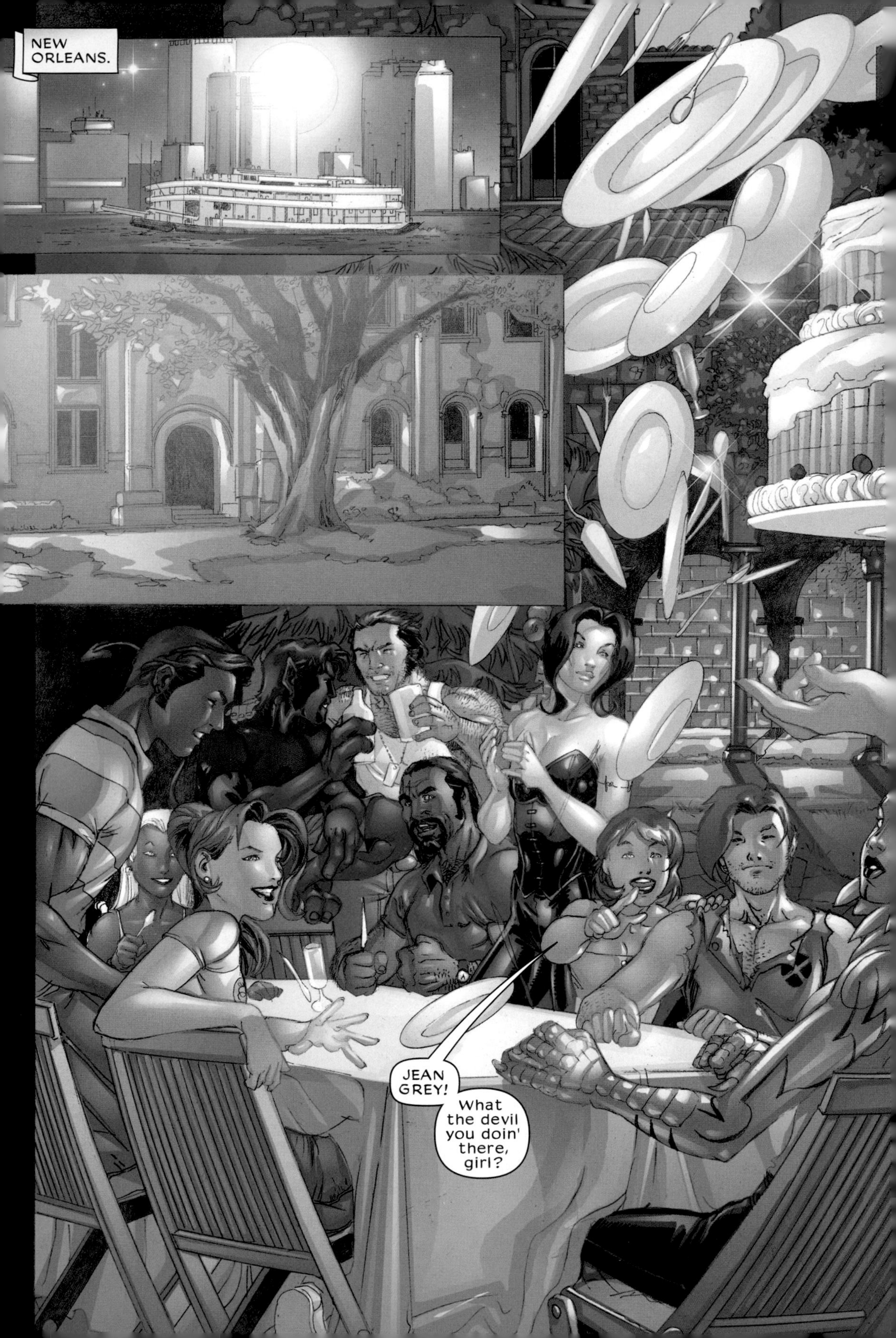
NEW ORLEANS.
JEAN GREY!
What the devil you doin' there, girl?

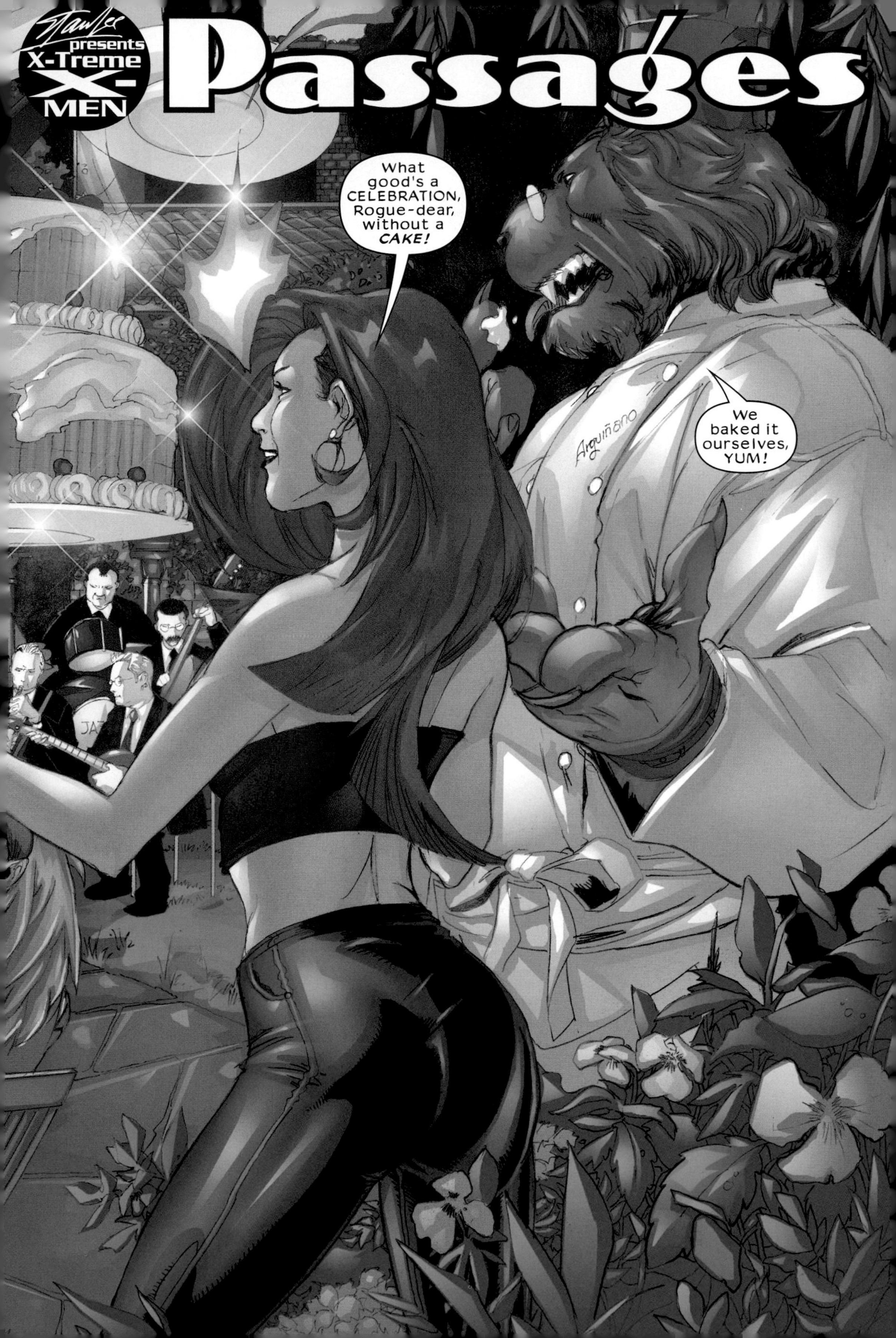
Stan Lee presents X-Treme X-Men
Passages
What good's a CELEBRATION, Rogue-dear, without a CAKE!
We baked it ourselves, YUM!
Arguiñano

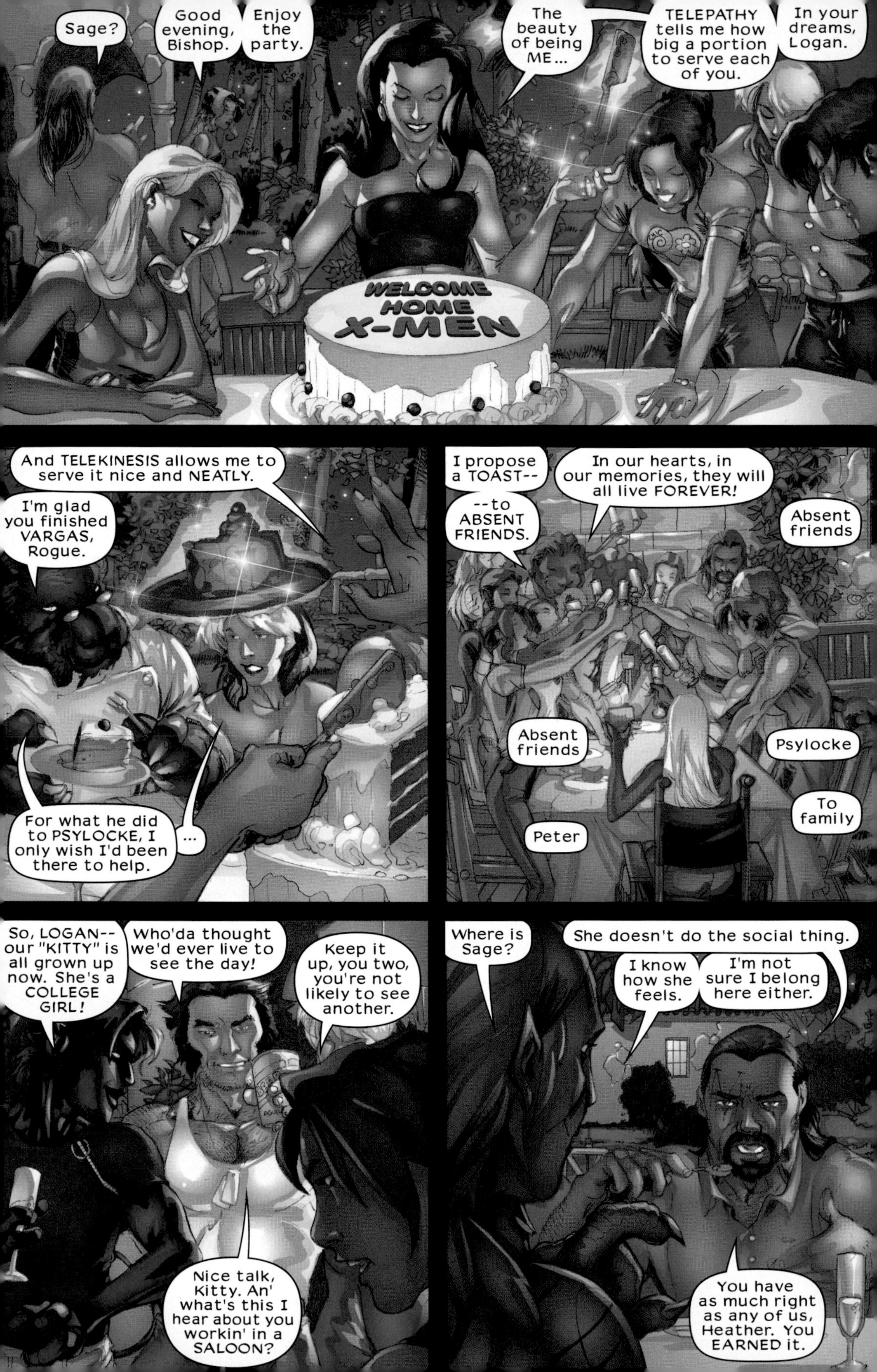
Sage?
Good evening, Bishop.
Enjoy the party.
The beauty of being ME...
TELEPATHY tells me how big a portion to serve each of you.
In your dreams, Logan.
WELCOME HOME X-MEN
And TELEKINESIS allows me to serve it nice and NEATLY.
I'm glad you finished VARGAS, Rogue.
For what he did to PSYLOCKE, I only wish I'd been there to help.
...
I propose a TOAST--
--to ABSENT FRIENDS.
In our hearts, in our memories, they will all live FOREVER!
Absent friends
Absent friends
Psylocke
To family
Peter
So, LOGAN-- our "KITTY" is all grown up now. She's a COLLEGE GIRL!
Who'da thought we'd ever live to see the day!
Keep it up, you two, you're not likely to see another.
Nice talk, Kitty. An' what's this I hear about you workin' in a SALOON?
Where is Sage?
She doesn't do the social thing.
I know how she feels.
I'm not sure I belong here either.
You have as much right as any of us, Heather. You EARNED it.

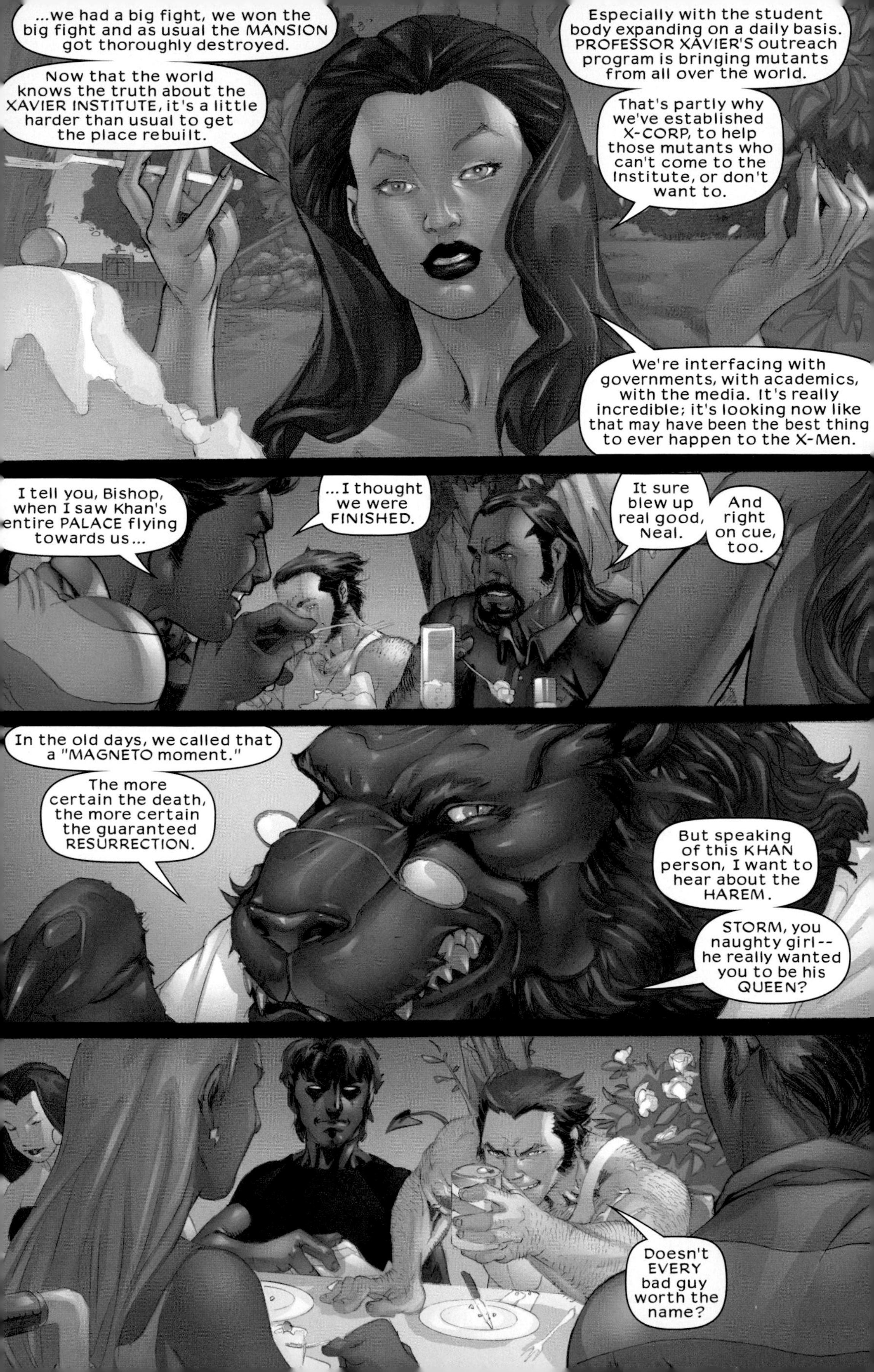
...we had a big fight, we won the big fight and as usual the MANSION got thoroughly destroyed.
Now that the world knows the truth about the XAVIER INSTITUTE, it's a little harder than usual to get the place rebuilt.
Especially with the student body expanding on a daily basis. PROFESSOR XAVIER'S outreach program is bringing mutants from all over the world.
That's partly why we've established X-CORP, to help those mutants who can't come to the Institute, or don't want to.
We're interfacing with governments, with academics, with the media. It's really incredible; it's looking now like that may have been the best thing to ever happen to the X-Men.
I tell you, Bishop, when I saw Khan's entire PALACE flying towards us...
...I thought we were FINISHED.
It sure blew up real good, Neal.
And right on cue, too.
In the old days, we called that a "MAGNETO moment."
The more certain the death, the more certain the guaranteed RESURRECTION.
But speaking of this KHAN person, I want to hear about the HAREM.
STORM, you naughty girl-- he really wanted you to be his QUEEN?
Doesn't EVERY bad guy worth the name?

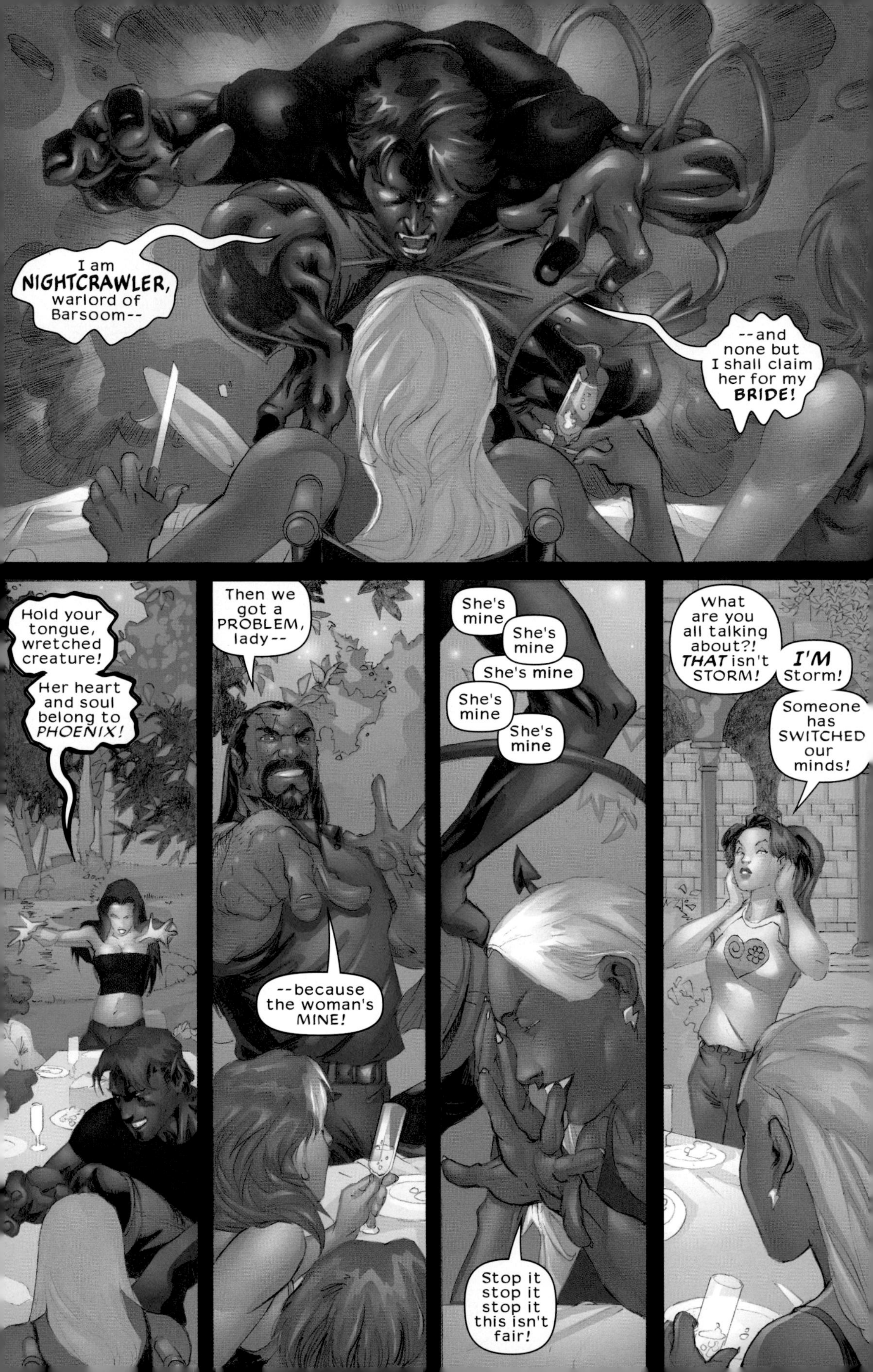
I am NIGHTCRAWLER, warlord of Barsoom--
--and none but I shall claim her for my BRIDE!
Hold your tongue, wretched creature!
Her heart and soul belong to PHOENIX!
Then we got a PROBLEM, lady--
--because the woman's MINE!
She's mine
She's mine
She's mine
She's mine
She's mine
Stop it stop it stop it this isn't fair!
What are you all talking about?! THAT isn't STORM!
I'M Storm!
Someone has SWITCHED our minds!

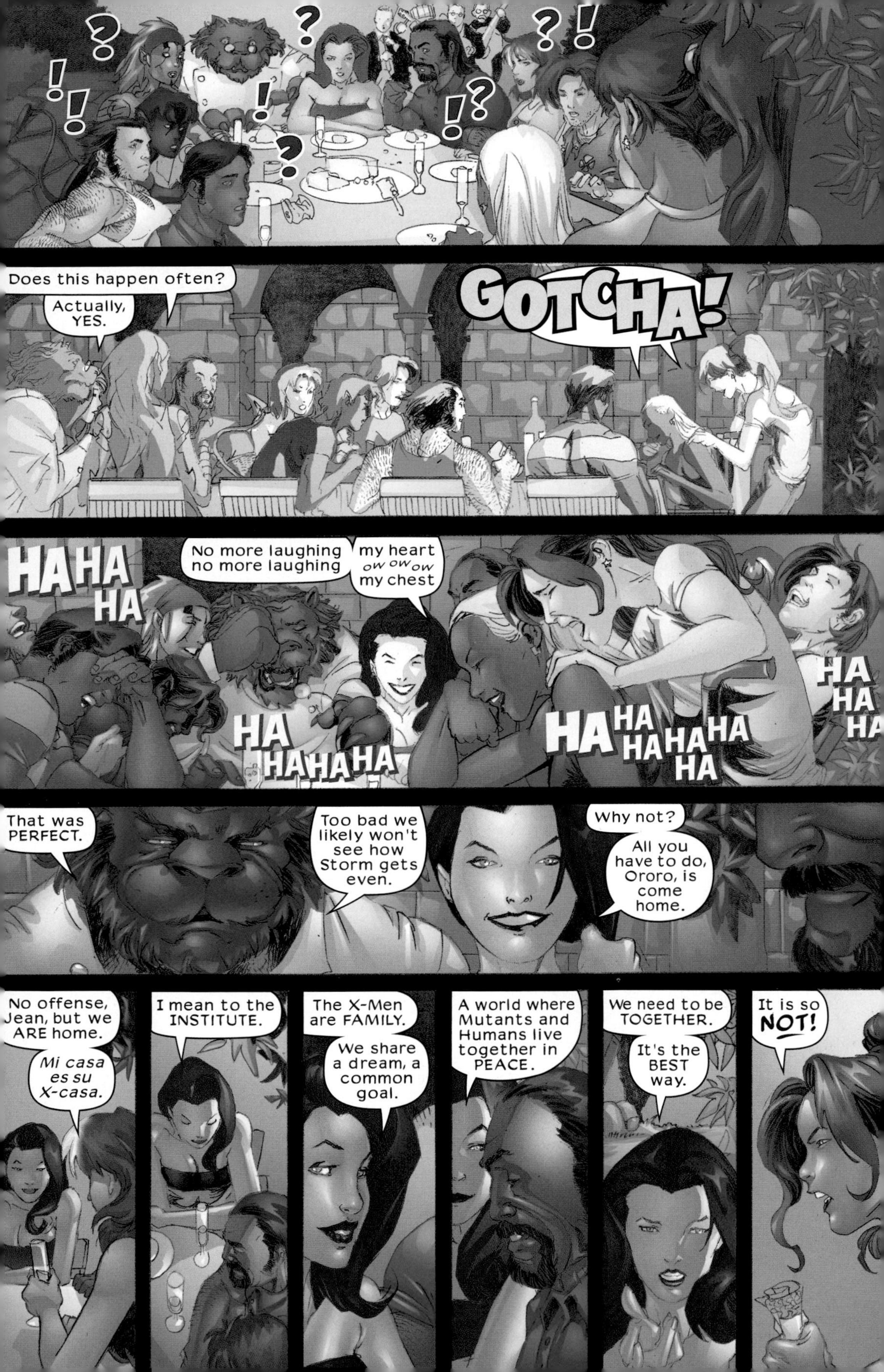
?
?
!
!
?
!
?!
!
?
!?
Does this happen often?
Actually, YES.
GOTCHA!
HAHA HA
No more laughing no more laughing
my heart ow ow ow my chest
HA HAHAHAHA
HA HA HA HAHA HA
HA HA HA
That was PERFECT.
Too bad we likely won't see how Storm gets even.
Why not?
All you have to do, Ororo, is come home.
No offense, Jean, but we ARE home.
Mi casa es su X-casa.
I mean to the INSTITUTE.
The X-Men are FAMILY.
We share a dream, a common goal.
A world where Mutants and Humans live together in PEACE.
We need to be TOGETHER.
It's the BEST way.
It is so NOT!

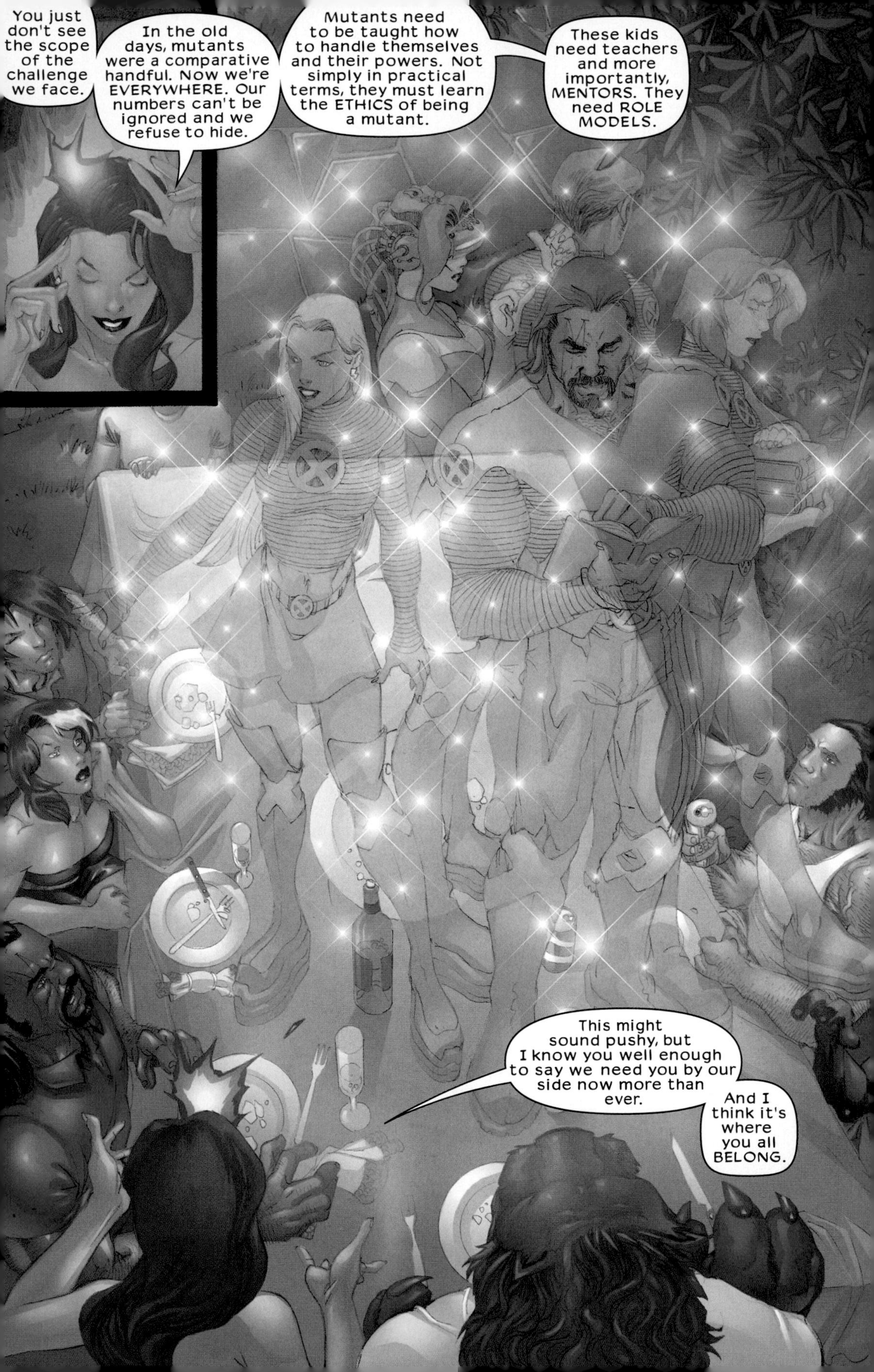
You just don't see the scope of the challenge we face.
In the old days, mutants were a comparative handful. Now we're EVERYWHERE. Our numbers can't be ignored and we refuse to hide.
Mutants need to be taught how to handle themselves and their powers. Not simply in practical terms, they must learn the ETHICS of being a mutant.
These kids need teachers and more importantly, MENTORS. They need ROLE MODELS.
This might sound pushy, but I know you well enough to say we need you by our side now more than ever.
And I think it's where you all BELONG.

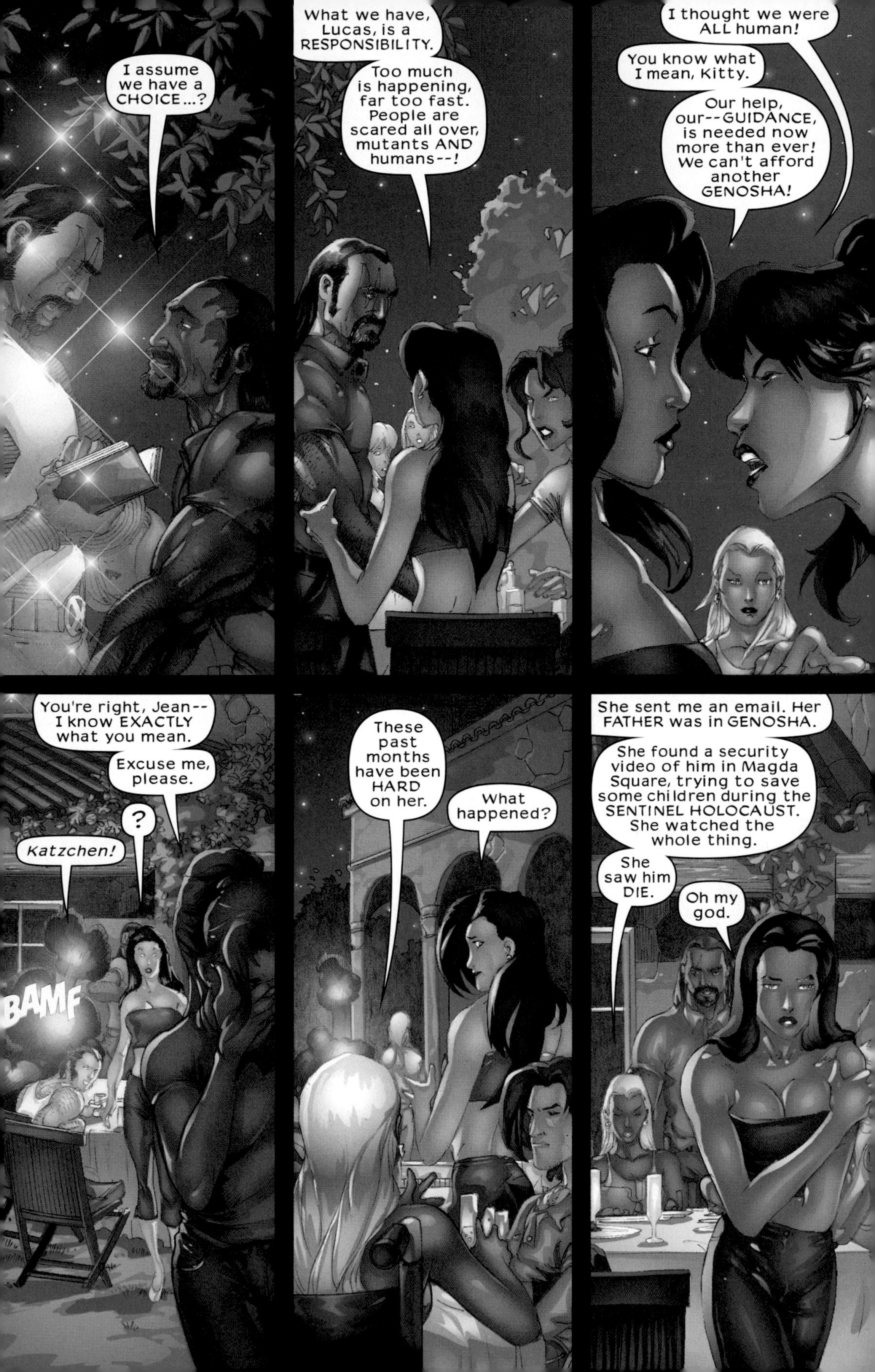
I assume we have a CHOICE...?
What we have, Lucas, is a RESPONSIBILITY.
Too much is happening, far too fast. People are scared all over, mutants AND humans--!
I thought we were ALL human!
You know what I mean, Kitty.
Our help, our--GUIDANCE, is needed now more than ever! We can't afford another GENOSHA!
You're right, Jean-- I know EXACTLY what you mean.
Excuse me, please.
?
Katzchen!
BAMF
These past months have been HARD on her.
What happened?
She sent me an email. Her FATHER was in GENOSHA.
She found a security video of him in Magda Square, trying to save some children during the SENTINEL HOLOCAUST. She watched the whole thing.
She saw him DIE.
Oh my god.

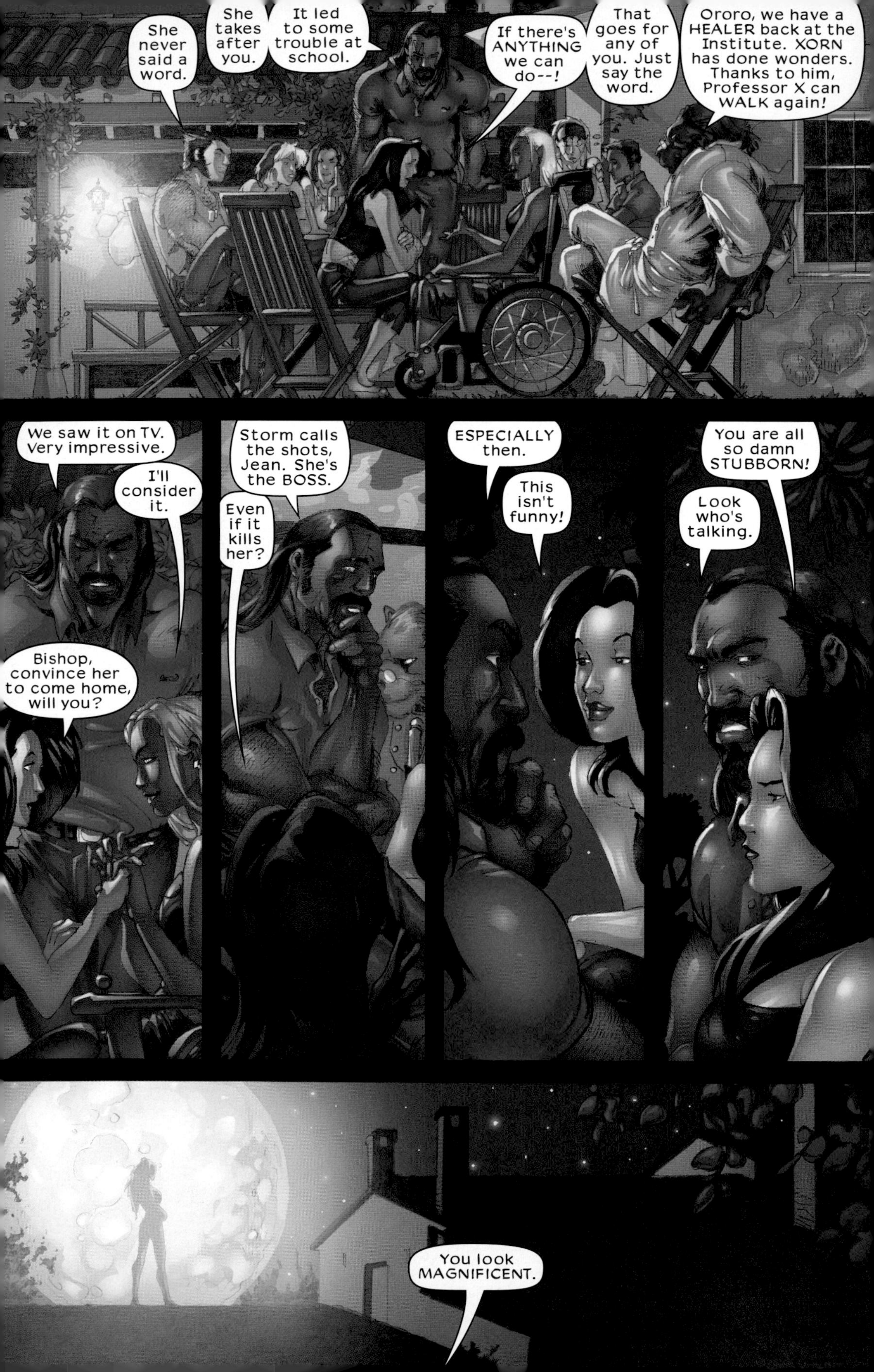
She never said a word.
She takes after you.
It led to some trouble at school.
If there's ANYTHING we can do--!
That goes for any of you. Just say the word.
Ororo, we have a HEALER back at the Institute. XORN has done wonders. Thanks to him, Professor X can WALK again!
We saw it on TV. Very impressive.
I'll consider it.
Bishop, convince her to come home, will you?
Storm calls the shots, Jean. She's the BOSS.
Even if it kills her?
ESPECIALLY then.
This isn't funny!
You are all so damn STUBBORN!
Look who's talking.
You look MAGNIFICENT.

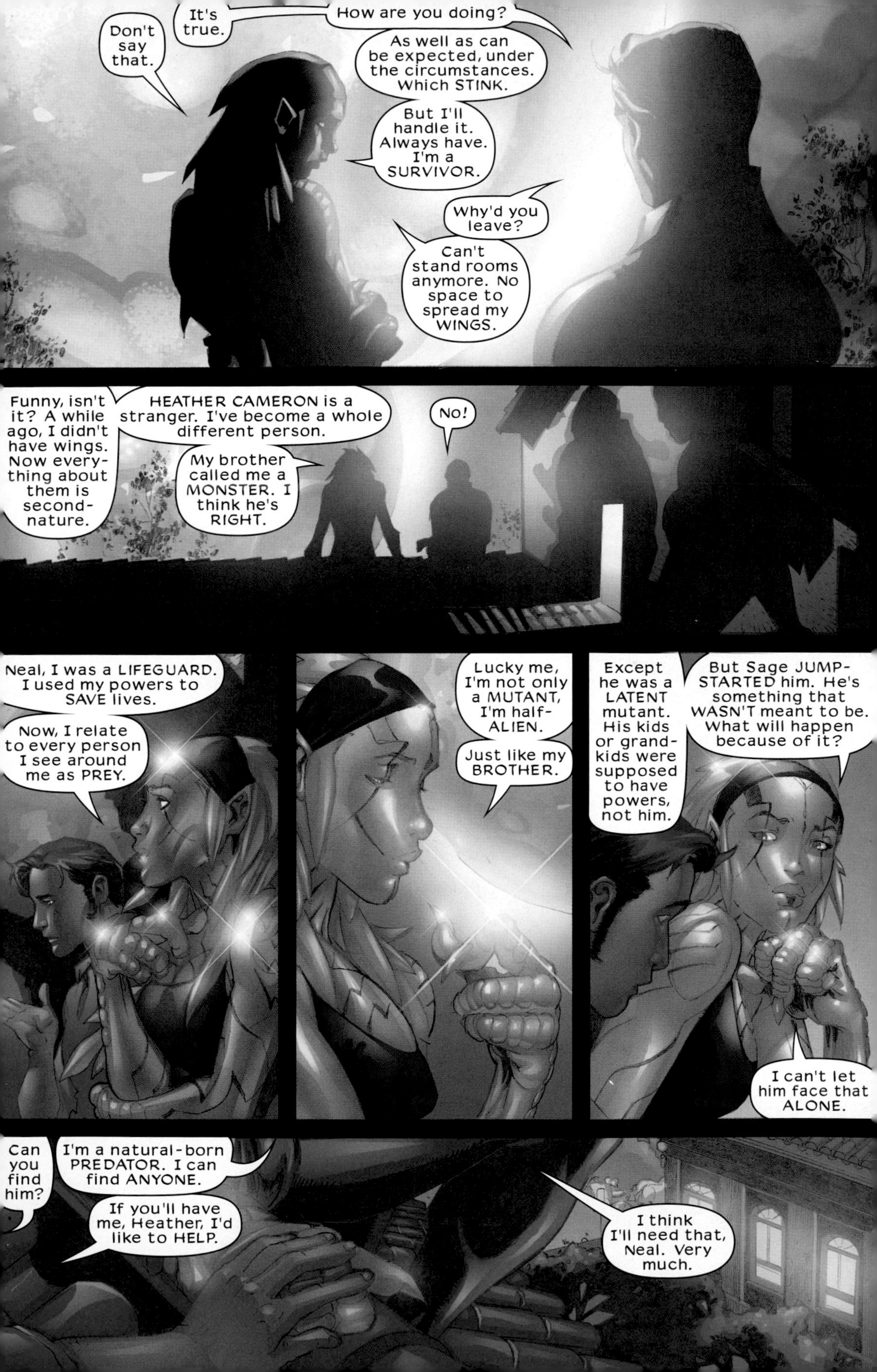
Don't say that.
It's true.
How are you doing?
As well as can be expected, under the circumstances. Which STINK.
But I'll handle it. Always have. I'm a SURVIVOR.
Why'd you leave?
Can't stand rooms anymore. No space to spread my WINGS.
Funny, isn't it? A while ago, I didn't have wings. Now everything about them is second-nature.
HEATHER CAMERON is a stranger. I've become a whole different person.
No!
My brother called me a MONSTER. I think he's RIGHT.
Neal, I was a LIFEGUARD. I used my powers to SAVE lives.
Now, I relate to every person I see around me as PREY.
Lucky me, I'm not only a MUTANT, I'm half-ALIEN.
Just like my BROTHER.
Except he was a LATENT mutant. His kids or grand-kids were supposed to have powers, not him.
But Sage JUMP-STARTED him. He's something that WASN'T meant to be. What will happen because of it?
I can't let him face that ALONE.
Can you find him?
I'm a natural-born PREDATOR. I can find ANYONE.
If you'll have me, Heather, I'd like to HELP.
I think I'll need that, Neal. Very much.

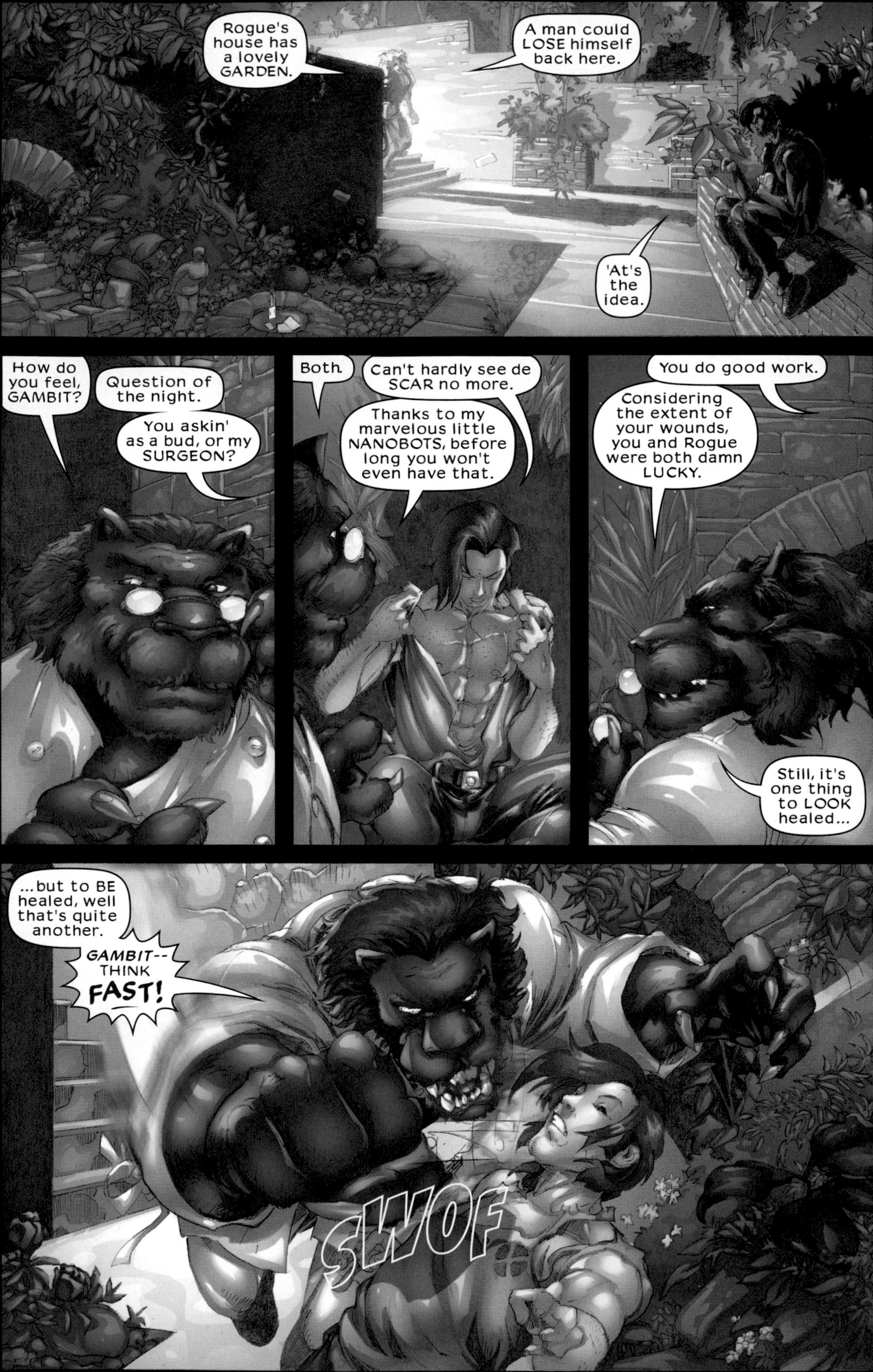

Rogue's house has a lovely GARDEN.
A man could LOSE himself back here.
'At's the idea.
How do you feel, GAMBIT?
Question of the night.
You askin' as a bud, or my SURGEON?
Both.
Can't hardly see de SCAR no more.
Thanks to my marvelous little NANOBOTS, before long you won't even have that.
You do good work.
Considering the extent of your wounds, you and Rogue were both damn LUCKY.
Still, it's one thing to LOOK healed...
...but to BE healed, well that's quite another.
GAMBIT-- THINK FAST!
SWOF

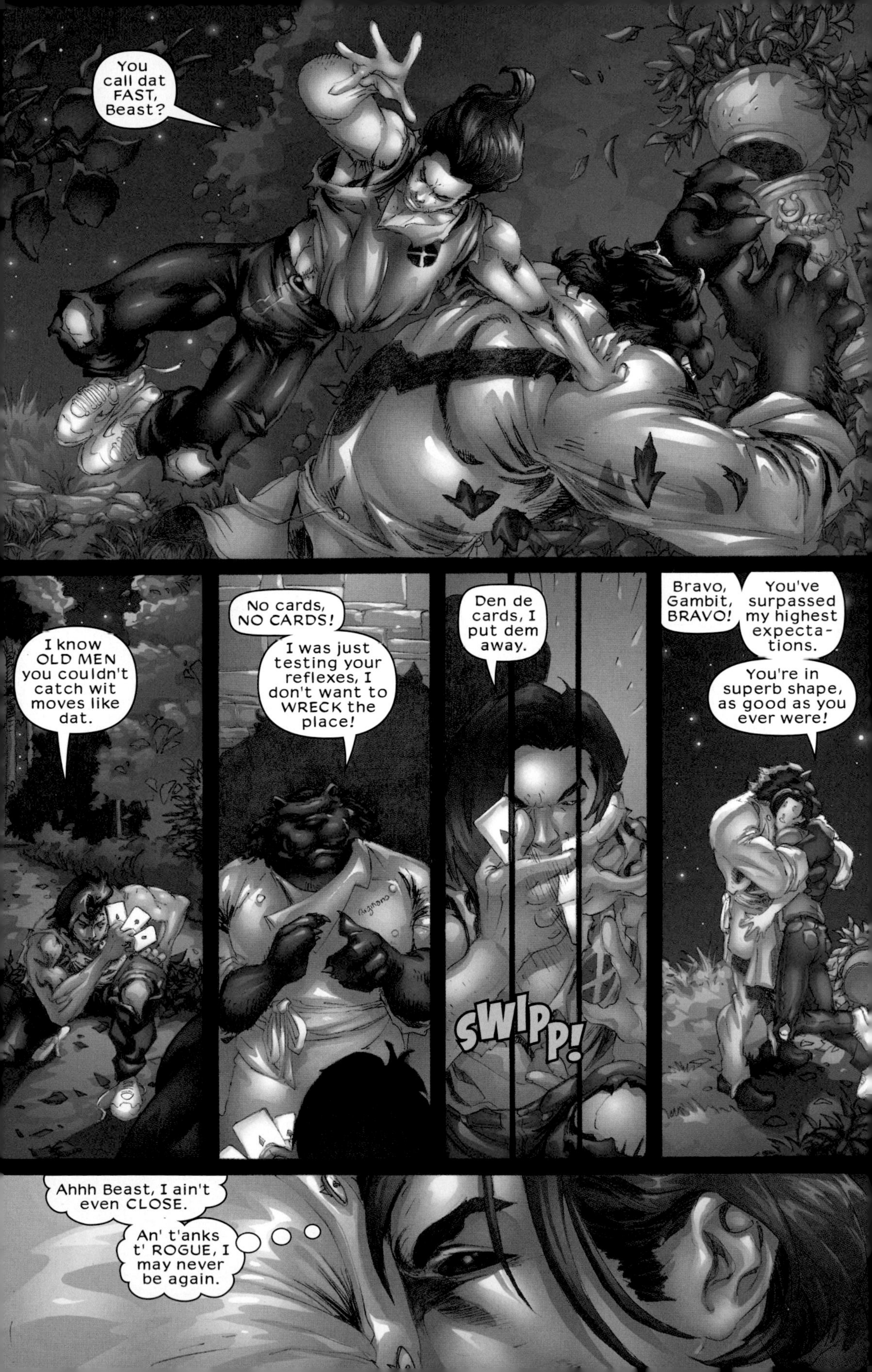

You call dat FAST, Beast?
I know OLD MEN you couldn't catch wit moves like dat.
No cards, NO CARDS!
I was just testing your reflexes, I don't want to WRECK the place!
Den de cards, I put dem away.
SWIPP!
Bravo, Gambit, BRAVO!
You've surpassed my highest expecta-tions.
You're in superb shape, as good as you ever were!
Ahhh Beast, I ain't even CLOSE.
An' t'anks t' ROGUE, I may never be again.

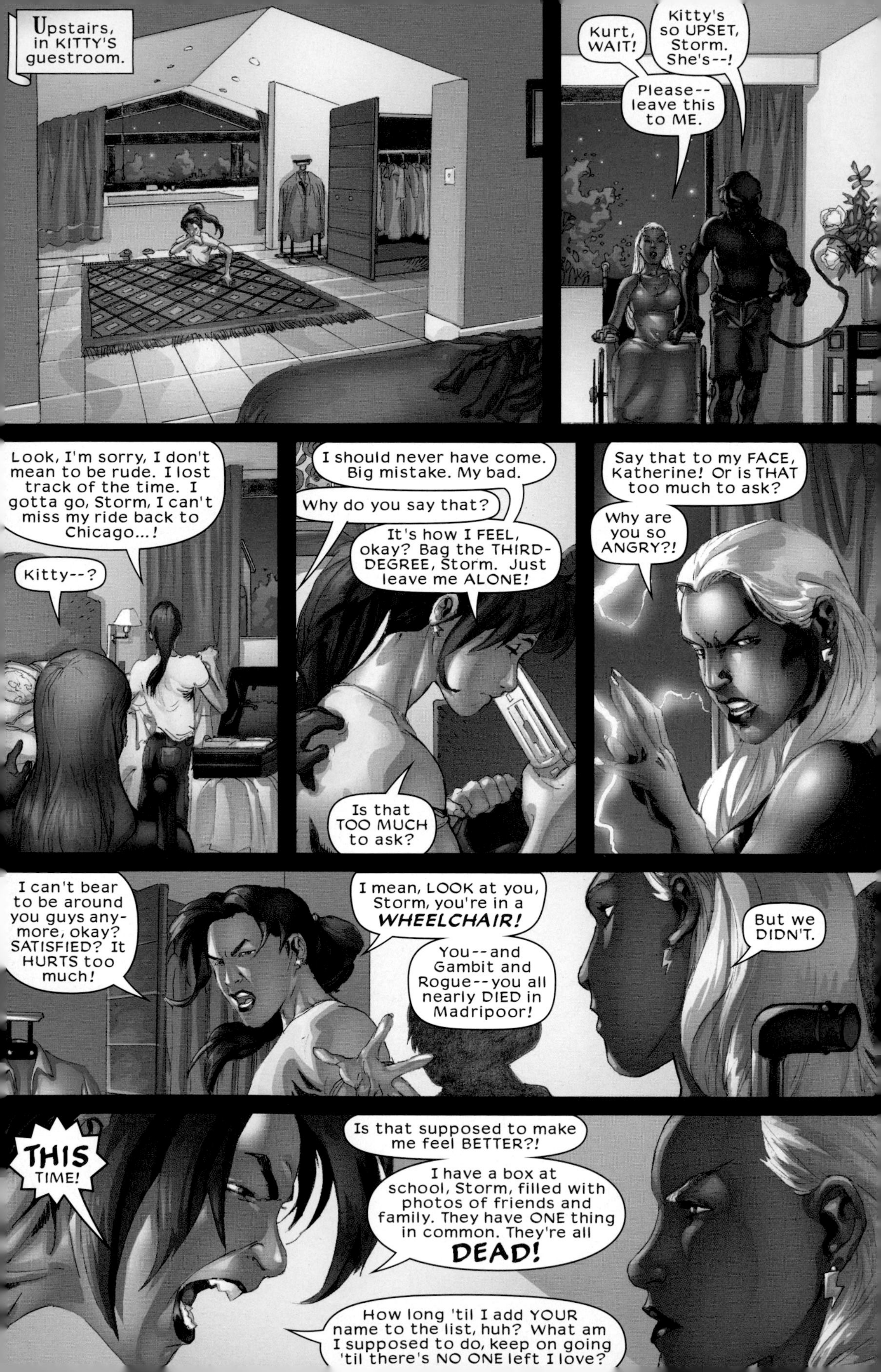

Upstairs, in KITTY'S guestroom.
Kurt, WAIT!
Kitty's so UPSET, Storm. She's--!
Please--leave this to ME.
Look, I'm sorry, I don't mean to be rude. I lost track of the time. I gotta go, Storm, I can't miss my ride back to Chicago...!
Kitty--?
I should never have come. Big mistake. My bad.
Why do you say that?
It's how I FEEL, okay? Bag the THIRD-DEGREE, Storm. Just leave me ALONE!
Is that TOO MUCH to ask?
Say that to my FACE, Katherine! Or is THAT too much to ask?
Why are you so ANGRY?!
I can't bear to be around you guys any-more, okay? SATISFIED? It HURTS too much!
I mean, LOOK at you, Storm, you're in a WHEELCHAIR!
You--and Gambit and Rogue--you all nearly DIED in Madripoor!
But we DIDN'T.
THIS TIME!
Is that supposed to make me feel BETTER?!
I have a box at school, Storm, filled with photos of friends and family. They have ONE thing in common. They're all DEAD!
How long 'til I add YOUR name to the list, huh? What am I supposed to do, keep on going 'til there's NO ONE left I love?

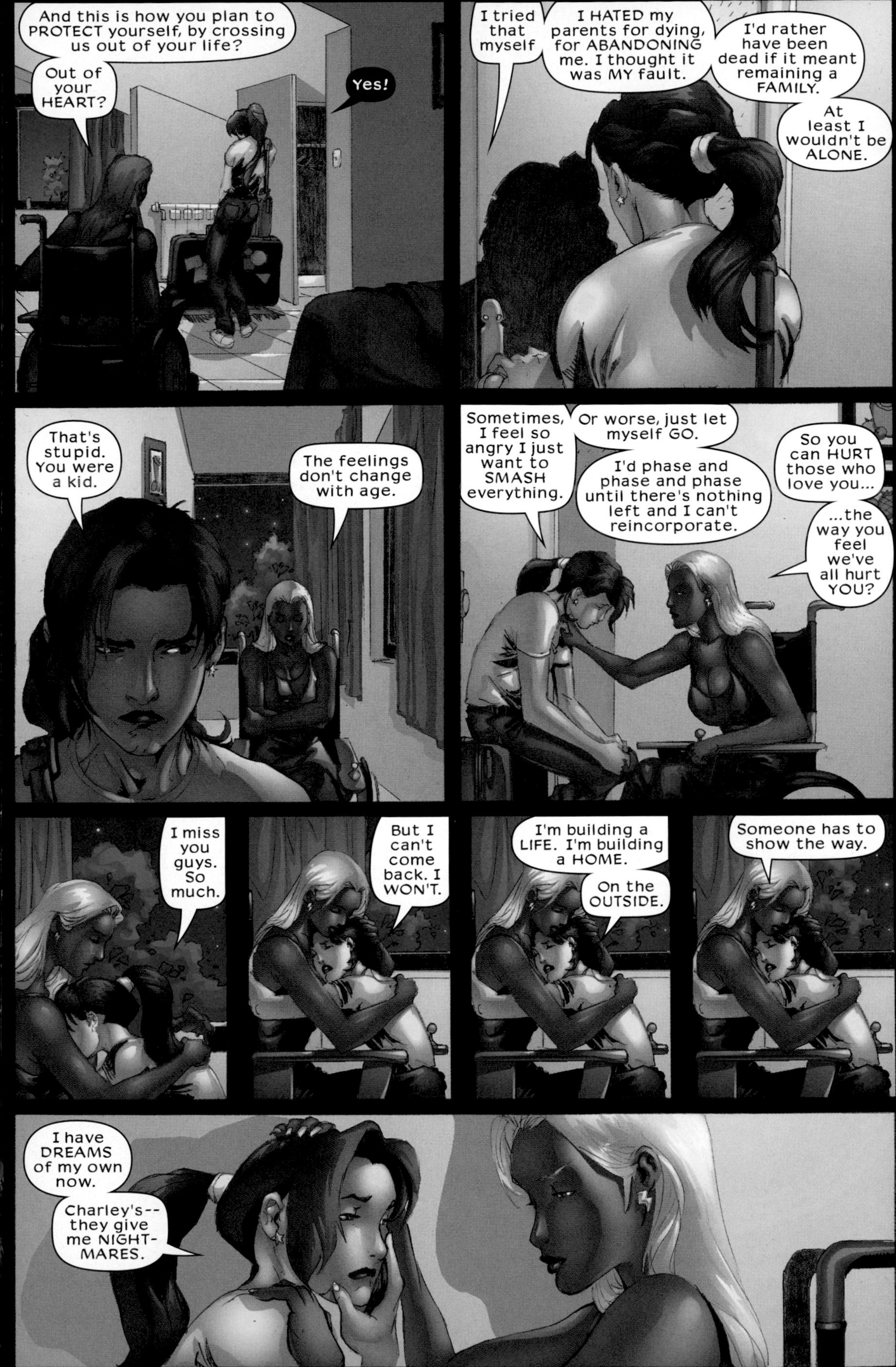
And this is how you plan to PROTECT yourself, by crossing us out of your life?
Out of your HEART?
Yes!
I tried that myself
I HATED my parents for dying, for ABANDONING me. I thought it was MY fault.
I'd rather have been dead if it meant remaining a FAMILY.
At least I wouldn't be ALONE.
That's stupid. You were a kid.
The feelings don't change with age.
Sometimes, I feel so angry I just want to SMASH everything.
Or worse, just let myself GO.
I'd phase and phase and phase until there's nothing left and I can't reincorporate.
So you can HURT those who love you...
...the way you feel we've all hurt YOU?
I miss you guys. So much.
But I can't come back. I WON'T.
I'm building a LIFE. I'm building a HOME.
On the OUTSIDE.
Someone has to show the way.
I have DREAMS of my own now.
Charley's-- they give me NIGHT-MARES.

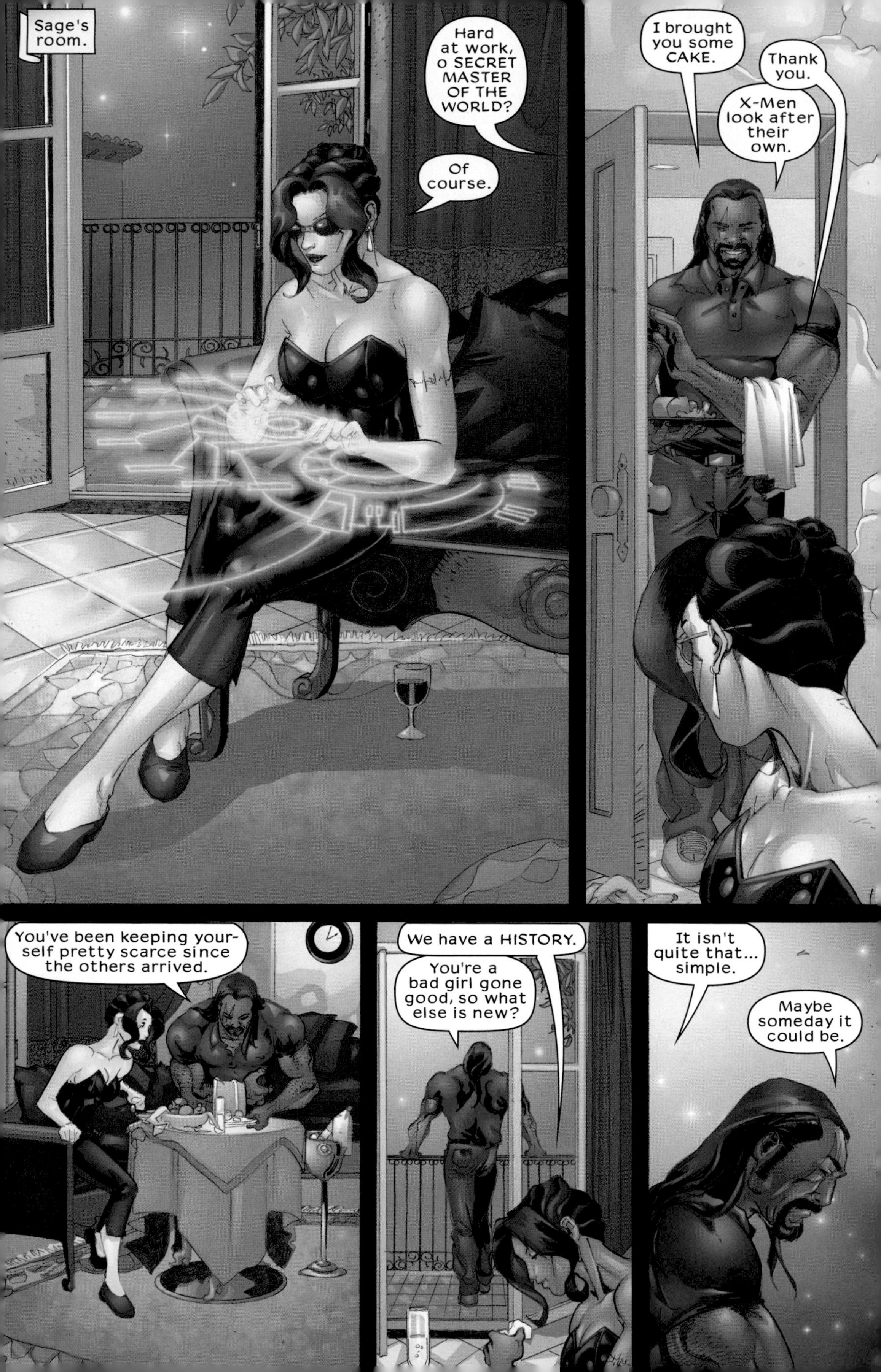
Sage's room.
Hard at work, o SECRET MASTER OF THE WORLD?
Of course.
I brought you some CAKE.
Thank you.
X-Men look after their own.
You've been keeping yourself pretty scarce since the others arrived.
We have a HISTORY.
You're a bad girl gone good, so what else is new?
It isn't quite that... simple.
Maybe someday it could be.

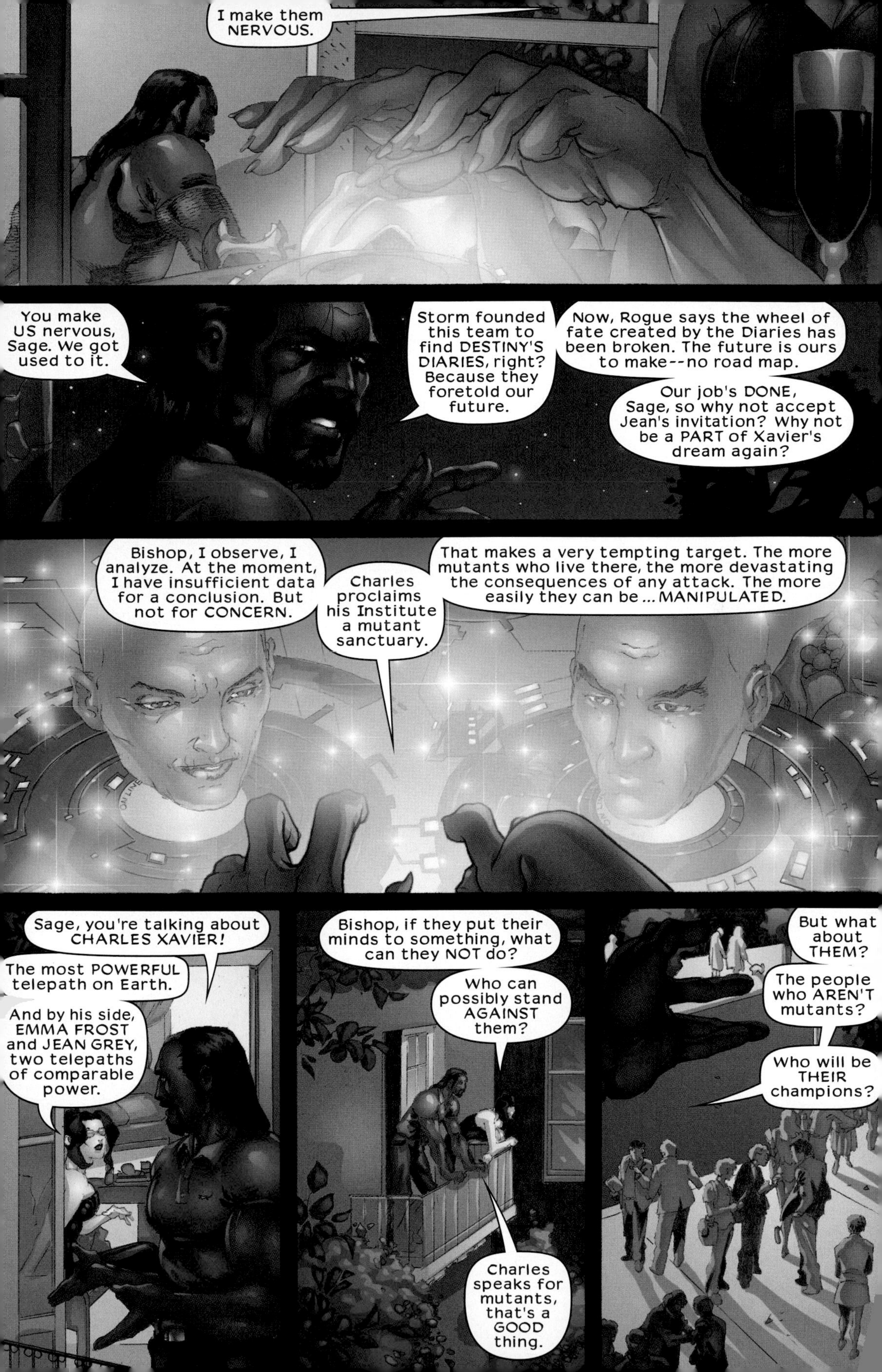
I make them NERVOUS.
You make US nervous, Sage. We got used to it.
Storm founded this team to find DESTINY'S DIARIES, right? Because they foretold our future.
Now, Rogue says the wheel of fate created by the Diaries has been broken. The future is ours to make--no road map.
Our job's DONE, Sage, so why not accept Jean's invitation? Why not be a PART of Xavier's dream again?
Bishop, I observe, I analyze. At the moment, I have insufficient data for a conclusion. But not for CONCERN.
Charles proclaims his Institute a mutant sanctuary.
That makes a very tempting target. The more mutants who live there, the more devastating the consequences of any attack. The more easily they can be ... MANIPULATED.
Sage, you're talking about CHARLES XAVIER!
The most POWERFUL telepath on Earth.
And by his side, EMMA FROST and JEAN GREY, two telepaths of comparable power.
Bishop, if they put their minds to something, what can they NOT do?
Who can possibly stand AGAINST them?
Charles speaks for mutants, that's a GOOD thing.
But what about THEM?
The people who AREN'T mutants?
Who will be THEIR champions?

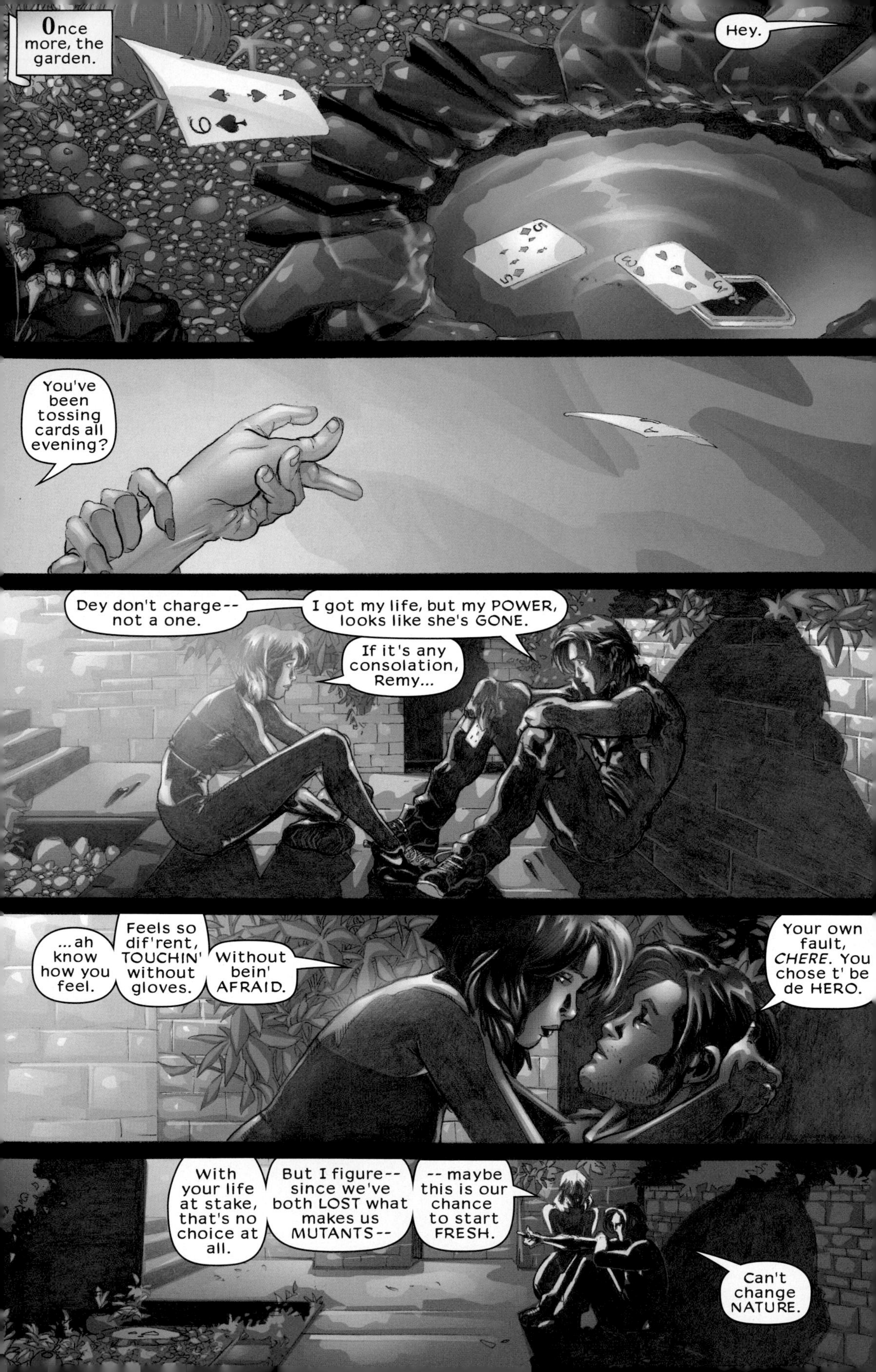
Once more, the garden.
Hey.
You've been tossing cards all evening?
Dey don't charge-- not a one.
I got my life, but my POWER, looks like she's GONE.
If it's any consolation, Remy...
...ah know how you feel.
Feels so dif'rent, TOUCHIN' without gloves.
Without bein' AFRAID.
Your own fault, CHERE. You chose t' be de HERO.
With your life at stake, that's no choice at all.
But I figure-- since we've both LOST what makes us MUTANTS--
--maybe this is our chance to start FRESH.
Can't change NATURE.

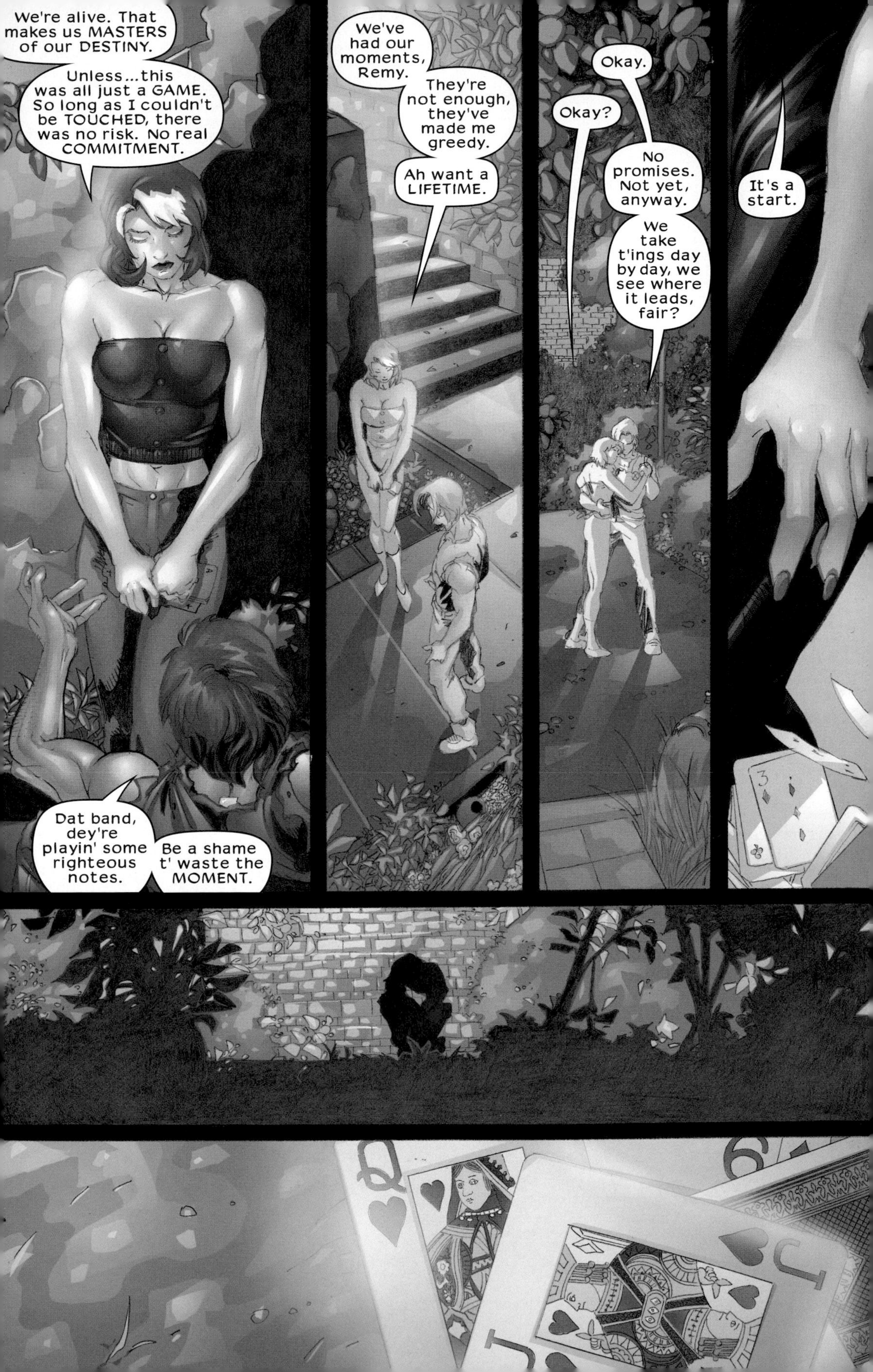
We're alive. That makes us MASTERS of our DESTINY.
Unless...this was all just a GAME. So long as I couldn't be TOUCHED, there was no risk. No real COMMITMENT.
Dat band, dey're playin' some righteous notes.
Be a shame t' waste the MOMENT.
We've had our moments, Remy.
They're not enough, they've made me greedy.
Ah want a LIFETIME.
Okay.
Okay?
No promises. Not yet, anyway.
We take t'ings day by day, we see where it leads, fair?
It's a start.

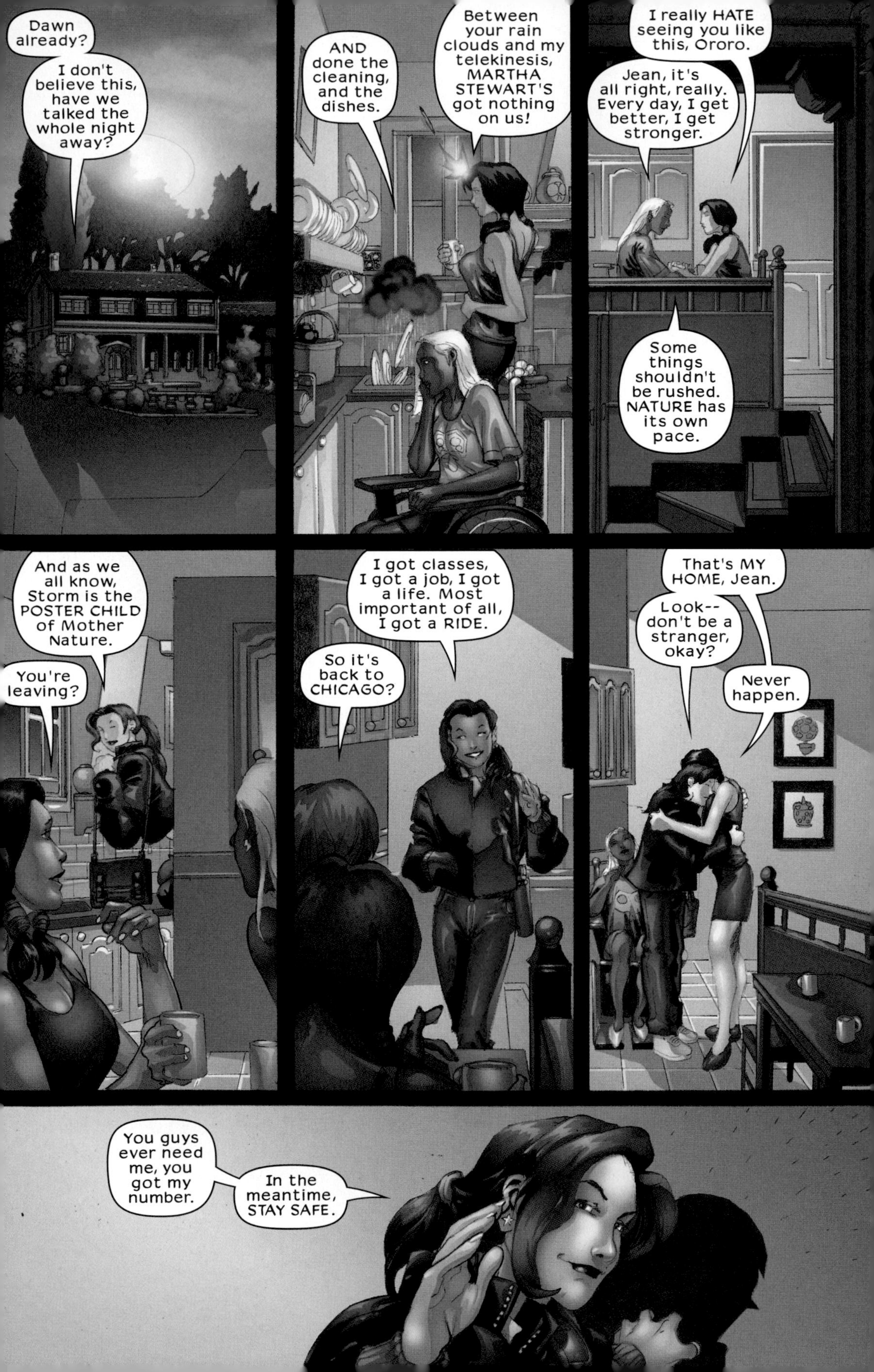

Dawn already?
I don't believe this, have we talked the whole night away?
AND done the cleaning, and the dishes.
Between your rain clouds and my telekinesis, MARTHA STEWART'S got nothing on us!
I really HATE seeing you like this, Ororo.
Jean, it's all right, really. Every day, I get better, I get stronger.
Some things shouldn't be rushed. NATURE has its own pace.
And as we all know, Storm is the POSTER CHILD of Mother Nature.
You're leaving?
I got classes, I got a job, I got a life. Most important of all, I got a RIDE.
So it's back to CHICAGO?
That's MY HOME, Jean.
Look--don't be a stranger, okay?
Never happen.
You guys ever need me, you got my number.
In the meantime, STAY SAFE.

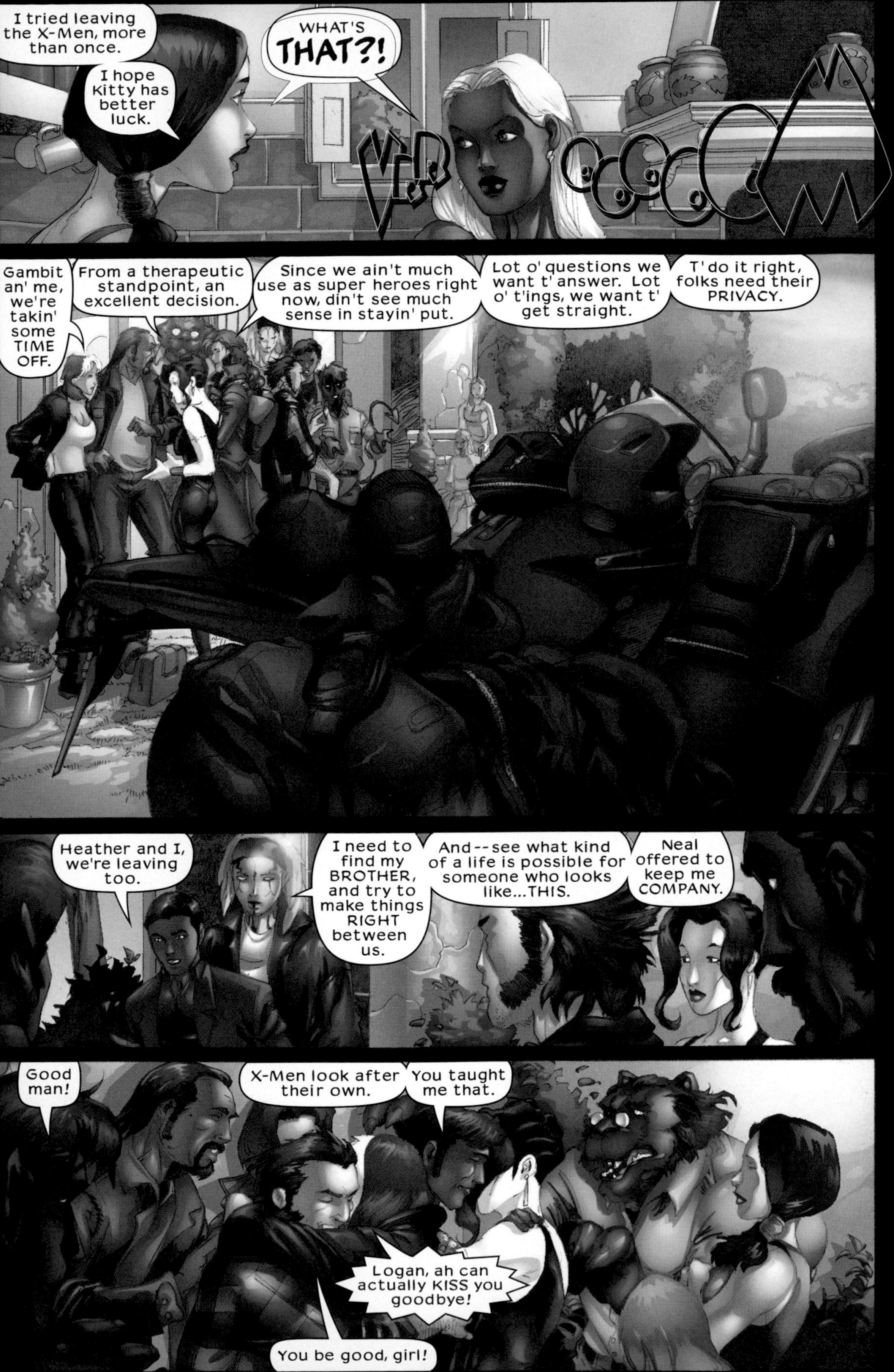
I tried leaving the X-Men, more than once.
I hope Kitty has better luck.
WHAT'S THAT?!
VRROOOOOM
Gambit an' me, we're takin' some TIME OFF.
From a therapeutic standpoint, an excellent decision.
Since we ain't much use as super heroes right now, din't see much sense in stayin' put.
Lot o' questions we want t' answer. Lot o' t'ings, we want t' get straight.
T' do it right, folks need their PRIVACY.
Heather and I, we're leaving too.
I need to find my BROTHER, and try to make things RIGHT between us.
And--see what kind of a life is possible for someone who looks like...THIS.
Neal offered to keep me COMPANY.
Good man!
X-Men look after their own.
You taught me that.
Logan, ah can actually KISS you goodbye!
You be good, girl!

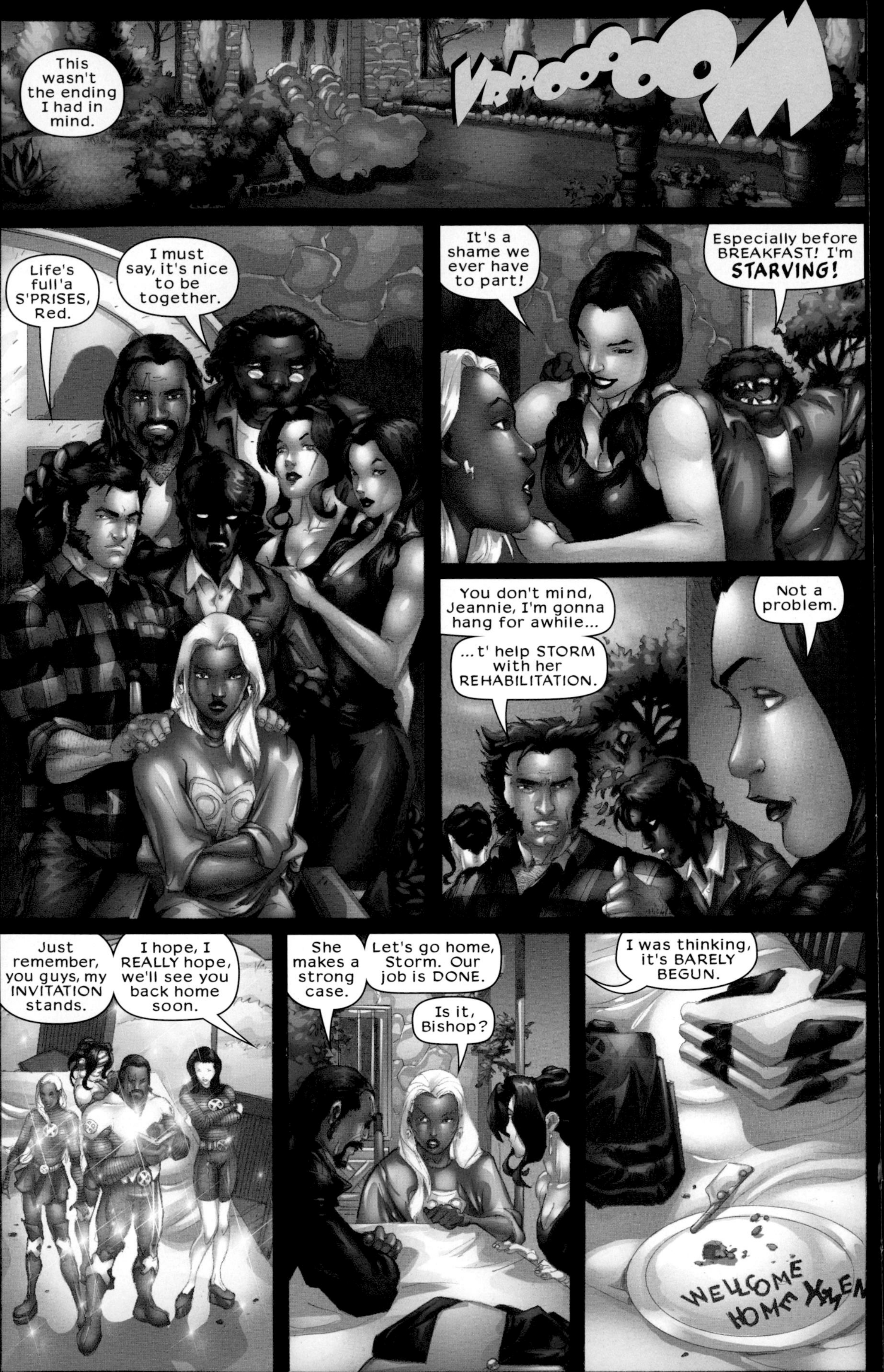
This wasn't the ending I had in mind.
VRROOOOOOM
Life's full'a S'PRISES, Red.
I must say, it's nice to be together.
It's a shame we ever have to part!
Especially before BREAKFAST! I'm STARVING!
You don't mind, Jeannie, I'm gonna hang for awhile...
...t' help STORM with her REHABILITATION.
Not a problem.
Just remember, you guys, my INVITATION stands.
I hope, I REALLY hope, we'll see you back home soon.
She makes a strong case.
Let's go home, Storm. Our job is DONE.
Is it, Bishop?
I was thinking, it's BARELY BEGUN.
WELLCOME HOME X-MEN

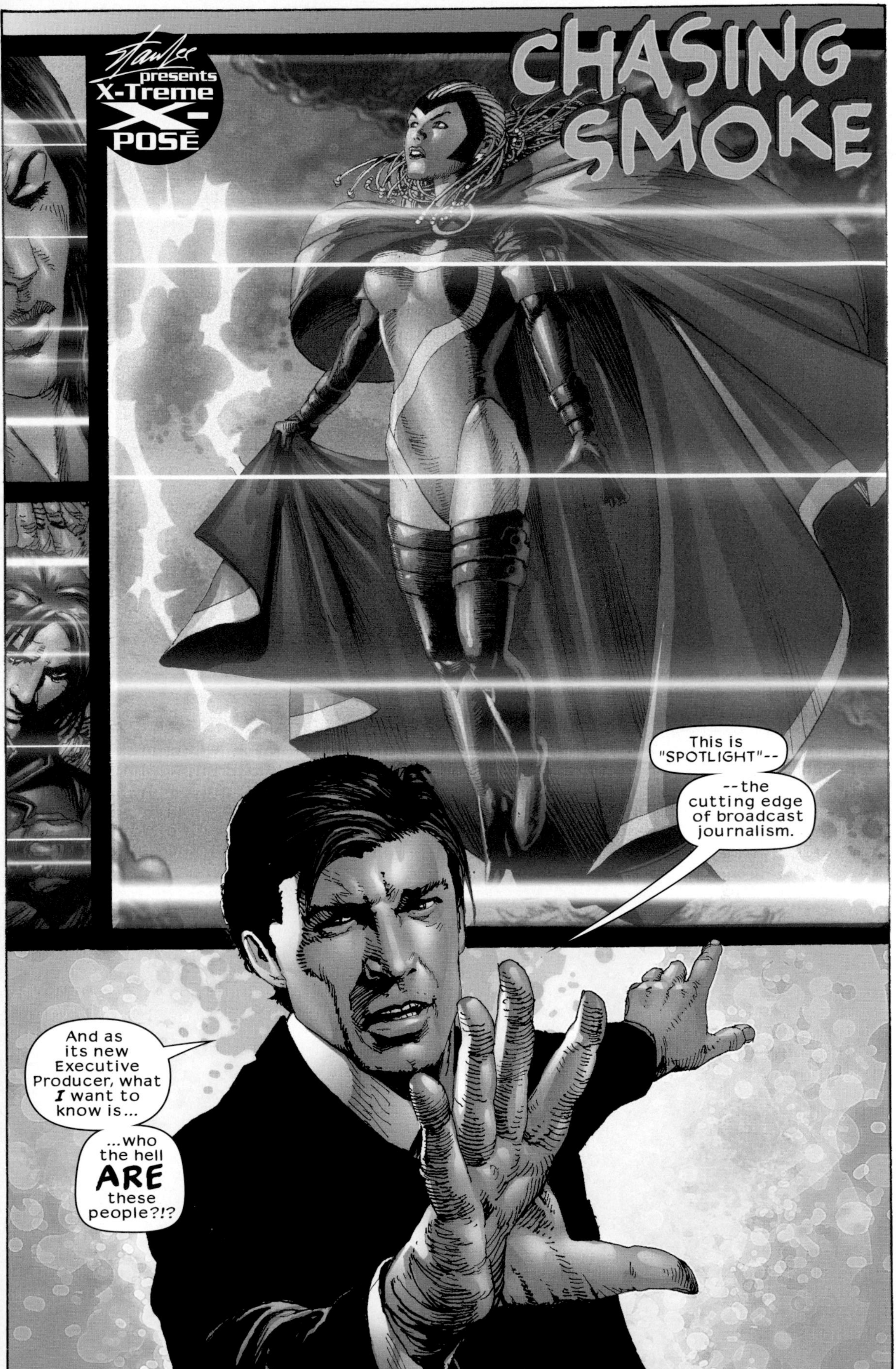
Stan Lee presents X-Treme X-POSÉ
CHASING SMOKE
This is "SPOTLIGHT"--
--the cutting edge of broadcast journalism.
And as its new Executive Producer, what I want to know is...
...who the hell ARE these people?!?

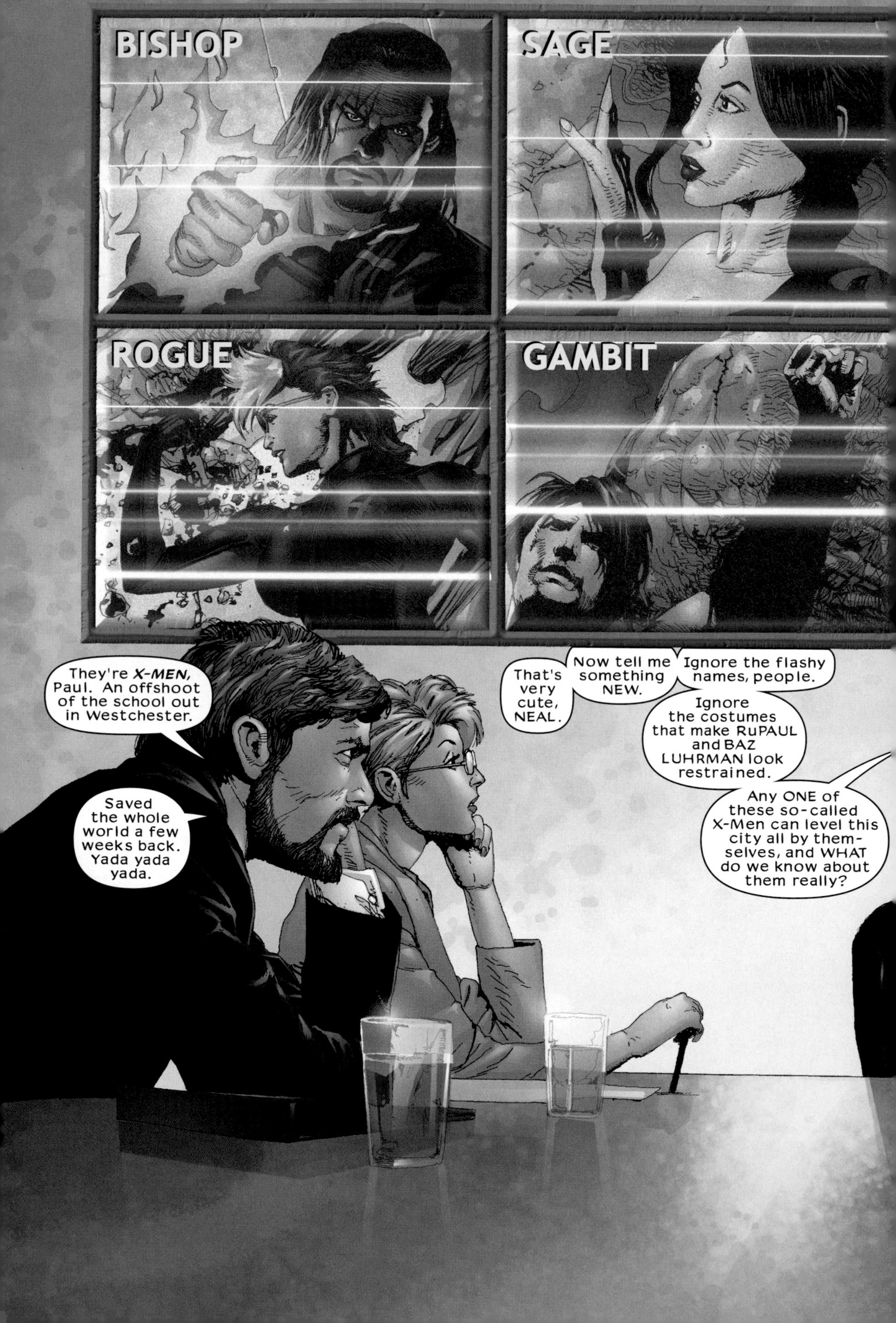
BISHOP
SAGE
ROGUE
GAMBIT
They're X-MEN, Paul. An offshoot of the school out in Westchester.
Saved the whole world a few weeks back. Yada yada yada.
That's very cute, NEAL.
Now tell me something NEW.
Ignore the flashy names, people.
Ignore the costumes that make RuPAUL and BAZ LUHRMAN look restrained.
Any ONE of these so-called X-Men can level this city all by them-selves, and WHAT do we know about them really?

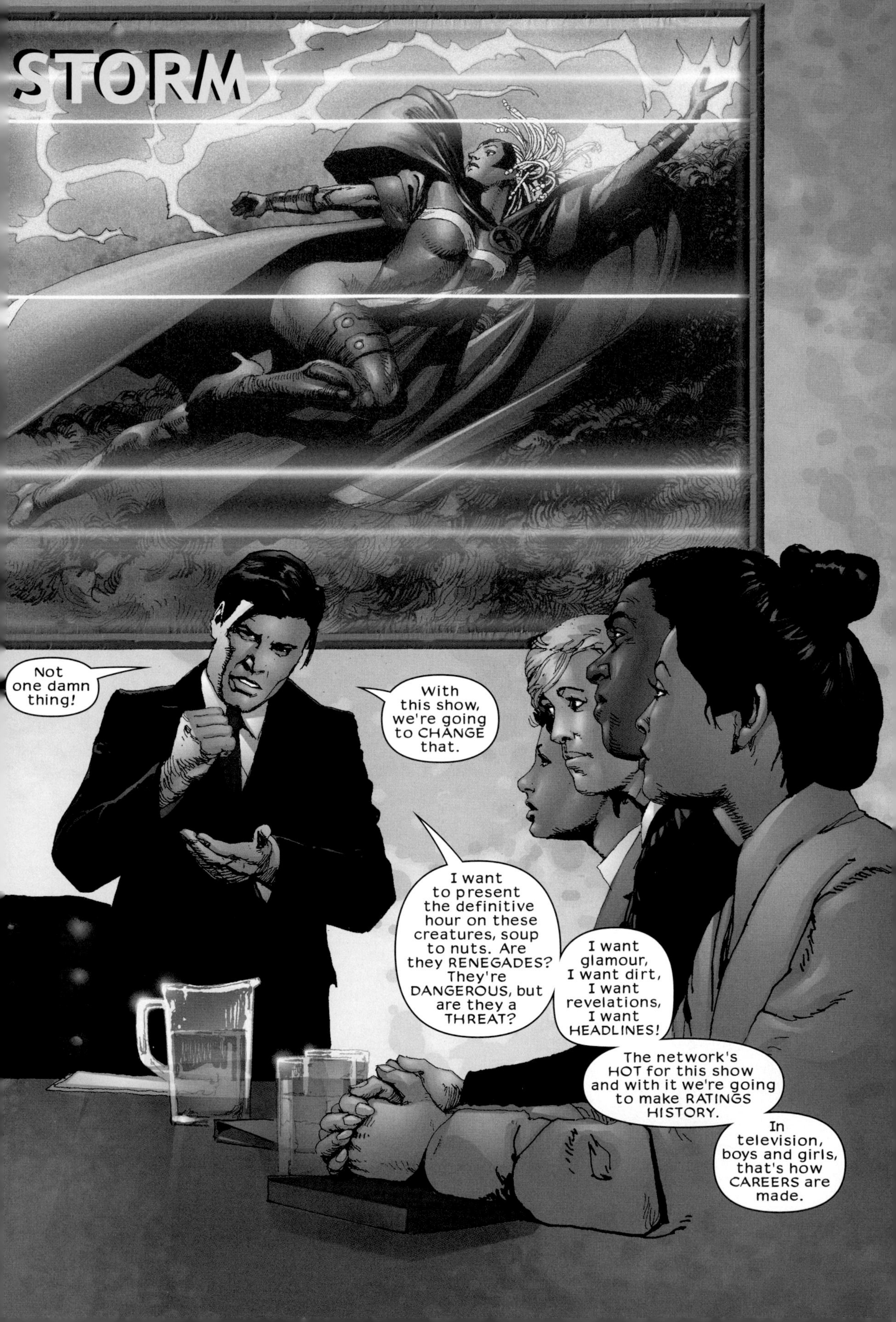
STORM
Not one damn thing!
With this show, we're going to CHANGE that.
I want to present the definitive hour on these creatures, soup to nuts. Are they RENEGADES? They're DANGEROUS, but are they a THREAT?
I want glamour, I want dirt, I want revelations, I want HEADLINES!
The network's HOT for this show and with it we're going to make RATINGS HISTORY.
In television, boys and girls, that's how CAREERS are made.

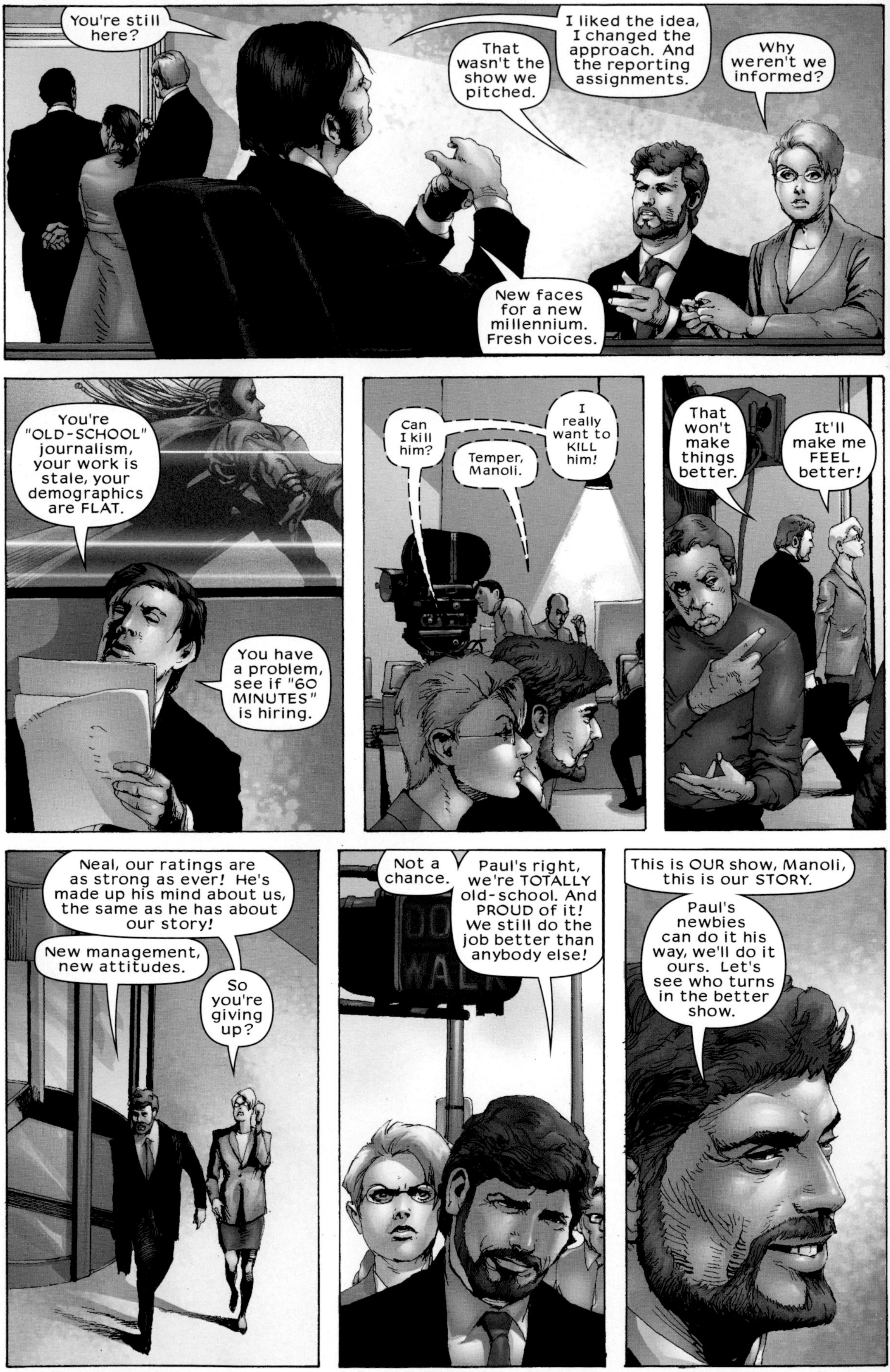
You're still here?
I liked the idea, I changed the approach. And the reporting assignments.
That wasn't the show we pitched.
Why weren't we informed?
New faces for a new millennium. Fresh voices.
You're "OLD-SCHOOL" journalism, your work is stale, your demographics are FLAT.
You have a problem, see if "60 MINUTES" is hiring.
Can I kill him?
I really want to KILL him!
Temper, Manoli.
That won't make things better.
It'll make me FEEL better!
Neal, our ratings are as strong as ever! He's made up his mind about us, the same as he has about our story!
New management, new attitudes.
So you're giving up?
Not a chance.
Paul's right, we're TOTALLY old-school. And PROUD of it! We still do the job better than anybody else!
This is OUR show, Manoli, this is our STORY.
Paul's newbies can do it his way, we'll do it ours. Let's see who turns in the better show.

8:53 AM. PARIS.

Bonjour, and welcome to X-CORP...

...dedicated to worldwide economic and business support for mutant entrepreneurs.

I'm HOLLY. How may I HELP you?

I'm a correspondent; I'm here to interview your BOSS.

Craig Damaski, SPOTLIGHT.

Mr. Jorgenson in Facilities Management?

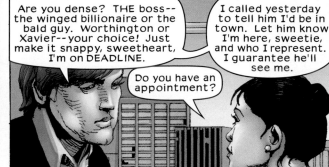

Are you dense? THE boss-- the winged billionaire or the bald guy. Worthington or Xavier-- your choice! Just make it snappy, sweetheart, I'm on DEADLINE.

Do you have an appointment?

I called yesterday to tell him I'd be in town. Let him know I'm here, sweetie, and who I represent. I guarantee he'll see me.

Have a seat, then. I'll see what I can do.

11:17 AM

12:29 PM

3:00 PM

5:09 PM

Hey!

Where's that other girl, the one from this morning--?

That's me. Same girl, different face. I'M a mutant.

I flew all the way to Paris for this!

Monsieur Worthington and Monsieur Xavier are very busy men. I'm terribly sorry.

They'll REGRET that decision--

--and so will YOU!

Have a nice day.

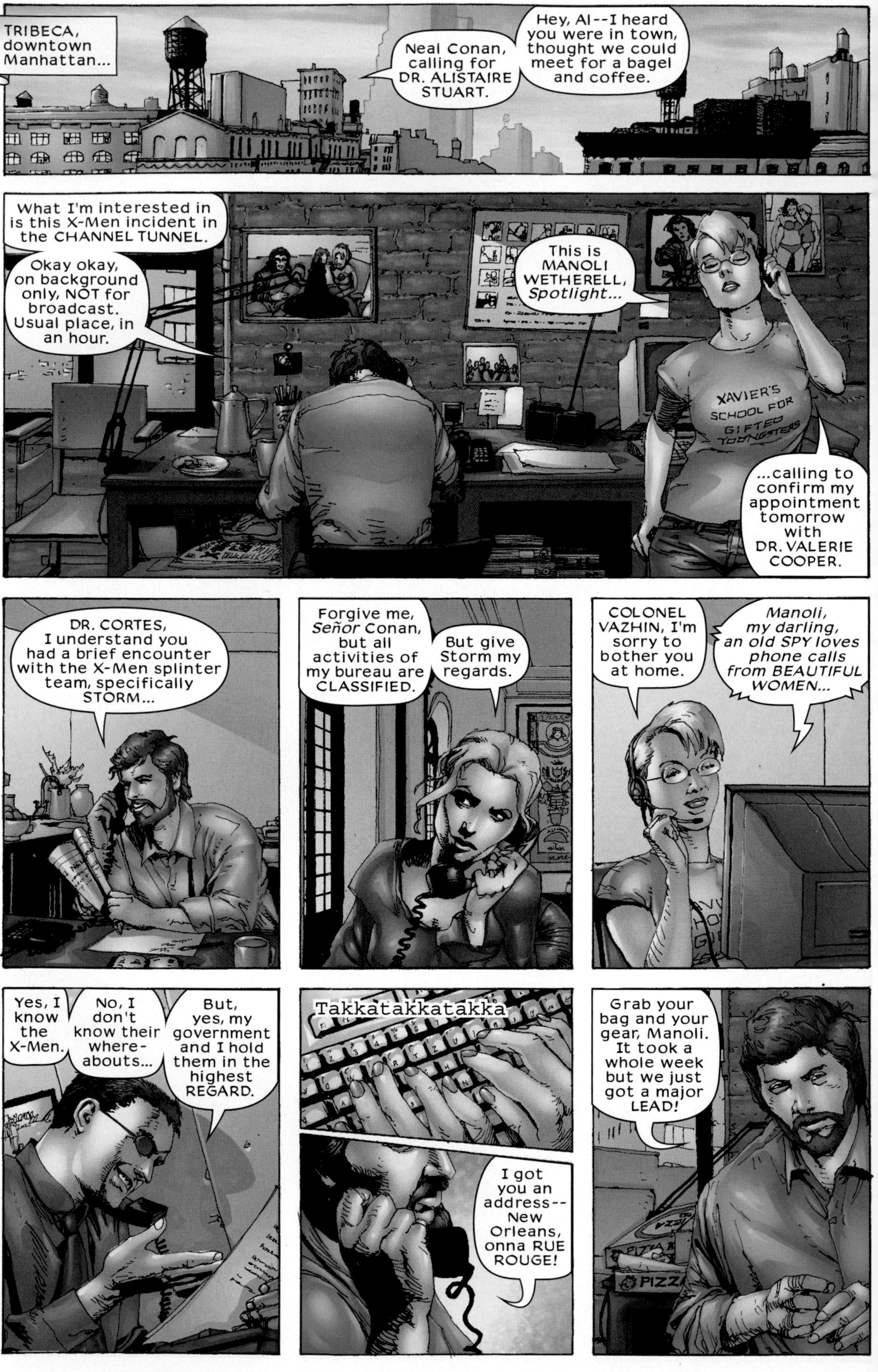
TRIBECA, downtown Manhattan...
Neal Conan, calling for DR. ALISTAIRE STUART.
Hey, Al--I heard you were in town, thought we could meet for a bagel and coffee.
What I'm interested in is this X-Men incident in the CHANNEL TUNNEL.
Okay okay, on background only, NOT for broadcast. Usual place, in an hour.
This is MANOLI WETHERELL, *Spotlight*...
XAVIER'S SCHOOL FOR GIFTED YOUNGSTERS
...calling to confirm my appointment tomorrow with DR. VALERIE COOPER.
DR. CORTES, I understand you had a brief encounter with the X-Men splinter team, specifically STORM...
Forgive me, *Señor* Conan, but all activities of my bureau are CLASSIFIED.
But give Storm my regards.
COLONEL VAZHIN, I'm sorry to bother you at home.
Manoli, my darling, an old SPY loves phone calls from BEAUTIFUL WOMEN...
Yes, I know the X-Men.
No, I don't know their where-abouts...
But, yes, my government and I hold them in the highest REGARD.
Takkatakkatakka
I got you an address-- New Orleans, onna RUE ROUGE!
Grab your bag and your gear, Manoli. It took a whole week but we just got a major LEAD!
PIZZA

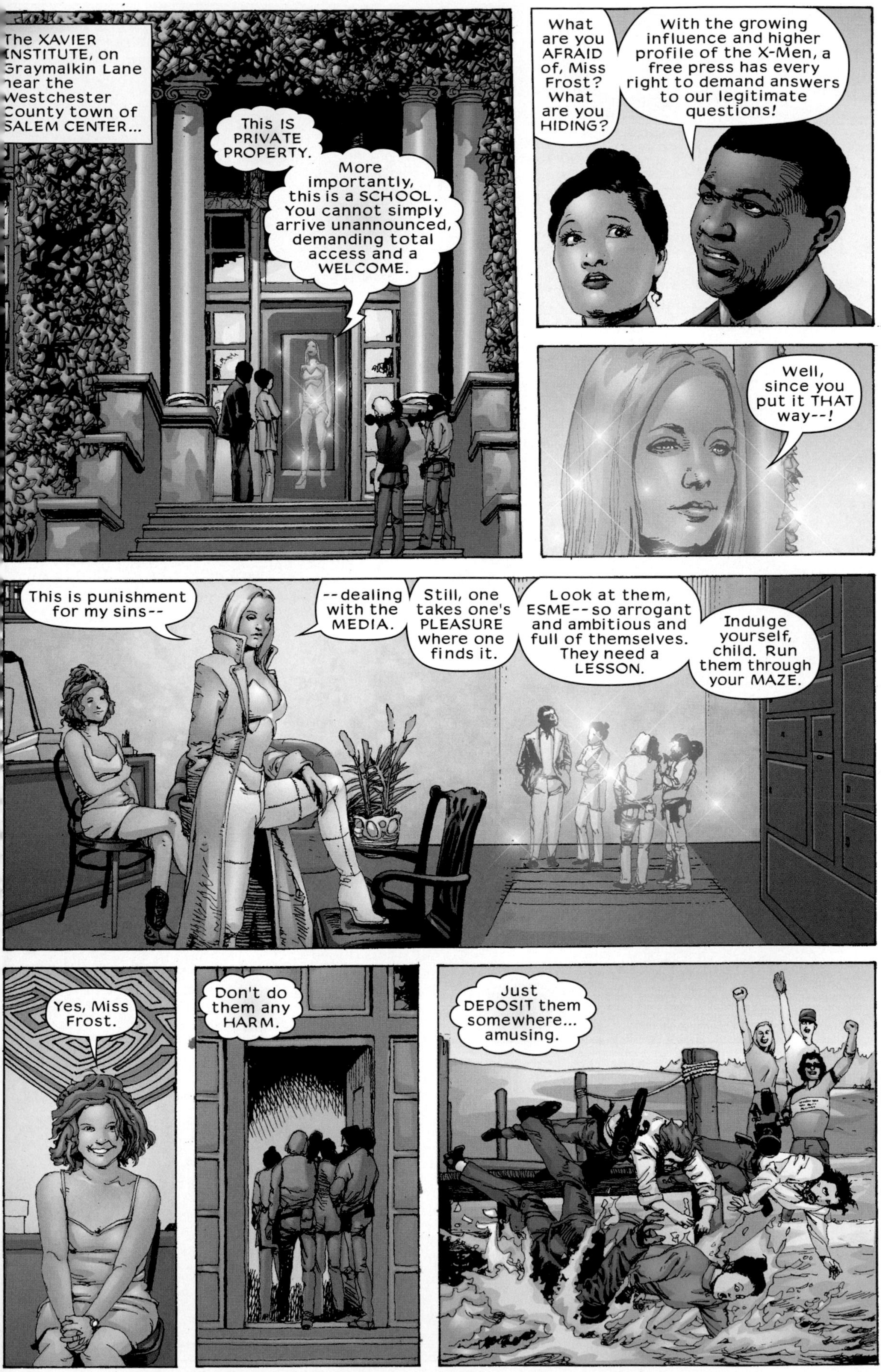
The XAVIER INSTITUTE, on Graymalkin Lane near the Westchester County town of SALEM CENTER...
This IS PRIVATE PROPERTY.
More importantly, this is a SCHOOL. You cannot simply arrive unannounced, demanding total access and a WELCOME.
What are you AFRAID of, Miss Frost? What are you HIDING?
With the growing influence and higher profile of the X-Men, a free press has every right to demand answers to our legitimate questions!
Well, since you put it THAT way--!
This is punishment for my sins--
--dealing with the MEDIA.
Still, one takes one's PLEASURE where one finds it.
Look at them, ESME--so arrogant and ambitious and full of themselves. They need a LESSON.
Indulge yourself, child. Run them through your MAZE.
Yes, Miss Frost.
Don't do them any HARM.
Just DEPOSIT them somewhere... amusing.

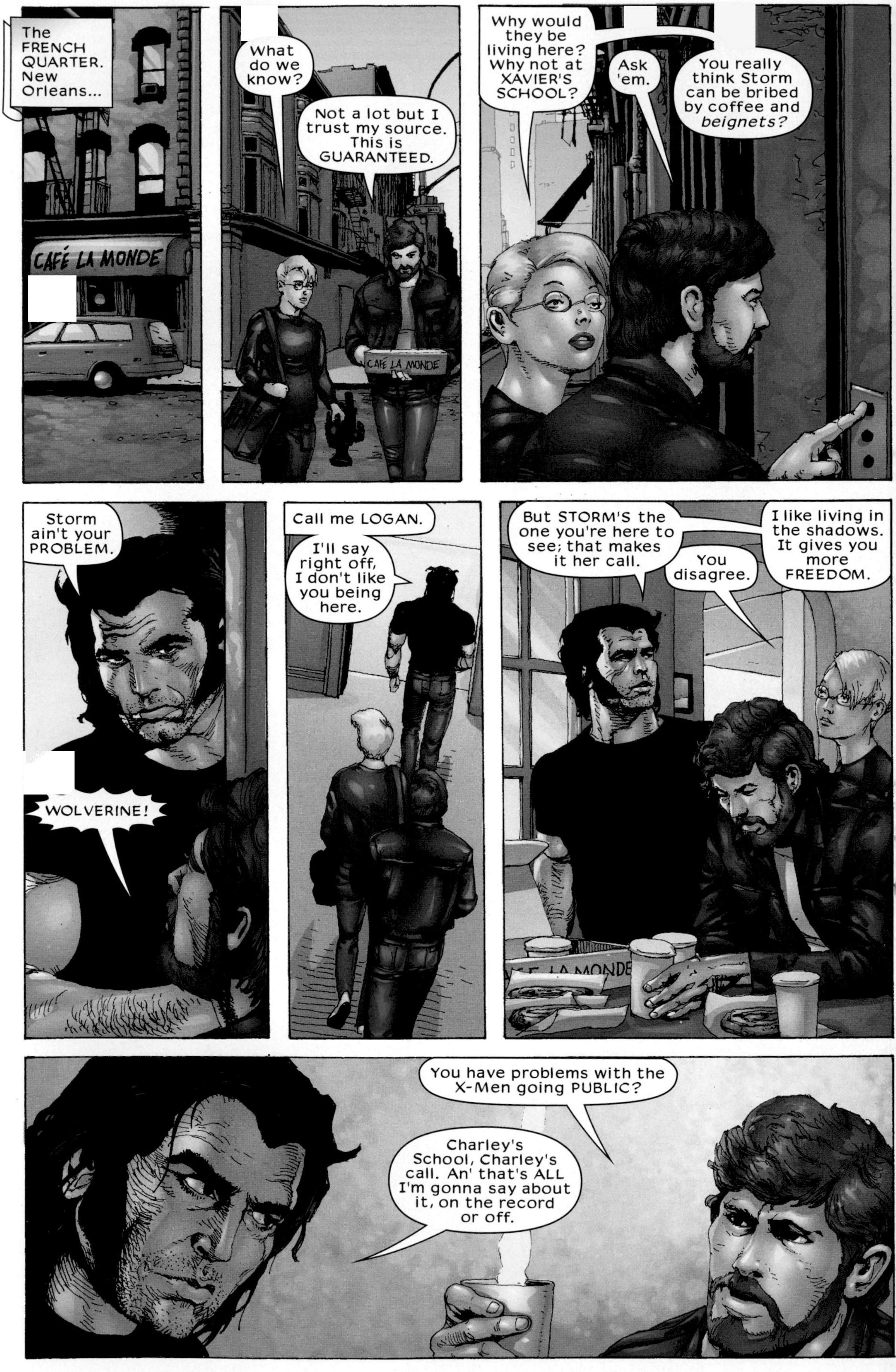
The FRENCH QUARTER. New Orleans...
CAFÉ LA MONDE
What do we know?
Not a lot but I trust my source. This is GUARANTEED.
CAFÉ LA MONDE
Why would they be living here? Why not at XAVIER'S SCHOOL?
Ask 'em.
You really think Storm can be bribed by coffee and *beignets?*
Storm ain't your PROBLEM.
WOLVERINE!
Call me LOGAN.
I'll say right off, I don't like you being here.
But STORM'S the one you're here to see; that makes it her call.
You disagree.
I like living in the shadows. It gives you more FREEDOM.
You have problems with the X-Men going PUBLIC?
Charley's School, Charley's call. An' that's ALL I'm gonna say about it, on the record or off.

Your guests are here, ORORO. Bearing GIFTS.

Gimme a decent workout this morning, I'll consider letting you eat 'em.

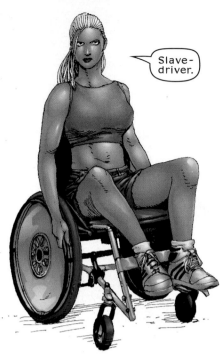

Slave-driver.

News reports said you'd been INJURED in Madripoor, but we had no idea it was so SERIOUS.

What, you think we'd ADVERTISE this?

It's just-- it was always comforting to think of the X-Men as UNTOUCHABLE.

Seeing you VULNERABLE, seeing you hurt--it makes you too much like US.

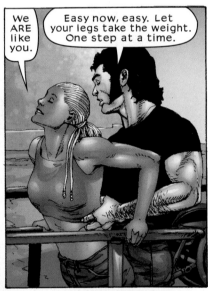

We ARE like you.

Easy now, easy. Let your legs take the weight. One step at a time.

We're HUMAN, Manoli. We're ALL human!

That's the TRAGEDY of racism. It makes you think people are something less than they are.

You mean mutants and... everyone else?

Sadly, yes.

However, thanks to recent events, the public profile and standing of the X-Men is HIGHER than it's been in years.

We're not in it for the MEDALS, bub.

STORM--!

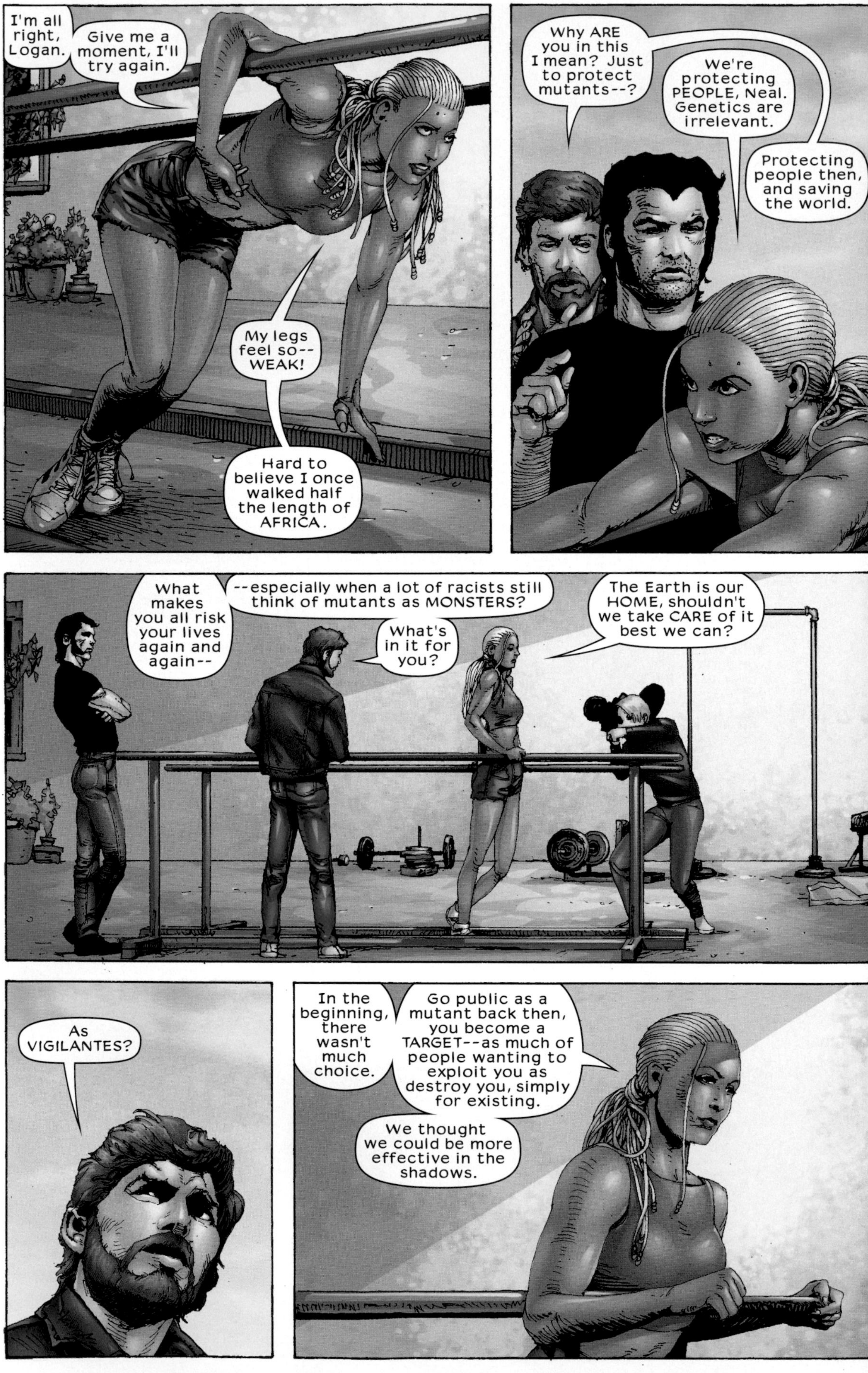
I'm all right, Logan.
Give me a moment, I'll try again.
My legs feel so-- WEAK!
Hard to believe I once walked half the length of AFRICA.
Why ARE you in this I mean? Just to protect mutants--?
We're protecting PEOPLE, Neal. Genetics are irrelevant.
Protecting people then, and saving the world.
What makes you all risk your lives again and again--
--especially when a lot of racists still think of mutants as MONSTERS?
What's in it for you?
The Earth is our HOME, shouldn't we take CARE of it best we can?
As VIGILANTES?
In the beginning, there wasn't much choice.
Go public as a mutant back then, you become a TARGET--as much of people wanting to exploit you as destroy you, simply for existing.
We thought we could be more effective in the shadows.

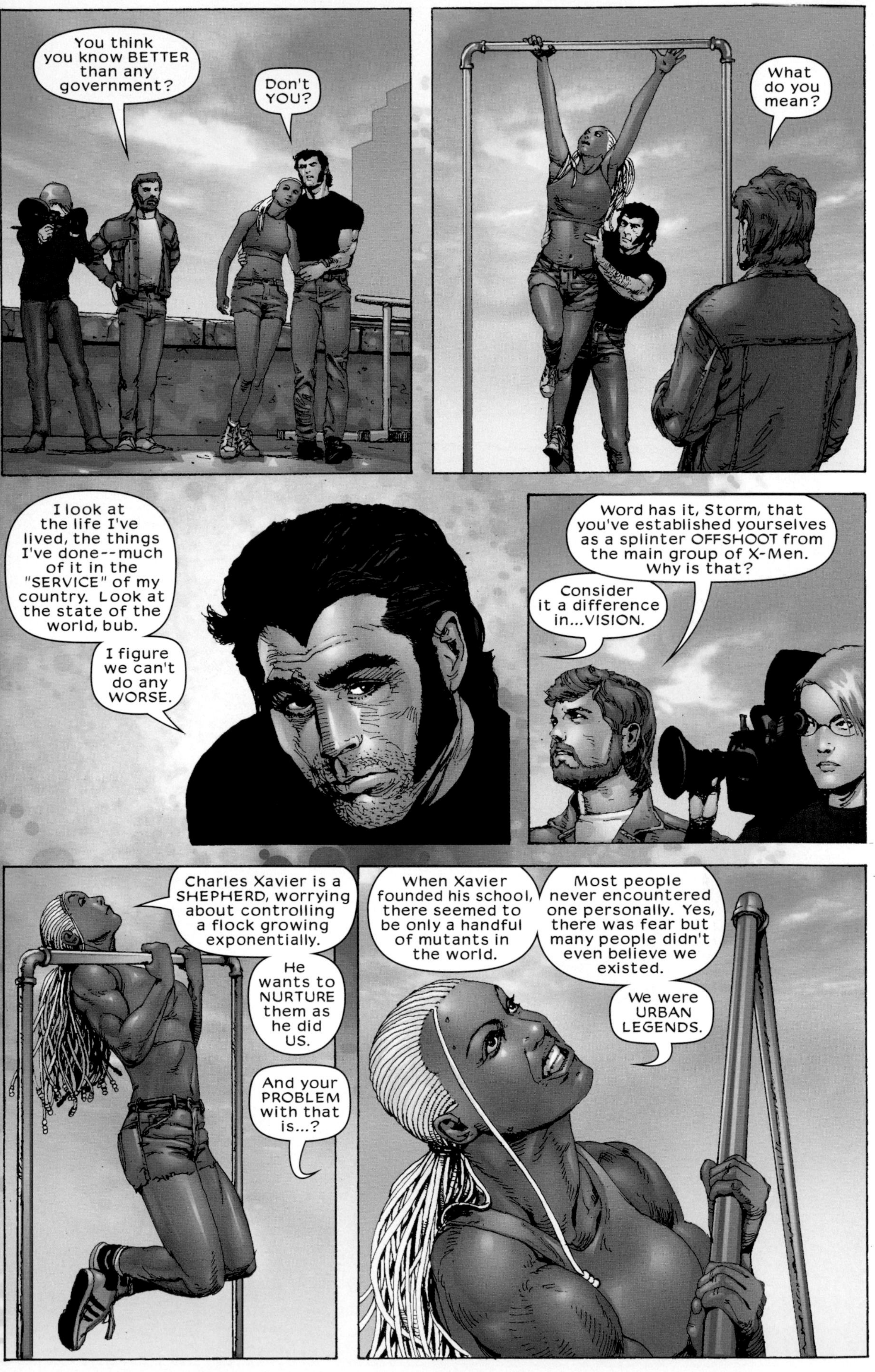

You think you know BETTER than any government?
Don't YOU?
What do you mean?
I look at the life I've lived, the things I've done--much of it in the "SERVICE" of my country. Look at the state of the world, bub.
I figure we can't do any WORSE.
Word has it, Storm, that you've established yourselves as a splinter OFFSHOOT from the main group of X-Men. Why is that?
Consider it a difference in...VISION.
Charles Xavier is a SHEPHERD, worrying about controlling a flock growing exponentially.
He wants to NURTURE them as he did US.
And your PROBLEM with that is...?
When Xavier founded his school, there seemed to be only a handful of mutants in the world.
Most people never encountered one personally. Yes, there was fear but many people didn't even believe we existed.
We were URBAN LEGENDS.

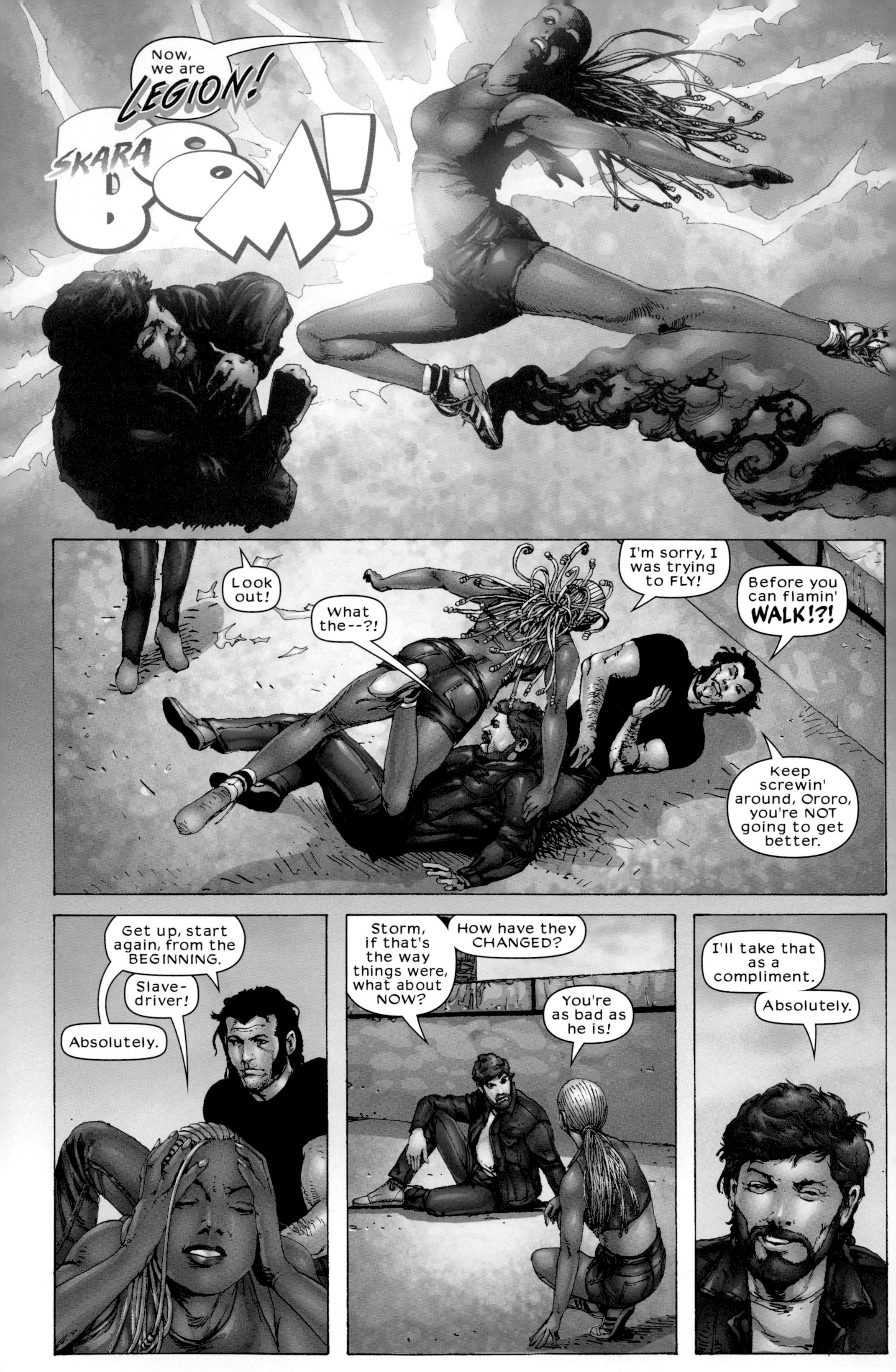
Now, we are LEGION!
SKARA BOOM!
Look out!
What the--?!
I'm sorry, I was trying to FLY!
Before you can flamin' WALK!?!
Keep screwin' around, Ororo, you're NOT going to get better.
Get up, start again, from the BEGINNING.
Slave-driver!
Absolutely.
Storm, if that's the way things were, what about NOW?
How have they CHANGED?
You're as bad as he is!
I'll take that as a compliment.
Absolutely.

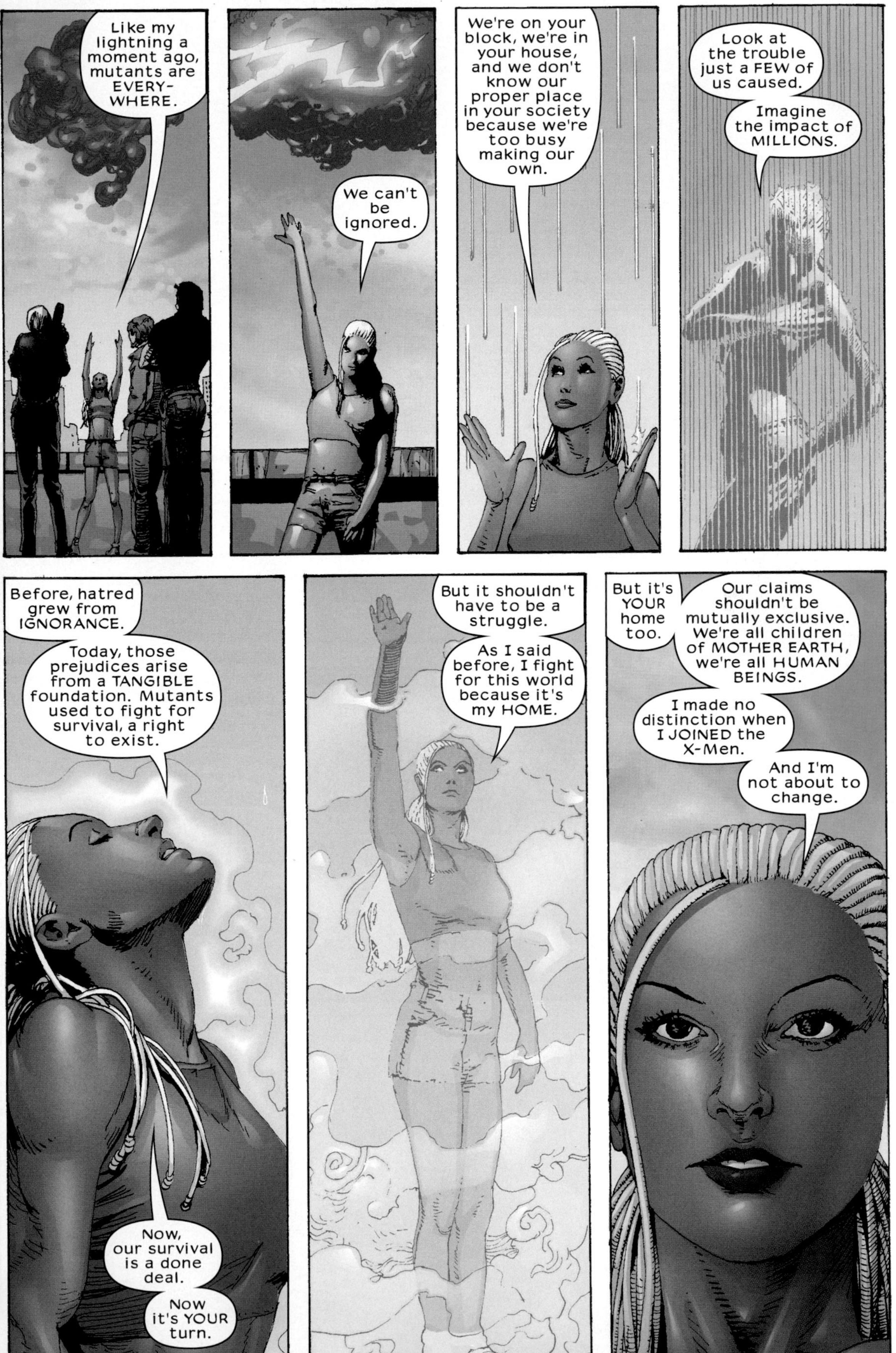
Like my lightning a moment ago, mutants are EVERY-WHERE.
We can't be ignored.
We're on your block, we're in your house, and we don't know our proper place in your society because we're too busy making our own.
Look at the trouble just a FEW of us caused.
Imagine the impact of MILLIONS.
Before, hatred grew from IGNORANCE.
Today, those prejudices arise from a TANGIBLE foundation. Mutants used to fight for survival, a right to exist.
Now, our survival is a done deal.
Now it's YOUR turn.
But it shouldn't have to be a struggle.
As I said before, I fight for this world because it's my HOME.
But it's YOUR home too.
Our claims shouldn't be mutually exclusive. We're all children of MOTHER EARTH, we're all HUMAN BEINGS.
I made no distinction when I JOINED the X-Men.
And I'm not about to change.

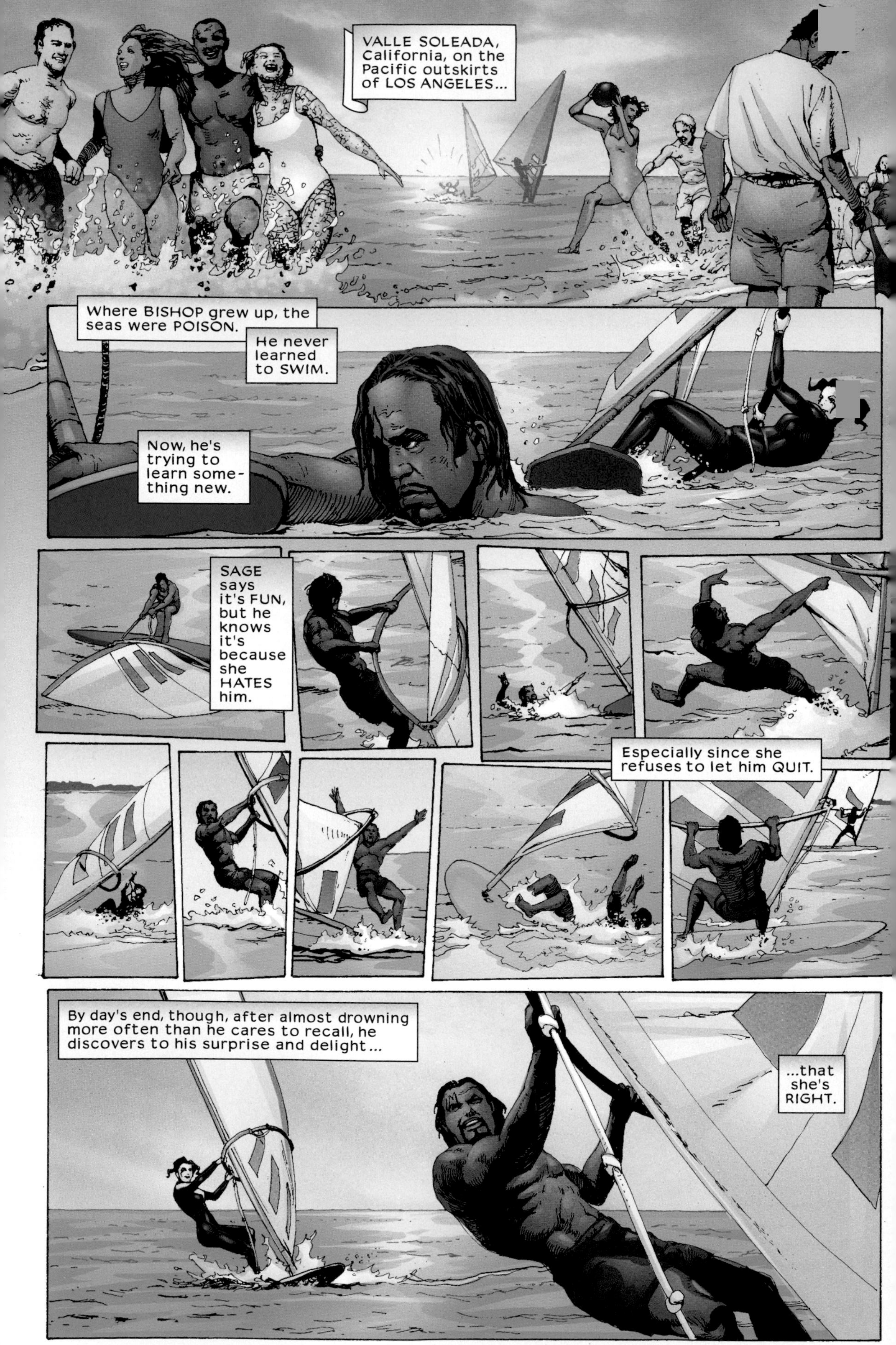

VALLE SOLEADA, California, on the Pacific outskirts of LOS ANGELES...
Where BISHOP grew up, the seas were POISON.
He never learned to SWIM.
Now, he's trying to learn something new.
SAGE says it's FUN, but he knows it's because she HATES him.
Especially since she refuses to let him QUIT.
By day's end, though, after almost drowning more often than he cares to recall, he discovers to his surprise and delight...
...that she's RIGHT.

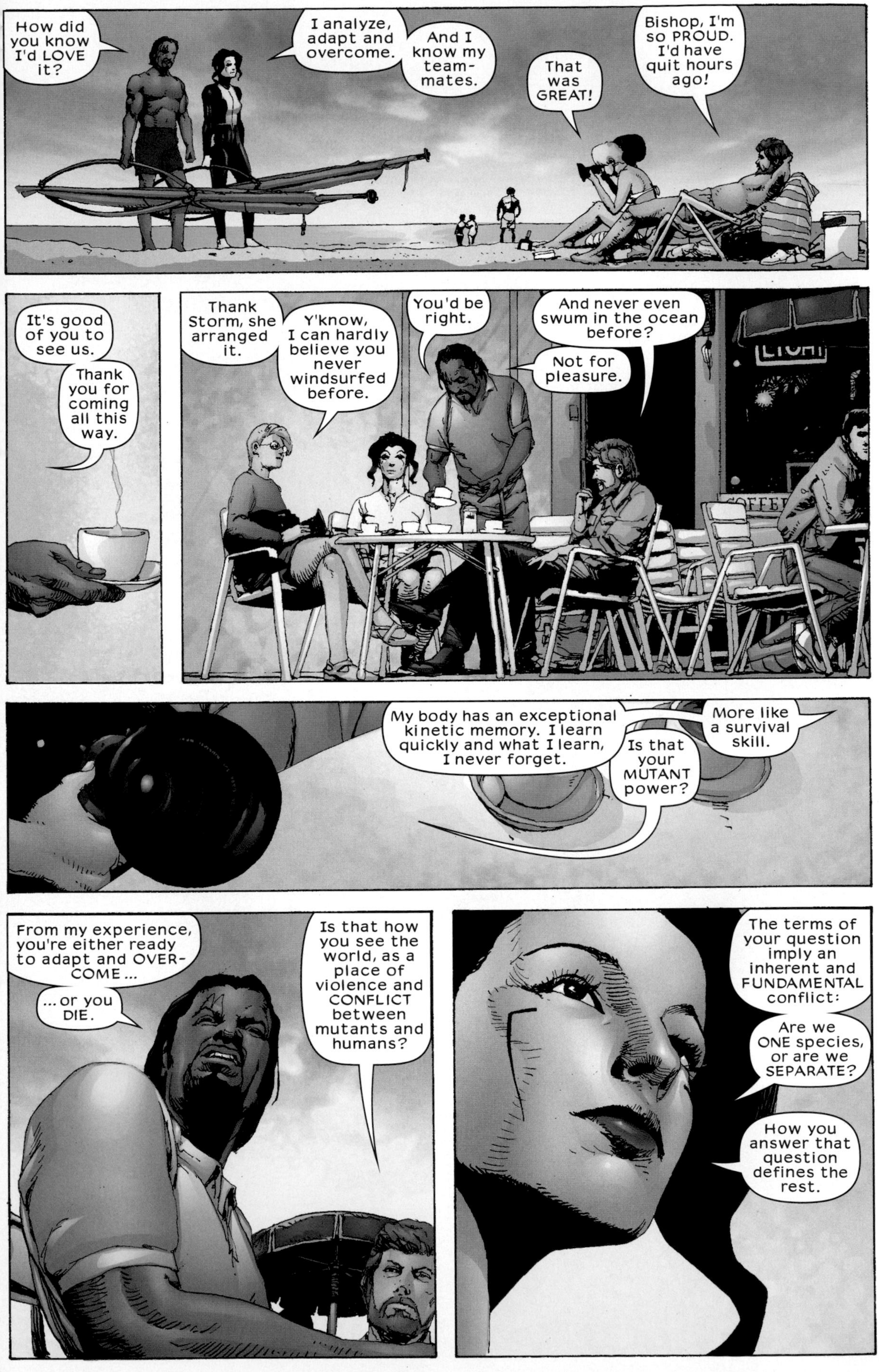

How did you know I'd LOVE it?
I analyze, adapt and overcome.
And I know my team-mates.
That was GREAT!
Bishop, I'm so PROUD. I'd have quit hours ago!
It's good of you to see us.
Thank you for coming all this way.
Thank Storm, she arranged it.
Y'know, I can hardly believe you never windsurfed before.
You'd be right.
And never even swum in the ocean before?
Not for pleasure.
My body has an exceptional kinetic memory. I learn quickly and what I learn, I never forget.
Is that your MUTANT power?
More like a survival skill.
From my experience, you're either ready to adapt and OVER-COME...
...or you DIE.
Is that how you see the world, as a place of violence and CONFLICT between mutants and humans?
The terms of your question imply an inherent and FUNDAMENTAL conflict:
Are we ONE species, or are we SEPARATE?
How you answer that question defines the rest.

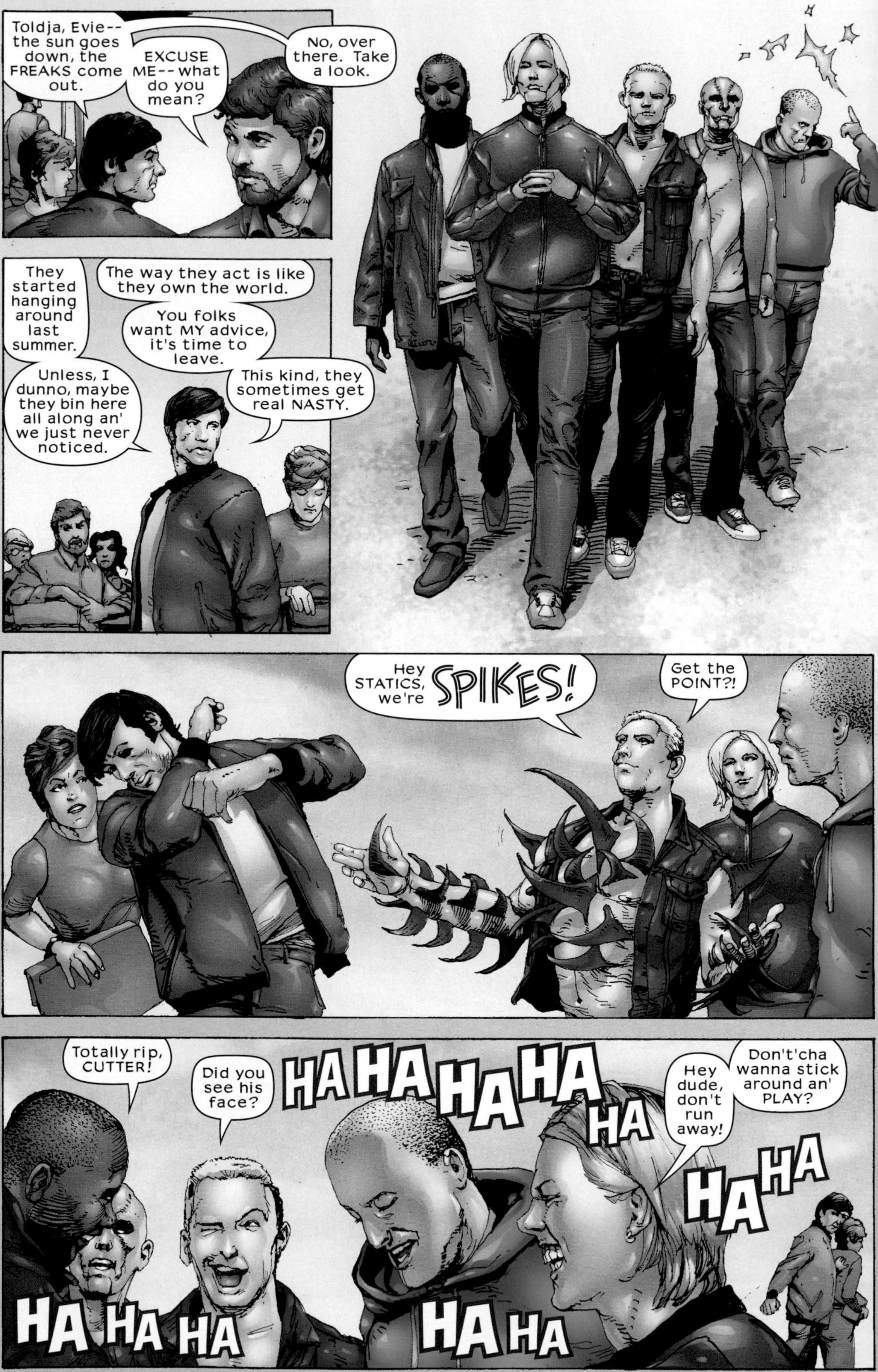

Toldja, Evie-- the sun goes down, the FREAKS come out.
EXCUSE ME--what do you mean?
No, over there. Take a look.
They started hanging around last summer.
The way they act is like they own the world.
You folks want MY advice, it's time to leave.
Unless, I dunno, maybe they bin here all along an' we just never noticed.
This kind, they sometimes get real NASTY.
Hey STATICS, we're SPIKES!
Get the POINT?!
Totally rip, CUTTER!
Did you see his face?
HA HA HA HA HA HA
Hey dude, don't run away!
Don't'cha wanna stick around an' PLAY?
HA HA
HA HA HA
HA HA

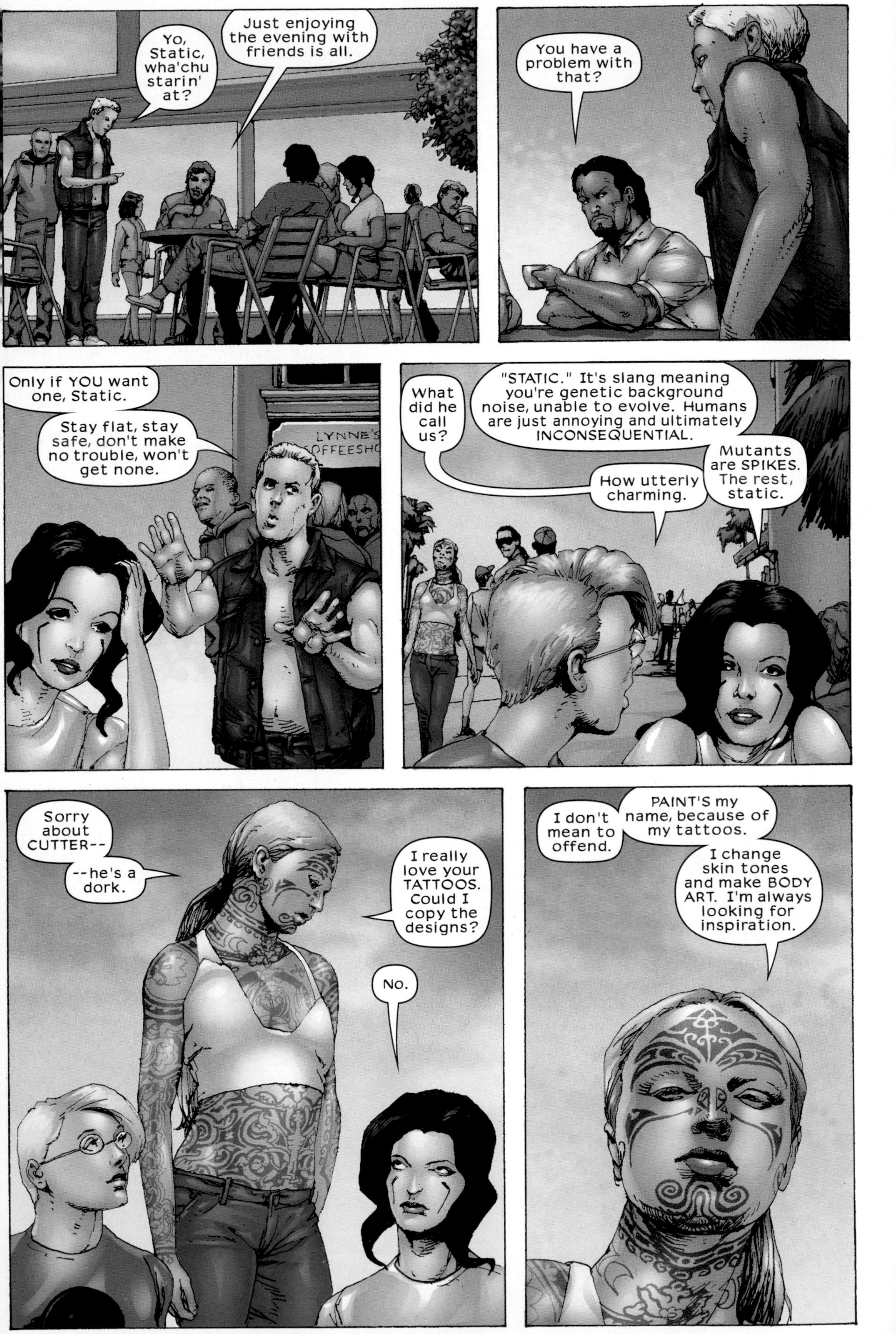
Yo, Static, wha'chu starin' at?
Just enjoying the evening with friends is all.
You have a problem with that?
Only if YOU want one, Static.
Stay flat, stay safe, don't make no trouble, won't get none.
LYNNE'S COFFEESHO
What did he call us?
"STATIC." It's slang meaning you're genetic background noise, unable to evolve. Humans are just annoying and ultimately INCONSEQUENTIAL.
Mutants are SPIKES. The rest, static.
How utterly charming.
Sorry about CUTTER--
--he's a dork.
I really love your TATTOOS. Could I copy the designs?
No.
I don't mean to offend.
PAINT'S my name, because of my tattoos.
I change skin tones and make BODY ART. I'm always looking for inspiration.

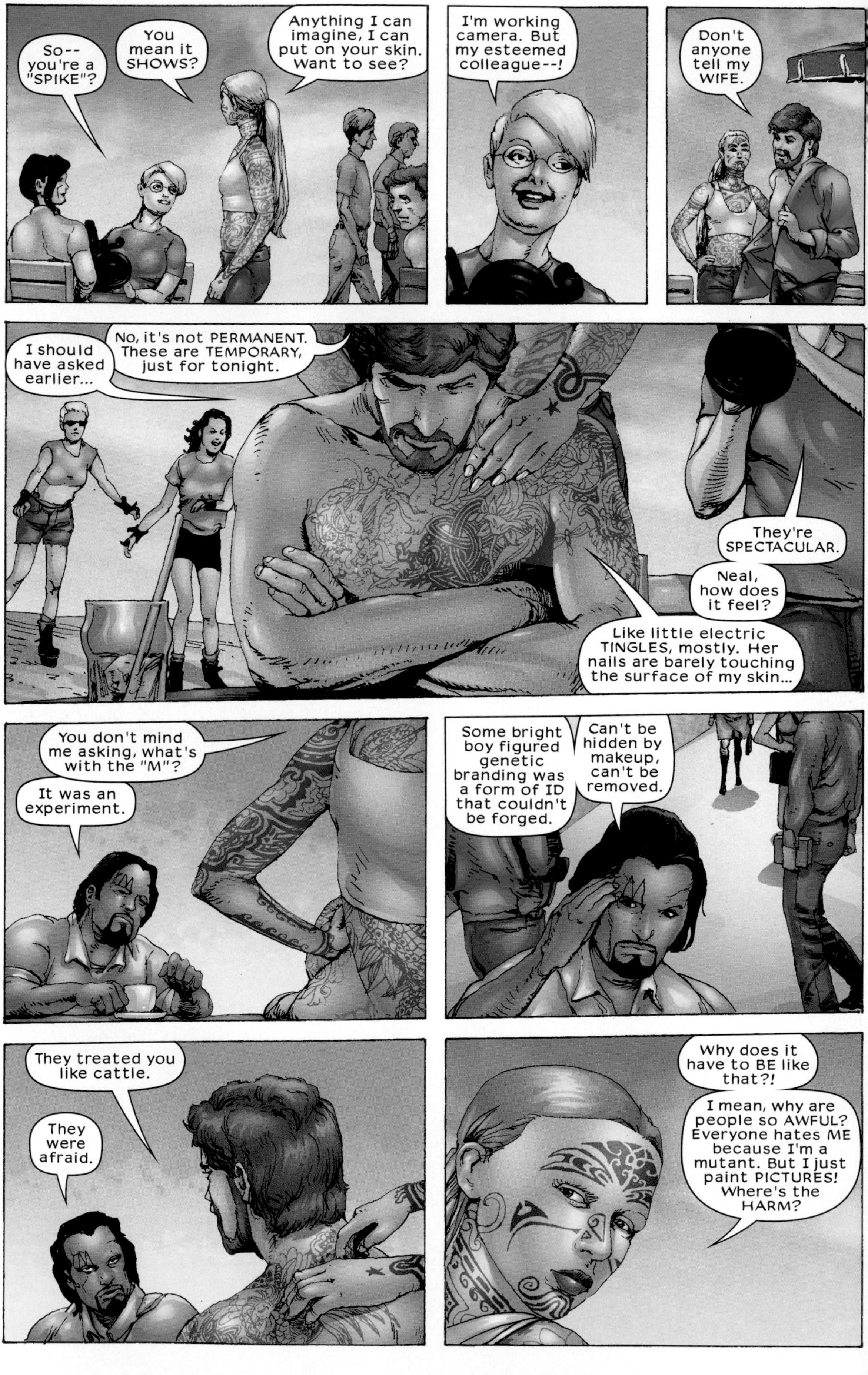
So-- you're a "SPIKE"?
You mean it SHOWS?
Anything I can imagine, I can put on your skin. Want to see?
I'm working camera. But my esteemed colleague--!
Don't anyone tell my WIFE.
I should have asked earlier...
No, it's not PERMANENT. These are TEMPORARY, just for tonight.
They're SPECTACULAR.
Neal, how does it feel?
Like little electric TINGLES, mostly. Her nails are barely touching the surface of my skin...
You don't mind me asking, what's with the "M"?
It was an experiment.
Some bright boy figured genetic branding was a form of ID that couldn't be forged.
Can't be hidden by makeup, can't be removed.
They treated you like cattle.
They were afraid.
Why does it have to BE like that?!
I mean, why are people so AWFUL? Everyone hates ME because I'm a mutant. But I just paint PICTURES! Where's the HARM?

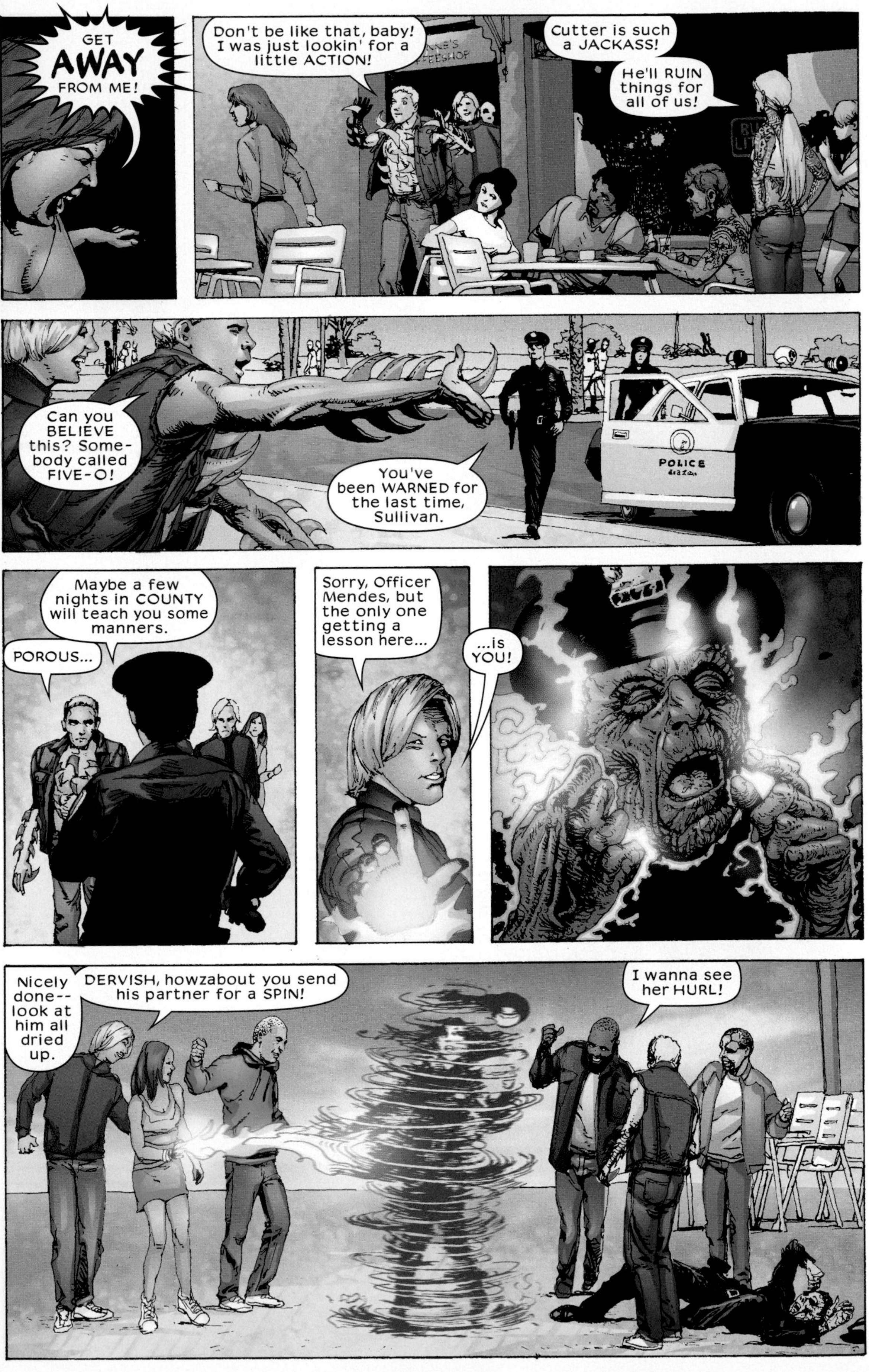
GET AWAY FROM ME!
Don't be like that, baby! I was just lookin' for a little ACTION!
Cutter is such a JACKASS!
He'll RUIN things for all of us!
Can you BELIEVE this? Somebody called FIVE-O!
You've been WARNED for the last time, Sullivan.
POLICE
Maybe a few nights in COUNTY will teach you some manners.
POROUS...
Sorry, Officer Mendes, but the only one getting a lesson here...
...is YOU!
Nicely done-- look at him all dried up.
DERVISH, howzabout you send his partner for a SPIN!
I wanna see her HURL!

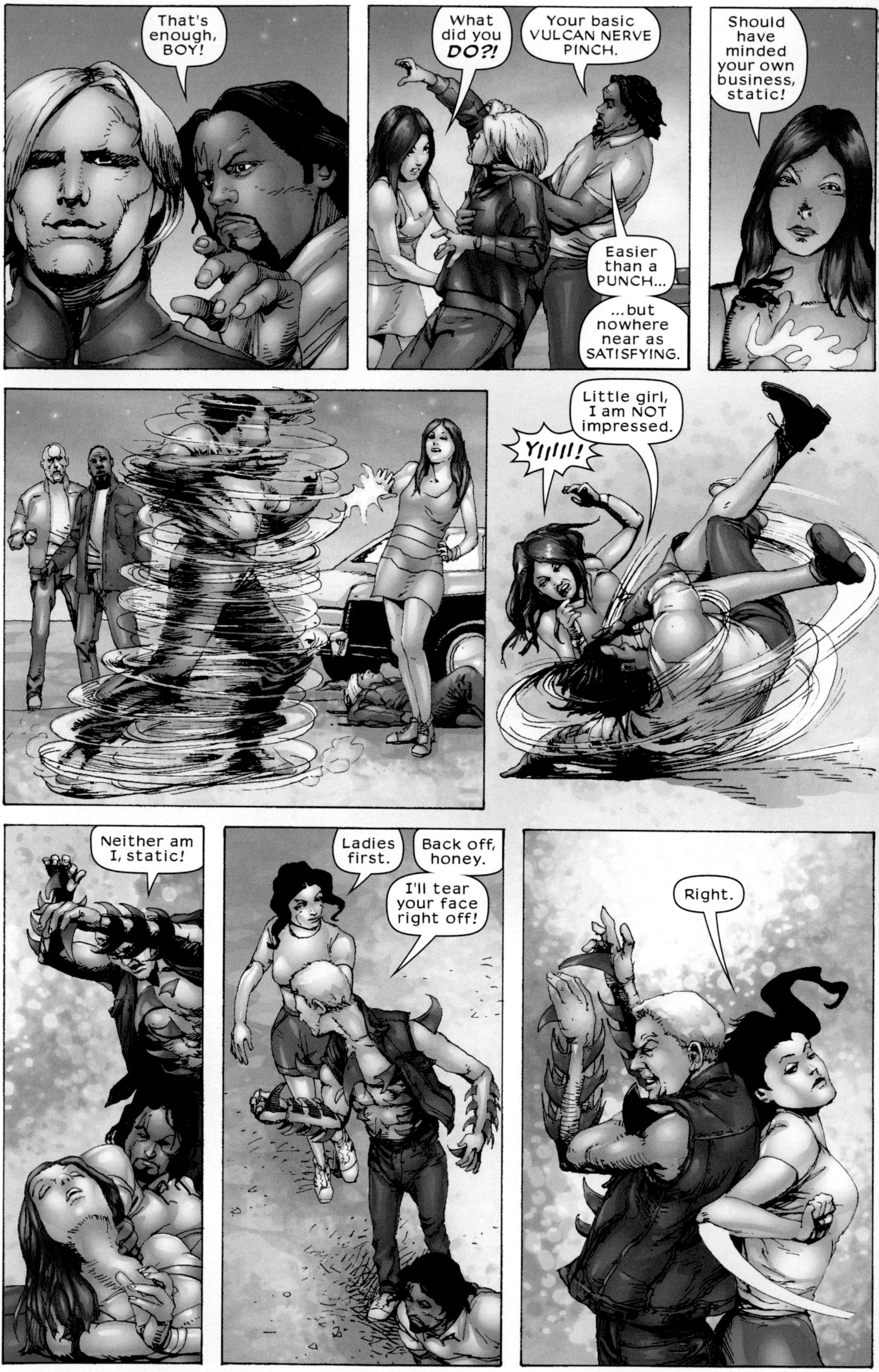
That's enough, BOY!
What did you DO?!
Your basic VULCAN NERVE PINCH.
Easier than a PUNCH...
...but nowhere near as SATISFYING.
Should have minded your own business, static!
YIIIII!
Little girl, I am NOT impressed.
Neither am I, static!
Ladies first.
Back off, honey.
I'll tear your face right off!
Right.

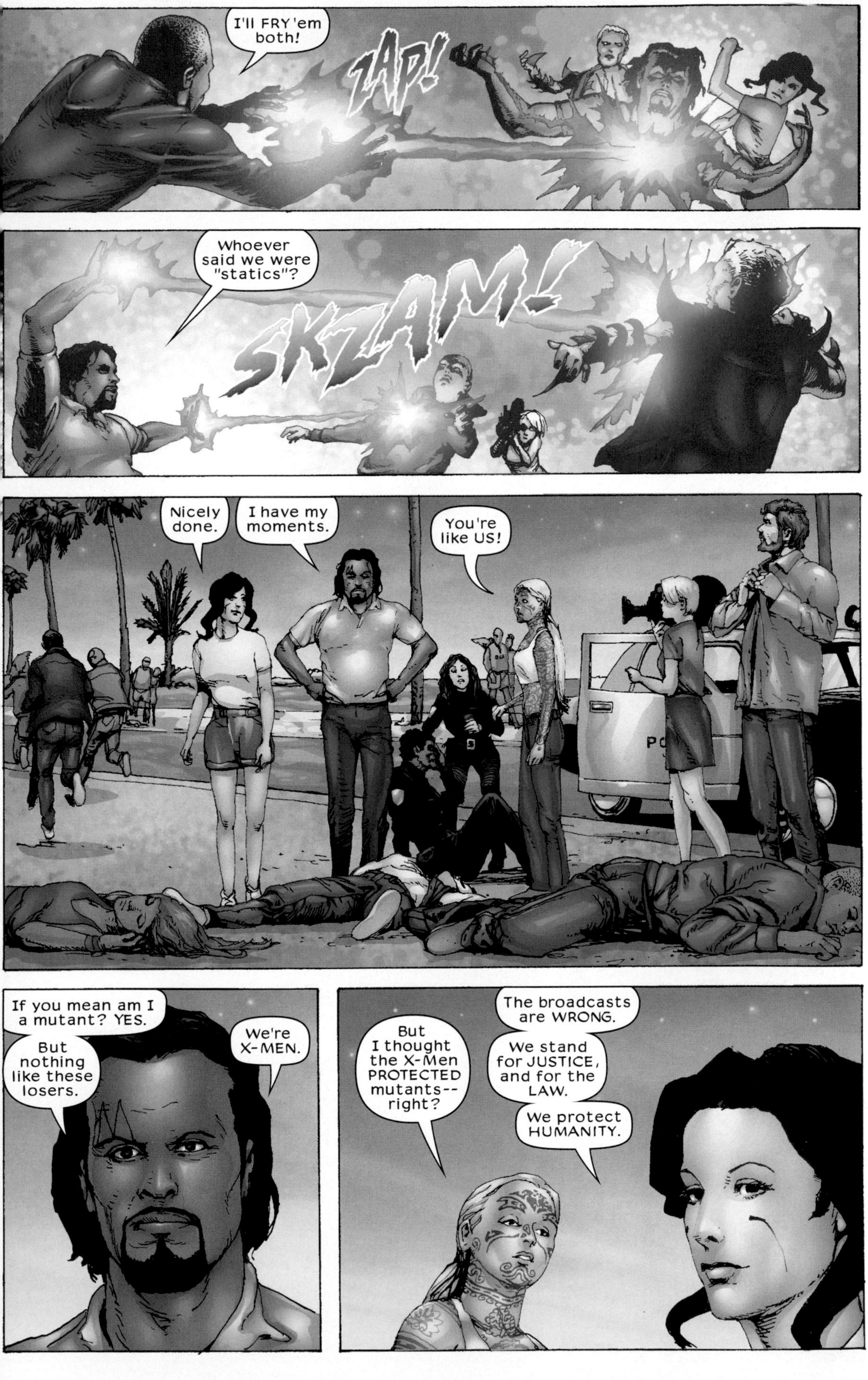
I'll FRY 'em both!
ZAP!
Whoever said we were "statics"?
SKZAM!
Nicely done.
I have my moments.
You're like US!
If you mean am I a mutant? YES.
But nothing like these losers.
We're X-MEN.
But I thought the X-Men PROTECTED mutants--right?
The broadcasts are WRONG.
We stand for JUSTICE, and for the LAW.
We protect HUMANITY.

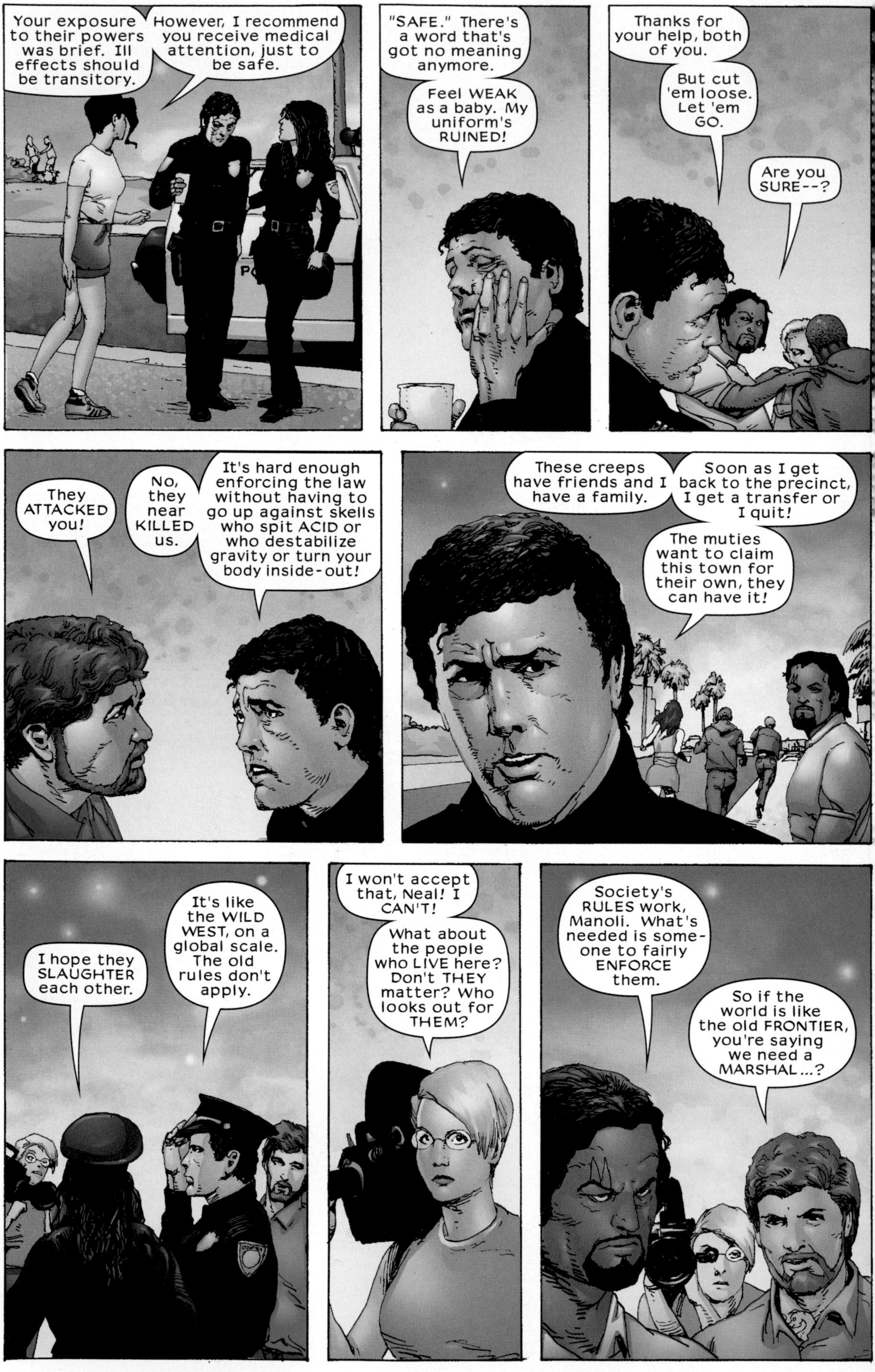

Your exposure to their powers was brief. Ill effects should be transitory.
However, I recommend you receive medical attention, just to be safe.
"SAFE." There's a word that's got no meaning anymore.
Feel WEAK as a baby. My uniform's RUINED!
Thanks for your help, both of you.
But cut 'em loose. Let 'em GO.
Are you SURE--?
They ATTACKED you!
No, they near KILLED us.
It's hard enough enforcing the law without having to go up against skells who spit ACID or who destabilize gravity or turn your body inside-out!
These creeps have friends and I have a family.
Soon as I get back to the precinct, I get a transfer or I quit!
The muties want to claim this town for their own, they can have it!
I hope they SLAUGHTER each other.
It's like the WILD WEST, on a global scale. The old rules don't apply.
I won't accept that, Neal! I CAN'T!
What about the people who LIVE here? Don't THEY matter? Who looks out for THEM?
Society's RULES work, Manoli. What's needed is some-one to fairly ENFORCE them.
So if the world is like the old FRONTIER, you're saying we need a MARSHAL...?

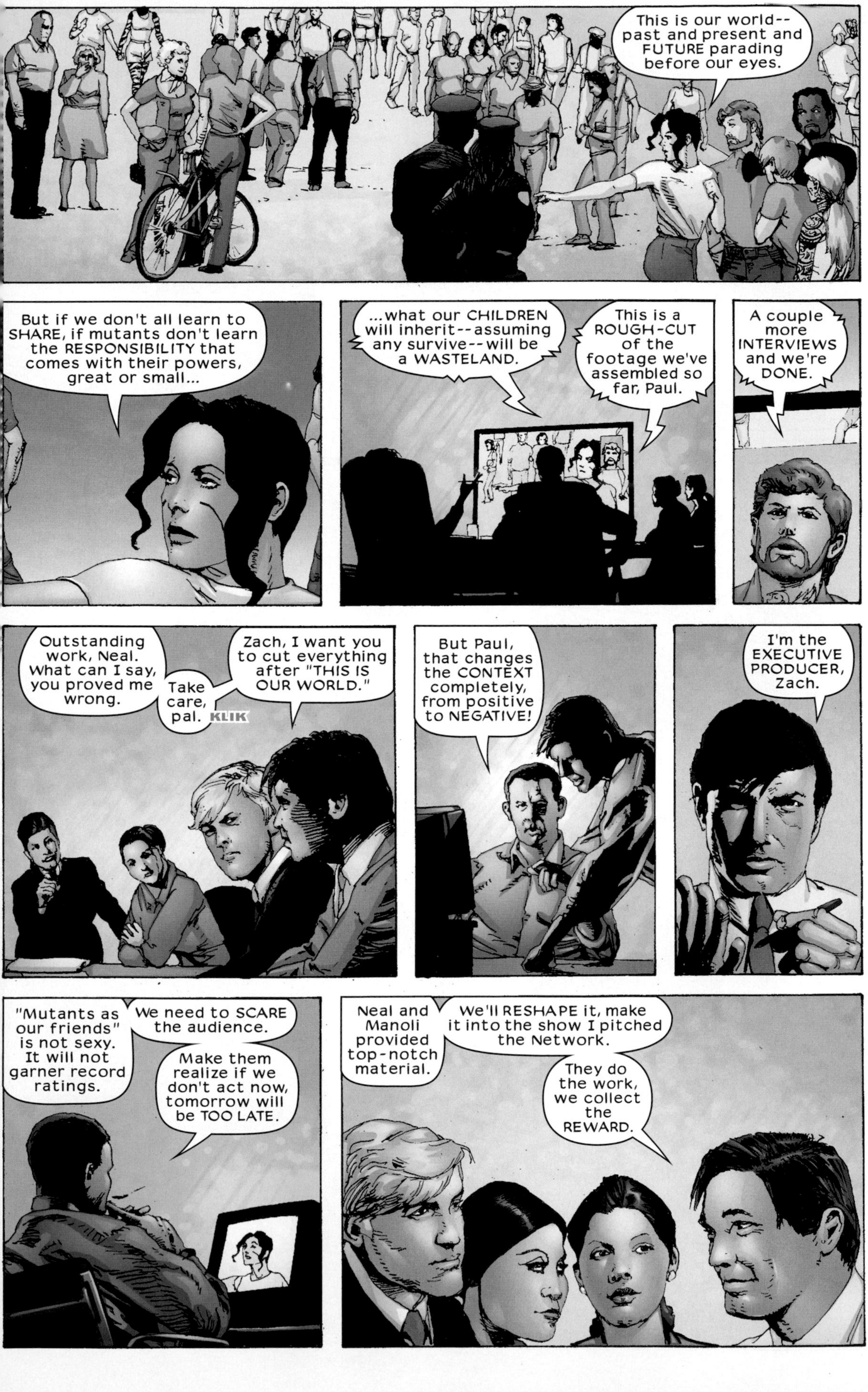
This is our world-- past and present and FUTURE parading before our eyes.
But if we don't all learn to SHARE, if mutants don't learn the RESPONSIBILITY that comes with their powers, great or small...
...what our CHILDREN will inherit--assuming any survive--will be a WASTELAND.
This is a ROUGH-CUT of the footage we've assembled so far, Paul.
A couple more INTERVIEWS and we're DONE.
Outstanding work, Neal. What can I say, you proved me wrong.
Take care, pal.
KLIK
Zach, I want you to cut everything after "THIS IS OUR WORLD."
But Paul, that changes the CONTEXT completely, from positive to NEGATIVE!
I'm the EXECUTIVE PRODUCER, Zach.
"Mutants as our friends" is not sexy. It will not garner record ratings.
We need to SCARE the audience.
Make them realize if we don't act now, tomorrow will be TOO LATE.
Neal and Manoli provided top-notch material.
We'll RESHAPE it, make it into the show I pitched the Network.
They do the work, we collect the REWARD.

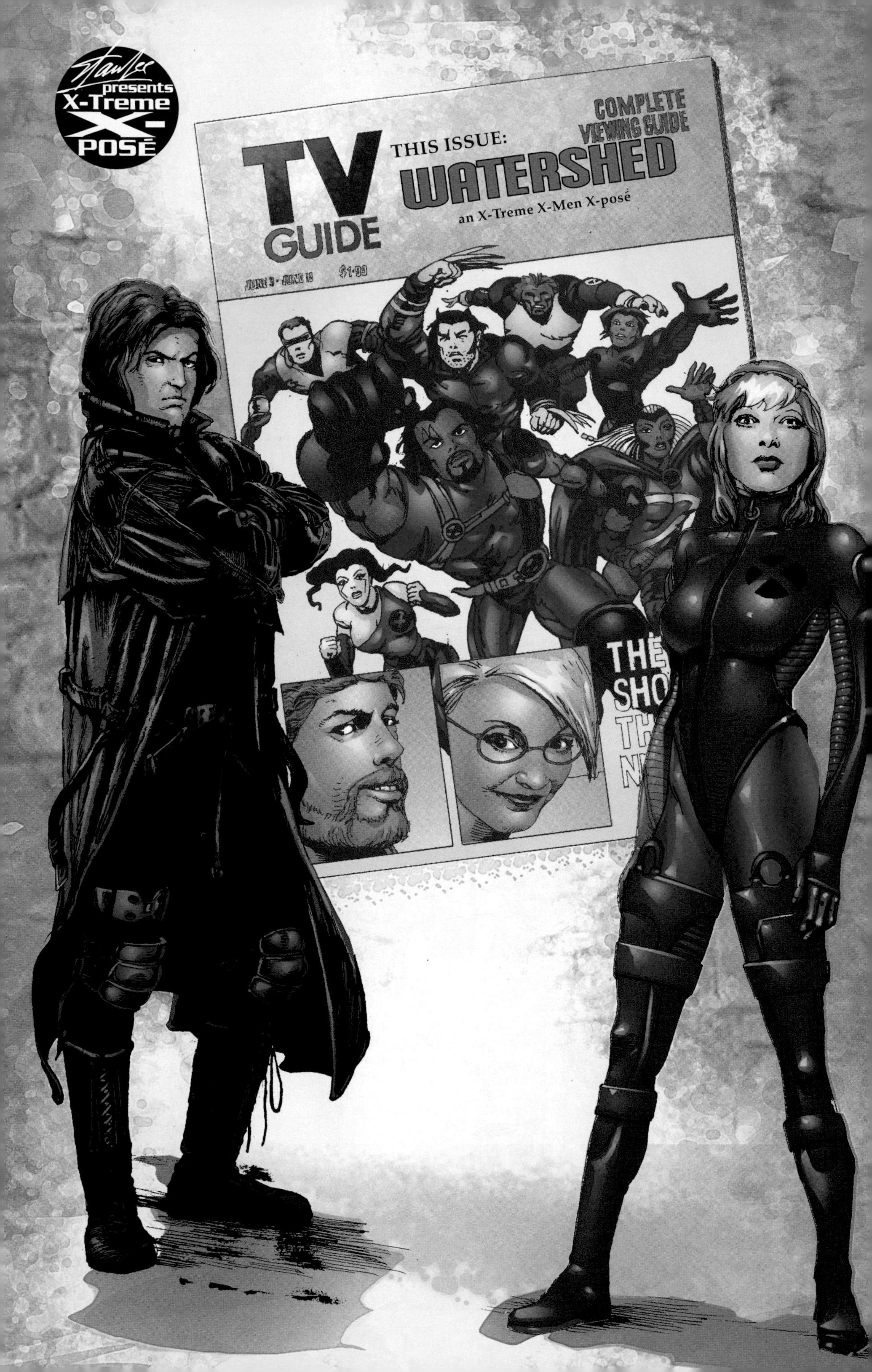

Stan Lee presents X-Treme X-Posé
TV GUIDE
THIS ISSUE:
WATERSHED
an X-Treme X-Men X-posé
COMPLETE VIEWING GUIDE
JUNE 3 • JUNE 10
$1.99

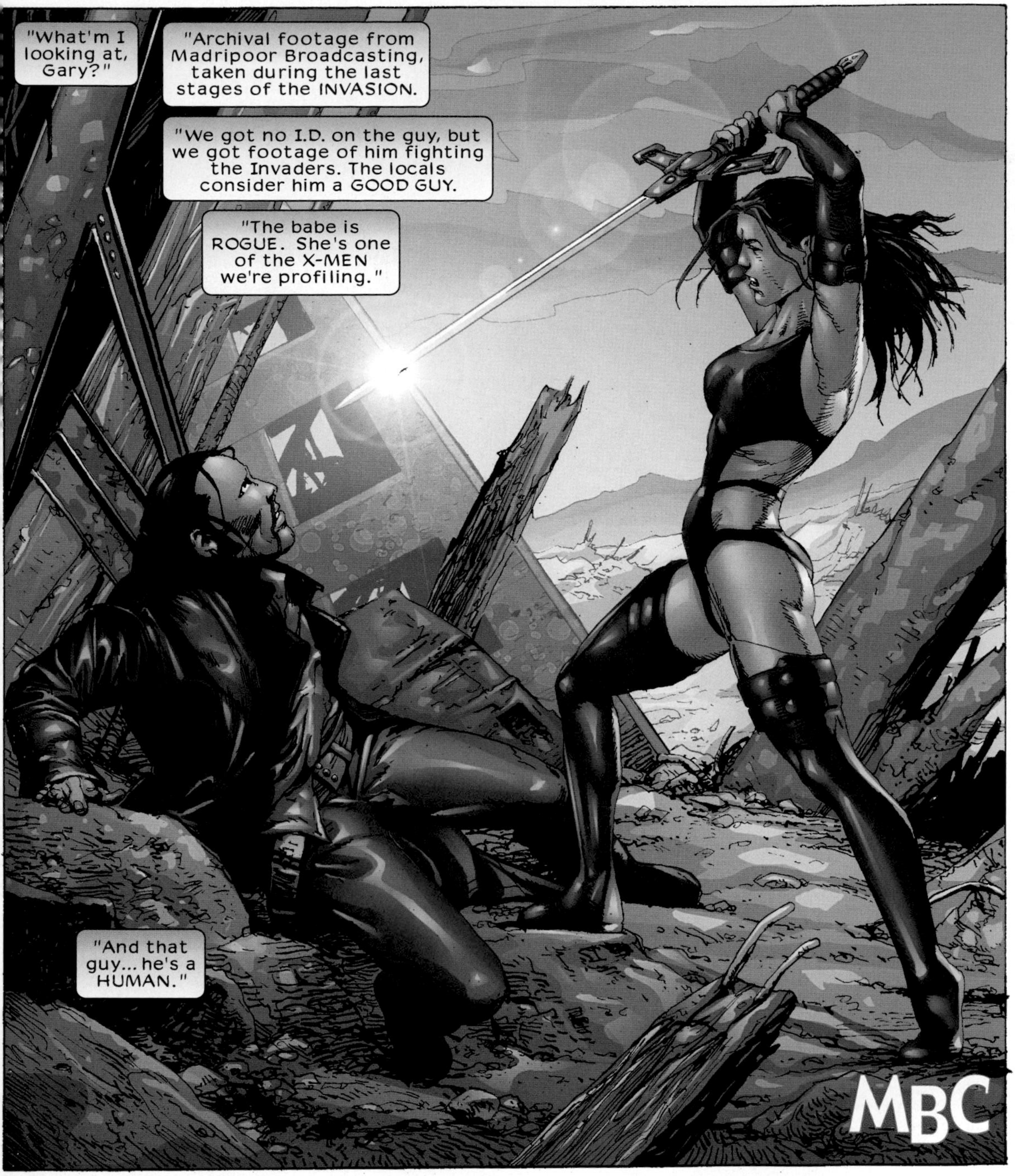
"What'm I looking at, Gary?"
"Archival footage from Madripoor Broadcasting, taken during the last stages of the INVASION.
"We got no I.D. on the guy, but we got footage of him fighting the Invaders. The locals consider him a GOOD GUY.
"The babe is ROGUE. She's one of the X-MEN we're profiling."
"And that guy... he's a HUMAN."
MBC

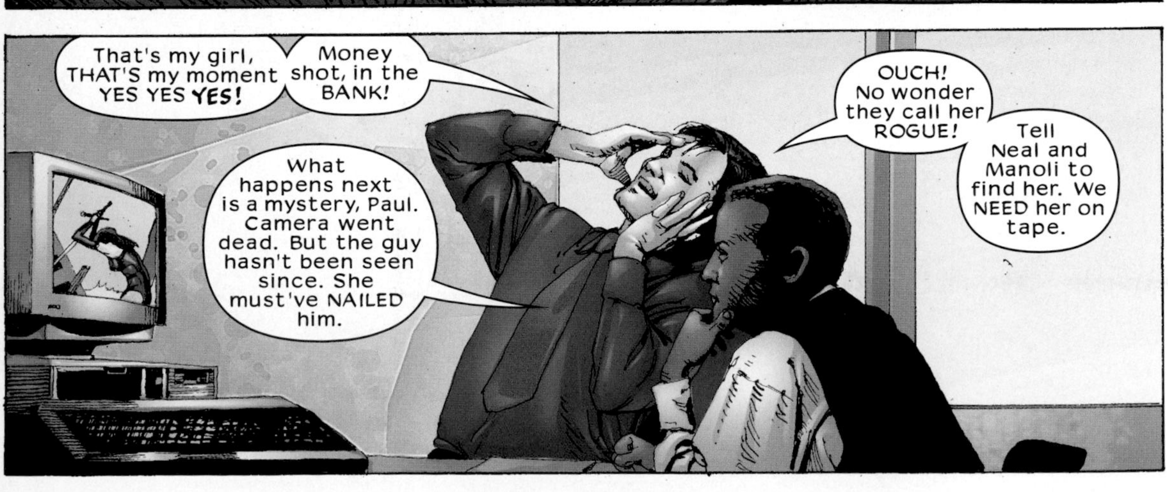
That's my girl, THAT'S my moment YES YES YES!
Money shot, in the BANK!
What happens next is a mystery, Paul. Camera went dead. But the guy hasn't been seen since. She must've NAILED him.
OUCH! No wonder they call her ROGUE!
Tell Neal and Manoli to find her. We NEED her on tape.

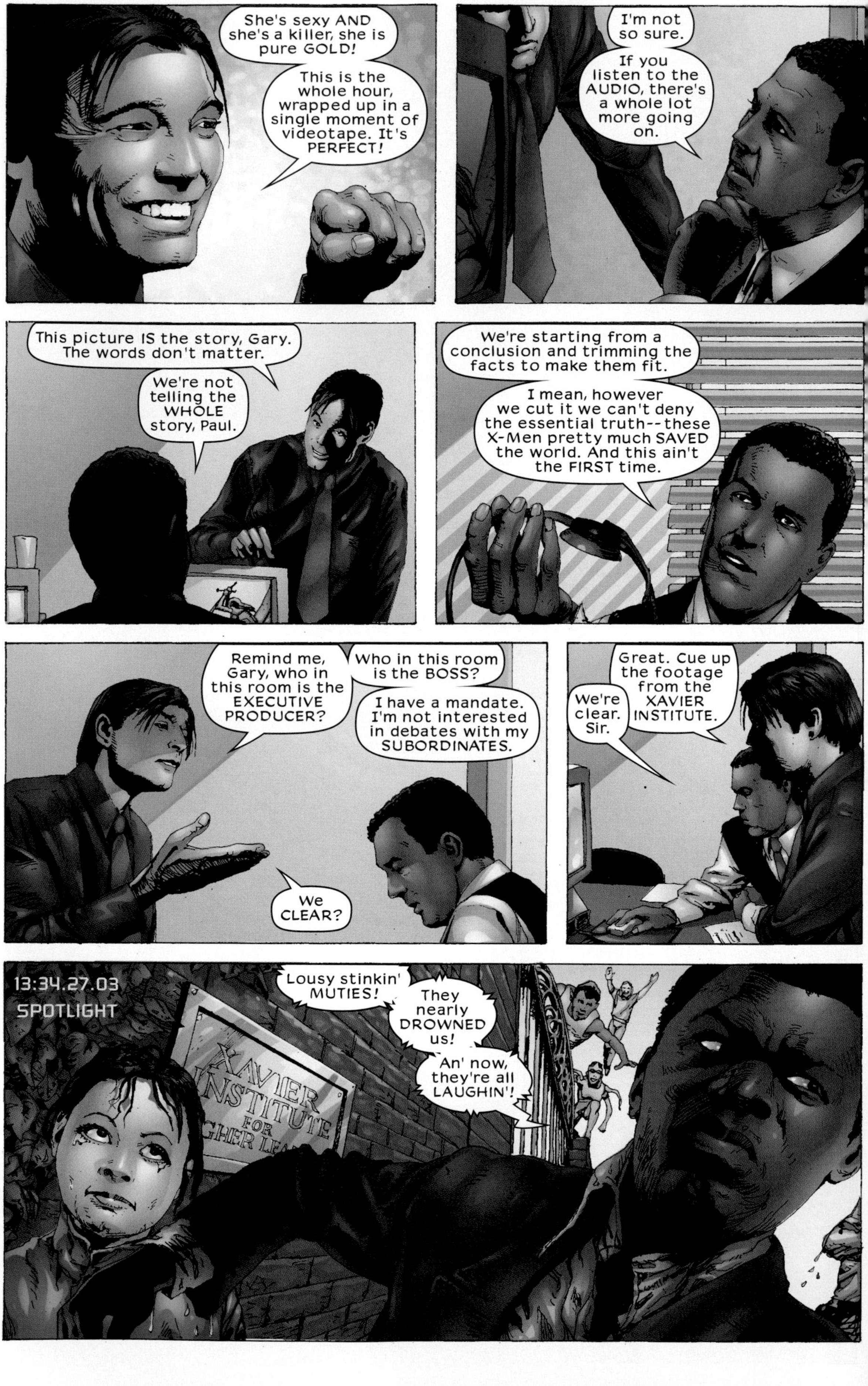

She's sexy AND she's a killer, she is pure GOLD!
This is the whole hour, wrapped up in a single moment of videotape. It's PERFECT!
I'm not so sure.
If you listen to the AUDIO, there's a whole lot more going on.
This picture IS the story, Gary. The words don't matter.
We're not telling the WHOLE story, Paul.
We're starting from a conclusion and trimming the facts to make them fit.
I mean, however we cut it we can't deny the essential truth--these X-Men pretty much SAVED the world. And this ain't the FIRST time.
Remind me, Gary, who in this room is the EXECUTIVE PRODUCER?
Who in this room is the BOSS?
I have a mandate. I'm not interested in debates with my SUBORDINATES.
We CLEAR?
We're clear. Sir.
Great. Cue up the footage from the XAVIER INSTITUTE.
13:34.27.03
SPOTLIGHT
Lousy stinkin' MUTIES!
They nearly DROWNED us!
An' now, they're all LAUGHIN'!
XAVIER INSTITUTE FOR

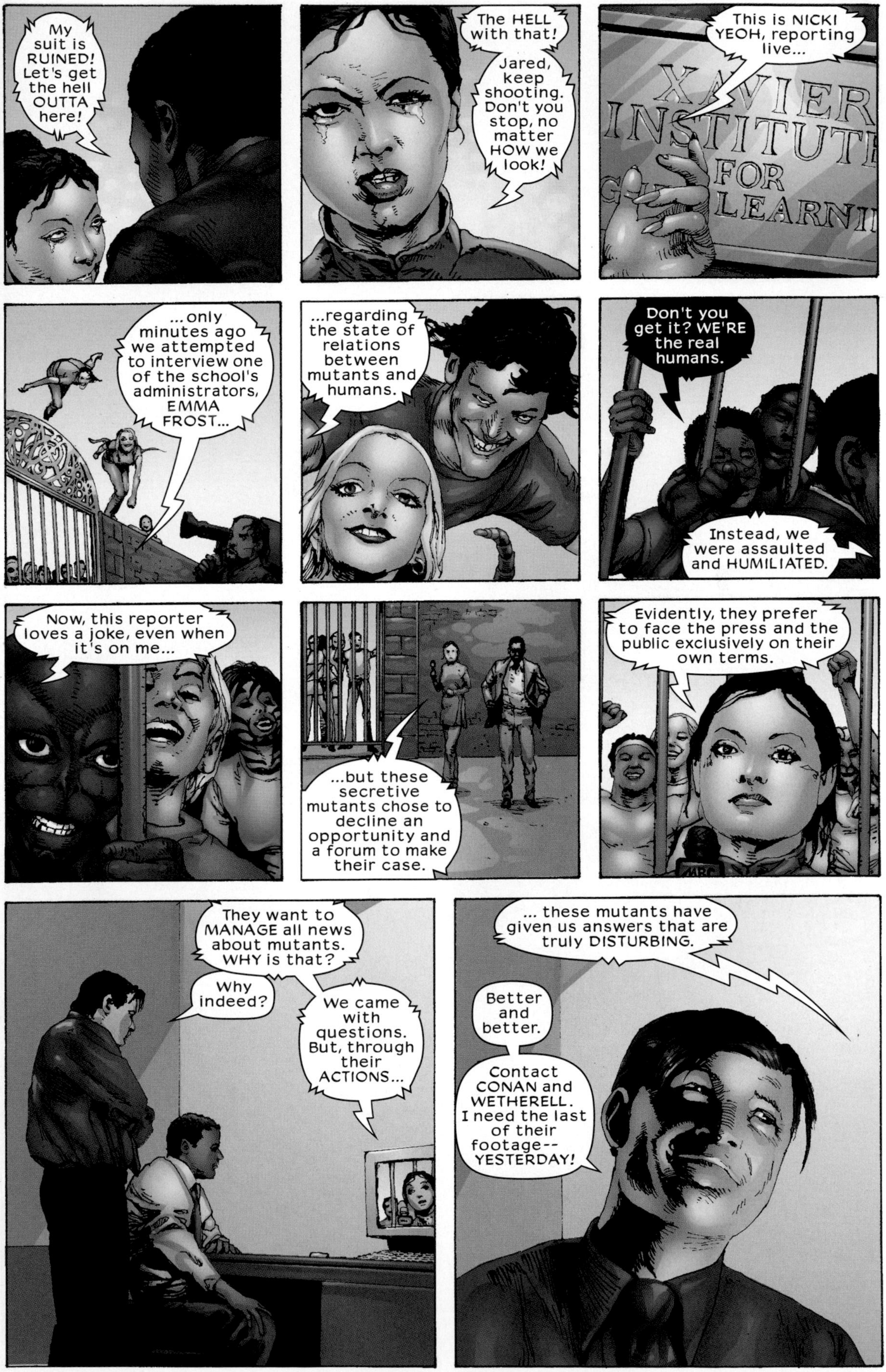
My suit is RUINED! Let's get the hell OUTTA here!
The HELL with that!
Jared, keep shooting. Don't you stop, no matter HOW we look!
This is NICKI YEOH, reporting live...
XAVIER INSTITUTE FOR LEARNI
...only minutes ago we attempted to interview one of the school's administrators, EMMA FROST...
...regarding the state of relations between mutants and humans.
Don't you get it? WE'RE the real humans.
Instead, we were assaulted and HUMILIATED.
Now, this reporter loves a joke, even when it's on me...
...but these secretive mutants chose to decline an opportunity and a forum to make their case.
Evidently, they prefer to face the press and the public exclusively on their own terms.
They want to MANAGE all news about mutants. WHY is that?
Why indeed?
We came with questions. But, through their ACTIONS...
... these mutants have given us answers that are truly DISTURBING.
Better and better.
Contact CONAN and WETHERELL. I need the last of their footage-- YESTERDAY!

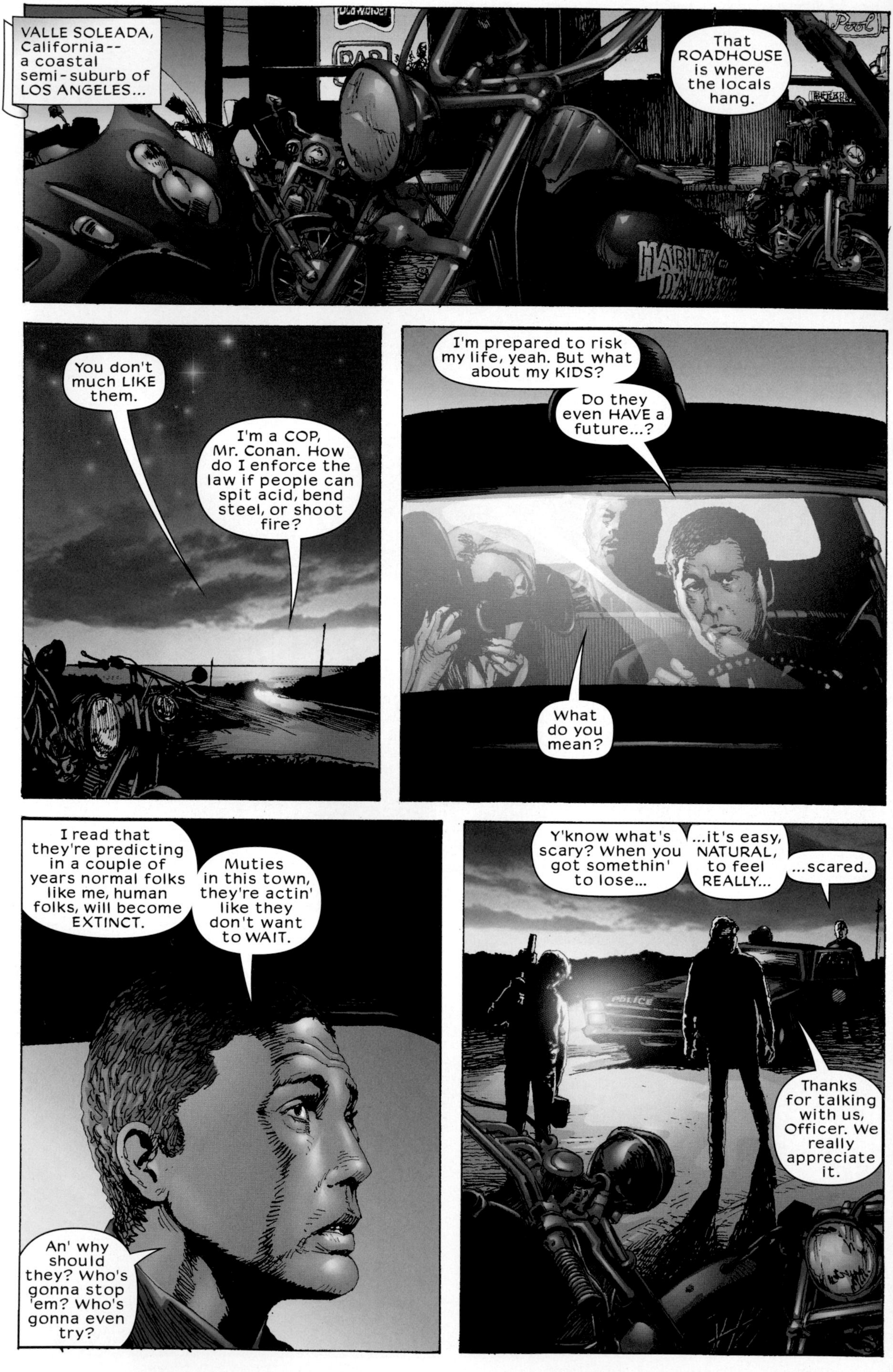

VALLE SOLEADA, California-- a coastal semi-suburb of LOS ANGELES...
That ROADHOUSE is where the locals hang.
You don't much LIKE them.
I'm a COP, Mr. Conan. How do I enforce the law if people can spit acid, bend steel, or shoot fire?
I'm prepared to risk my life, yeah. But what about my KIDS?
Do they even HAVE a future...?
What do you mean?
I read that they're predicting in a couple of years normal folks like me, human folks, will become EXTINCT.
Muties in this town, they're actin' like they don't want to WAIT.
An' why should they? Who's gonna stop 'em? Who's gonna even try?
Y'know what's scary? When you got somethin' to lose...
...it's easy, NATURAL, to feel REALLY...
...scared.
Thanks for talking with us, Officer. We really appreciate it.

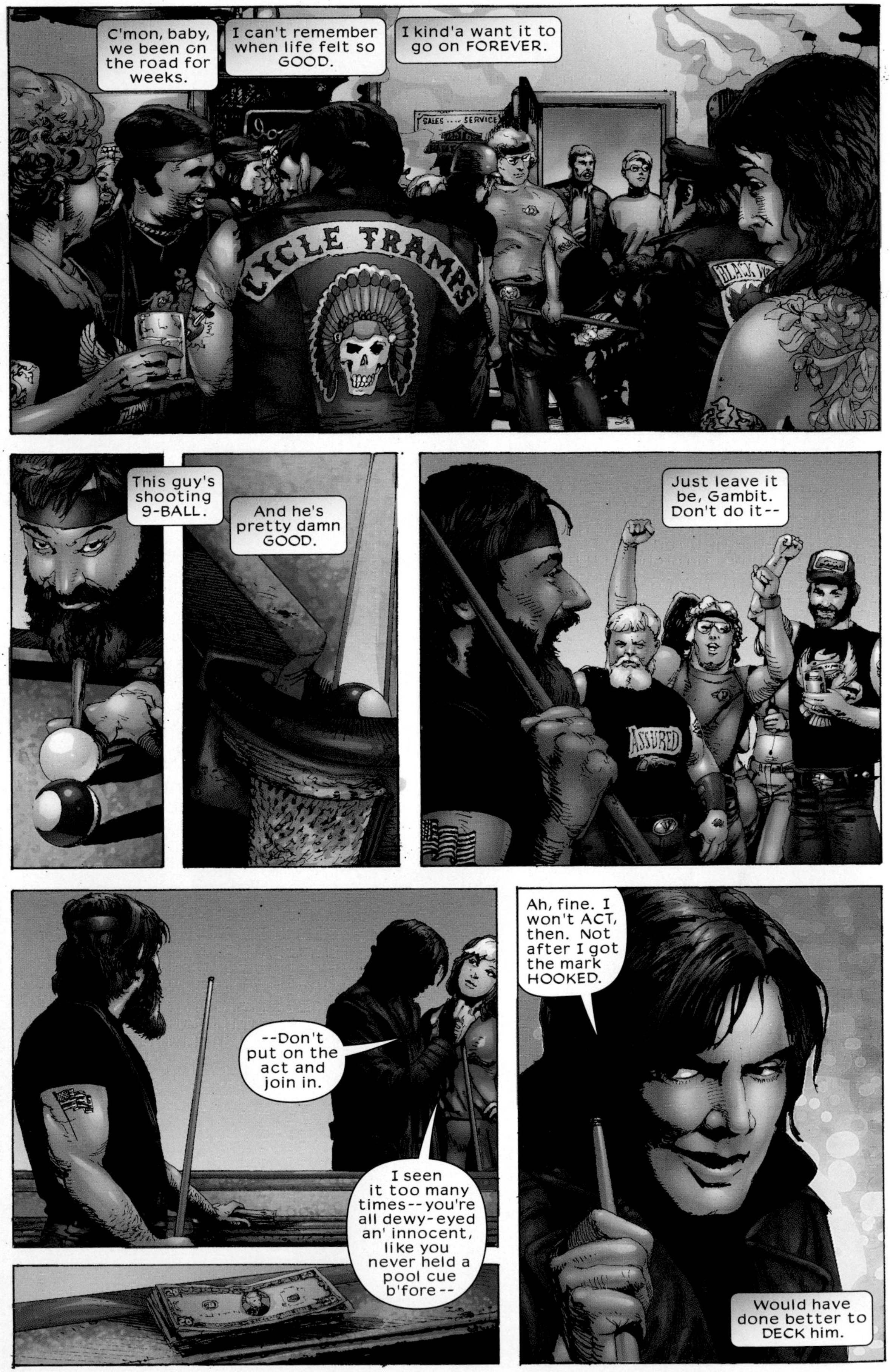

C'mon, baby, we been on the road for weeks.
I can't remember when life felt so GOOD.
I kind'a want it to go on FOREVER.
CYCLE TRAMPS
SALES .... SERVICE
This guy's shooting 9-BALL.
And he's pretty damn GOOD.
Just leave it be, Gambit. Don't do it--
ASSURED
--Don't put on the act and join in.
I seen it too many times--you're all dewy-eyed an' innocent, like you never held a pool cue b'fore--
Ah, fine. I won't ACT, then. Not after I got the mark HOOKED.
Would have done better to DECK him.

Nice shot...

PLIK!

PLOOK!

PLOP!

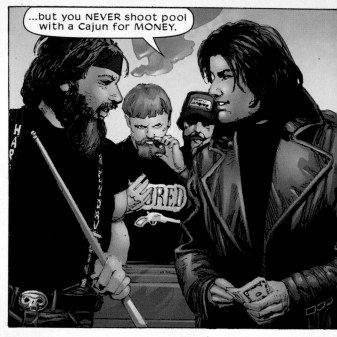

...but you NEVER shoot pool with a Cajun for MONEY.

We don't like bein' HUSTLED, Cajun.

DORKING Angels

Name's REMY. A Cajun's just a natural, an' a natural charmer...

Buy you a BEER?

All of you?

All right, friend. Good game. I'm JACK.

CAMERA!

REPORTERS!

CLEAR OUT!

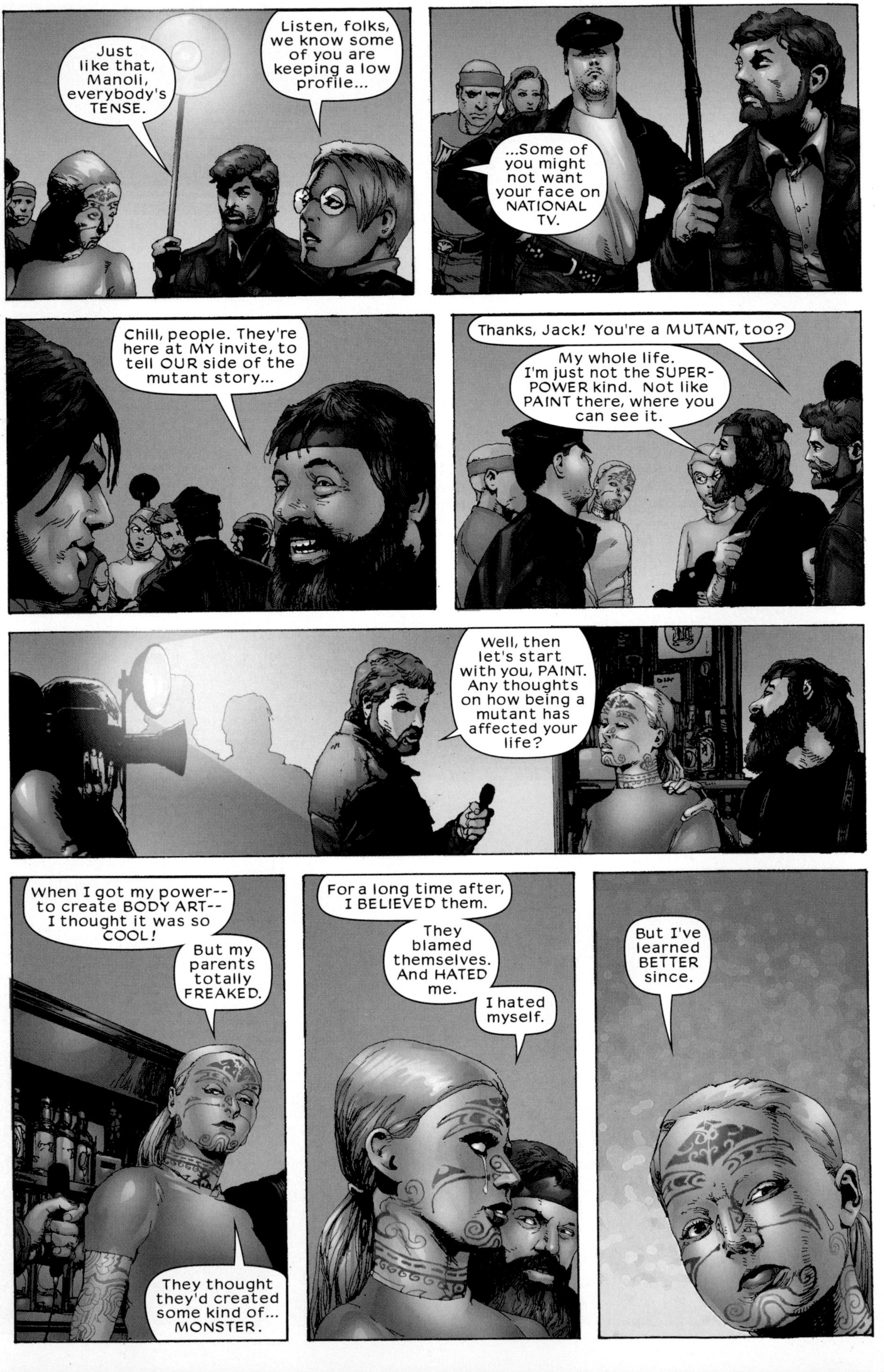
Just like that, Manoli, everybody's TENSE.
Listen, folks, we know some of you are keeping a low profile...
...Some of you might not want your face on NATIONAL TV.
Chill, people. They're here at MY invite, to tell OUR side of the mutant story...
Thanks, Jack! You're a MUTANT, too?
My whole life. I'm just not the SUPER-POWER kind. Not like PAINT there, where you can see it.
Well, then let's start with you, PAINT. Any thoughts on how being a mutant has affected your life?
When I got my power--to create BODY ART--I thought it was so COOL!
But my parents totally FREAKED.
They thought they'd created some kind of... MONSTER.
For a long time after, I BELIEVED them.
They blamed themselves. And HATED me.
I hated myself.
But I've learned BETTER since.

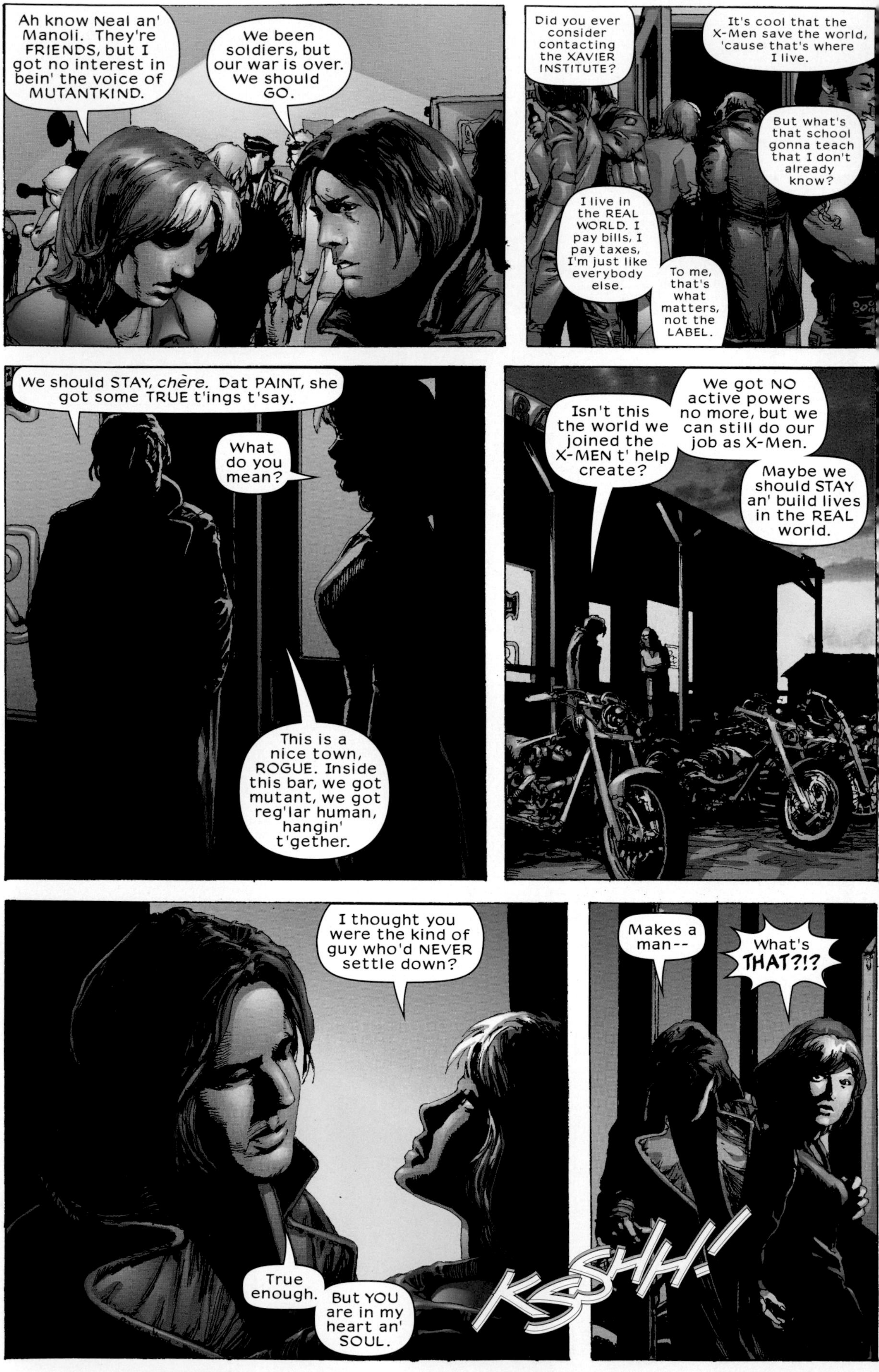
Ah know Neal an' Manoli. They're FRIENDS, but I got no interest in bein' the voice of MUTANTKIND.
We been soldiers, but our war is over. We should GO.
Did you ever consider contacting the XAVIER INSTITUTE?
It's cool that the X-Men save the world, 'cause that's where I live.
But what's that school gonna teach that I don't already know?
I live in the REAL WORLD. I pay bills, I pay taxes, I'm just like everybody else.
To me, that's what matters, not the LABEL.
We should STAY, chère. Dat PAINT, she got some TRUE t'ings t'say.
What do you mean?
This is a nice town, ROGUE. Inside this bar, we got mutant, we got reg'lar human, hangin' t'gether.
Isn't this the world we joined the X-MEN t' help create?
We got NO active powers no more, but we can still do our job as X-Men.
Maybe we should STAY an' build lives in the REAL world.
I thought you were the kind of guy who'd NEVER settle down?
True enough.
But YOU are in my heart an' SOUL.
KSSHH!
Makes a man--
What's THAT?!?

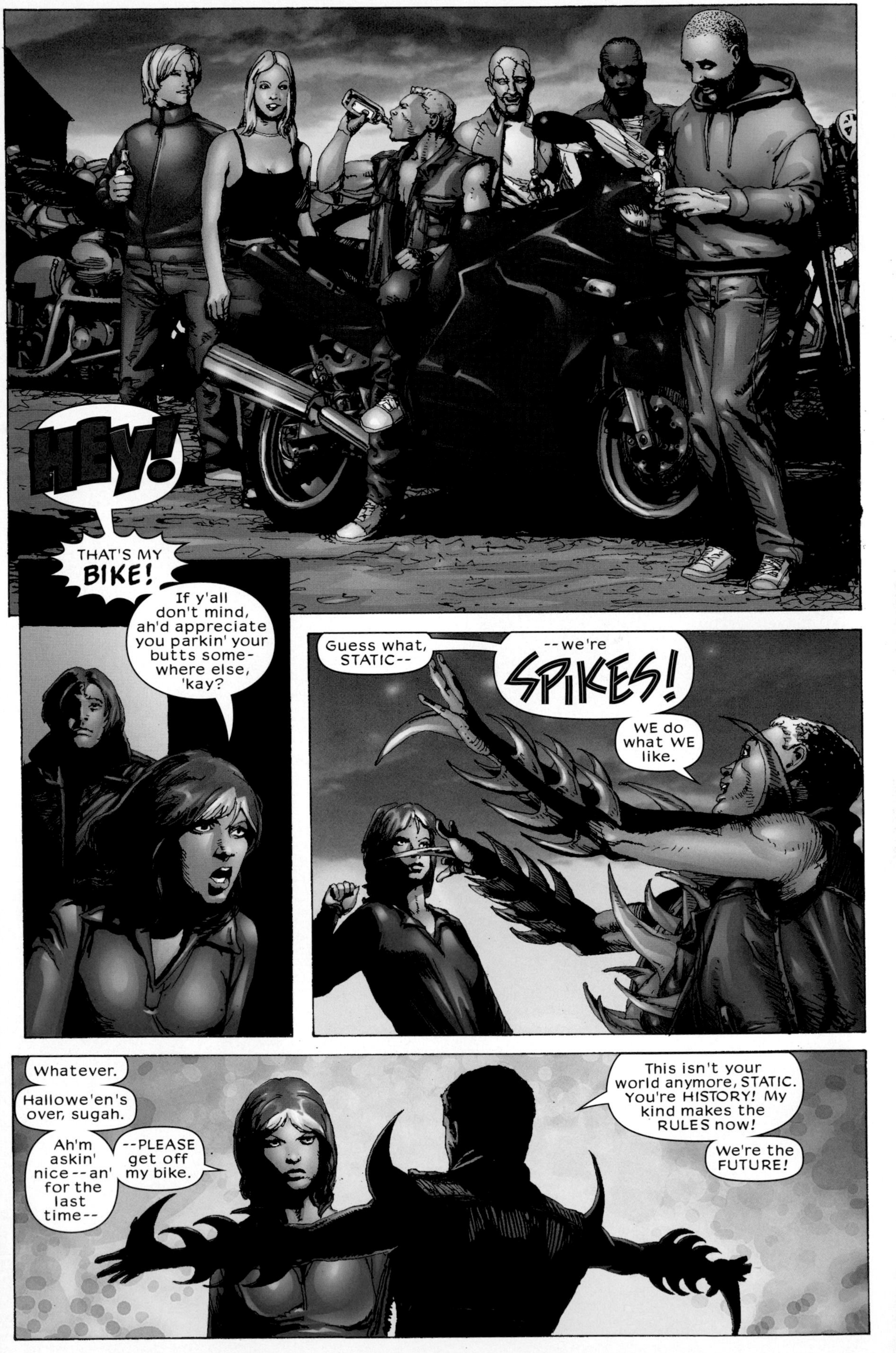
HEY!
THAT'S MY BIKE!
If y'all don't mind, ah'd appreciate you parkin' your butts some-where else, 'kay?
Guess what, STATIC--
--we're SPIKES!
WE do what WE like.
Whatever.
Hallowe'en's over, sugah.
Ah'm askin' nice--an' for the last time--
--PLEASE get off my bike.
This isn't your world anymore, STATIC. You're HISTORY! My kind makes the RULES now!
We're the FUTURE!

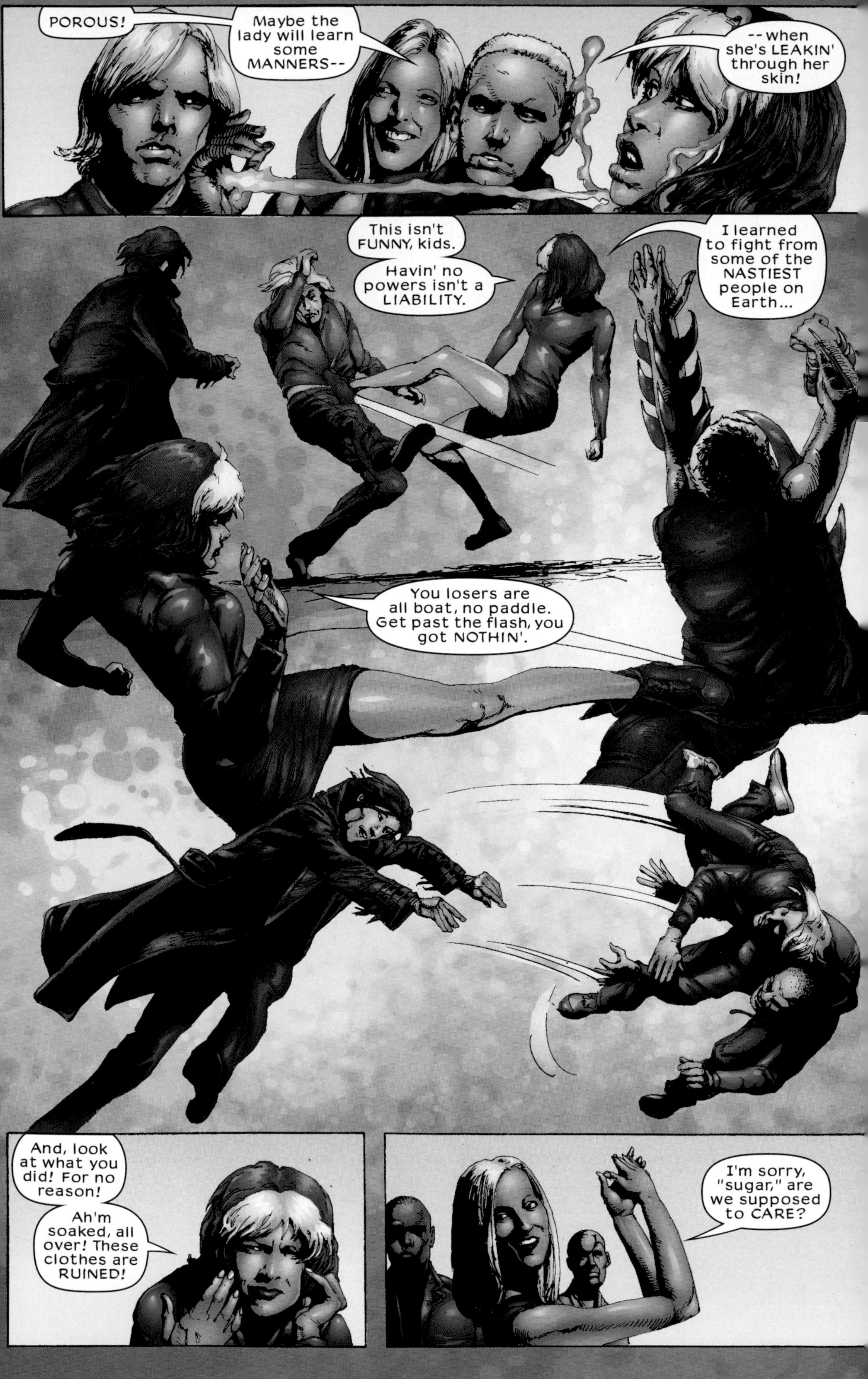

POROUS!
Maybe the lady will learn some MANNERS--
--when she's LEAKIN' through her skin!
This isn't FUNNY, kids.
Havin' no powers isn't a LIABILITY.
I learned to fight from some of the NASTIEST people on Earth...
You losers are all boat, no paddle. Get past the flash, you got NOTHIN'.
And, look at what you did! For no reason!
Ah'm soaked, all over! These clothes are RUINED!
I'm sorry, "sugar," are we supposed to CARE?

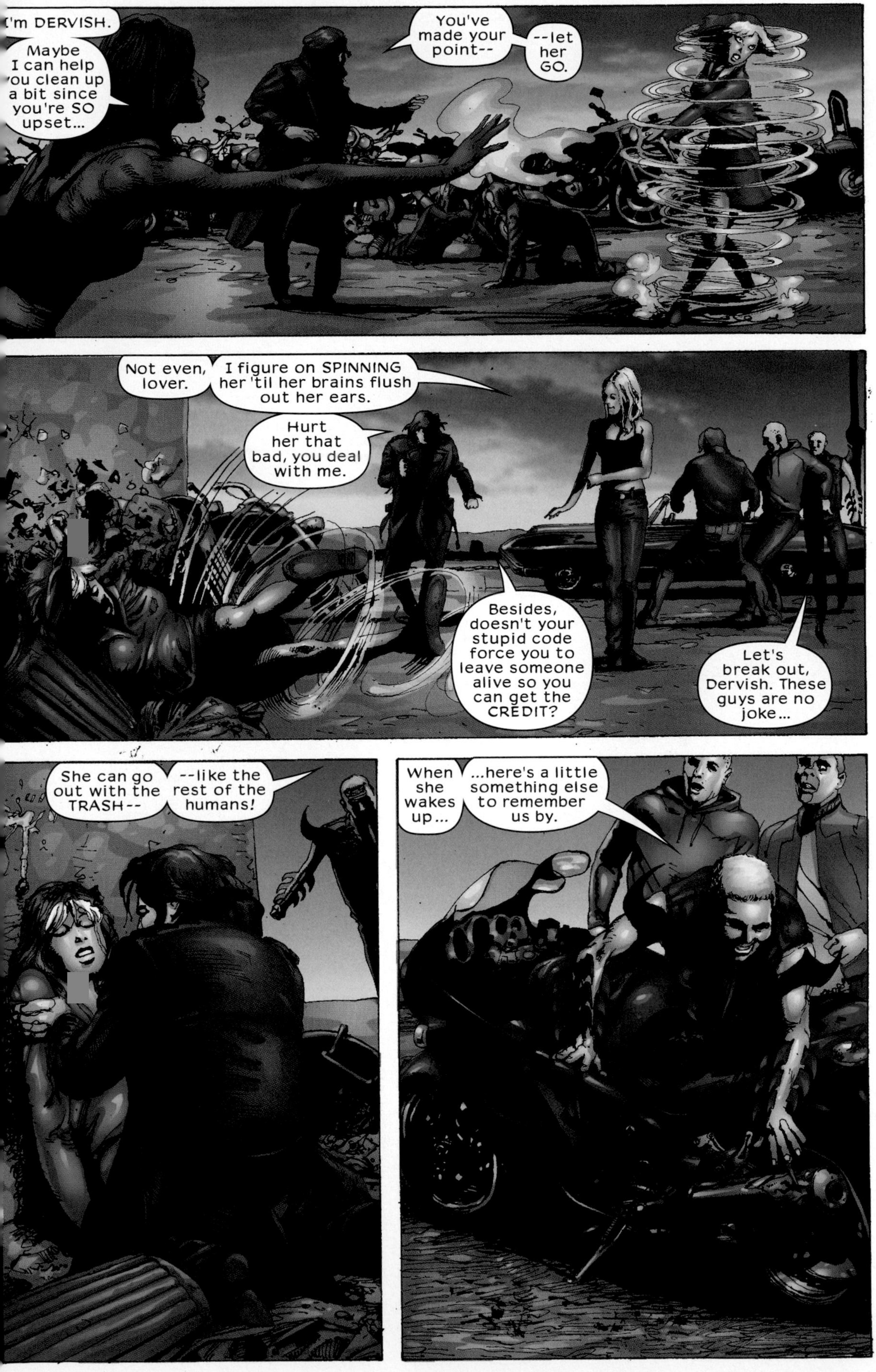
I'm DERVISH.
Maybe I can help you clean up a bit since you're SO upset...
You've made your point--
--let her GO.
Not even, lover.
I figure on SPINNING her 'til her brains flush out her ears.
Hurt her that bad, you deal with me.
Besides, doesn't your stupid code force you to leave someone alive so you can get the CREDIT?
Let's break out, Dervish. These guys are no joke...
She can go out with the TRASH--
--like the rest of the humans!
When she wakes up...
...here's a little something else to remember us by.

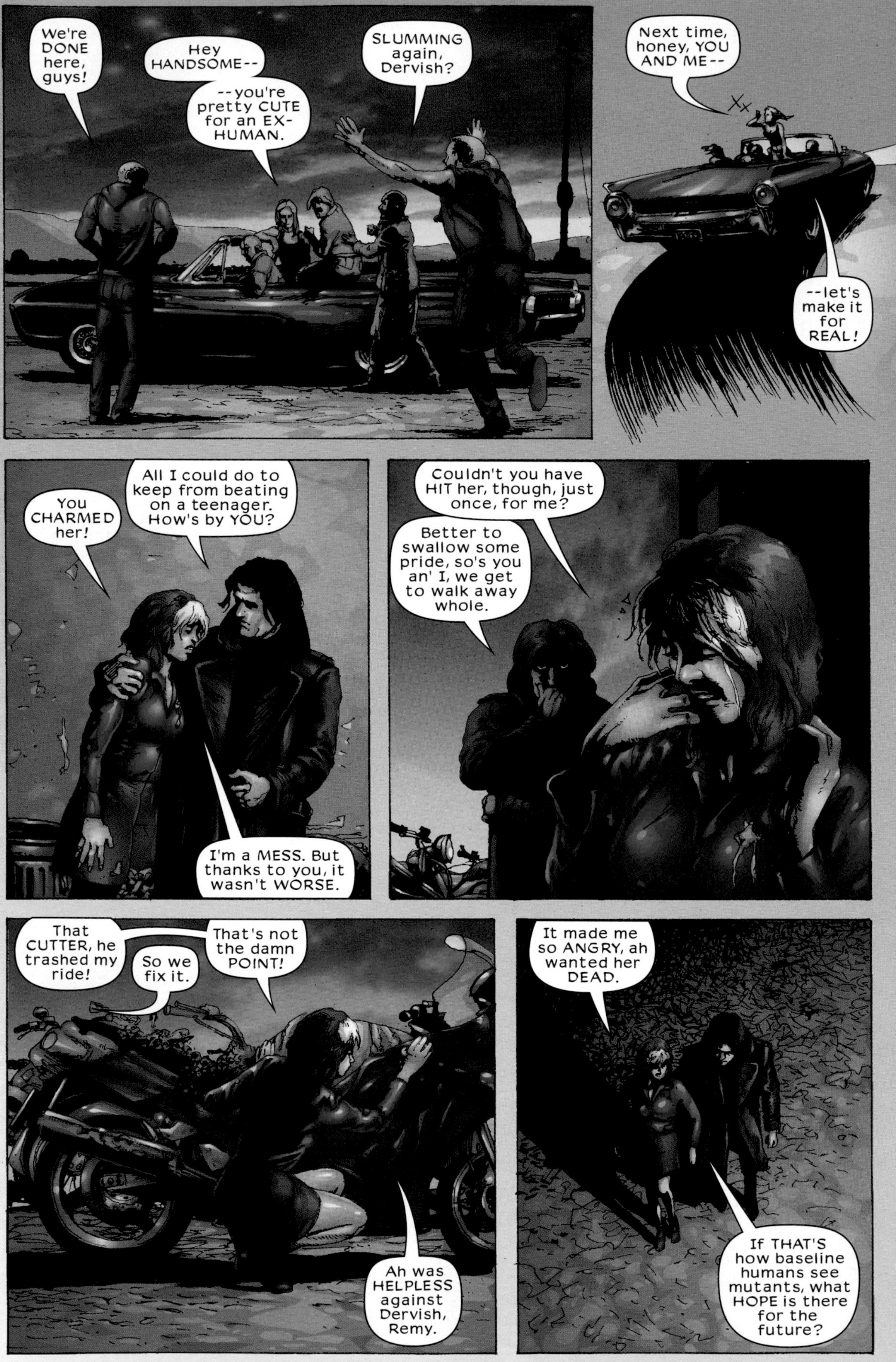
We're DONE here, guys!
Hey HANDSOME--
--you're pretty CUTE for an EX-HUMAN.
SLUMMING again, Dervish?
Next time, honey, YOU AND ME--
--let's make it for REAL!
You CHARMED her!
All I could do to keep from beating on a teenager. How's by YOU?
I'm a MESS. But thanks to you, it wasn't WORSE.
Couldn't you have HIT her, though, just once, for me?
Better to swallow some pride, so's you an' I, we get to walk away whole.
That CUTTER, he trashed my ride!
So we fix it.
That's not the damn POINT!
Ah was HELPLESS against Dervish, Remy.
It made me so ANGRY, ah wanted her DEAD.
If THAT'S how baseline humans see mutants, what HOPE is there for the future?

Ah'm a mess... I guess it's back inside while ah get cleaned up...

On the BRIGHT side, the way you look, no one's likely to RECOGNIZE, or even notice you.

What HAPPENED?!

We got jumped by some wannabe mutant gang-bangers.

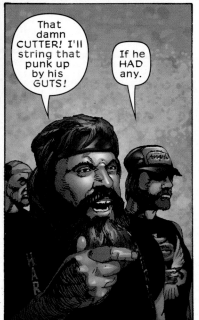

That damn CUTTER! I'll string that punk up by his GUTS!

If he HAD any.

They didn't really HURT anything, except my bike. Just let it go, okay?

You're a lot more COOL about this than I'D ever be.

Ah fight my own battles.

It ain't just YOUR fight, Miss.

This used to be a DECENT town. Folks treated each other with RESPECT. Kids figure bein' a mutant makes 'em king of the world!

It's like they think I should just hang with BIKERS, 'cause I ride one. Or web-designers, 'cause that's how I pay my mortgage.

Or HUMAN BEINGS, 'cause under the skin that's what we ALL are!

A-MEN, brother!

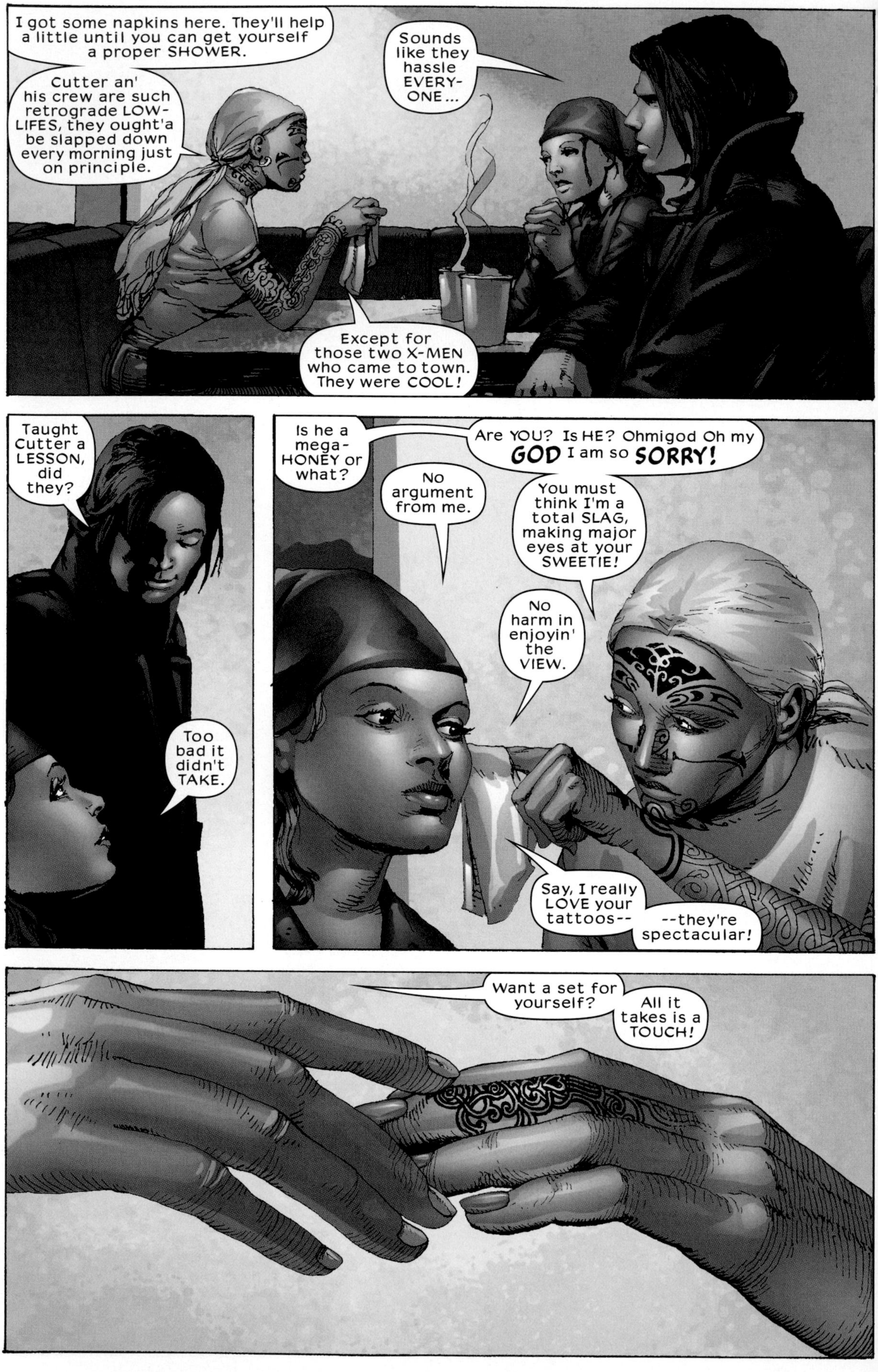
I got some napkins here. They'll help a little until you can get yourself a proper SHOWER.
Cutter an' his crew are such retrograde LOW-LIFES, they ought'a be slapped down every morning just on principle.
Sounds like they hassle EVERY-ONE...
Except for those two X-MEN who came to town. They were COOL!
Taught Cutter a LESSON, did they?
Too bad it didn't TAKE.
Is he a mega-HONEY or what?
Are YOU? Is HE? Ohmigod Oh my GOD I am so SORRY!
No argument from me.
You must think I'm a total SLAG, making major eyes at your SWEETIE!
No harm in enjoyin' the VIEW.
Say, I really LOVE your tattoos--
--they're spectacular!
Want a set for yourself?
All it takes is a TOUCH!

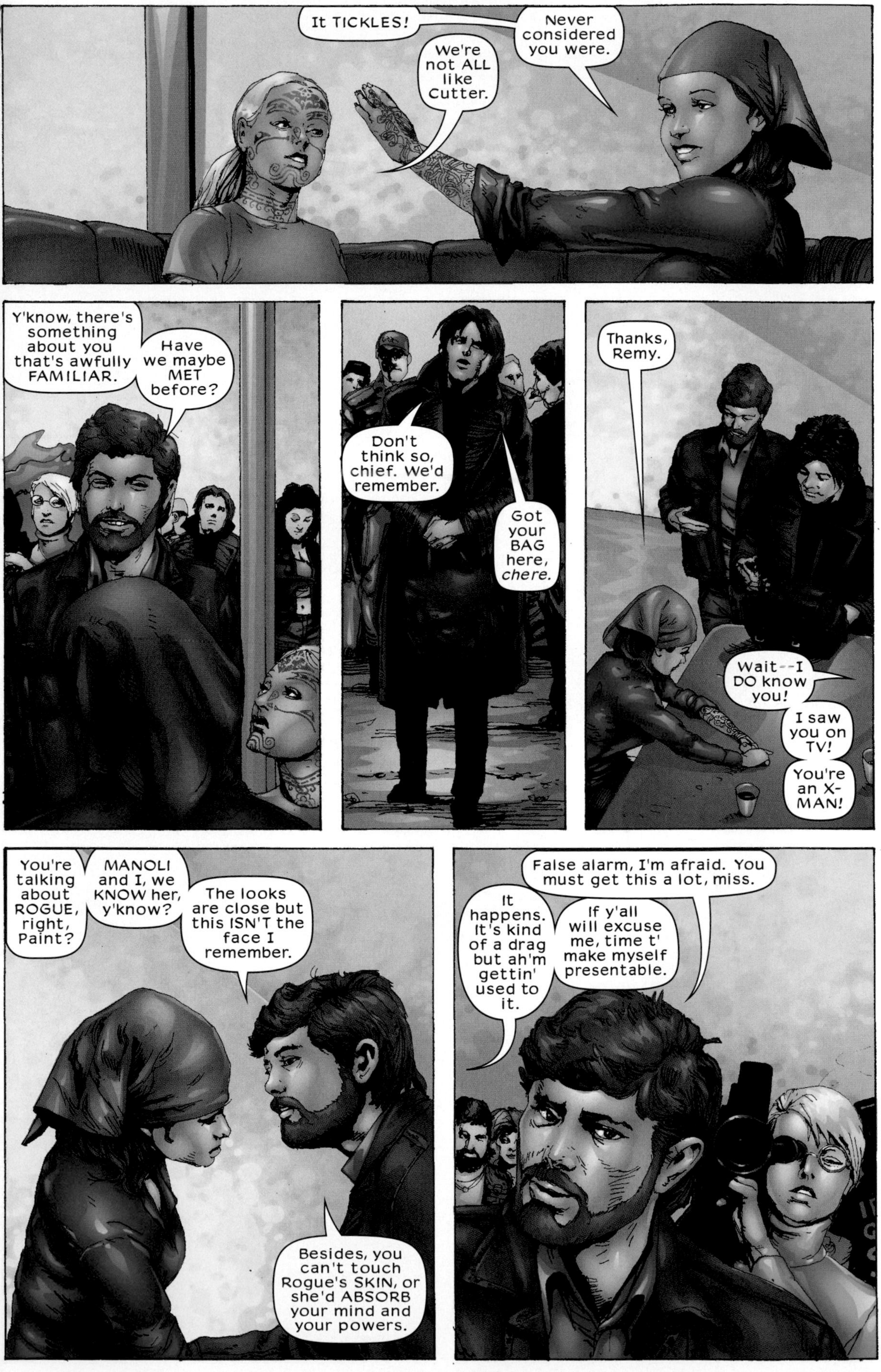
It TICKLES!
Never considered you were.
We're not ALL like Cutter.
Y'know, there's something about you that's awfully FAMILIAR.
Have we maybe MET before?
Don't think so, chief. We'd remember.
Got your BAG here, *chere.*
Thanks, Remy.
Wait--I DO know you!
I saw you on TV!
You're an X-MAN!
You're talking about ROGUE, right, Paint?
MANOLI and I, we KNOW her, y'know?
The looks are close but this ISN'T the face I remember.
Besides, you can't touch Rogue's SKIN, or she'd ABSORB your mind and your powers.
False alarm, I'm afraid. You must get this a lot, miss.
It happens. It's kind of a drag but ah'm gettin' used to it.
If y'all will excuse me, time t' make myself presentable.

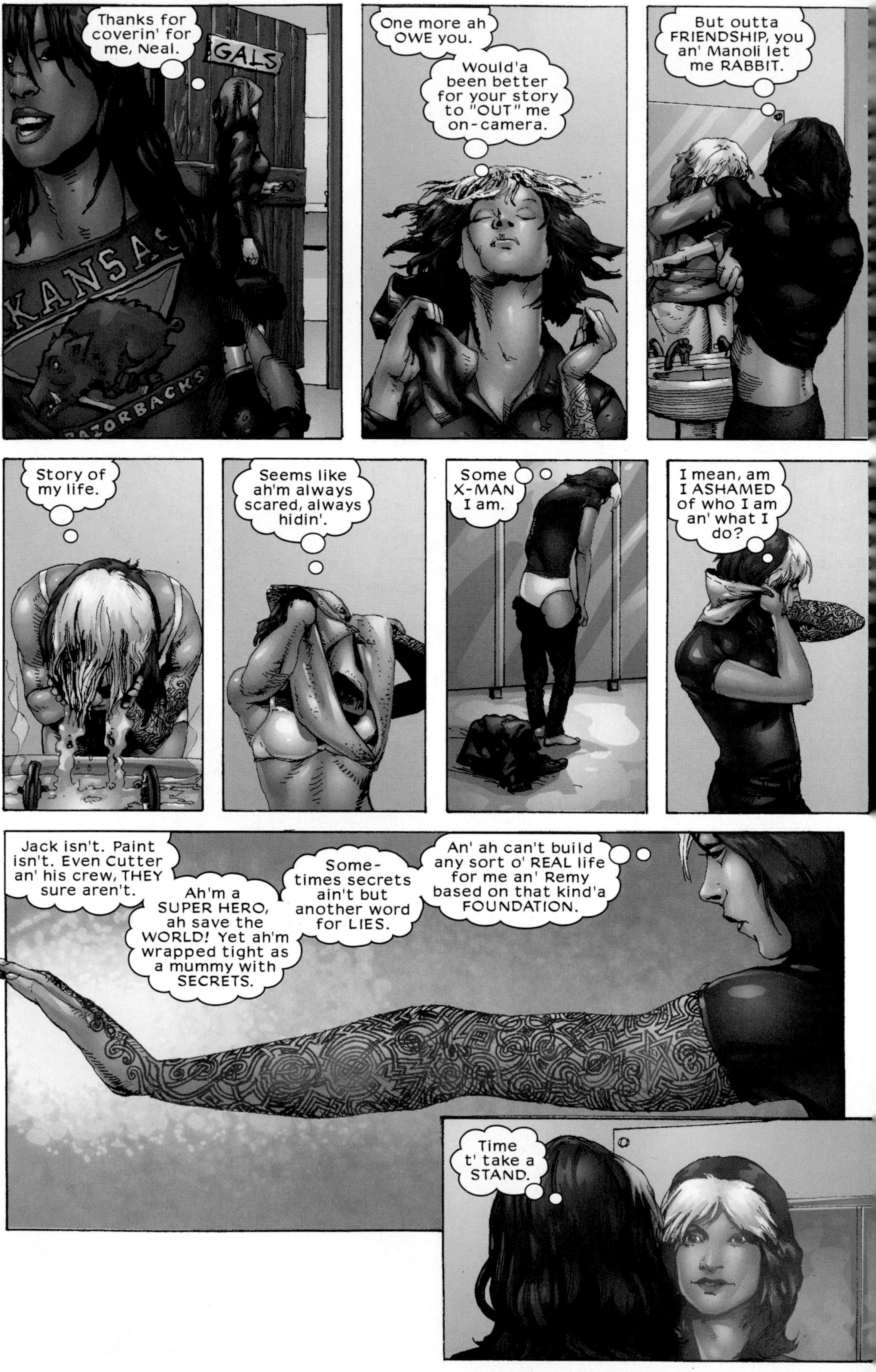

Thanks for coverin' for me, Neal.
GALS
One more ah OWE you.
Would'a been better for your story to "OUT" me on-camera.
But outta FRIENDSHIP, you an' Manoli let me RABBIT.
KANSAS
RAZORBACKS
Story of my life.
Seems like ah'm always scared, always hidin'.
Some X-MAN I am.
I mean, am I ASHAMED of who I am an' what I do?
Jack isn't. Paint isn't. Even Cutter an' his crew, THEY sure aren't.
Ah'm a SUPER HERO, ah save the WORLD! Yet ah'm wrapped tight as a mummy with SECRETS.
Some-times secrets ain't but another word for LIES.
An' ah can't build any sort o' REAL life for me an' Remy based on that kind'a FOUNDATION.
Time t' take a STAND.

GAL

?!

Yo, NEAL!

If y'all're still lookin' for an interview with ROGUE, ah'm ready!

Remy, what happened while ah was gone?

Place looks like ev'rybody's fav'rite DOG just died!

Neal just got a "head's-up" call from a friend at the network.

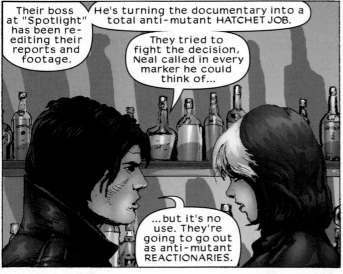

Their boss at "Spotlight" has been re-editing their reports and footage.

He's turning the documentary into a total anti-mutant HATCHET JOB.

They tried to fight the decision, Neal called in every marker he could think of...

...but it's no use. They're going to go out as anti-mutant REACTIONARIES.

Ah'm so sorry, guys!

I thought the quality of the work, the TRUTH of what we were reporting, would make a difference.

We've just got to decide now if it's even worth it to get back on that plane...

Buy y'all a drink?

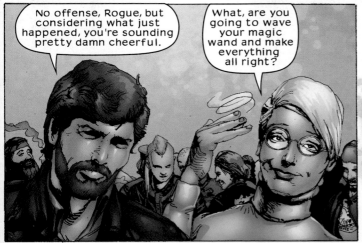

No offense, Rogue, but considering what just happened, you're sounding pretty damn cheerful.

What, are you going to wave your magic wand and make everything all right?

Somethin' like that, you betcha.

Let ME make a call-- call in some o' my OWN markers--

--we'll see if we can't do a little something for your SHOW!

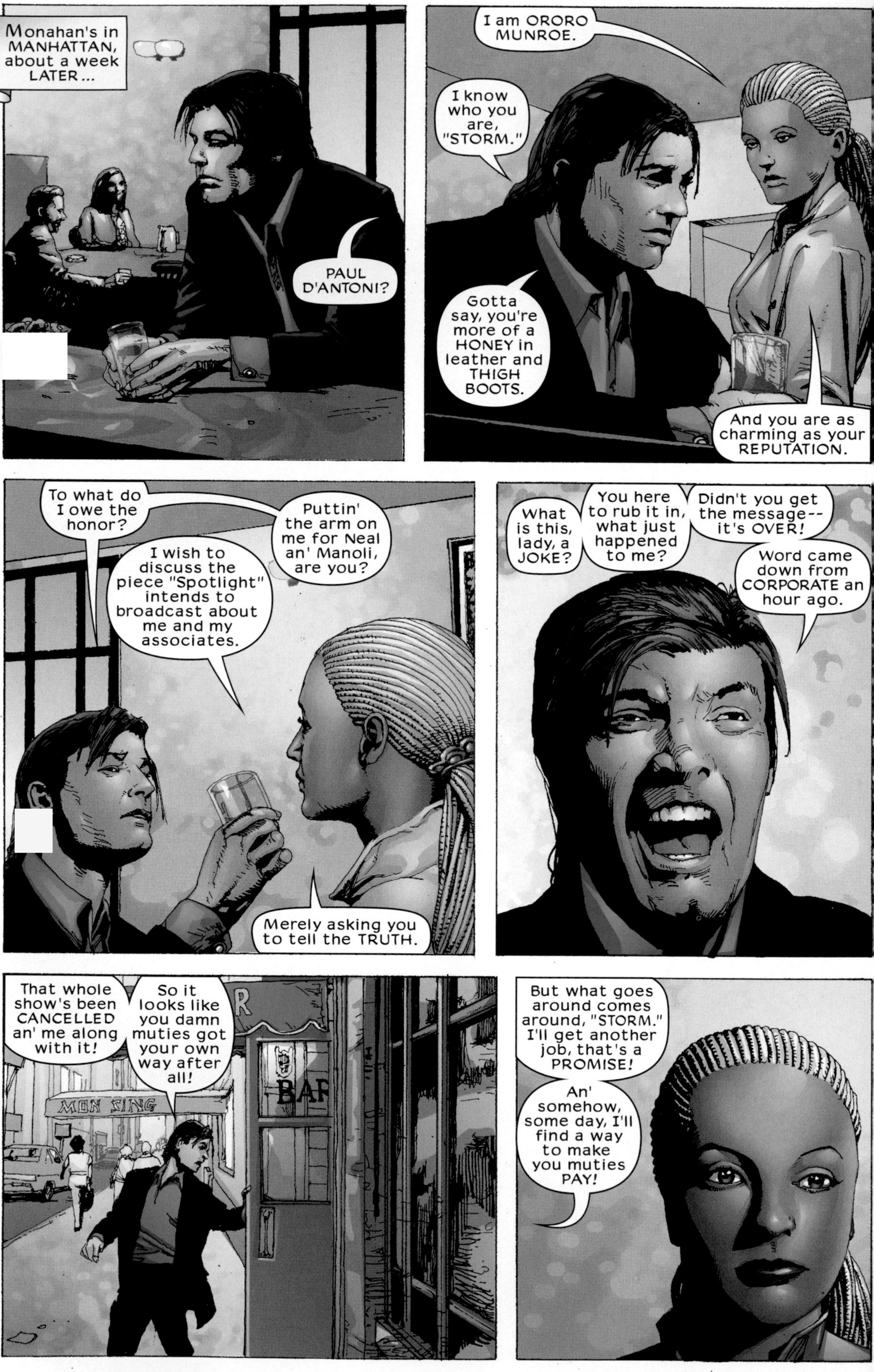

Monahan's in MANHATTAN, about a week LATER...
PAUL D'ANTONI?
I am ORORO MUNROE.
I know who you are, "STORM."
Gotta say, you're more of a HONEY in leather and THIGH BOOTS.
And you are as charming as your REPUTATION.
To what do I owe the honor?
Puttin' the arm on me for Neal an' Manoli, are you?
I wish to discuss the piece "Spotlight" intends to broadcast about me and my associates.
Merely asking you to tell the TRUTH.
What is this, lady, a JOKE?
You here to rub it in, what just happened to me?
Didn't you get the message--it's OVER!
Word came down from CORPORATE an hour ago.
That whole show's been CANCELLED an' me along with it!
So it looks like you damn muties got your own way after all!
MON SING
BAR
But what goes around comes around, "STORM." I'll get another job, that's a PROMISE!
An' somehow, some day, I'll find a way to make you muties PAY!

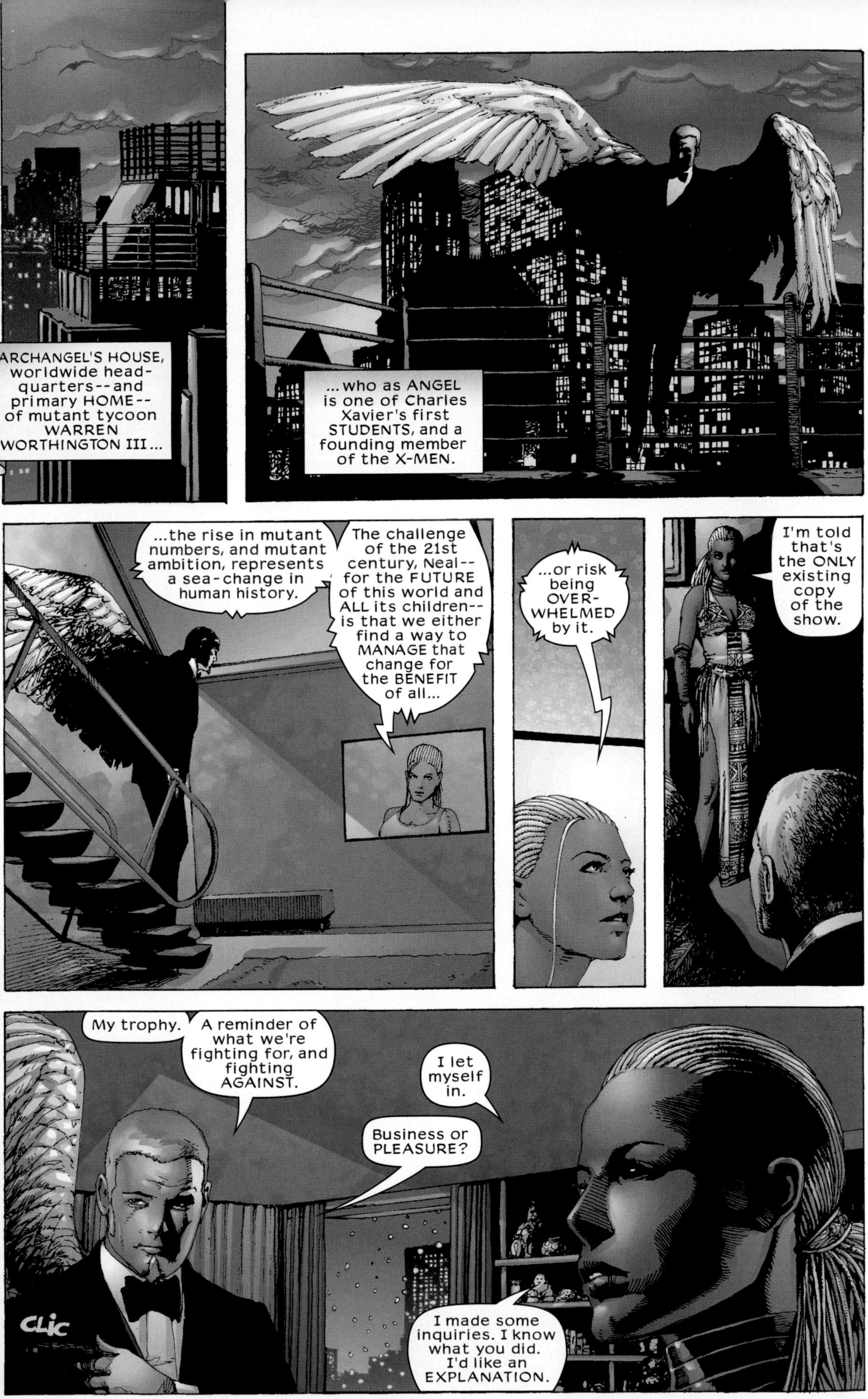

ARCHANGEL'S HOUSE, worldwide head-quarters--and primary HOME--of mutant tycoon WARREN WORTHINGTON III...
...who as ANGEL is one of Charles Xavier's first STUDENTS, and a founding member of the X-MEN.
...the rise in mutant numbers, and mutant ambition, represents a sea-change in human history.
The challenge of the 21st century, Neal--for the FUTURE of this world and ALL its children--is that we either find a way to MANAGE that change for the BENEFIT of all...
...or risk being OVER-WHELMED by it.
I'm told that's the ONLY existing copy of the show.
My trophy.
A reminder of what we're fighting for, and fighting AGAINST.
I let myself in.
Business or PLEASURE?
I made some inquiries. I know what you did. I'd like an EXPLANATION.
CLIC

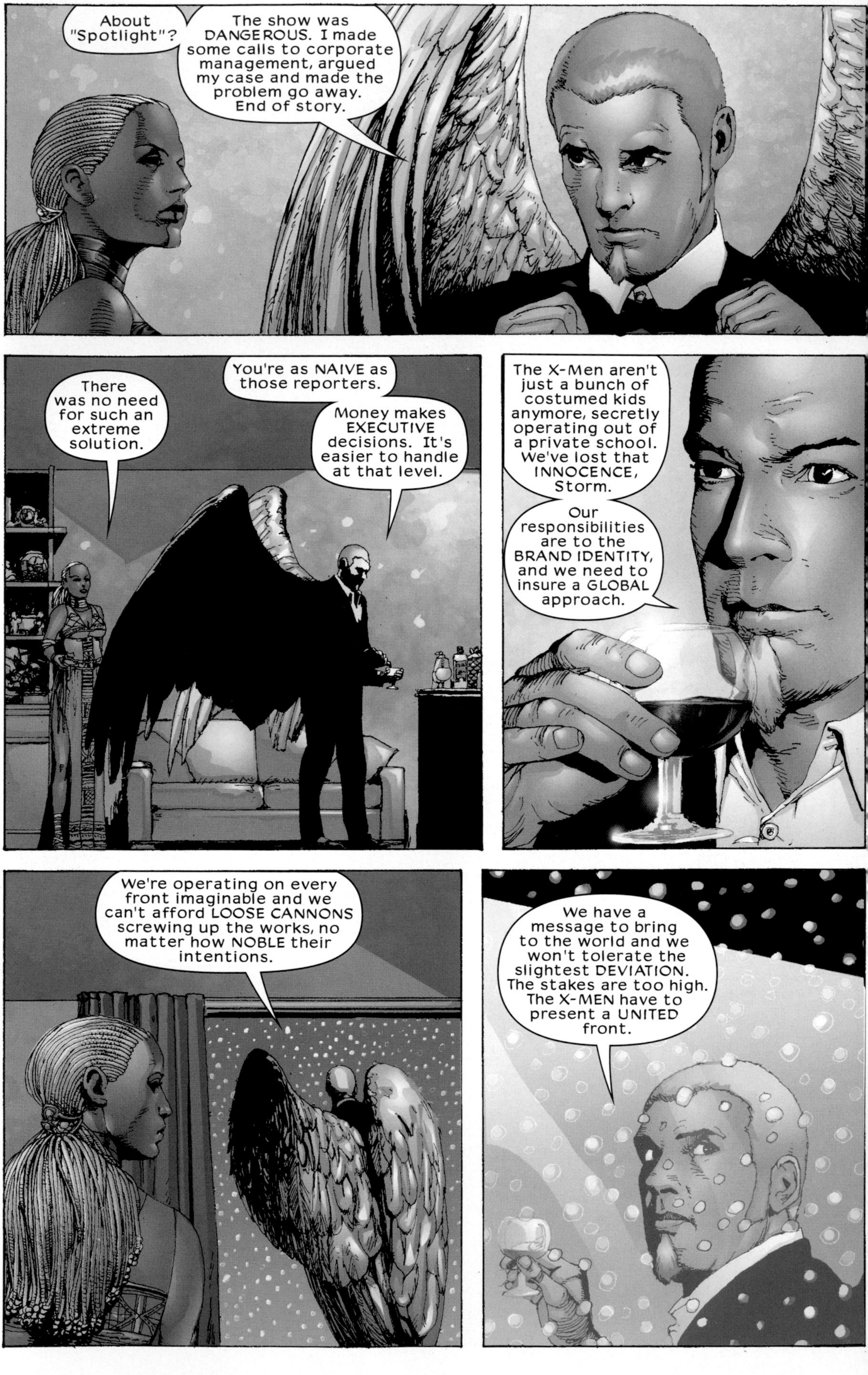
About "Spotlight"?
The show was DANGEROUS. I made some calls to corporate management, argued my case and made the problem go away. End of story.
There was no need for such an extreme solution.
You're as NAIVE as those reporters.
Money makes EXECUTIVE decisions. It's easier to handle at that level.
The X-Men aren't just a bunch of costumed kids anymore, secretly operating out of a private school. We've lost that INNOCENCE, Storm.
Our responsibilities are to the BRAND IDENTITY, and we need to insure a GLOBAL approach.
We're operating on every front imaginable and we can't afford LOOSE CANNONS screwing up the works, no matter how NOBLE their intentions.
We have a message to bring to the world and we won't tolerate the slightest DEVIATION. The stakes are too high. The X-MEN have to present a UNITED front.

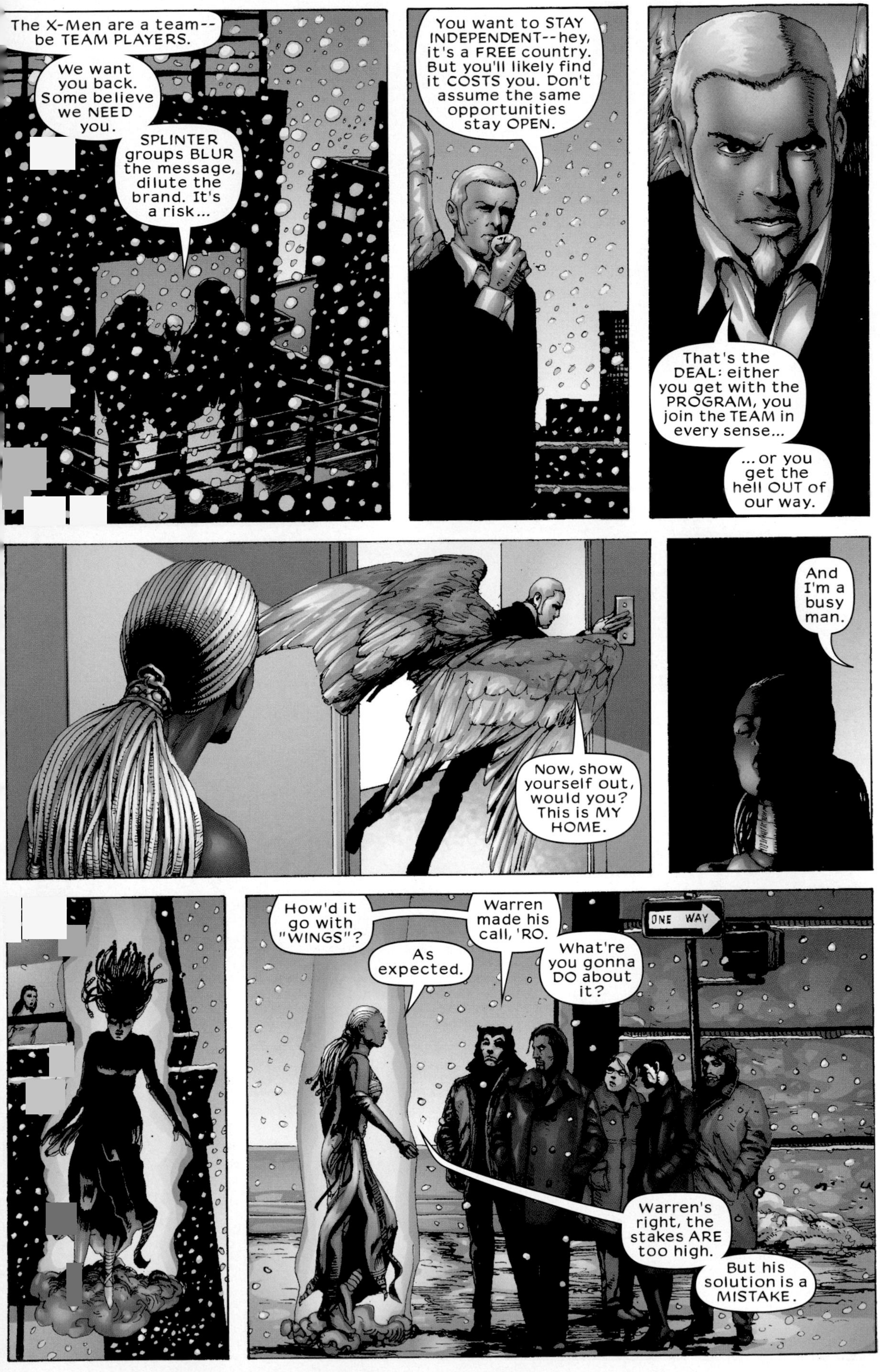
The X-Men are a team--
be TEAM PLAYERS.
We want you back. Some believe we NEED you.
SPLINTER groups BLUR the message, dilute the brand. It's a risk...
You want to STAY INDEPENDENT--hey, it's a FREE country. But you'll likely find it COSTS you. Don't assume the same opportunities stay OPEN.
That's the DEAL: either you get with the PROGRAM, you join the TEAM in every sense...
...or you get the hell OUT of our way.
Now, show yourself out, would you? This is MY HOME.
And I'm a busy man.
How'd it go with "WINGS"?
Warren made his call, 'RO.
As expected.
What're you gonna DO about it?
ONE WAY
Warren's right, the stakes ARE too high.
But his solution is a MISTAKE.

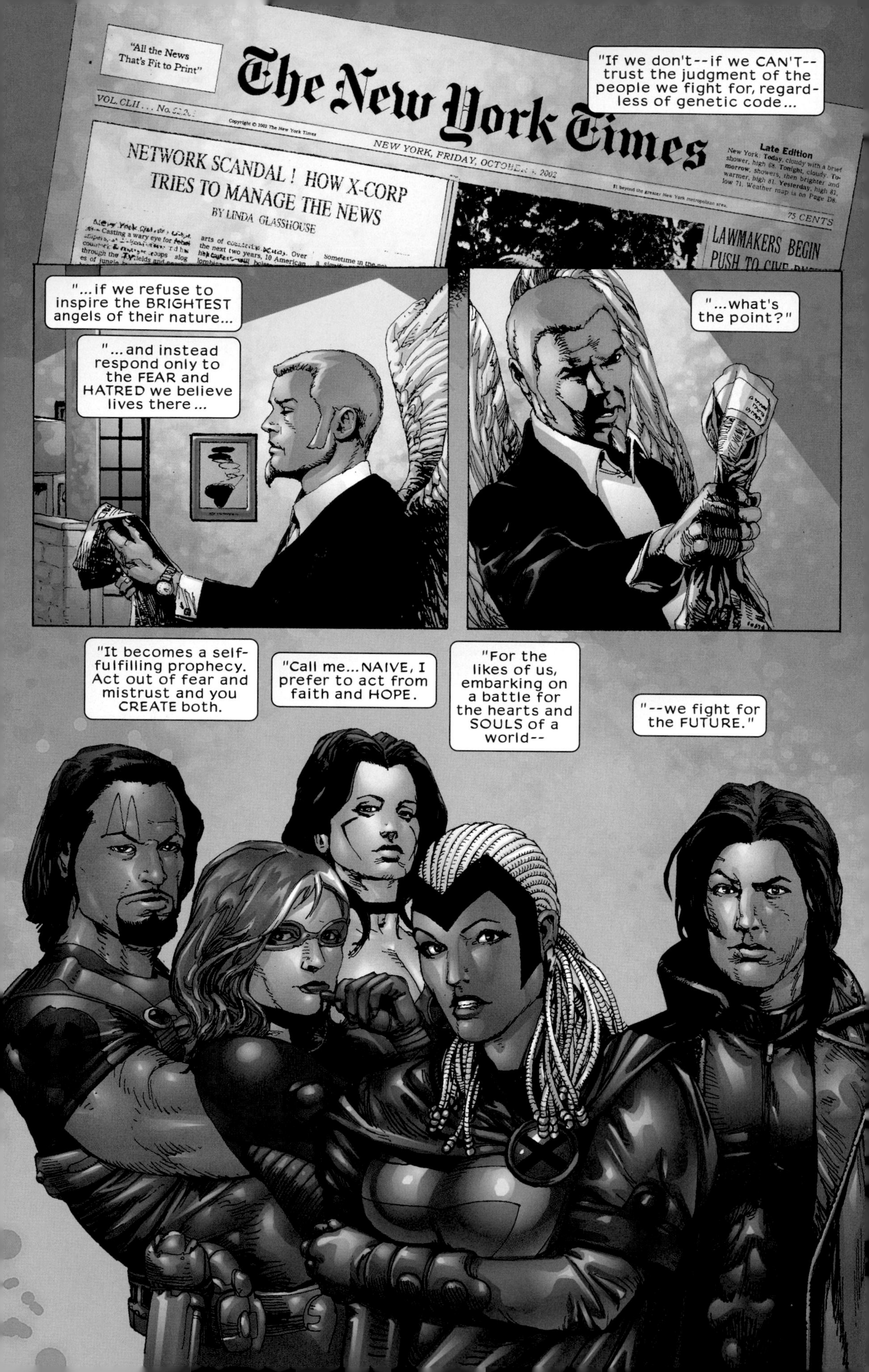
"All the News That's Fit to Print"
The New York Times
"If we don't--if we CAN'T--trust the judgment of the people we fight for, regardless of genetic code...
Late Edition
NETWORK SCANDAL ! HOW X-CORP TRIES TO MANAGE THE NEWS
BY LINDA GLASSHOUSE
75 CENTS
LAWMAKERS BEGIN
"...if we refuse to inspire the BRIGHTEST angels of their nature...
"...and instead respond only to the FEAR and HATRED we believe lives there...
"...what's the point?"
"It becomes a self-fulfilling prophecy. Act out of fear and mistrust and you CREATE both.
"Call me...NAIVE, I prefer to act from faith and HOPE.
"For the likes of us, embarking on a battle for the hearts and SOULS of a world--
"--we fight for the FUTURE."

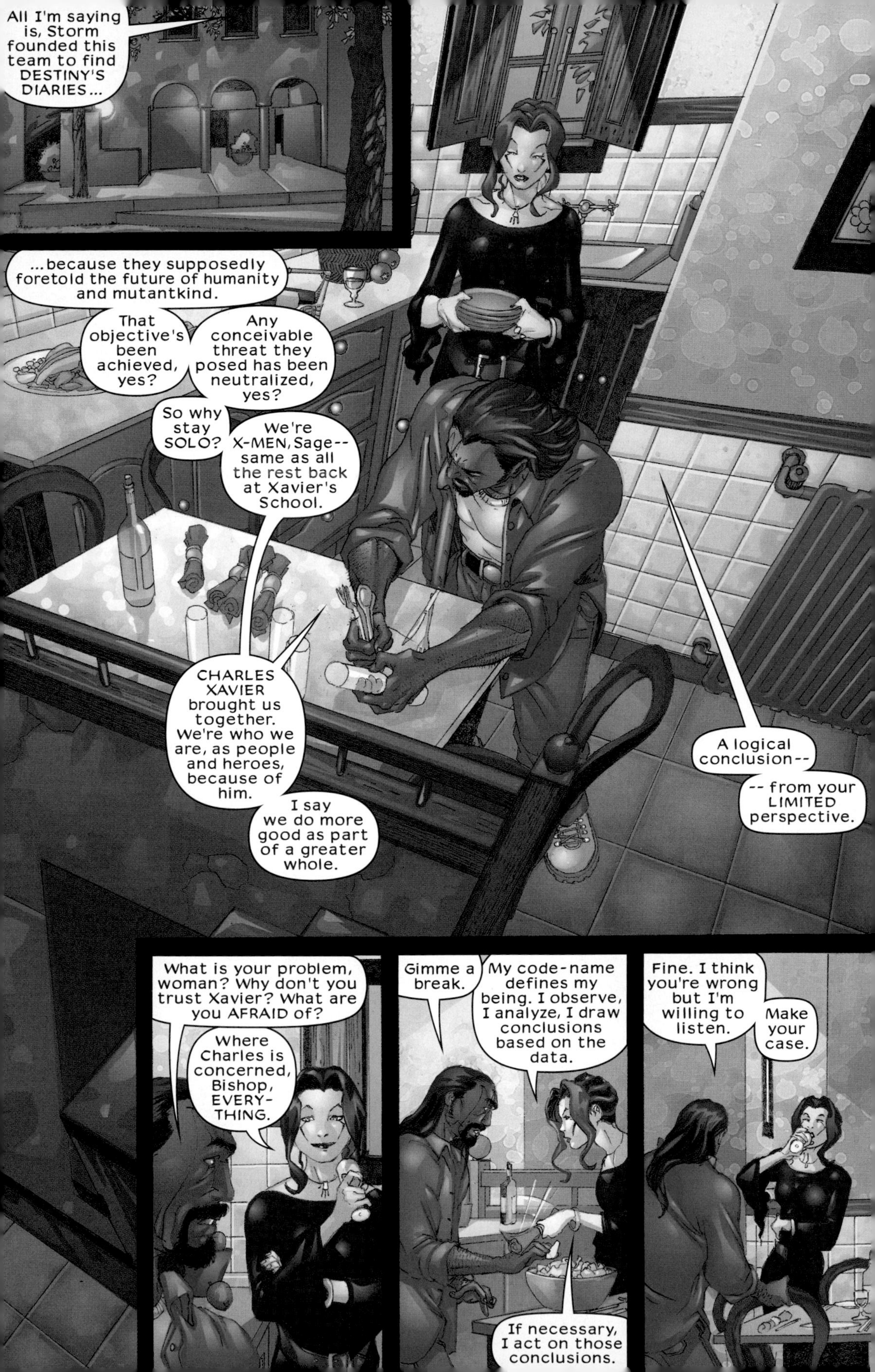
All I'm saying is, Storm founded this team to find DESTINY'S DIARIES...
...because they supposedly foretold the future of humanity and mutantkind.
That objective's been achieved, yes?
Any conceivable threat they posed has been neutralized, yes?
So why stay SOLO?
We're X-MEN, Sage--same as all the rest back at Xavier's School.
CHARLES XAVIER brought us together. We're who we are, as people and heroes, because of him.
I say we do more good as part of a greater whole.
A logical conclusion--
-- from your LIMITED perspective.
What is your problem, woman? Why don't you trust Xavier? What are you AFRAID of?
Where Charles is concerned, Bishop, EVERYTHING.
Gimme a break.
My code-name defines my being. I observe, I analyze, I draw conclusions based on the data.
If necessary, I act on those conclusions.
Fine. I think you're wrong but I'm willing to listen.
Make your case.

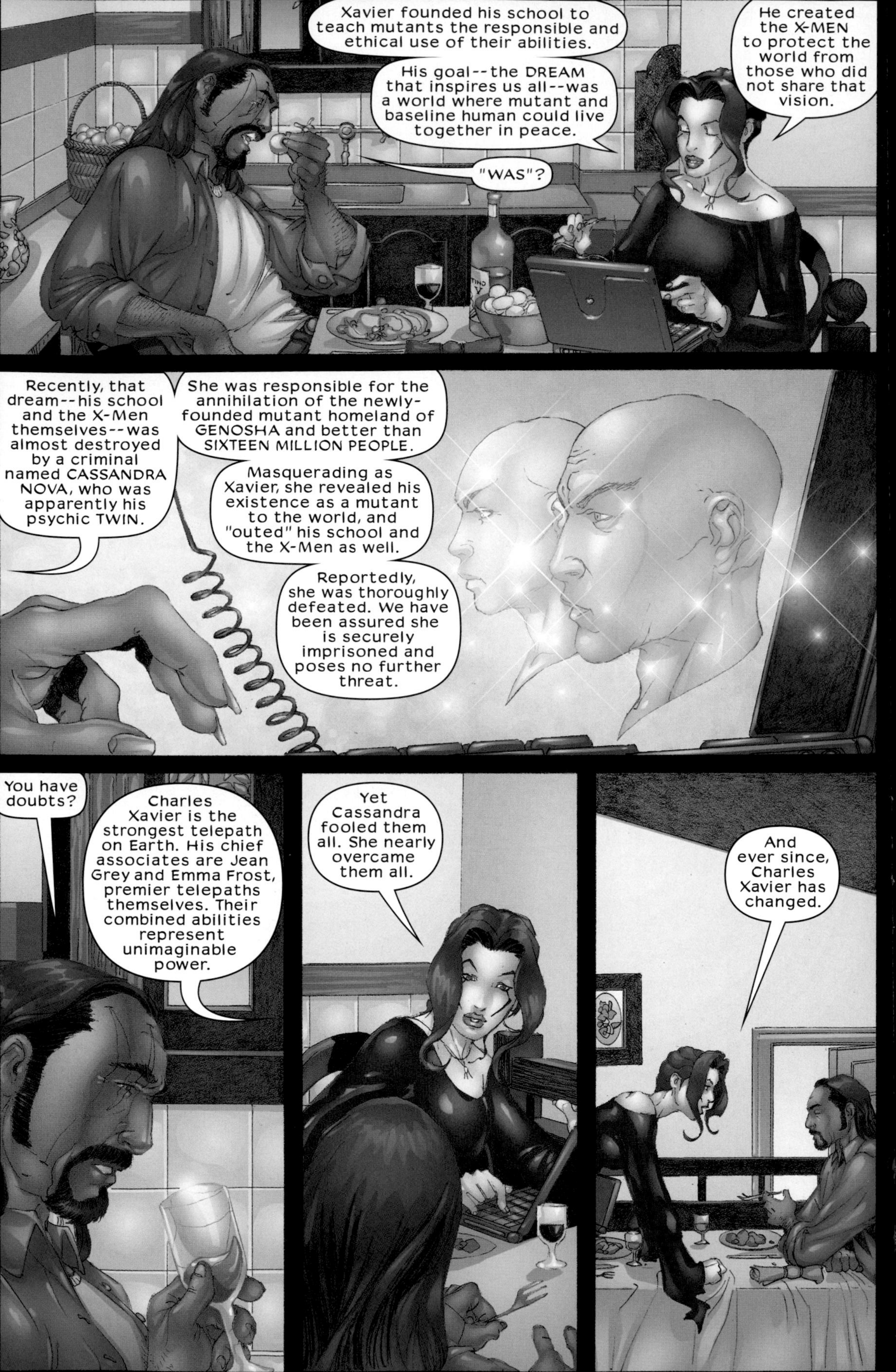
Xavier founded his school to teach mutants the responsible and ethical use of their abilities.
His goal--the DREAM that inspires us all--was a world where mutant and baseline human could live together in peace.
He created the X-MEN to protect the world from those who did not share that vision.
"WAS"?
Recently, that dream--his school and the X-Men themselves--was almost destroyed by a criminal named CASSANDRA NOVA, who was apparently his psychic TWIN.
She was responsible for the annihilation of the newly-founded mutant homeland of GENOSHA and better than SIXTEEN MILLION PEOPLE.
Masquerading as Xavier, she revealed his existence as a mutant to the world, and "outed" his school and the X-Men as well.
Reportedly, she was thoroughly defeated. We have been assured she is securely imprisoned and poses no further threat.
You have doubts?
Charles Xavier is the strongest telepath on Earth. His chief associates are Jean Grey and Emma Frost, premier telepaths themselves. Their combined abilities represent unimaginable power.
Yet Cassandra fooled them all. She nearly overcame them all.
And ever since, Charles Xavier has changed.

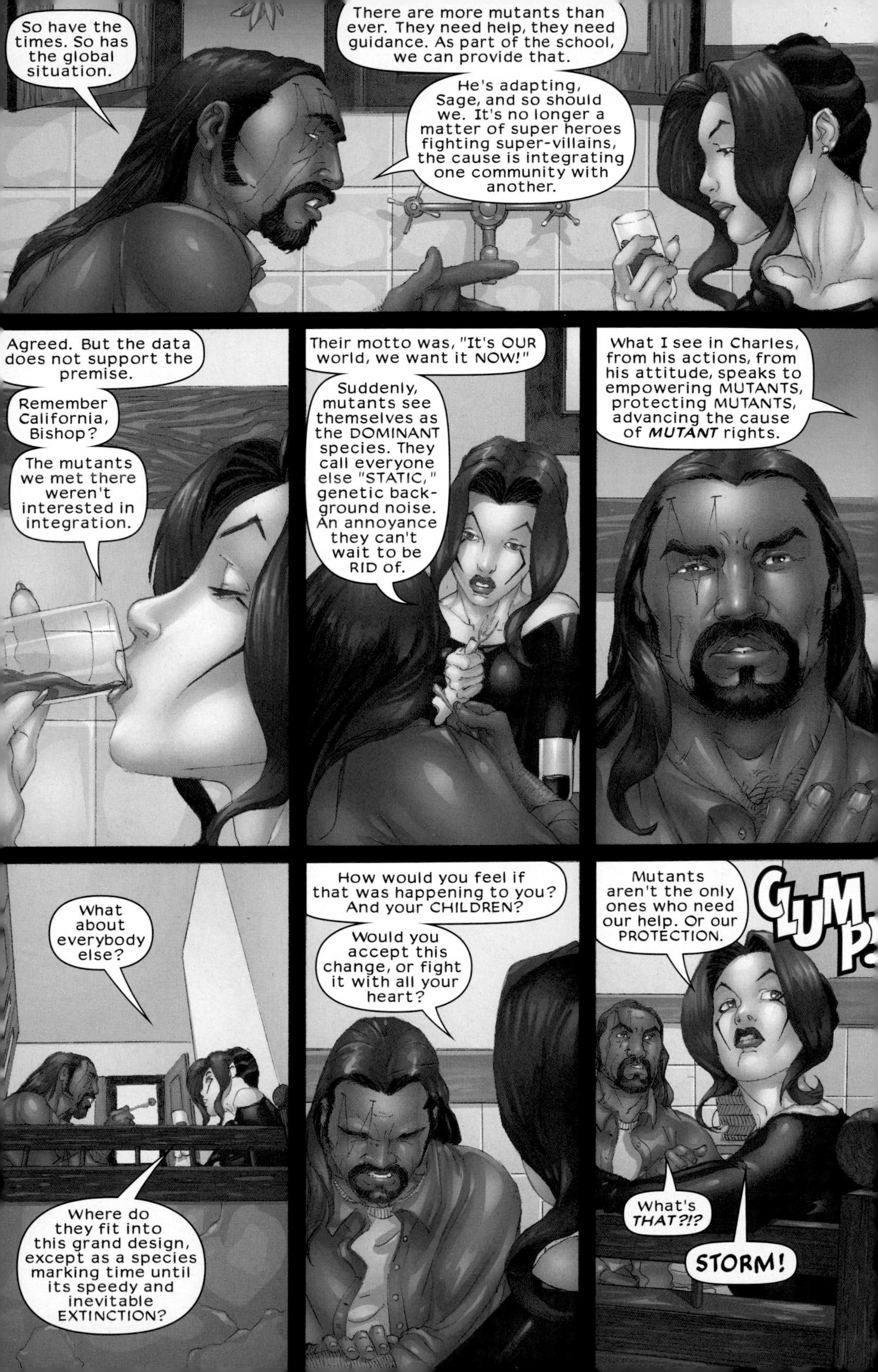
So have the times. So has the global situation.
There are more mutants than ever. They need help, they need guidance. As part of the school, we can provide that.
He's adapting, Sage, and so should we. It's no longer a matter of super heroes fighting super-villains, the cause is integrating one community with another.
Agreed. But the data does not support the premise.
Remember California, Bishop?
The mutants we met there weren't interested in integration.
Their motto was, "It's OUR world, we want it NOW!"
Suddenly, mutants see themselves as the DOMINANT species. They call everyone else "STATIC," genetic back-ground noise. An annoyance they can't wait to be RID of.
What I see in Charles, from his actions, from his attitude, speaks to empowering MUTANTS, protecting MUTANTS, advancing the cause of *MUTANT* rights.
What about everybody else?
Where do they fit into this grand design, except as a species marking time until its speedy and inevitable EXTINCTION?
How would you feel if that was happening to you? And your CHILDREN?
Would you accept this change, or fight it with all your heart?
Mutants aren't the only ones who need our help. Or our PROTECTION.
CLUMP.
What's *THAT?!?*
STORM!

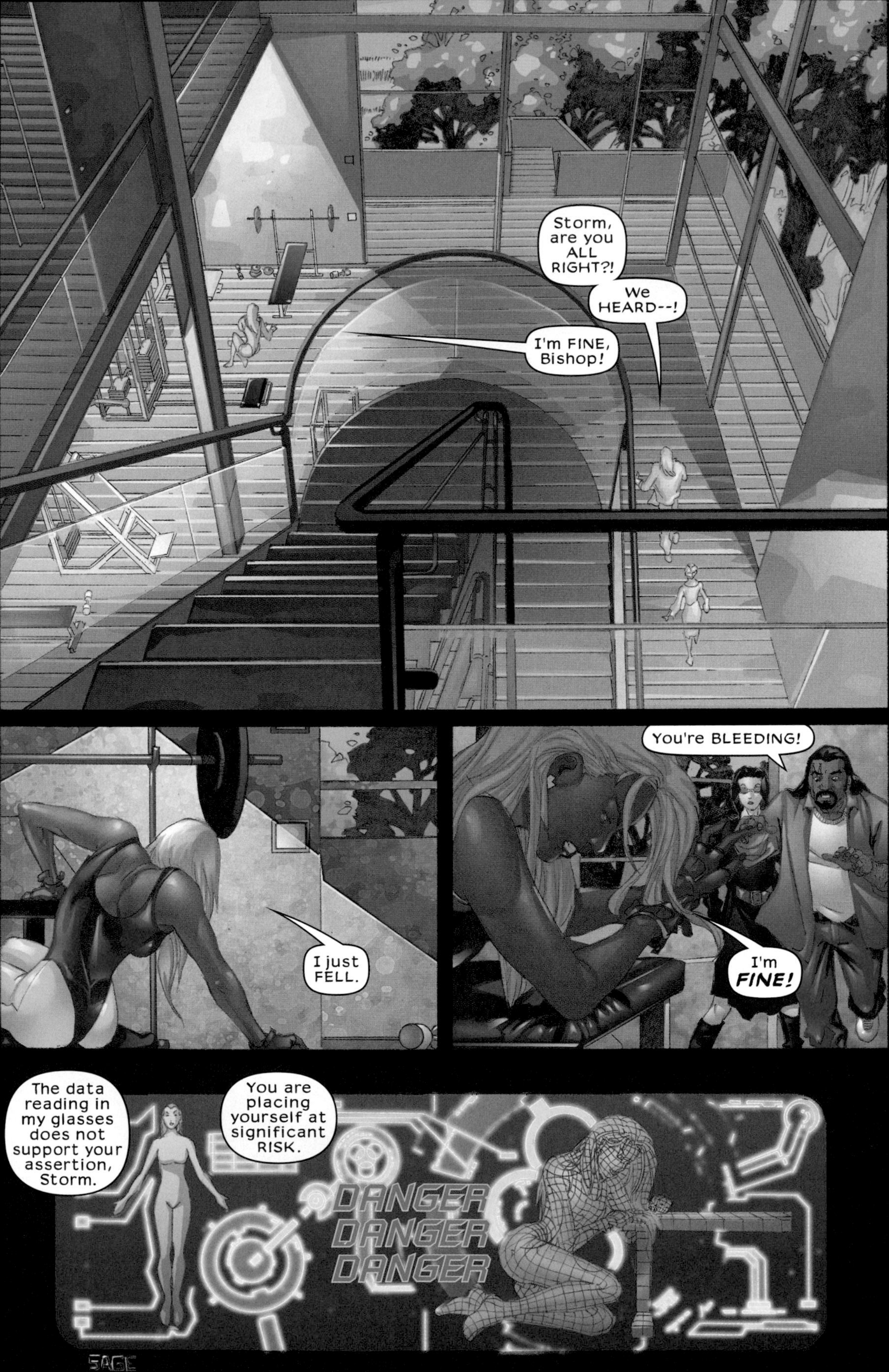
Storm, are you ALL RIGHT?!
We HEARD--!
I'm FINE, Bishop!
I just FELL.
You're BLEEDING!
I'm FINE!
The data reading in my glasses does not support your assertion, Storm.
You are placing yourself at significant RISK.
DANGER
DANGER
DANGER
SAGE

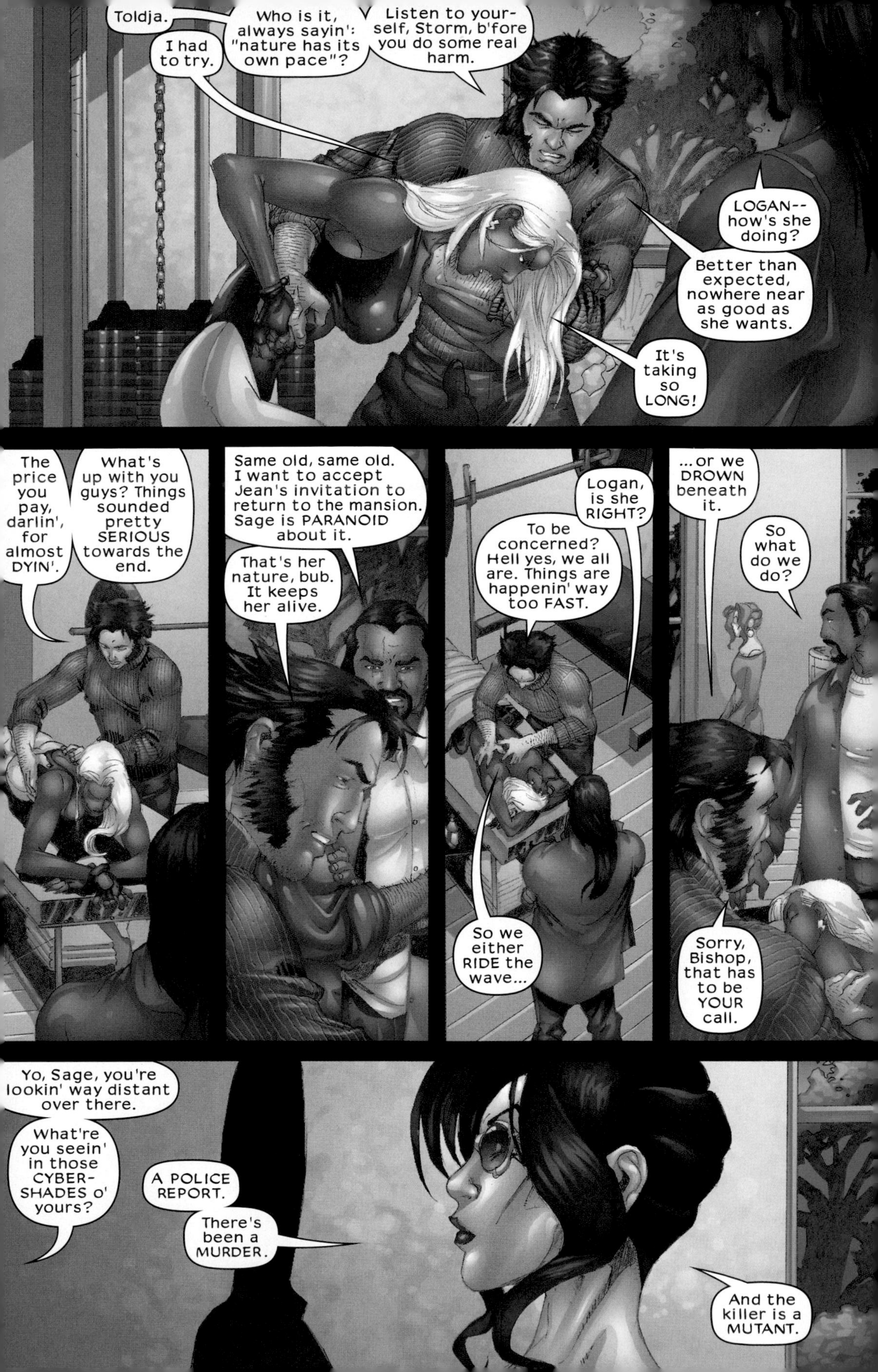
Toldja.
I had to try.
Who is it, always sayin': "nature has its own pace"?
Listen to yourself, Storm, b'fore you do some real harm.
LOGAN-- how's she doing?
Better than expected, nowhere near as good as she wants.
It's taking so LONG!
The price you pay, darlin', for almost DYIN'.
What's up with you guys? Things sounded pretty SERIOUS towards the end.
Same old, same old. I want to accept Jean's invitation to return to the mansion. Sage is PARANOID about it.
That's her nature, bub. It keeps her alive.
Logan, is she RIGHT?
To be concerned? Hell yes, we all are. Things are happenin' way too FAST.
So we either RIDE the wave...
...or we DROWN beneath it.
So what do we do?
Sorry, Bishop, that has to be YOUR call.
Yo, Sage, you're lookin' way distant over there.
What're you seein' in those CYBER-SHADES o' yours?
A POLICE REPORT.
There's been a MURDER.
And the killer is a MUTANT.

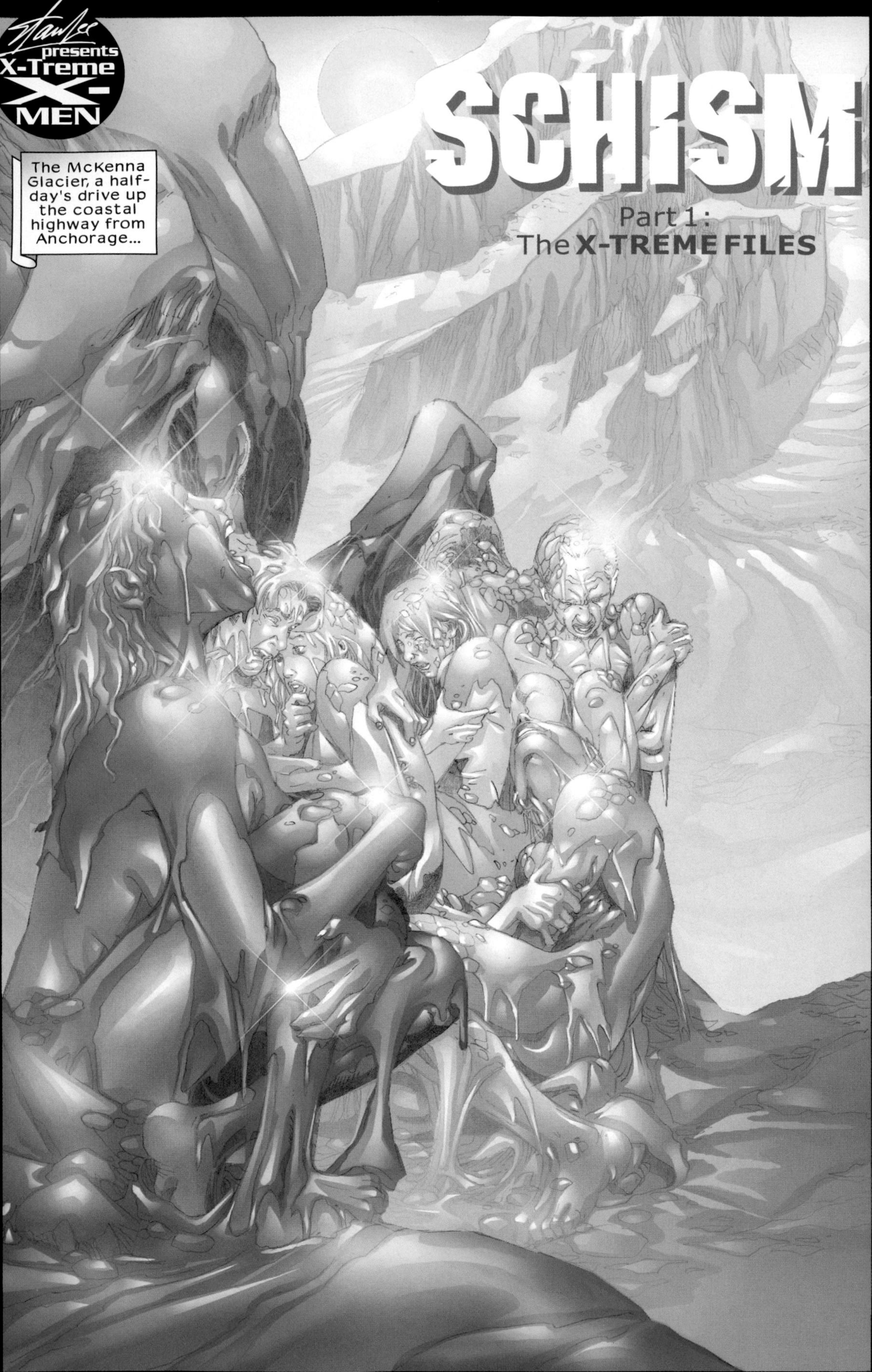
Stan Lee presents X-Treme X-MEN
SCHISM
Part 1: The X-TREME FILES
The McKenna Glacier, a half-day's drive up the coastal highway from Anchorage...

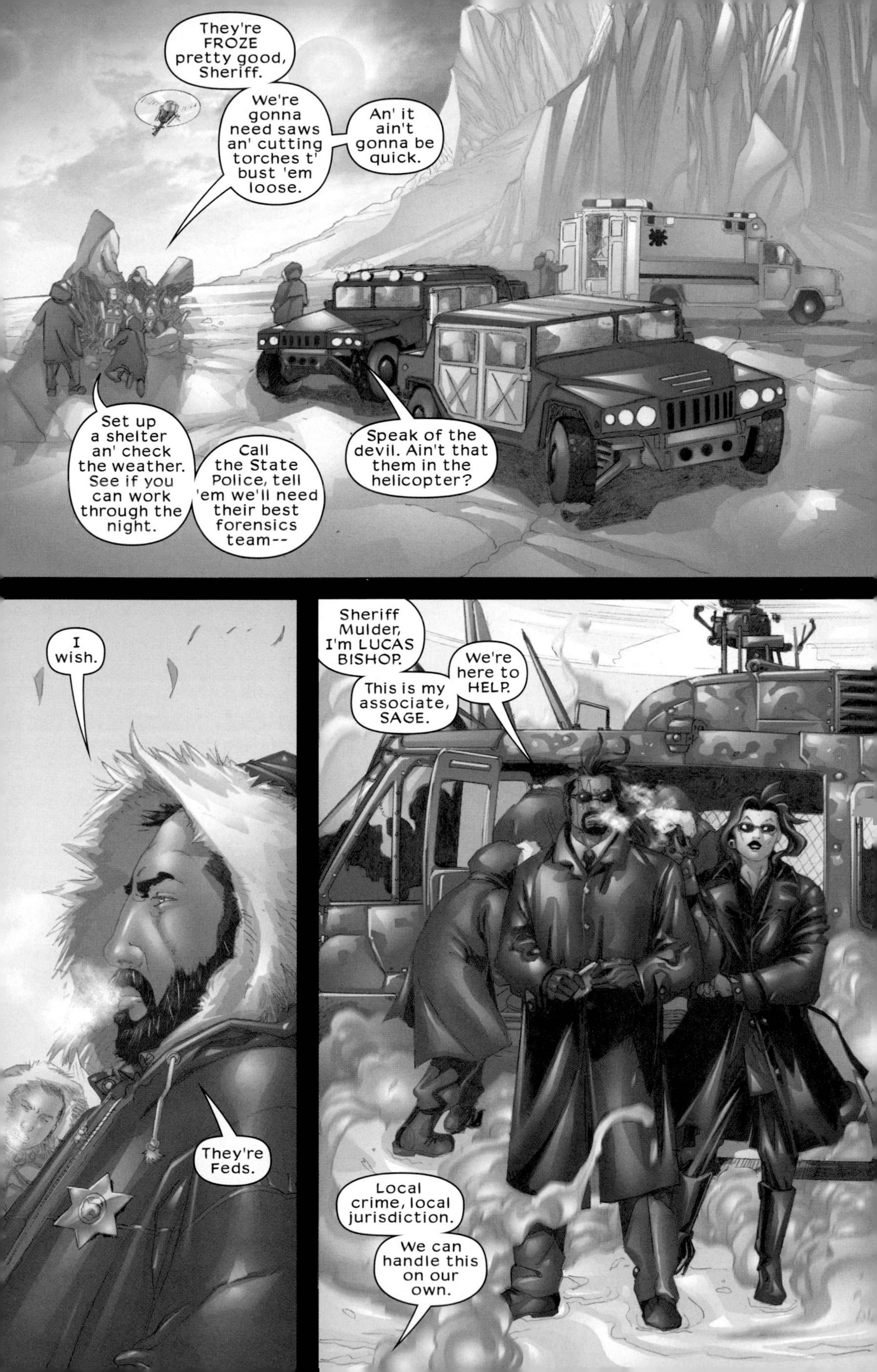
They're FROZE pretty good, Sheriff.
We're gonna need saws an' cutting torches t' bust 'em loose.
An' it ain't gonna be quick.
Set up a shelter an' check the weather. See if you can work through the night.
Call the State Police, tell 'em we'll need their best forensics team--
Speak of the devil. Ain't that them in the helicopter?
I wish.
They're Feds.
Sheriff Mulder, I'm LUCAS BISHOP.
This is my associate, SAGE.
We're here to HELP.
Local crime, local jurisdiction.
We can handle this on our own.

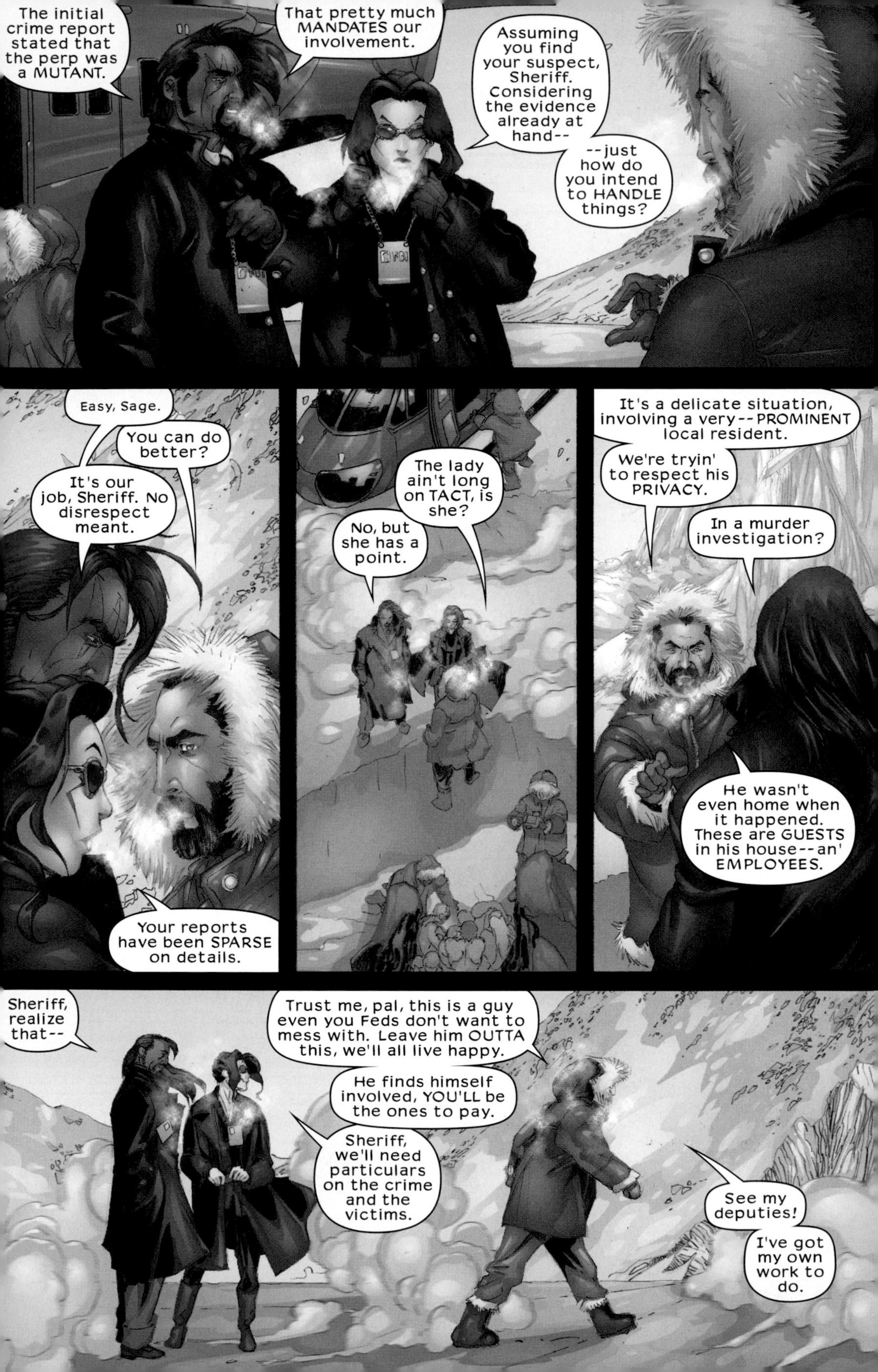

The initial crime report stated that the perp was a MUTANT.
That pretty much MANDATES our involvement.
Assuming you find your suspect, Sheriff. Considering the evidence already at hand--
--just how do you intend to HANDLE things?
Easy, Sage.
You can do better?
It's our job, Sheriff. No disrespect meant.
Your reports have been SPARSE on details.
The lady ain't long on TACT, is she?
No, but she has a point.
It's a delicate situation, involving a very--PROMINENT local resident.
We're tryin' to respect his PRIVACY.
In a murder investigation?
He wasn't even home when it happened. These are GUESTS in his house--an' EMPLOYEES.
Sheriff, realize that--
Trust me, pal, this is a guy even you Feds don't want to mess with. Leave him OUTTA this, we'll all live happy.
He finds himself involved, YOU'LL be the ones to pay.
Sheriff, we'll need particulars on the crime and the victims.
See my deputies!
I've got my own work to do.

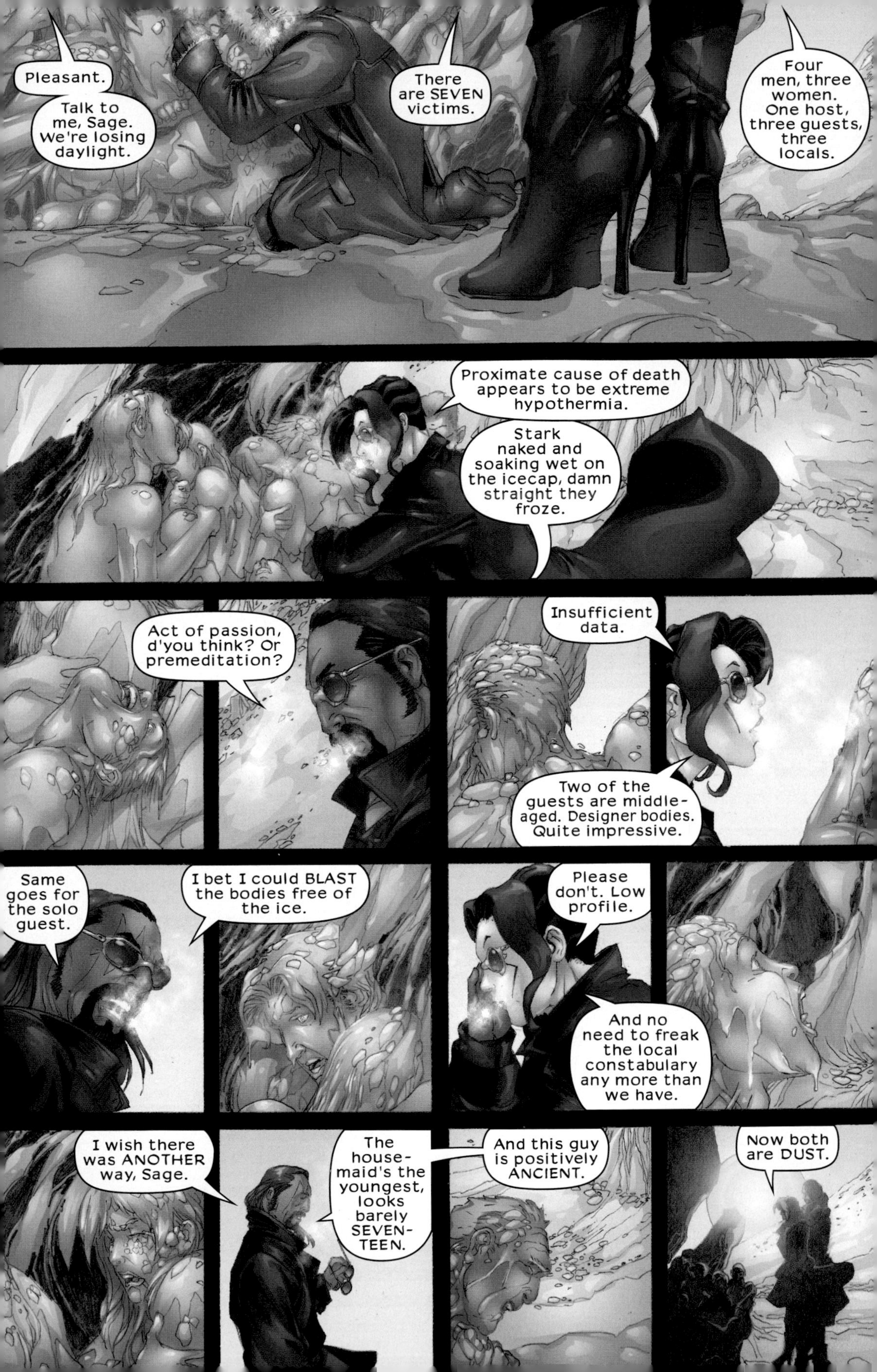

Pleasant.
Talk to me, Sage. We're losing daylight.
There are SEVEN victims.
Four men, three women. One host, three guests, three locals.
Proximate cause of death appears to be extreme hypothermia.
Stark naked and soaking wet on the icecap, damn straight they froze.
Act of passion, d'you think? Or premeditation?
Insufficient data.
Two of the guests are middle-aged. Designer bodies. Quite impressive.
Same goes for the solo guest.
I bet I could BLAST the bodies free of the ice.
Please don't. Low profile.
And no need to freak the local constabulary any more than we have.
I wish there was ANOTHER way, Sage.
The house-maid's the youngest, looks barely SEVEN-TEEN.
And this guy is positively ANCIENT.
Now both are DUST.

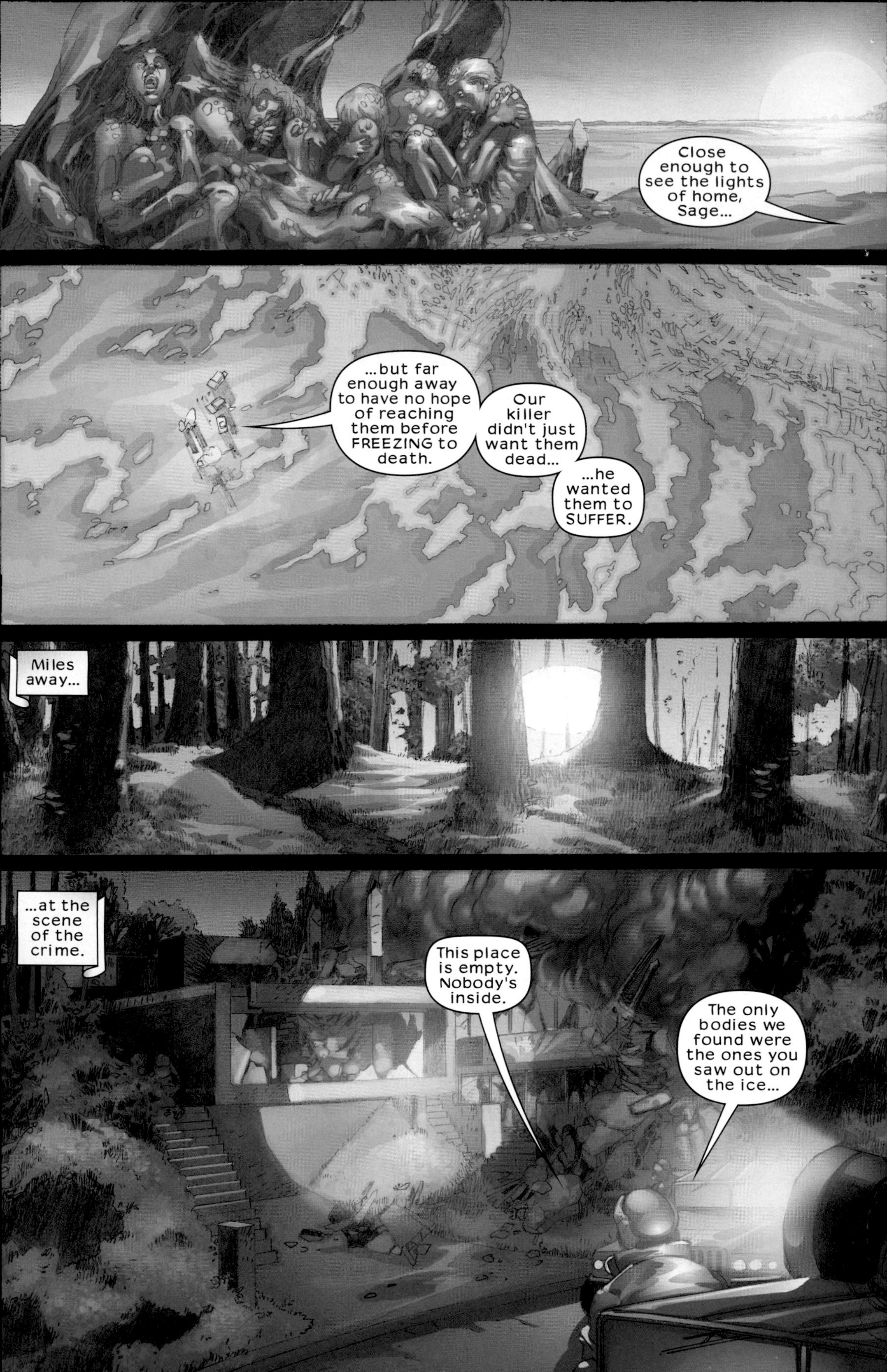
Close enough to see the lights of home, Sage...
...but far enough away to have no hope of reaching them before FREEZING to death.
Our killer didn't just want them dead...
...he wanted them to SUFFER.
Miles away...
...at the scene of the crime.
This place is empty. Nobody's inside.
The only bodies we found were the ones you saw out on the ice...

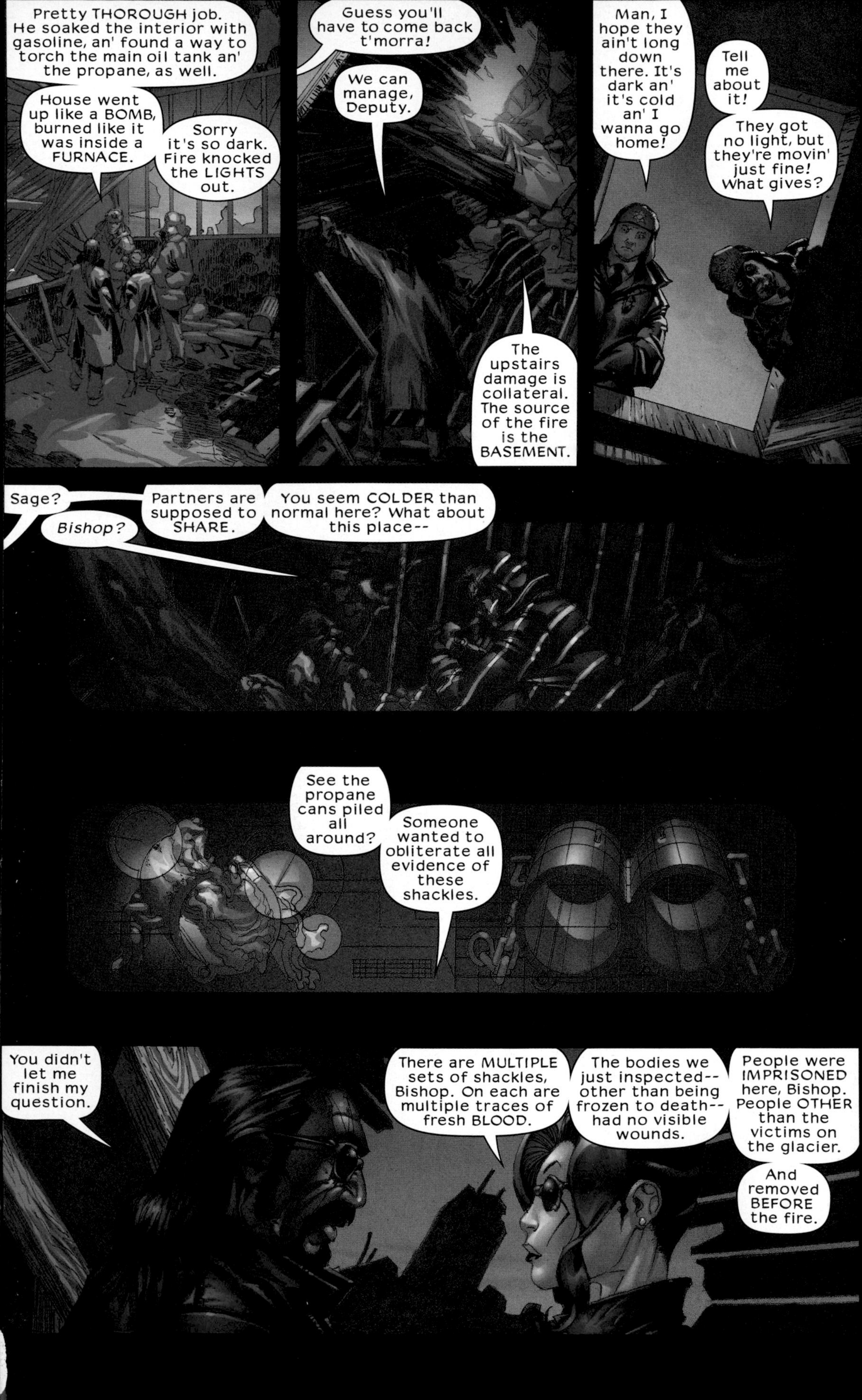
Pretty THOROUGH job. He soaked the interior with gasoline, an' found a way to torch the main oil tank an' the propane, as well.
House went up like a BOMB, burned like it was inside a FURNACE.
Sorry it's so dark. Fire knocked the LIGHTS out.
Guess you'll have to come back t'morra!
We can manage, Deputy.
The upstairs damage is collateral. The source of the fire is the BASEMENT.
Man, I hope they ain't long down there. It's dark an' it's cold an' I wanna go home!
Tell me about it!
They got no light, but they're movin' just fine! What gives?
Sage?
Bishop?
Partners are supposed to SHARE.
You seem COLDER than normal here? What about this place--
See the propane cans piled all around?
Someone wanted to obliterate all evidence of these shackles.
You didn't let me finish my question.
There are MULTIPLE sets of shackles, Bishop. On each are multiple traces of fresh BLOOD.
The bodies we just inspected-- other than being frozen to death-- had no visible wounds.
People were IMPRISONED here, Bishop. People OTHER than the victims on the glacier.
And removed BEFORE the fire.

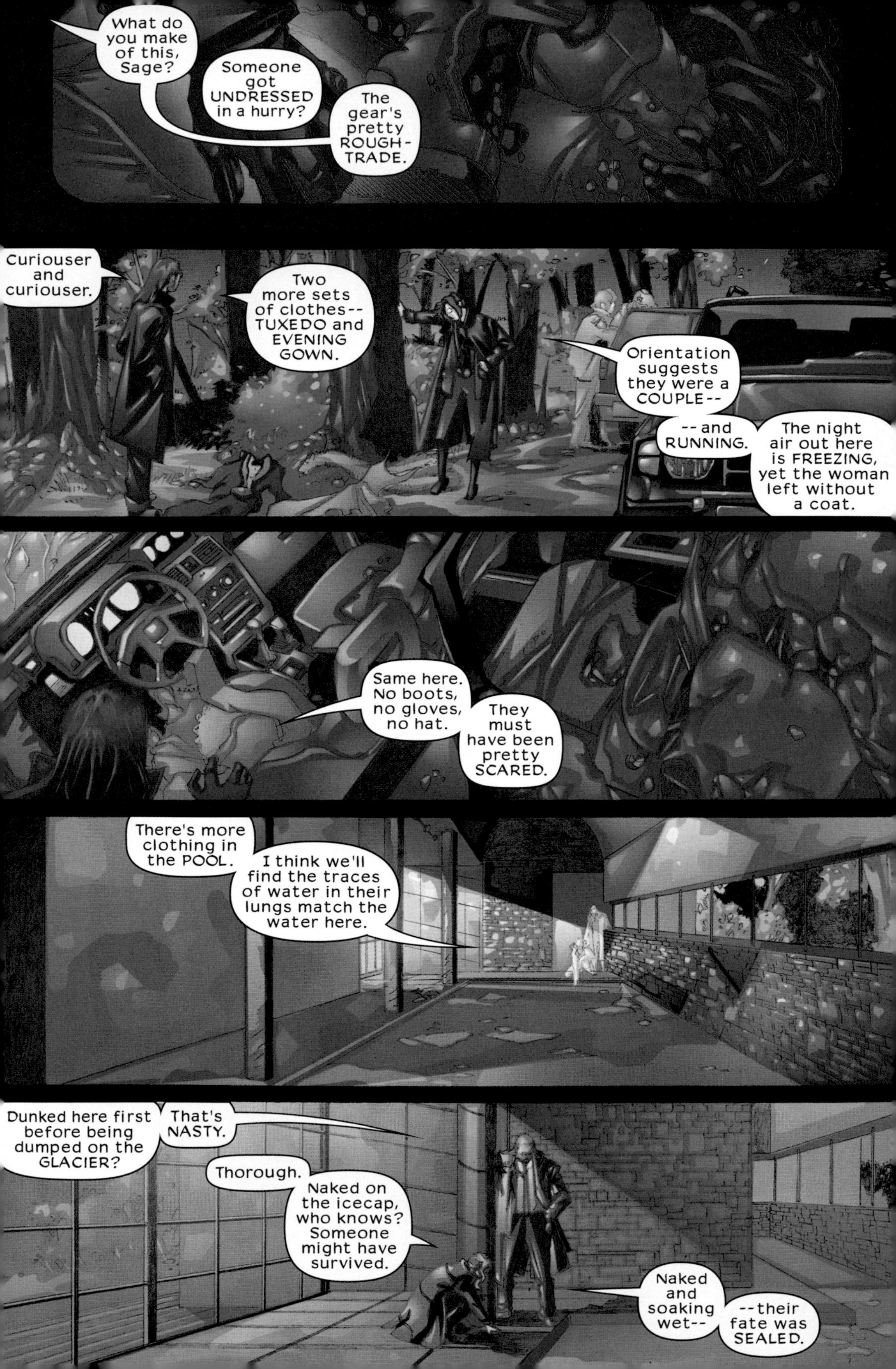

What do you make of this, Sage?
Someone got UNDRESSED in a hurry?
The gear's pretty ROUGH-TRADE.
Curiouser and curiouser.
Two more sets of clothes--TUXEDO and EVENING GOWN.
Orientation suggests they were a COUPLE--
--and RUNNING.
The night air out here is FREEZING, yet the woman left without a coat.
Same here. No boots, no gloves, no hat.
They must have been pretty SCARED.
There's more clothing in the POOL.
I think we'll find the traces of water in their lungs match the water here.
Dunked here first before being dumped on the GLACIER?
That's NASTY.
Thorough.
Naked on the icecap, who knows? Someone might have survived.
Naked and soaking wet--
--their fate was SEALED.

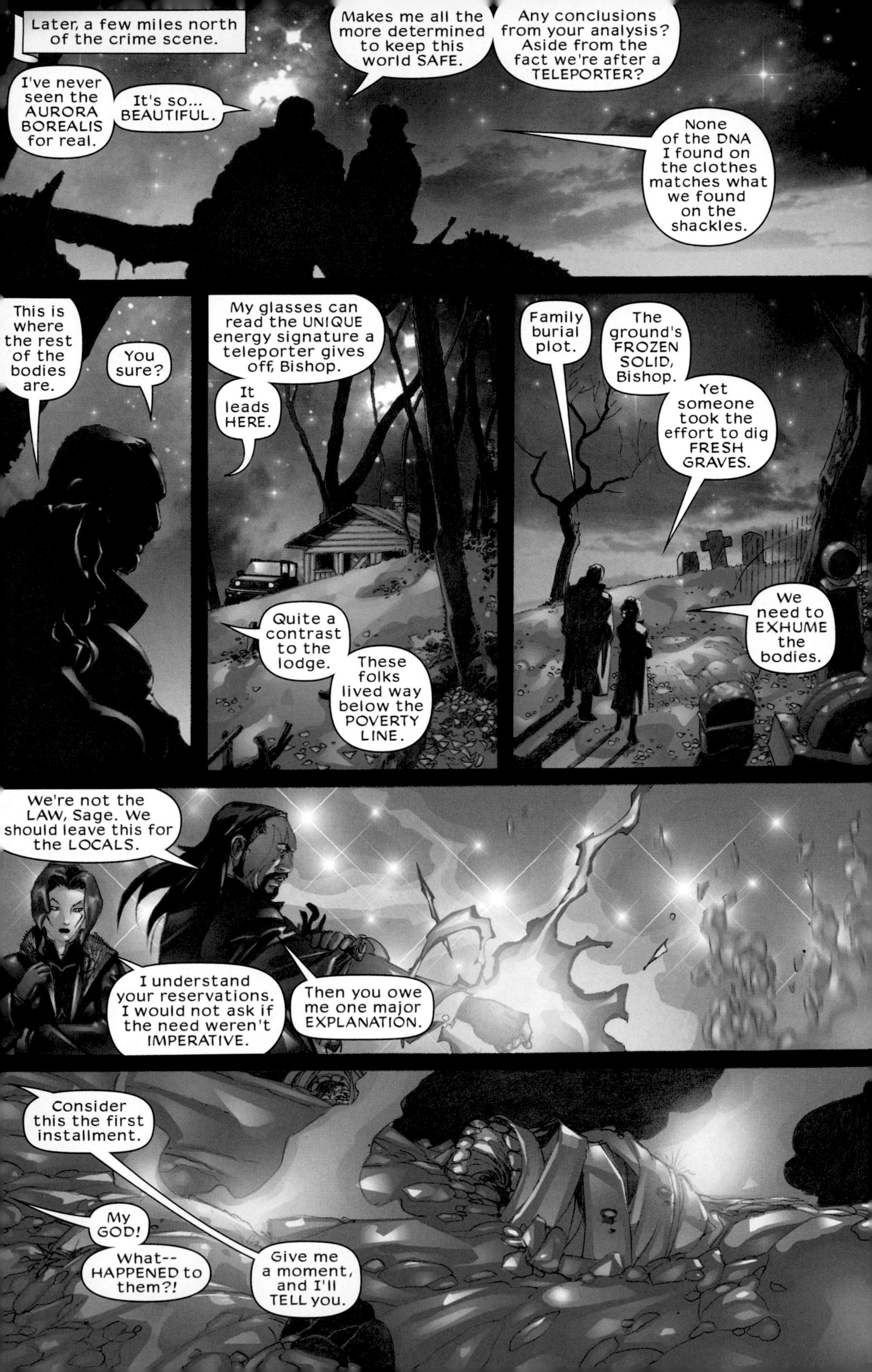

Later, a few miles north of the crime scene.
I've never seen the AURORA BOREALIS for real.
It's so... BEAUTIFUL.
Makes me all the more determined to keep this world SAFE.
Any conclusions from your analysis? Aside from the fact we're after a TELEPORTER?
None of the DNA I found on the clothes matches what we found on the shackles.
This is where the rest of the bodies are.
You sure?
My glasses can read the UNIQUE energy signature a teleporter gives off, Bishop.
It leads HERE.
Quite a contrast to the lodge.
These folks lived way below the POVERTY LINE.
Family burial plot.
The ground's FROZEN SOLID, Bishop.
Yet someone took the effort to dig FRESH GRAVES.
We need to EXHUME the bodies.
We're not the LAW, Sage. We should leave this for the LOCALS.
I understand your reservations. I would not ask if the need weren't IMPERATIVE.
Then you owe me one major EXPLANATION.
Consider this the first installment.
My GOD!
What--HAPPENED to them?!
Give me a moment, and I'll TELL you.

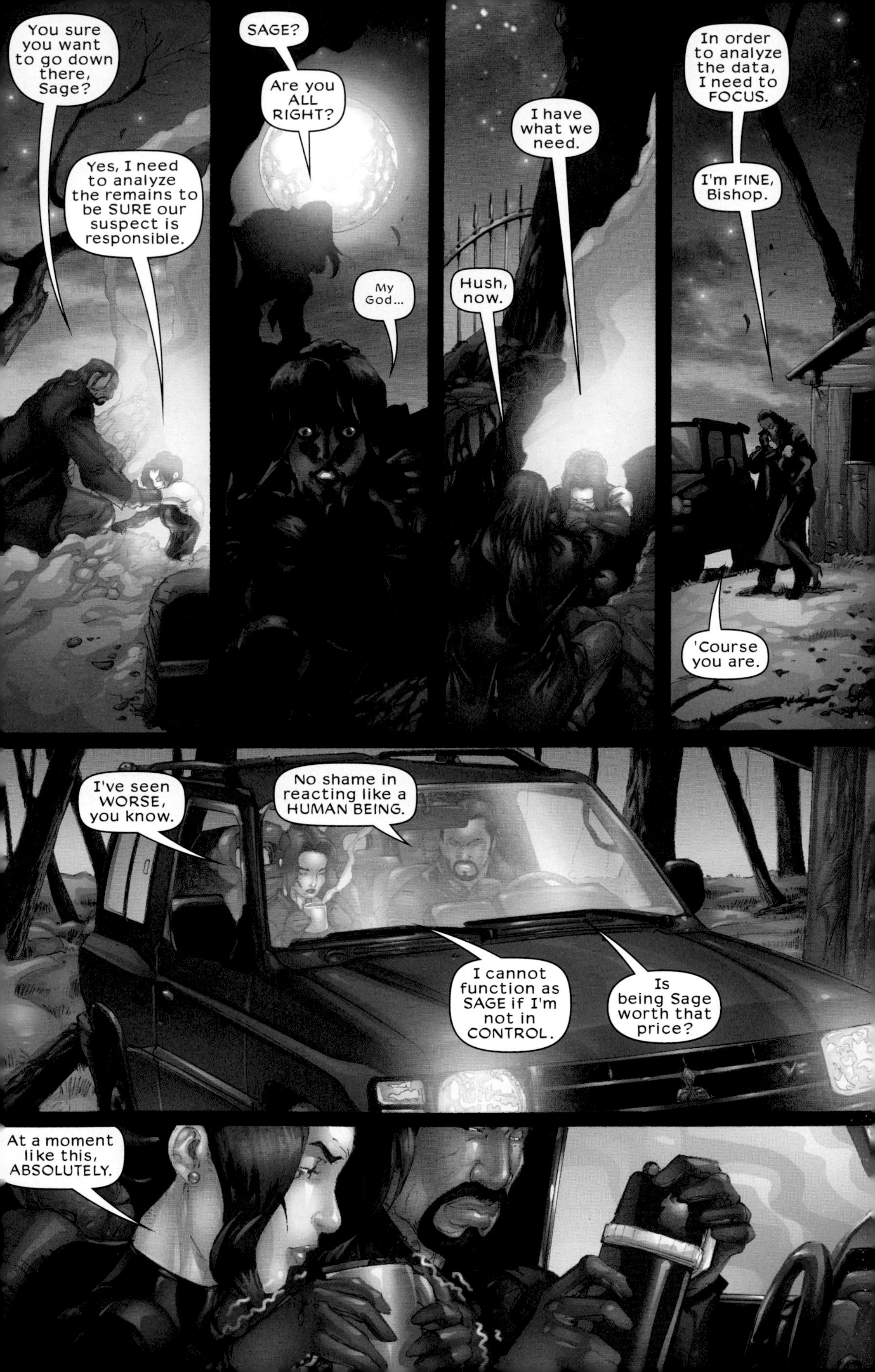
You sure you want to go down there, Sage?
Yes, I need to analyze the remains to be SURE our suspect is responsible.
SAGE?
Are you ALL RIGHT?
My God...
I have what we need.
Hush, now.
In order to analyze the data, I need to FOCUS.
I'm FINE, Bishop.
'Course you are.
I've seen WORSE, you know.
No shame in reacting like a HUMAN BEING.
I cannot function as SAGE if I'm not in CONTROL.
Is being Sage worth that price?
At a moment like this, ABSOLUTELY.

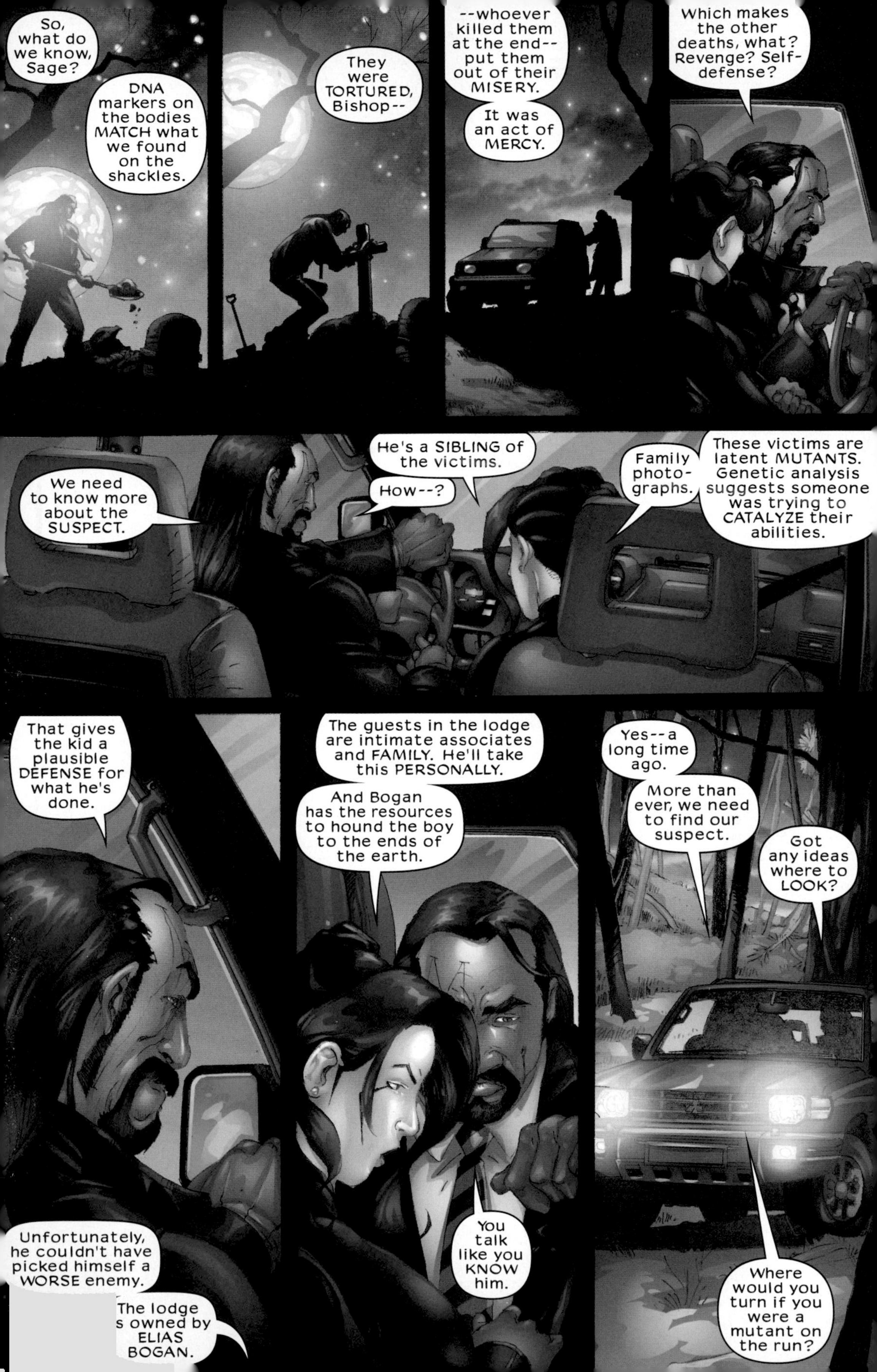
So, what do we know, Sage?
DNA markers on the bodies MATCH what we found on the shackles.
They were TORTURED, Bishop--
--whoever killed them at the end--put them out of their MISERY.
It was an act of MERCY.
Which makes the other deaths, what? Revenge? Self-defense?
We need to know more about the SUSPECT.
He's a SIBLING of the victims.
How--?
Family photo-graphs.
These victims are latent MUTANTS. Genetic analysis suggests someone was trying to CATALYZE their abilities.
That gives the kid a plausible DEFENSE for what he's done.
Unfortunately, he couldn't have picked himself a WORSE enemy.
The lodge s owned by ELIAS BOGAN.
The guests in the lodge are intimate associates and FAMILY. He'll take this PERSONALLY.
And Bogan has the resources to hound the boy to the ends of the earth.
You talk like you KNOW him.
Yes--a long time ago.
More than ever, we need to find our suspect.
Got any ideas where to LOOK?
Where would you turn if you were a mutant on the run?

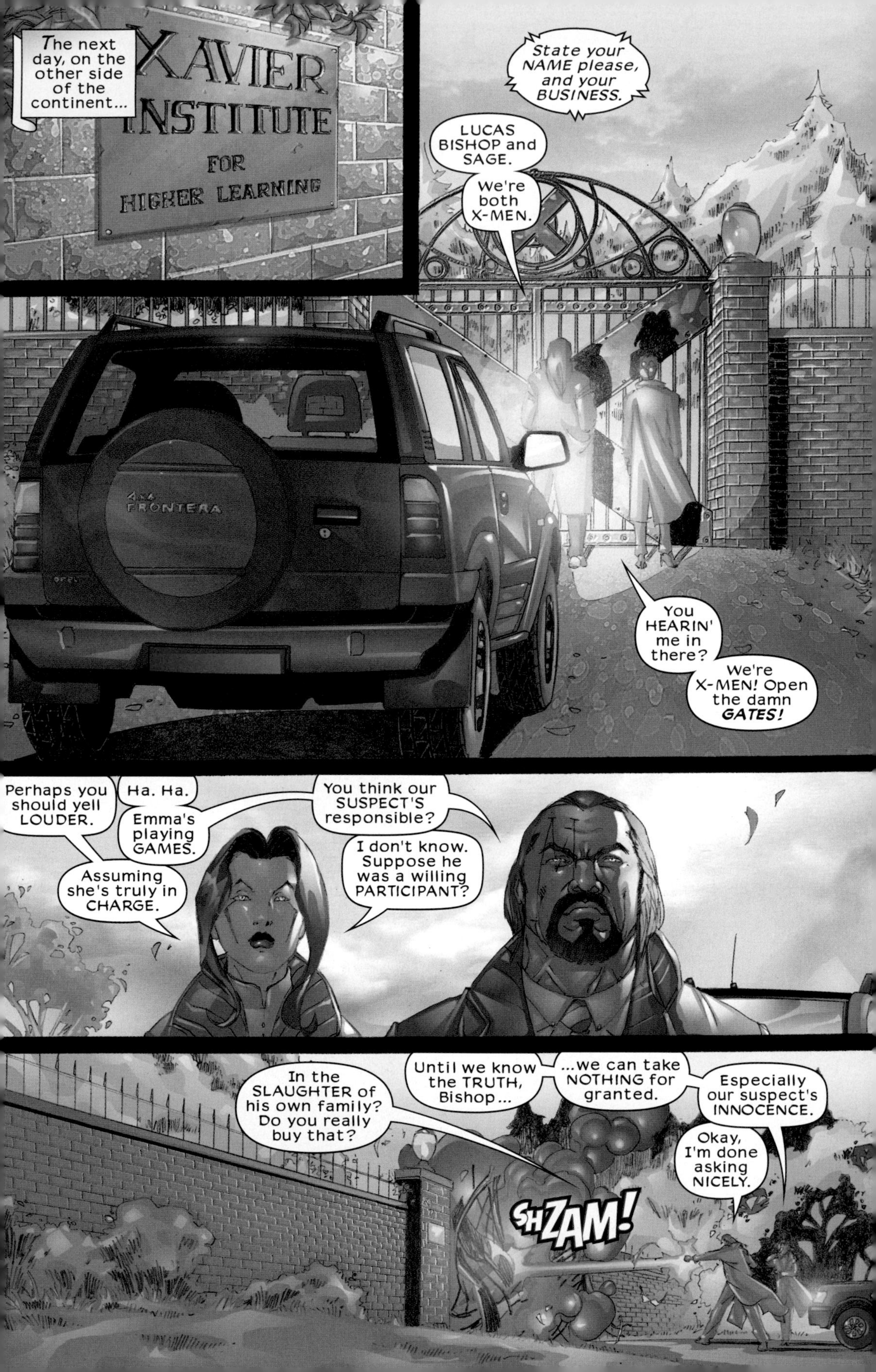
The next day, on the other side of the continent...
XAVIER INSTITUTE FOR HIGHER LEARNING
State your NAME please, and your BUSINESS.
LUCAS BISHOP and SAGE.
We're both X-MEN.
4x4 FRONTERA
You HEARIN' me in there?
We're X-MEN! Open the damn GATES!
Perhaps you should yell LOUDER.
Ha. Ha.
Emma's playing GAMES.
Assuming she's truly in CHARGE.
You think our SUSPECT'S responsible?
I don't know. Suppose he was a willing PARTICIPANT?
In the SLAUGHTER of his own family? Do you really buy that?
Until we know the TRUTH, Bishop...
...we can take NOTHING for granted.
Especially our suspect's INNOCENCE.
Okay, I'm done asking NICELY.
SHZAM!

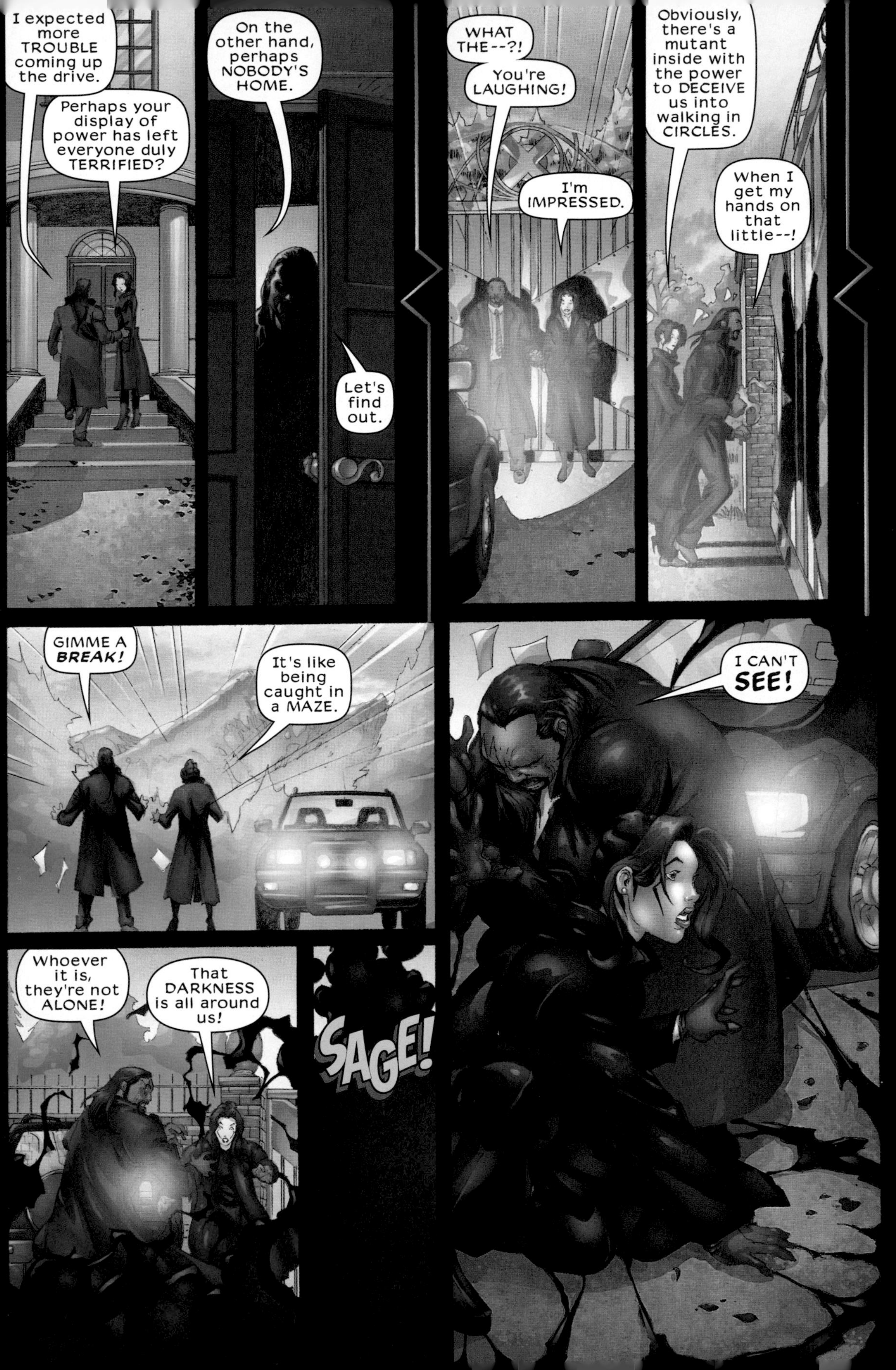
I expected more TROUBLE coming up the drive.
Perhaps your display of power has left everyone duly TERRIFIED?
On the other hand, perhaps NOBODY'S HOME.
Let's find out.
WHAT THE--?!
You're LAUGHING!
I'm IMPRESSED.
Obviously, there's a mutant inside with the power to DECEIVE us into walking in CIRCLES.
When I get my hands on that little--!
GIMME A BREAK!
It's like being caught in a MAZE.
I CAN'T SEE!
Whoever it is, they're not ALONE!
That DARKNESS is all around us!
SAGE!

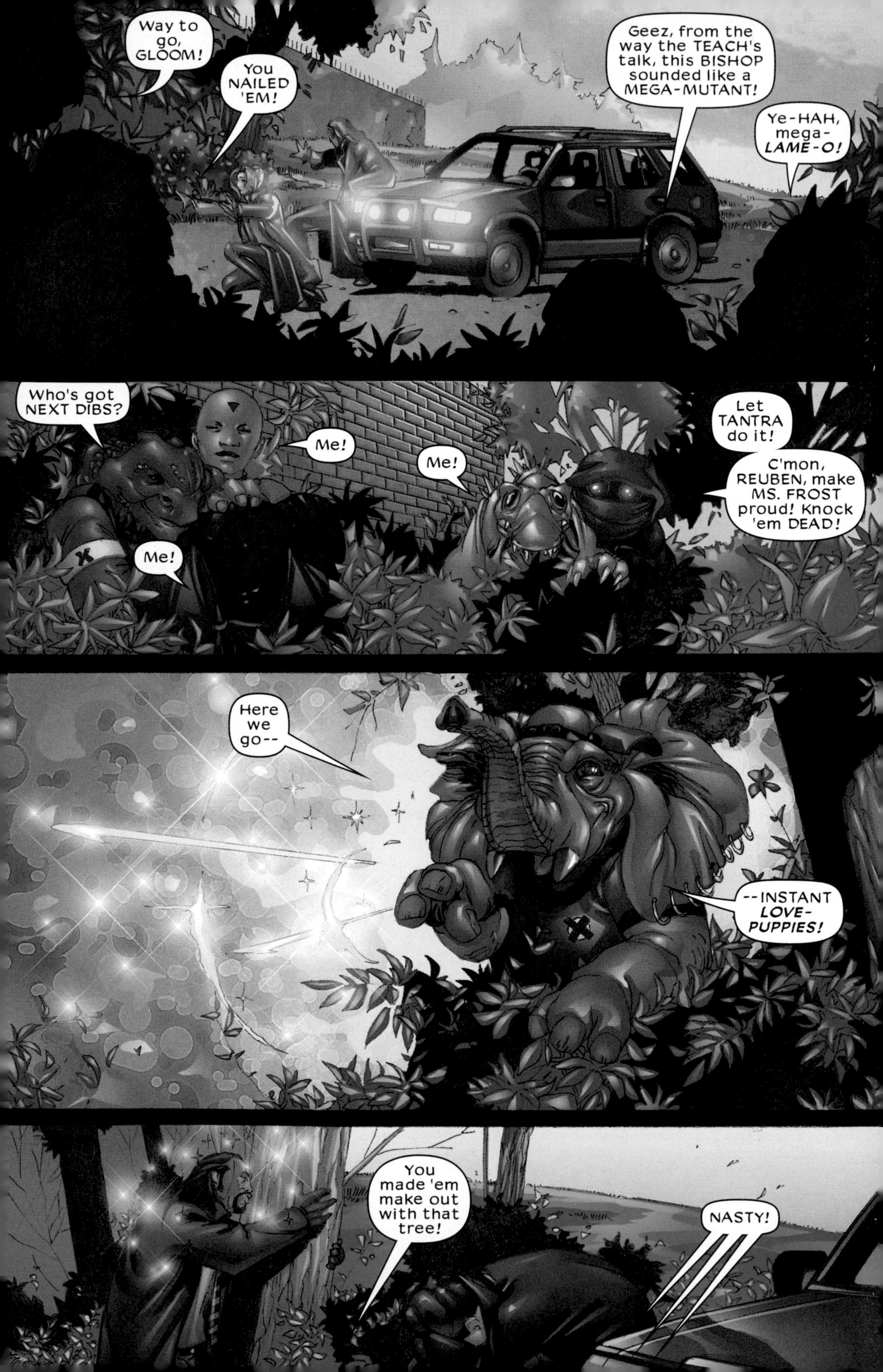
Way to go, GLOOM!
You NAILED 'EM!
Geez, from the way the TEACH's talk, this BISHOP sounded like a MEGA-MUTANT!
Ye-HAH, mega-LAME-O!
Who's got NEXT DIBS?
Me!
Me!
Me!
Let TANTRA do it!
C'mon, REUBEN, make MS. FROST proud! Knock 'em DEAD!
Here we go--
--INSTANT LOVE-PUPPIES!
You made 'em make out with that tree!
NASTY!

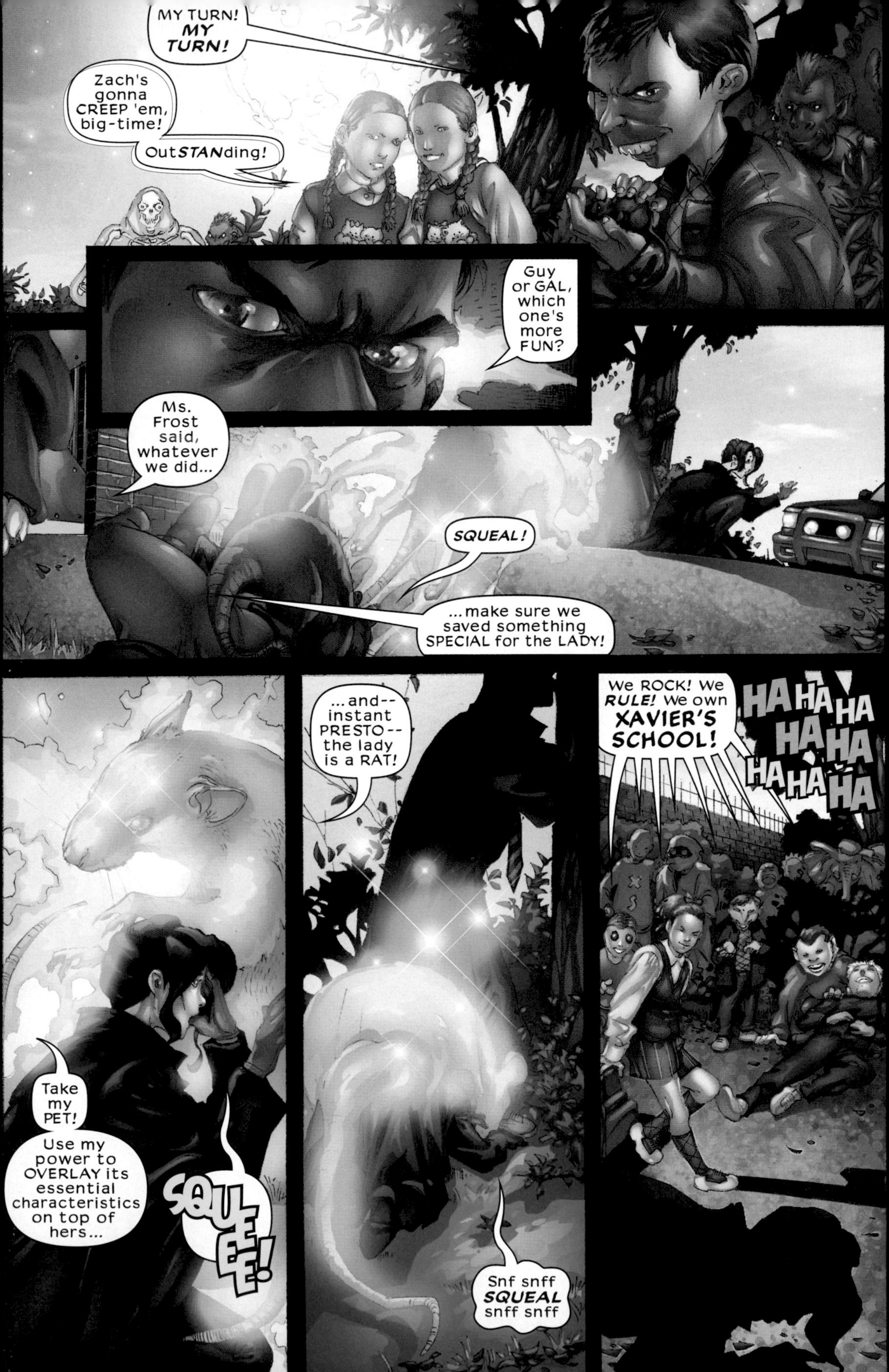
MY TURN! MY TURN!
Zach's gonna CREEP 'em, big-time!
OutSTANding!
Guy or GAL, which one's more FUN?
Ms. Frost said, whatever we did...
SQUEAL!
...make sure we saved something SPECIAL for the LADY!
Take my PET!
Use my power to OVERLAY its essential characteristics on top of hers...
SQUEEE!
...and-- instant PRESTO-- the lady is a RAT!
Snf snff SQUEAL snff snff
We ROCK! We RULE! We own XAVIER'S SCHOOL!
HA HA HA HA HA HA HA HA HA

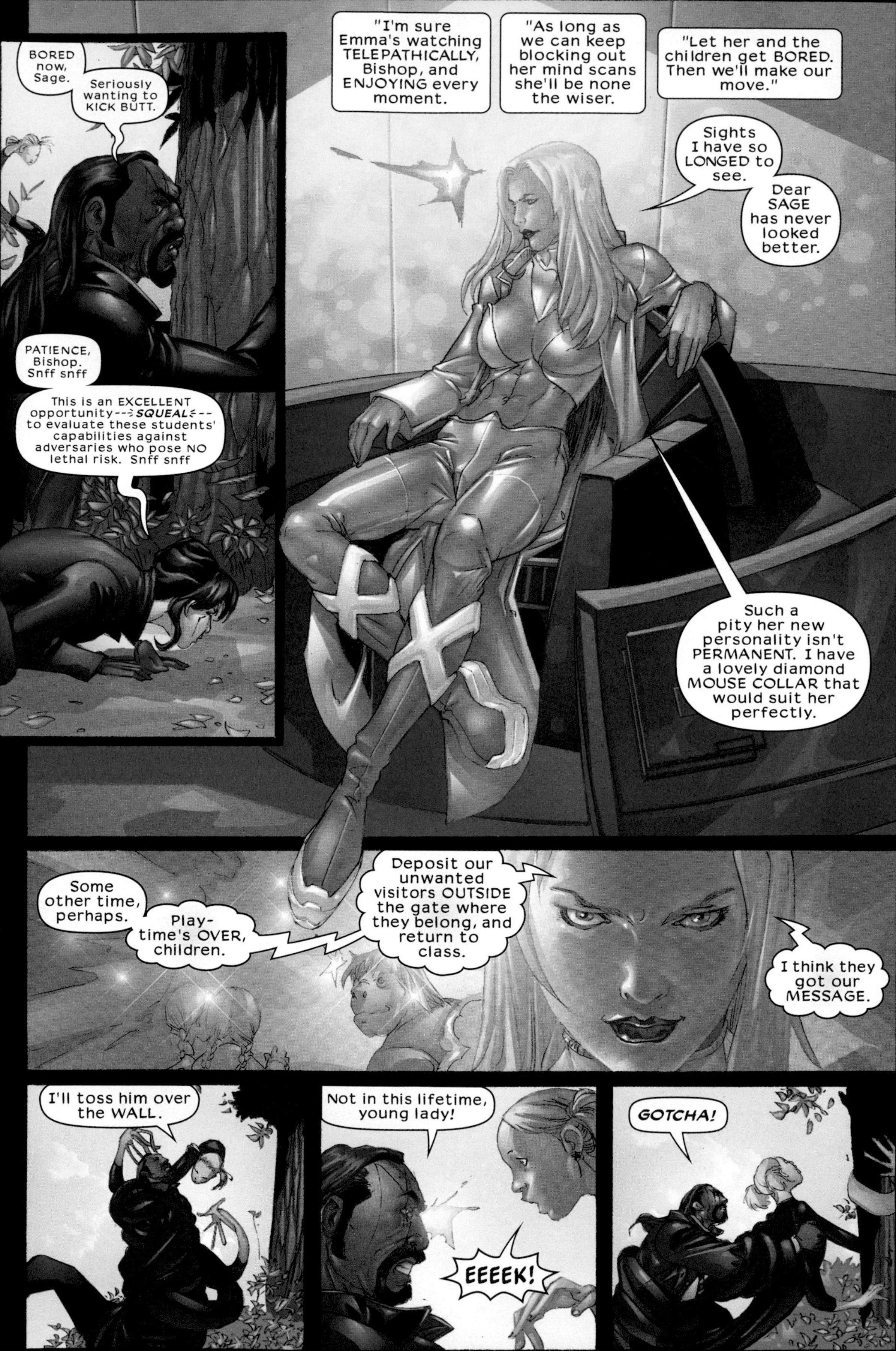
BORED now, Sage.
Seriously wanting to KICK BUTT.
PATIENCE, Bishop. Snff snff
This is an EXCELLENT opportunity--SQUEAL--to evaluate these students' capabilities against adversaries who pose NO lethal risk. Snff snff
"I'm sure Emma's watching TELEPATHICALLY, Bishop, and ENJOYING every moment.
"As long as we can keep blocking out her mind scans she'll be none the wiser.
"Let her and the children get BORED. Then we'll make our move."
Sights I have so LONGED to see.
Dear SAGE has never looked better.
Such a pity her new personality isn't PERMANENT. I have a lovely diamond MOUSE COLLAR that would suit her perfectly.
Some other time, perhaps.
Play-time's OVER, children.
Deposit our unwanted visitors OUTSIDE the gate where they belong, and return to class.
I think they got our MESSAGE.
I'll toss him over the WALL.
Not in this lifetime, young lady!
EEEEK!
GOTCHA!

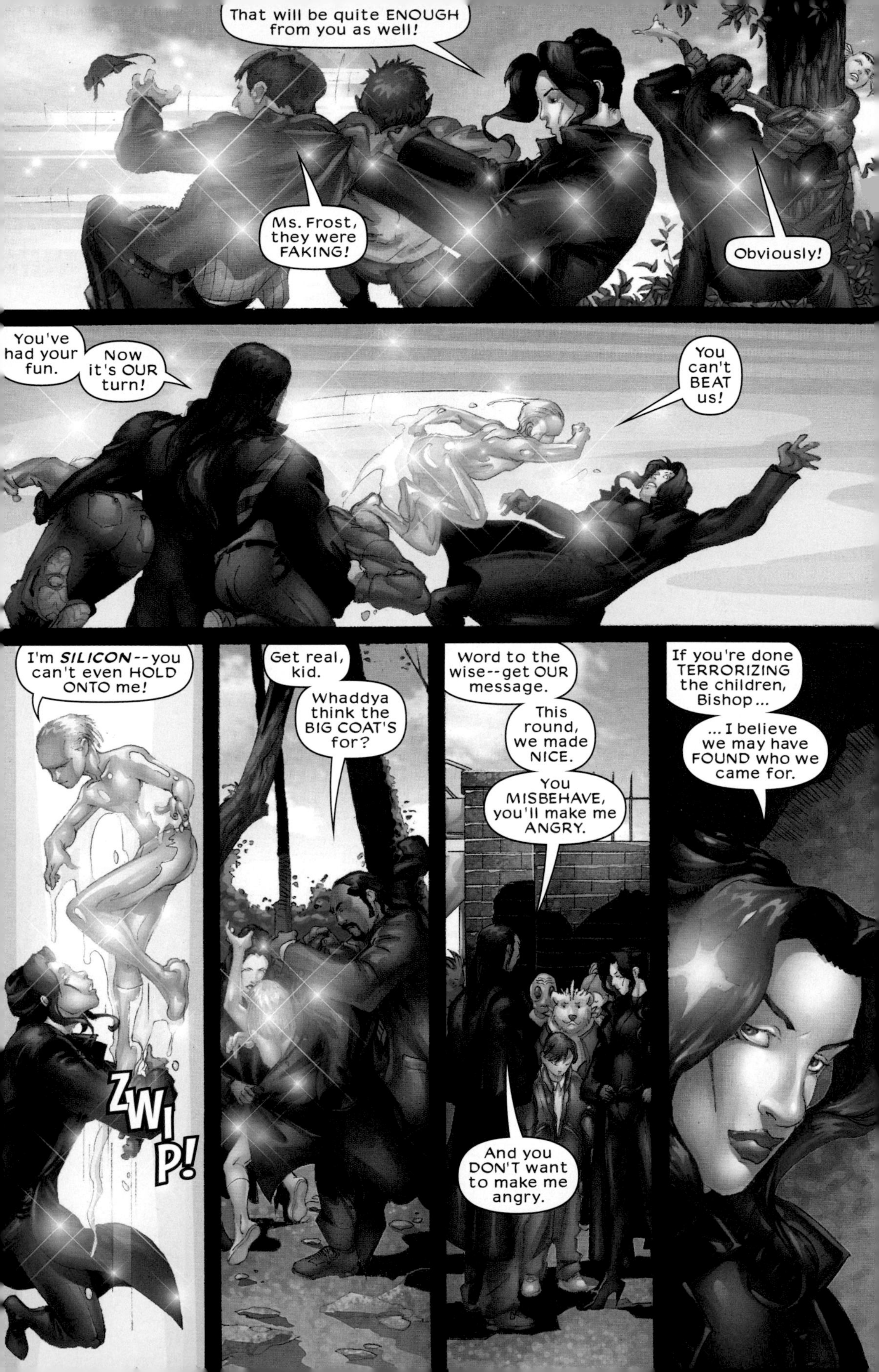
That will be quite ENOUGH from you as well!
Ms. Frost, they were FAKING!
Obviously!
You've had your fun.
Now it's OUR turn!
You can't BEAT us!
I'm SILICON--you can't even HOLD ONTO me!
ZWIP!
Get real, kid.
Whaddya think the BIG COAT'S for?
Word to the wise--get OUR message.
This round, we made NICE.
You MISBEHAVE, you'll make me ANGRY.
And you DON'T want to make me angry.
If you're done TERRORIZING the children, Bishop...
...I believe we may have FOUND who we came for.

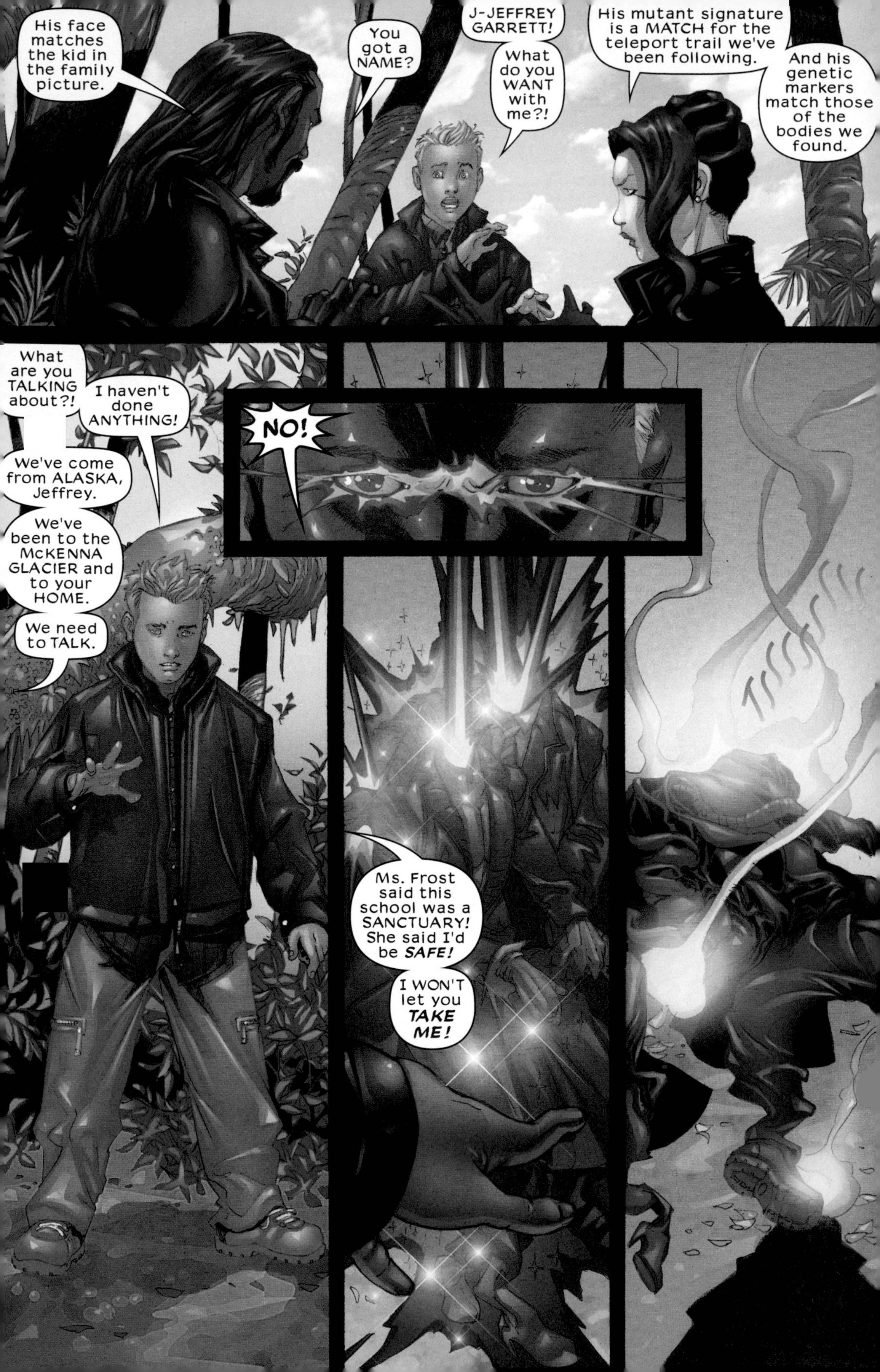
His face matches the kid in the family picture.
You got a NAME?
J-JEFFREY GARRETT!
What do you WANT with me?!
His mutant signature is a MATCH for the teleport trail we've been following.
And his genetic markers match those of the bodies we found.
What are you TALKING about?!
I haven't done ANYTHING!
We've come from ALASKA, Jeffrey.
We've been to the McKENNA GLACIER and to your HOME.
We need to TALK.
NO!
Ms. Frost said this school was a SANCTUARY! She said I'd be *SAFE!*
I WON'T let you *TAKE ME!*

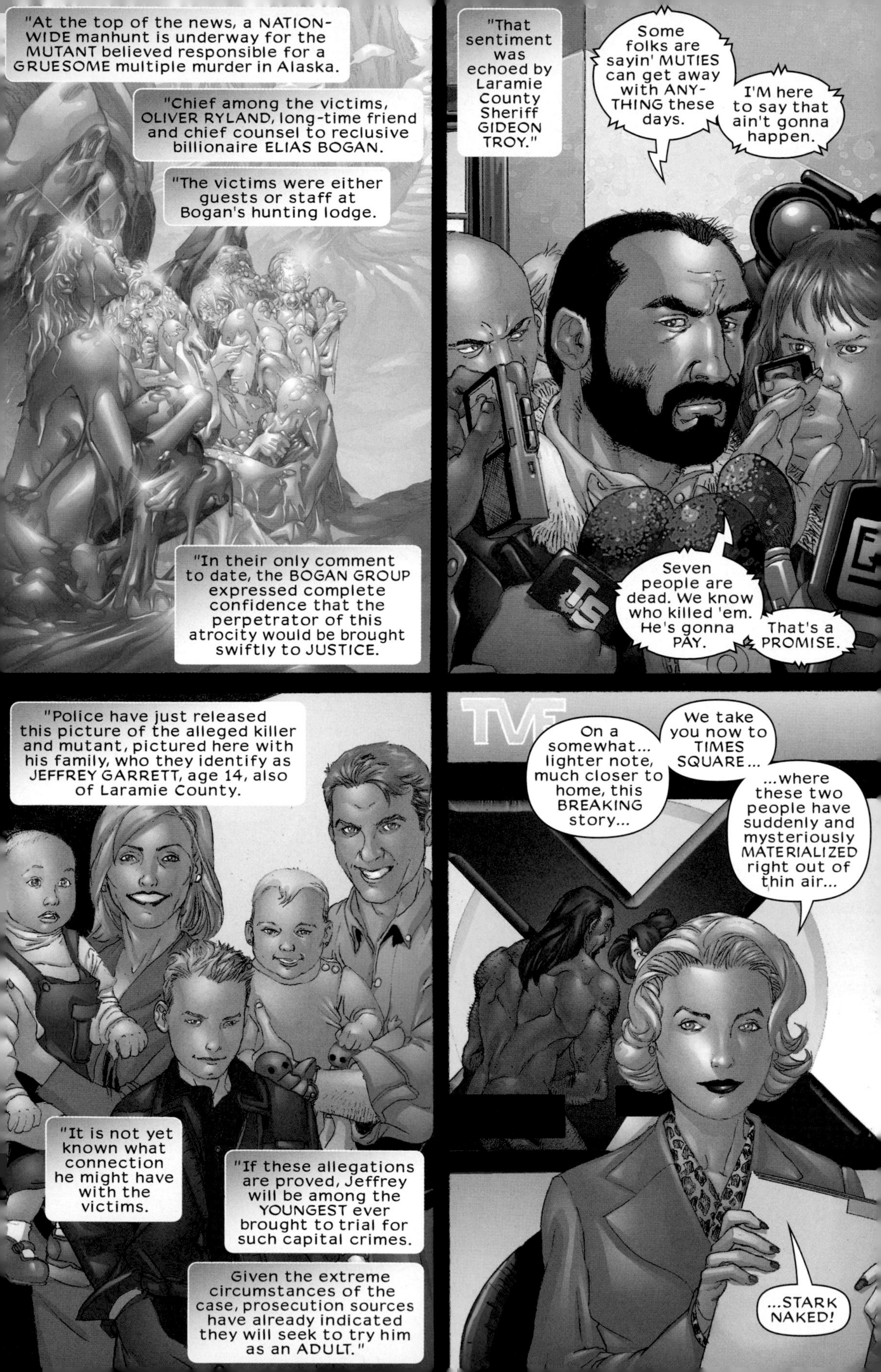
"At the top of the news, a NATION-WIDE manhunt is underway for the MUTANT believed responsible for a GRUESOME multiple murder in Alaska.
"Chief among the victims, OLIVER RYLAND, long-time friend and chief counsel to reclusive billionaire ELIAS BOGAN.
"The victims were either guests or staff at Bogan's hunting lodge.
"In their only comment to date, the BOGAN GROUP expressed complete confidence that the perpetrator of this atrocity would be brought swiftly to JUSTICE.
"That sentiment was echoed by Laramie County Sheriff GIDEON TROY."
Some folks are sayin' MUTIES can get away with ANY-THING these days.
I'M here to say that ain't gonna happen.
Seven people are dead. We know who killed 'em. He's gonna PAY.
That's a PROMISE.
"Police have just released this picture of the alleged killer and mutant, pictured here with his family, who they identify as JEFFREY GARRETT, age 14, also of Laramie County.
"It is not yet known what connection he might have with the victims.
"If these allegations are proved, Jeffrey will be among the YOUNGEST ever brought to trial for such capital crimes.
Given the extreme circumstances of the case, prosecution sources have already indicated they will seek to try him as an ADULT."
On a somewhat... lighter note, much closer to home, this BREAKING story...
We take you now to TIMES SQUARE...
...where these two people have suddenly and mysteriously MATERIALIZED right out of thin air...
...STARK NAKED!

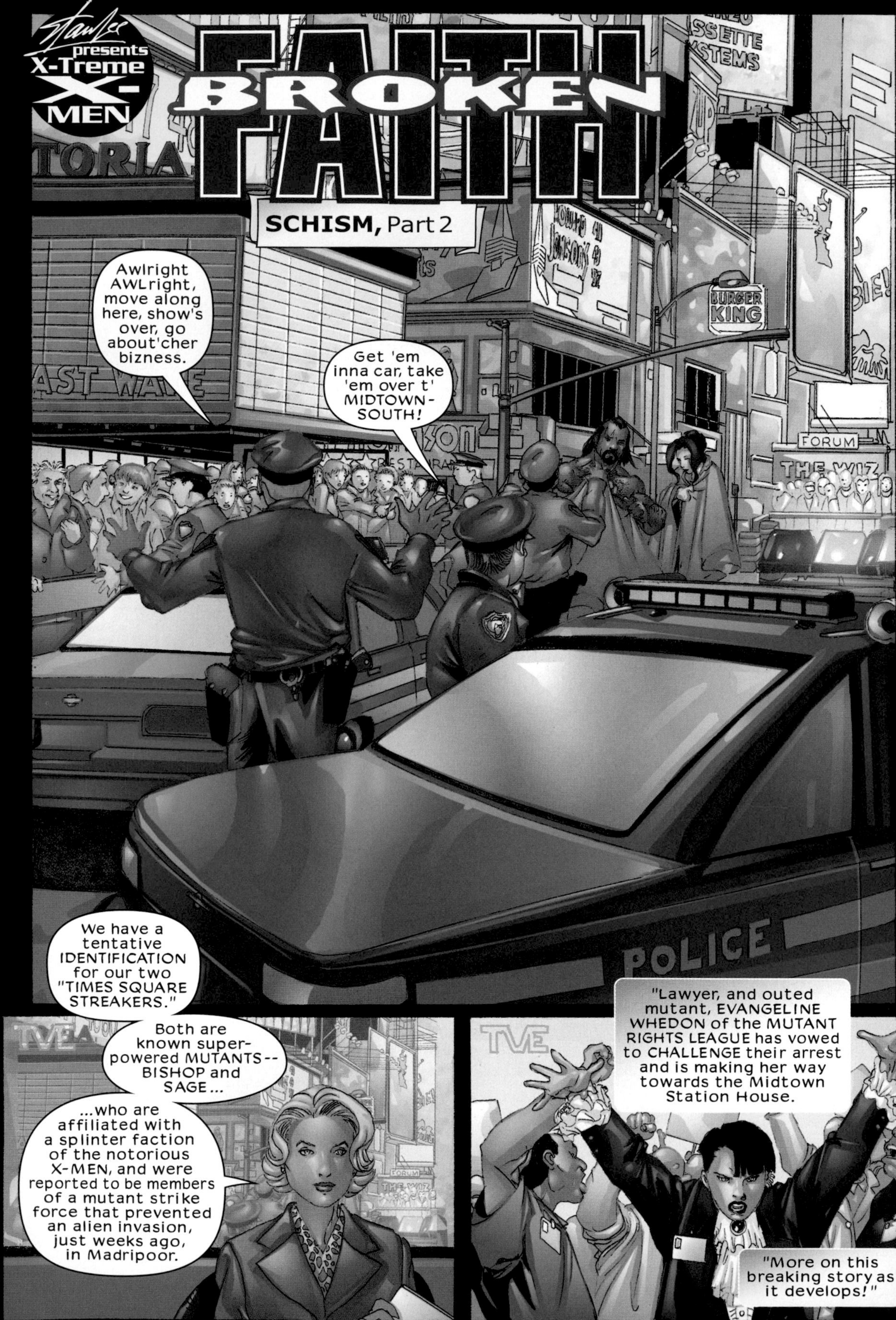
Stan Lee presents X-Treme X-MEN
FAITH BROKEN
SCHISM, Part 2
Awlright AWLright, move along here, show's over, go about'cher bizness.
Get 'em inna car, take 'em over t' MIDTOWN-SOUTH!
POLICE
We have a tentative IDENTIFICATION for our two "TIMES SQUARE STREAKERS."
Both are known super-powered MUTANTS -- BISHOP and SAGE...
...who are affiliated with a splinter faction of the notorious X-MEN, and were reported to be members of a mutant strike force that prevented an alien invasion, just weeks ago, in Madripoor.
"Lawyer, and outed mutant, EVANGELINE WHEDON of the MUTANT RIGHTS LEAGUE has vowed to CHALLENGE their arrest and is making her way towards the Midtown Station House.
"More on this breaking story as it develops!"

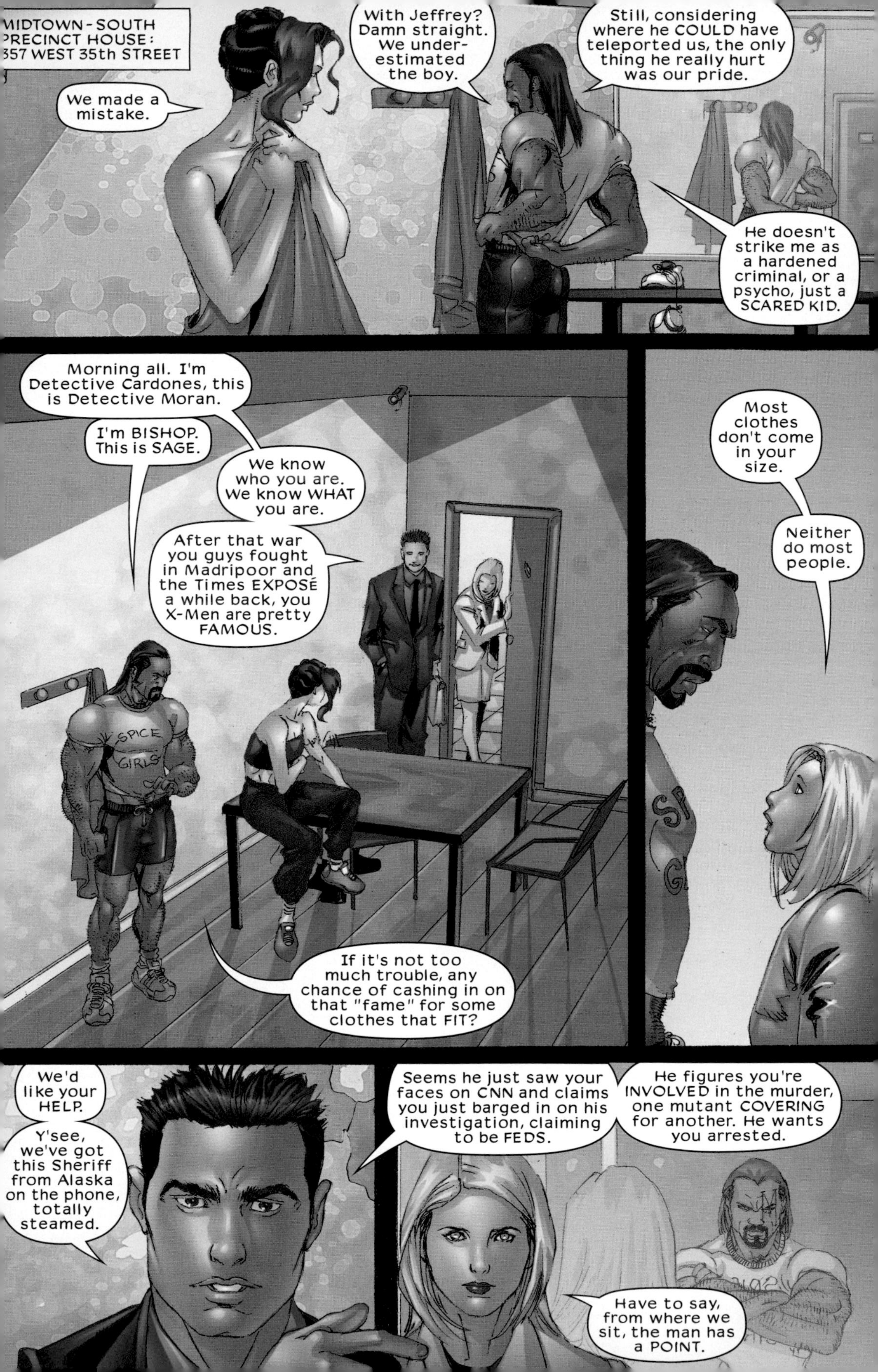
MIDTOWN-SOUTH PRECINCT HOUSE: 357 WEST 35th STREET
We made a mistake.
With Jeffrey? Damn straight. We under-estimated the boy.
Still, considering where he COULD have teleported us, the only thing he really hurt was our pride.
He doesn't strike me as a hardened criminal, or a psycho, just a SCARED KID.
Morning all. I'm Detective Cardones, this is Detective Moran.
I'm BISHOP. This is SAGE.
We know who you are. We know WHAT you are.
After that war you guys fought in Madripoor and the Times EXPOSÉ a while back, you X-Men are pretty FAMOUS.
SPICE GIRLS
If it's not too much trouble, any chance of cashing in on that "fame" for some clothes that FIT?
Most clothes don't come in your size.
Neither do most people.
We'd like your HELP.
Y'see, we've got this Sheriff from Alaska on the phone, totally steamed.
Seems he just saw your faces on CNN and claims you just barged in on his investigation, claiming to be FEDS.
He figures you're INVOLVED in the murder, one mutant COVERING for another. He wants you arrested.
Have to say, from where we sit, the man has a POINT.

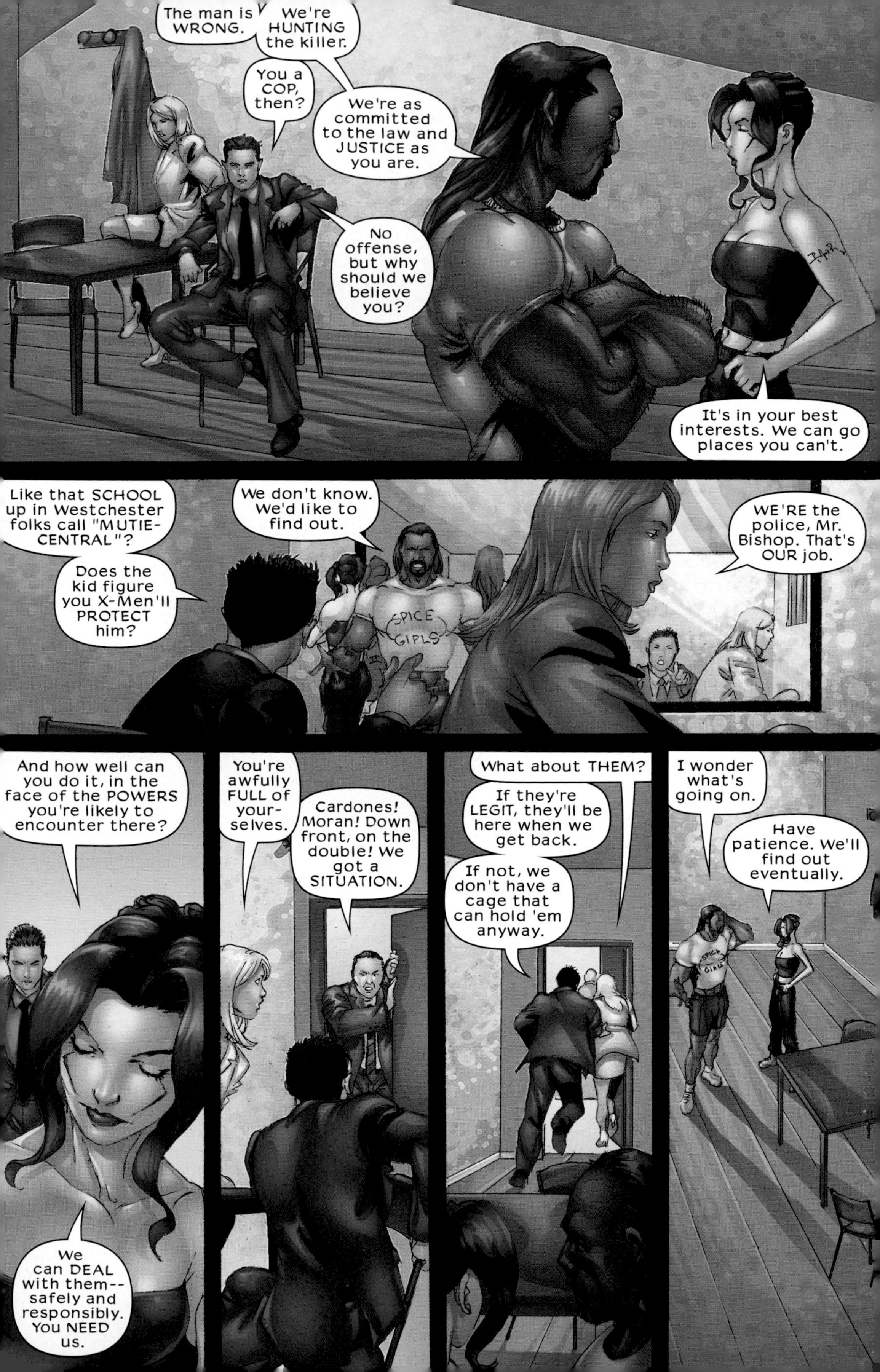
The man is WRONG.
We're HUNTING the killer.
You a COP, then?
We're as committed to the law and JUSTICE as you are.
No offense, but why should we believe you?
It's in your best interests. We can go places you can't.
Like that SCHOOL up in Westchester folks call "MUTIE-CENTRAL"?
Does the kid figure you X-Men'll PROTECT him?
We don't know. We'd like to find out.
SPICE GIRLS
WE'RE the police, Mr. Bishop. That's OUR job.
And how well can you do it, in the face of the POWERS you're likely to encounter there?
We can DEAL with them--safely and responsibly. You NEED us.
You're awfully FULL of your-selves.
Cardones! Moran! Down front, on the double! We got a SITUATION.
What about THEM?
If they're LEGIT, they'll be here when we get back.
If not, we don't have a cage that can hold 'em anyway.
I wonder what's going on.
Have patience. We'll find out eventually.

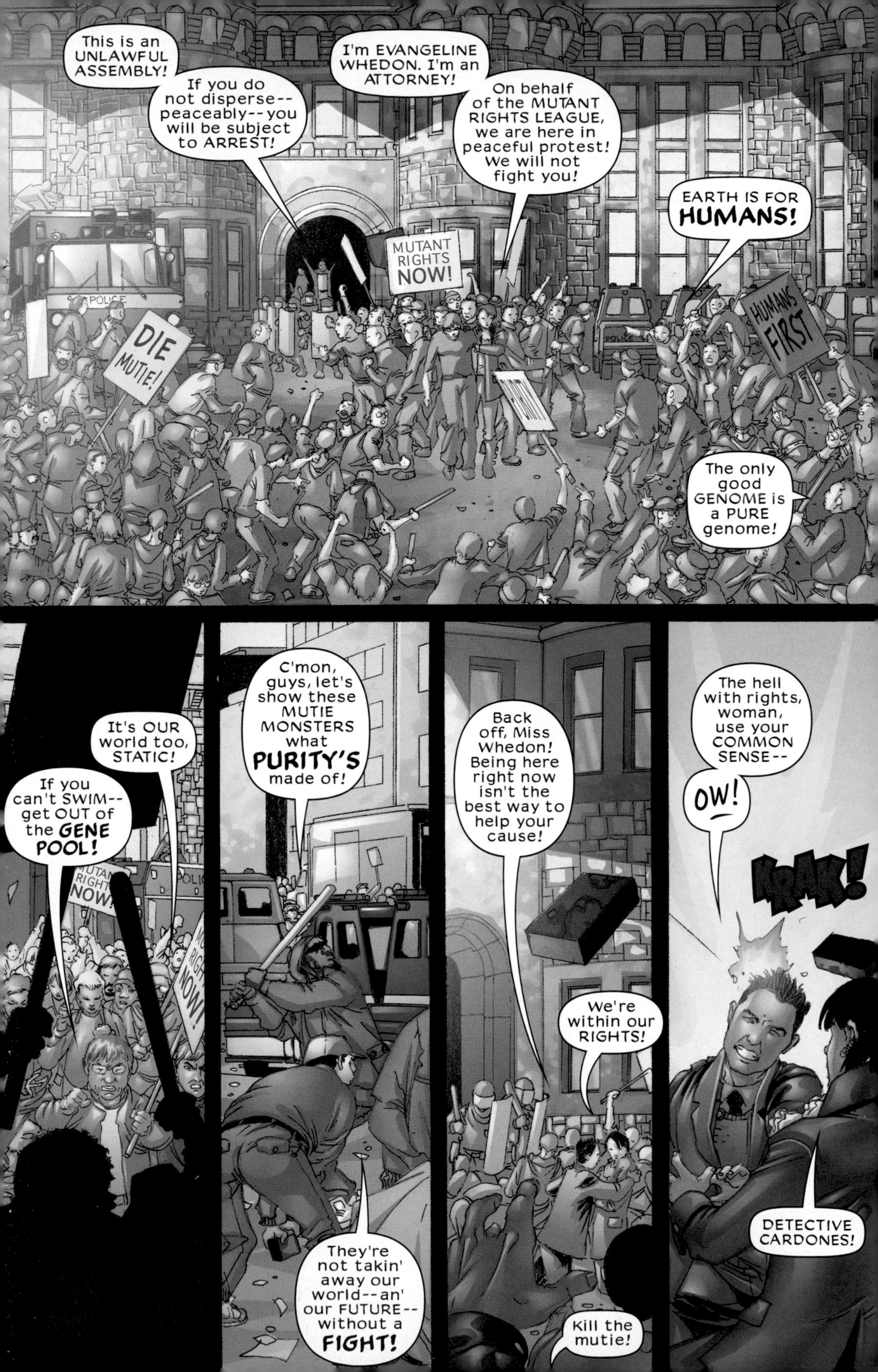
This is an UNLAWFUL ASSEMBLY!
If you do not disperse--peaceably--you will be subject to ARREST!
I'm EVANGELINE WHEDON. I'm an ATTORNEY!
On behalf of the MUTANT RIGHTS LEAGUE, we are here in peaceful protest! We will not fight you!
EARTH IS FOR HUMANS!
MUTANT RIGHTS NOW!
DIE MUTIE!
HUMANS FIRST
POLICE
The only good GENOME is a PURE genome!
It's OUR world too, STATIC!
If you can't SWIM--get OUT of the GENE POOL!
MUTANT RIGHTS NOW!
C'mon, guys, let's show these MUTIE MONSTERS what PURITY'S made of!
They're not takin' away our world--an' our FUTURE--without a FIGHT!
Back off, Miss Whedon! Being here right now isn't the best way to help your cause!
We're within our RIGHTS!
Kill the mutie!
The hell with rights, woman, use your COMMON SENSE--
OW!
KRAK!
DETECTIVE CARDONES!

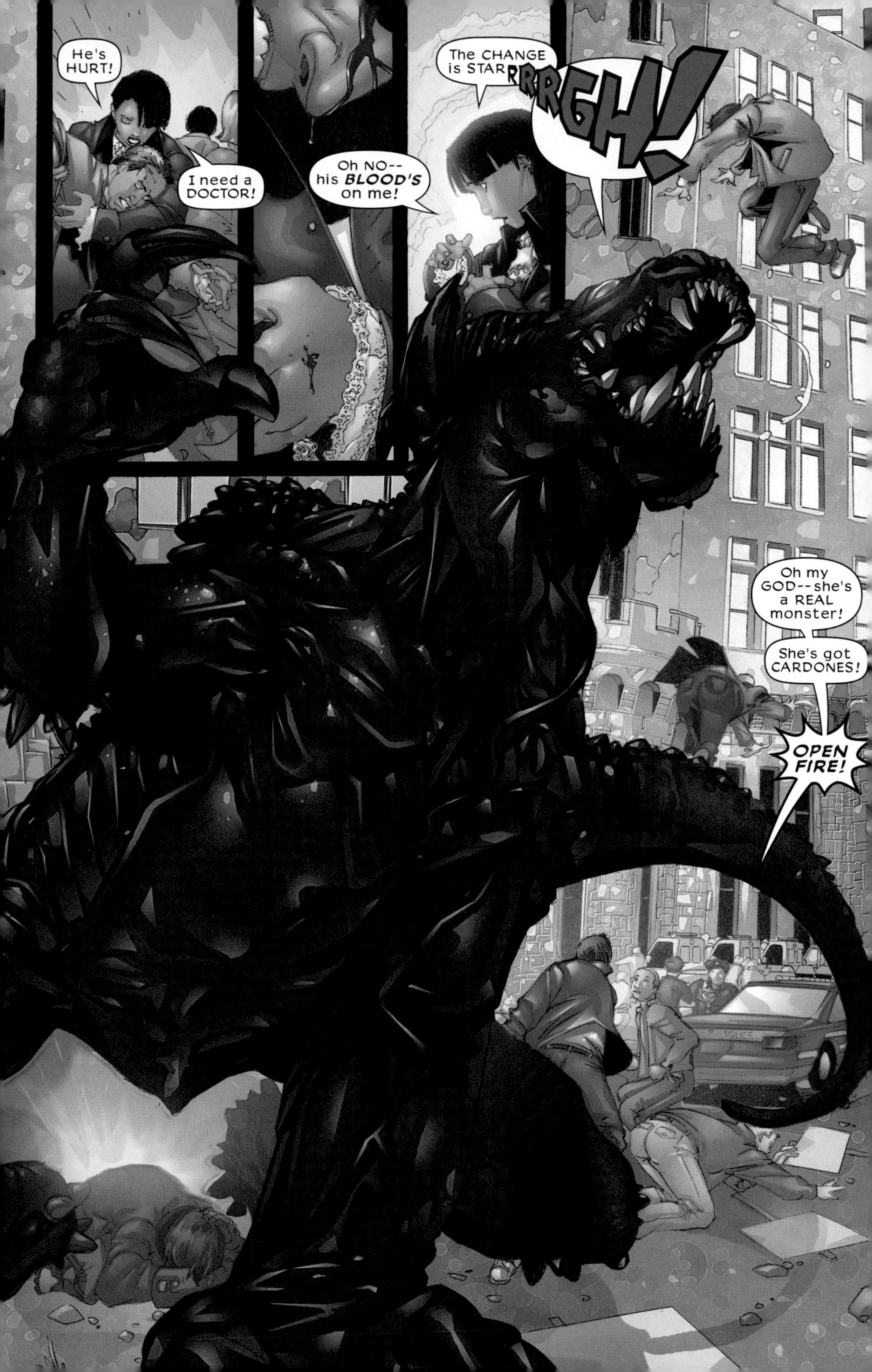
He's HURT!
I need a DOCTOR!
Oh NO-- his BLOOD'S on me!
The CHANGE is STARRRRGH!
Oh my GOD--she's a REAL monster!
She's got CARDONES!
OPEN FIRE!
POLICE

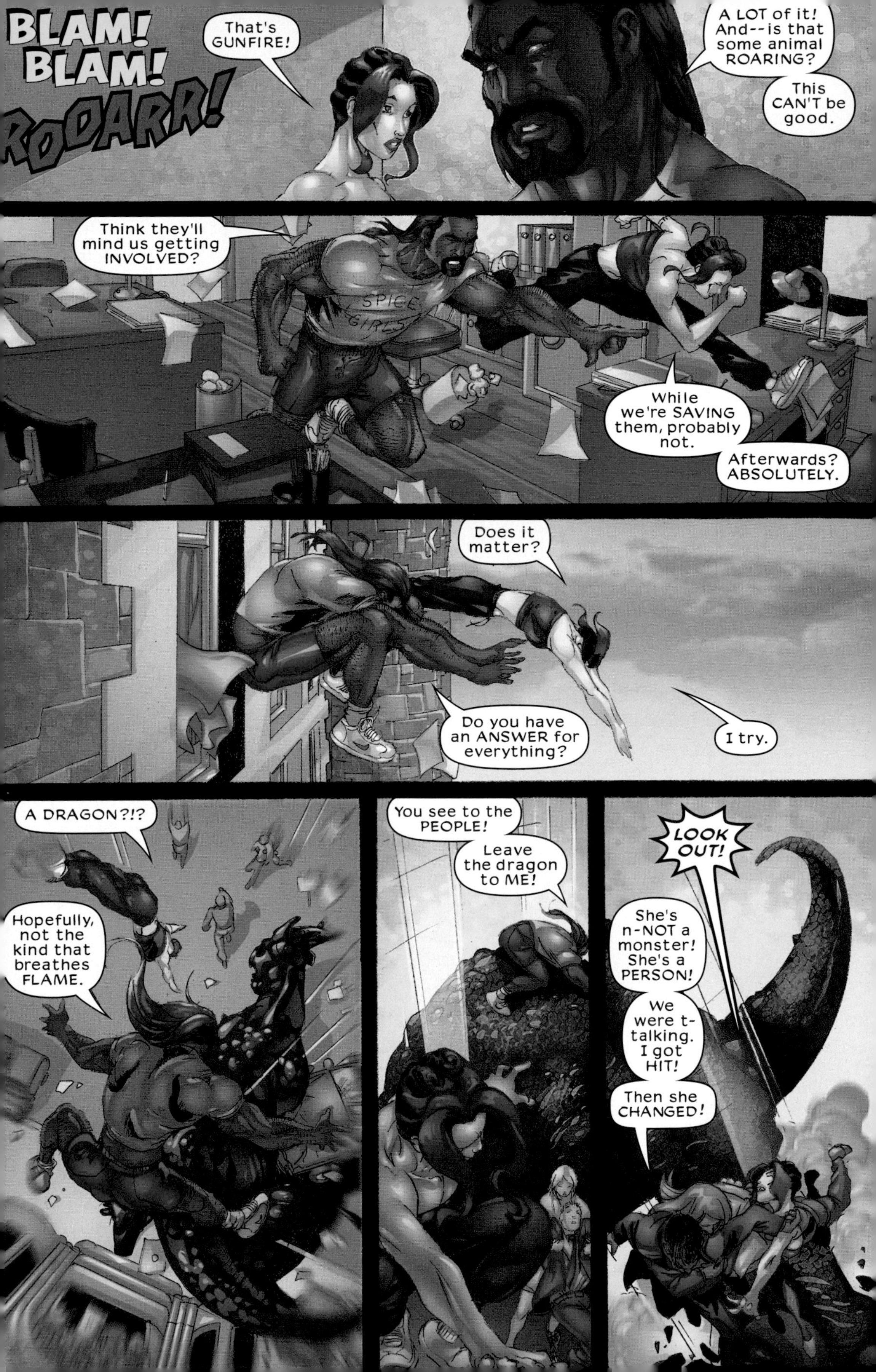
BLAM! BLAM!
ROOARR!
That's GUNFIRE!
A LOT of it! And--is that some animal ROARING?
This CAN'T be good.
Think they'll mind us getting INVOLVED?
SPICE GIRLS
While we're SAVING them, probably not.
Afterwards? ABSOLUTELY.
Does it matter?
Do you have an ANSWER for everything?
I try.
A DRAGON?!?
Hopefully, not the kind that breathes FLAME.
You see to the PEOPLE!
Leave the dragon to ME!
LOOK OUT!
She's n-NOT a monster! She's a PERSON!
We were t-talking. I got HIT!
Then she CHANGED!

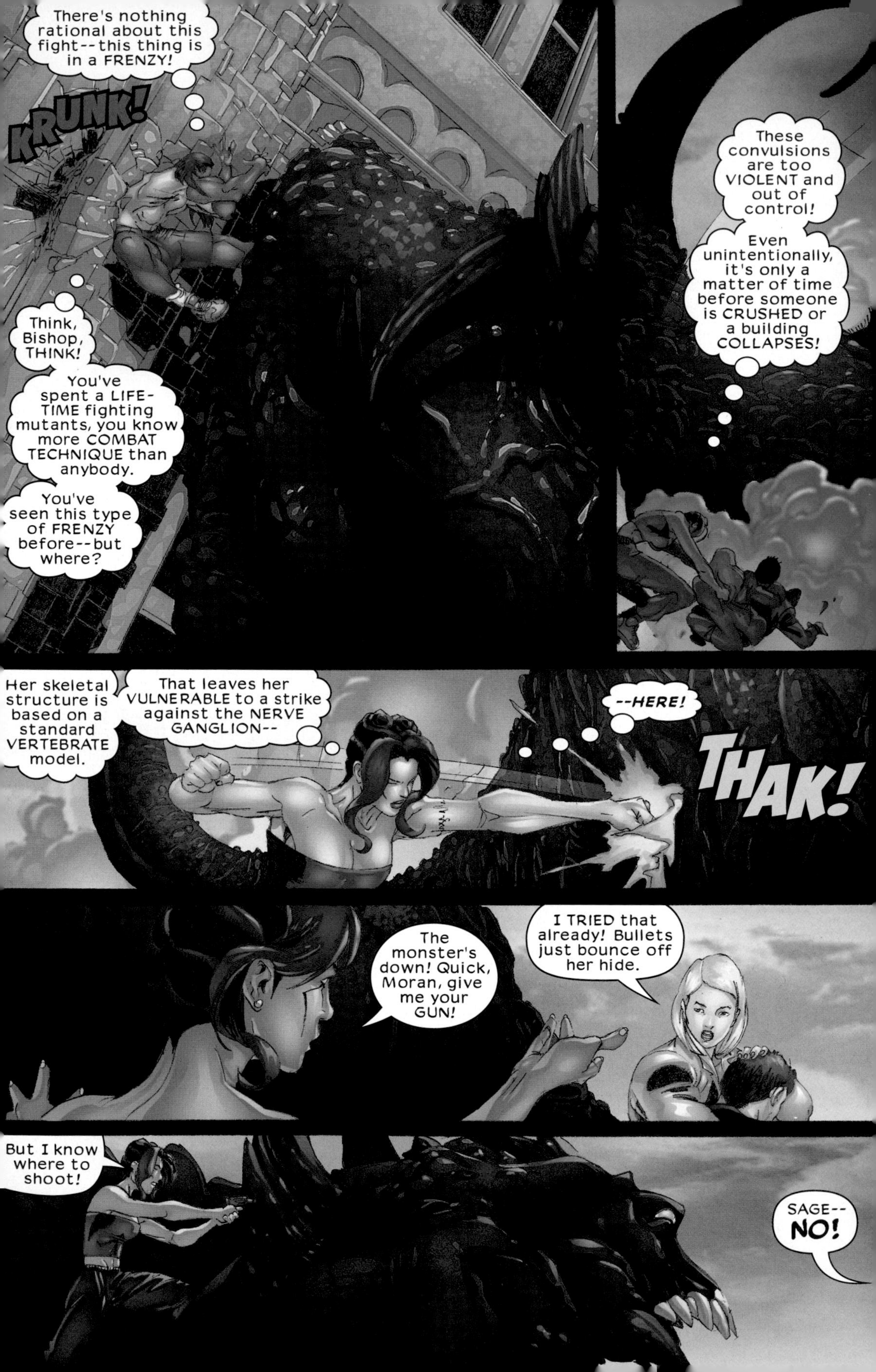
There's nothing rational about this fight--this thing is in a FRENZY!
KRUNK!
Think, Bishop, THINK!
You've spent a LIFE-TIME fighting mutants, you know more COMBAT TECHNIQUE than anybody.
You've seen this type of FRENZY before--but where?
These convulsions are too VIOLENT and out of control!
Even unintentionally, it's only a matter of time before someone is CRUSHED or a building COLLAPSES!
Her skeletal structure is based on a standard VERTEBRATE model.
That leaves her VULNERABLE to a strike against the NERVE GANGLION--
--HERE!
THAK!
The monster's down! Quick, Moran, give me your GUN!
I TRIED that already! Bullets just bounce off her hide.
But I know where to shoot!
SAGE--NO!

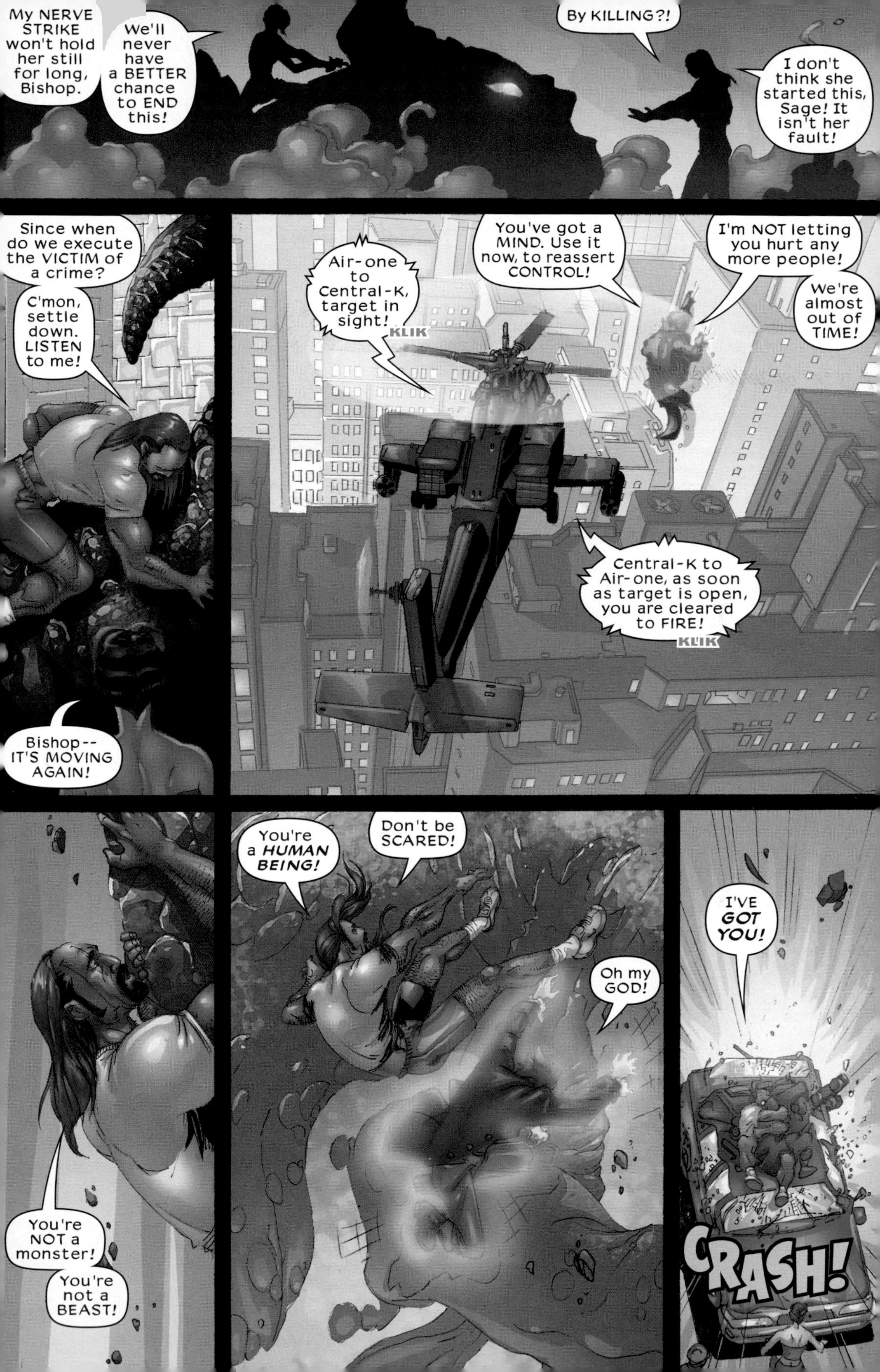
My NERVE STRIKE won't hold her still for long, Bishop.
We'll never have a BETTER chance to END this!
By KILLING?!
I don't think she started this, Sage! It isn't her fault!
Since when do we execute the VICTIM of a crime?
C'mon, settle down. LISTEN to me!
Bishop-- IT'S MOVING AGAIN!
Air-one to Central-K, target in sight!
KLIK
You've got a MIND. Use it now, to reassert CONTROL!
I'm NOT letting you hurt any more people!
We're almost out of TIME!
Central-K to Air-one, as soon as target is open, you are cleared to FIRE!
KLIK
You're NOT a monster!
You're not a BEAST!
You're a HUMAN BEING!
Don't be SCARED!
Oh my GOD!
I'VE GOT YOU!
CRASH!

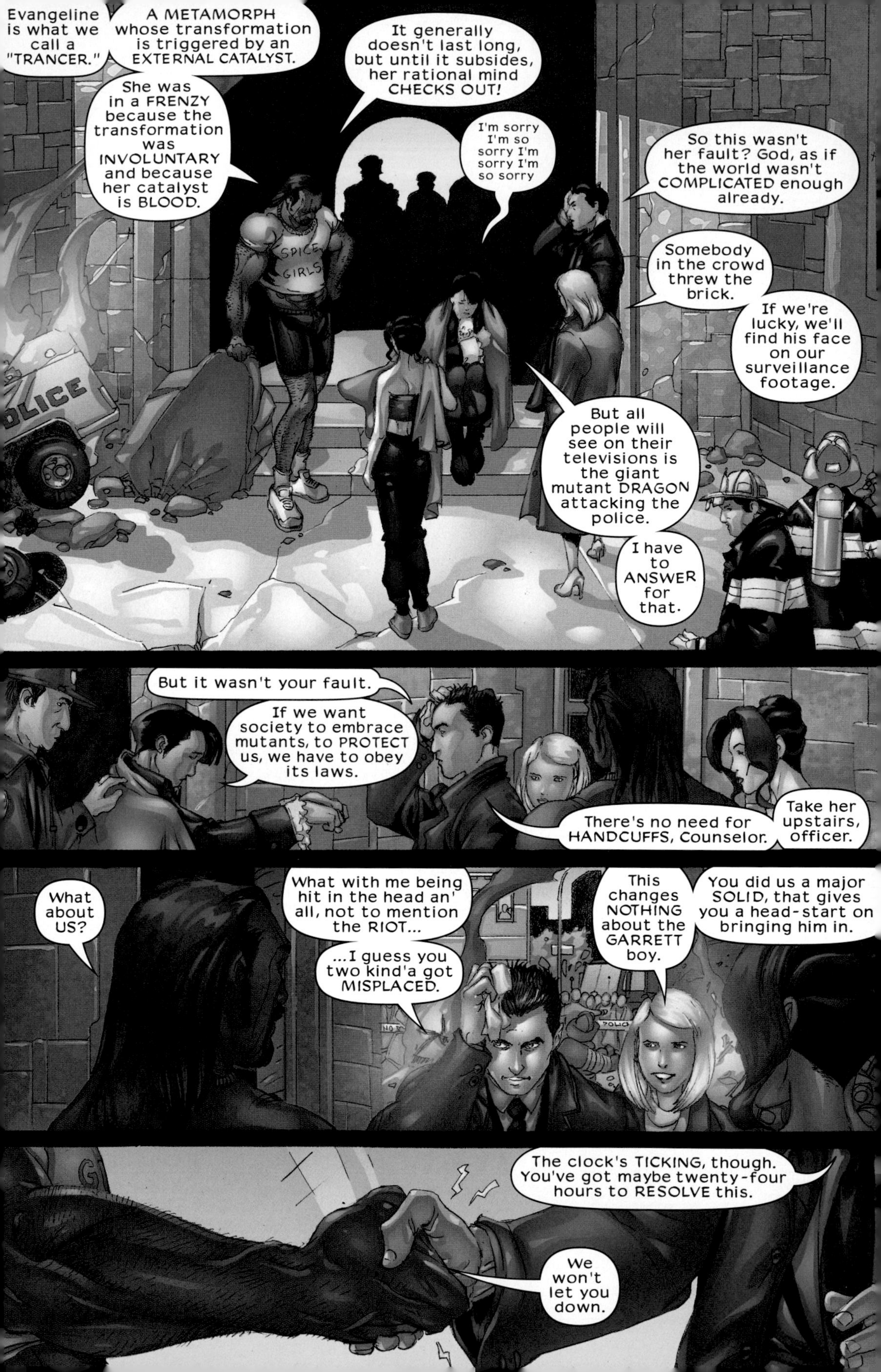

Evangeline is what we call a "TRANCER."
A METAMORPH whose transformation is triggered by an EXTERNAL CATALYST.
She was in a FRENZY because the transformation was INVOLUNTARY and because her catalyst is BLOOD.
It generally doesn't last long, but until it subsides, her rational mind CHECKS OUT!
I'm sorry I'm so sorry I'm sorry I'm so sorry
SPICE GIRLS
POLICE
So this wasn't her fault? God, as if the world wasn't COMPLICATED enough already.
Somebody in the crowd threw the brick.
If we're lucky, we'll find his face on our surveillance footage.
But all people will see on their televisions is the giant mutant DRAGON attacking the police.
I have to ANSWER for that.
But it wasn't your fault.
If we want society to embrace mutants, to PROTECT us, we have to obey its laws.
There's no need for HANDCUFFS, Counselor.
Take her upstairs, officer.
What about US?
What with me being hit in the head an' all, not to mention the RIOT...
...I guess you two kind'a got MISPLACED.
This changes NOTHING about the GARRETT boy.
You did us a major SOLID, that gives you a head-start on bringing him in.
The clock's TICKING, though. You've got maybe twenty-four hours to RESOLVE this.
We won't let you down.

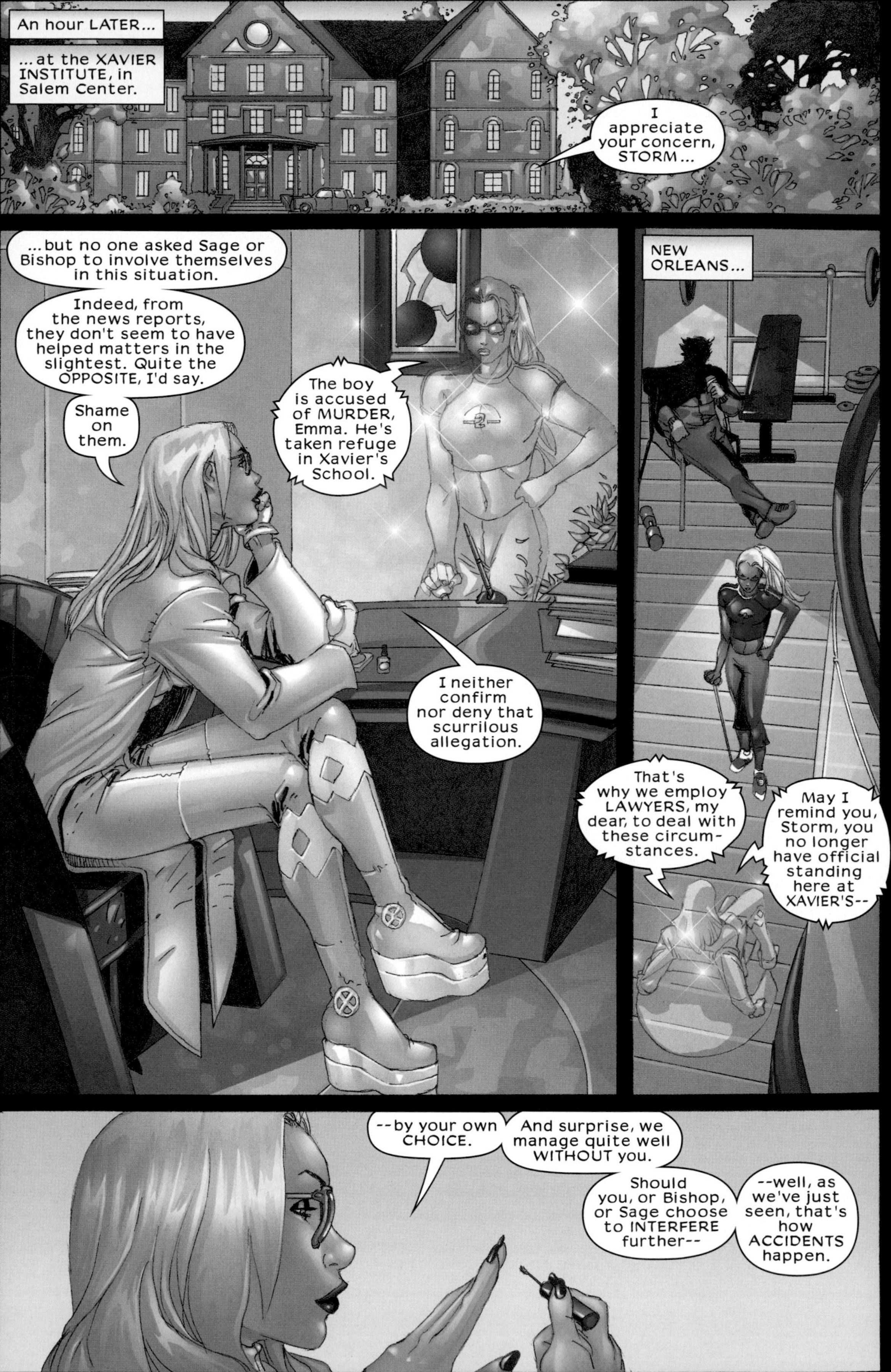
An hour LATER...
...at the XAVIER INSTITUTE, in Salem Center.
I appreciate your concern, STORM...
...but no one asked Sage or Bishop to involve themselves in this situation.
Indeed, from the news reports, they don't seem to have helped matters in the slightest. Quite the OPPOSITE, I'd say.
Shame on them.
The boy is accused of MURDER, Emma. He's taken refuge in Xavier's School.
I neither confirm nor deny that scurrilous allegation.
NEW ORLEANS...
That's why we employ LAWYERS, my dear, to deal with these circum-stances.
May I remind you, Storm, you no longer have official standing here at XAVIER'S--
--by your own CHOICE.
And surprise, we manage quite well WITHOUT you.
Should you, or Bishop, or Sage choose to INTERFERE further--
--well, as we've just seen, that's how ACCIDENTS happen.

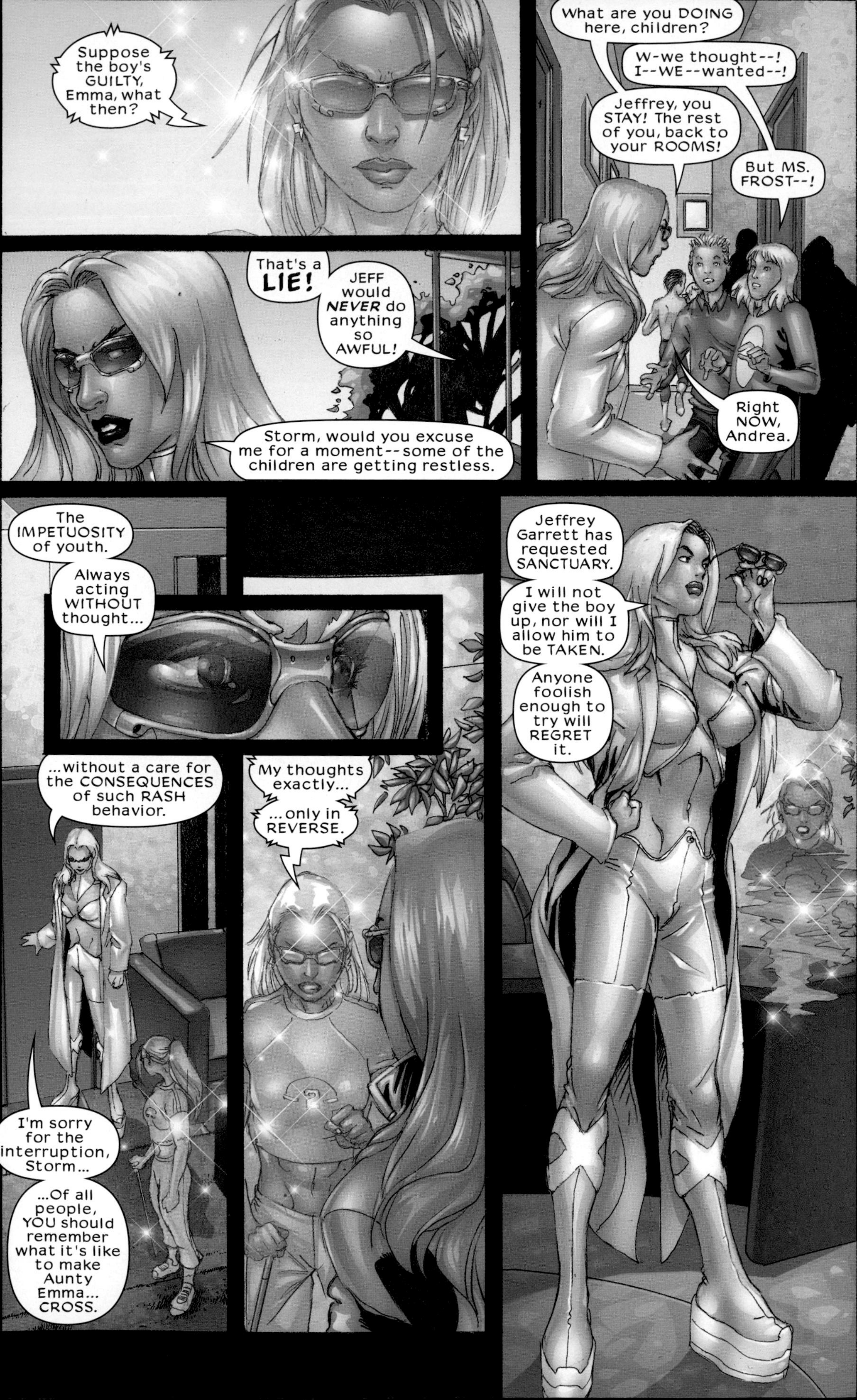
Suppose the boy's GUILTY, Emma, what then?
That's a LIE!
JEFF would NEVER do anything so AWFUL!
Storm, would you excuse me for a moment--some of the children are getting restless.
What are you DOING here, children?
W-we thought--! I--WE--wanted--!
Jeffrey, you STAY! The rest of you, back to your ROOMS!
But MS. FROST--!
Right NOW, Andrea.
The IMPETUOSITY of youth.
Always acting WITHOUT thought...
...without a care for the CONSEQUENCES of such RASH behavior.
I'm sorry for the interruption, Storm...
...Of all people, YOU should remember what it's like to make Aunty Emma... CROSS.
My thoughts exactly...
...only in REVERSE.
Jeffrey Garrett has requested SANCTUARY.
I will not give the boy up, nor will I allow him to be TAKEN.
Anyone foolish enough to try will REGRET it.

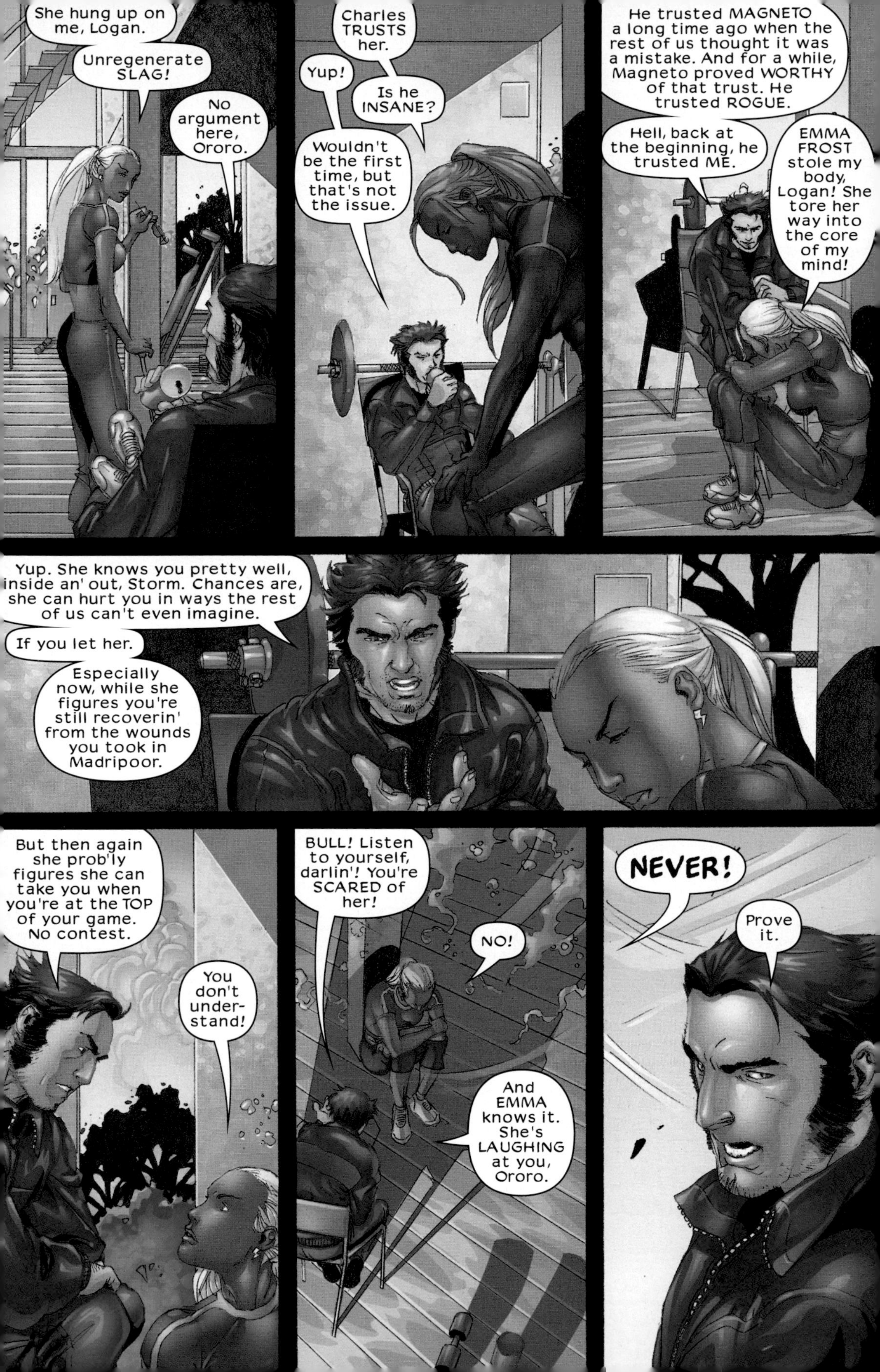
She hung up on me, Logan.
Unregenerate SLAG!
No argument here, Ororo.
Charles TRUSTS her.
Yup!
Is he INSANE?
Wouldn't be the first time, but that's not the issue.
He trusted MAGNETO a long time ago when the rest of us thought it was a mistake. And for a while, Magneto proved WORTHY of that trust. He trusted ROGUE.
Hell, back at the beginning, he trusted ME.
EMMA FROST stole my body, Logan! She tore her way into the core of my mind!
Yup. She knows you pretty well, inside an' out, Storm. Chances are, she can hurt you in ways the rest of us can't even imagine.
If you let her.
Especially now, while she figures you're still recoverin' from the wounds you took in Madripoor.
But then again she prob'ly figures she can take you when you're at the TOP of your game. No contest.
You don't under-stand!
BULL! Listen to yourself, darlin'! You're SCARED of her!
NO!
And EMMA knows it. She's LAUGHING at you, Ororo.
NEVER!
Prove it.

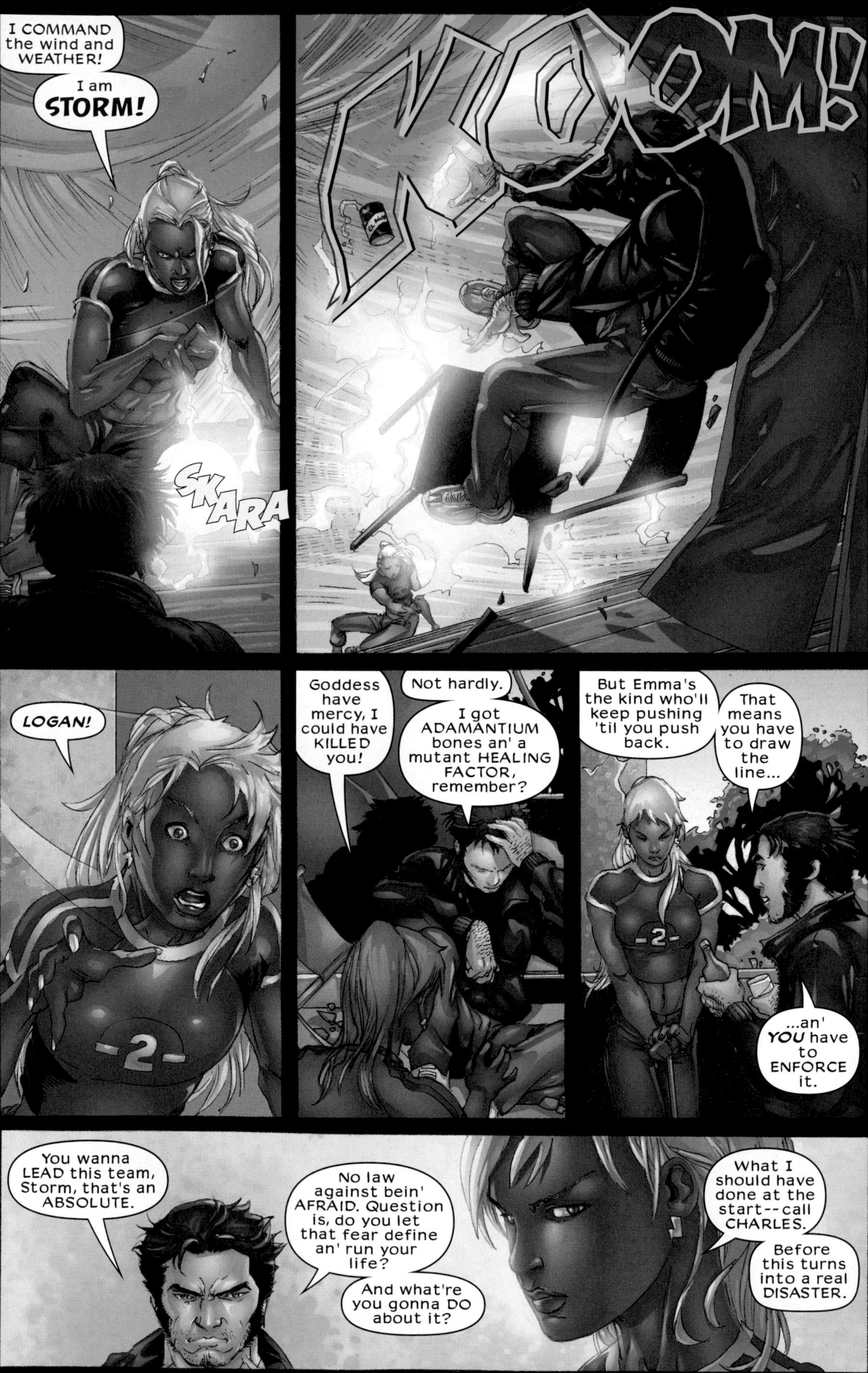

I COMMAND the wind and WEATHER!
I am STORM!
SKARA
KROOOM!
LOGAN!
Goddess have mercy, I could have KILLED you!
Not hardly.
I got ADAMANTIUM bones an' a mutant HEALING FACTOR, remember?
But Emma's the kind who'll keep pushing 'til you push back.
That means you have to draw the line...
...an' YOU have to ENFORCE it.
You wanna LEAD this team, Storm, that's an ABSOLUTE.
No law against bein' AFRAID. Question is, do you let that fear define an' run your life?
And what're you gonna DO about it?
What I should have done at the start--call CHARLES.
Before this turns into a real DISASTER.

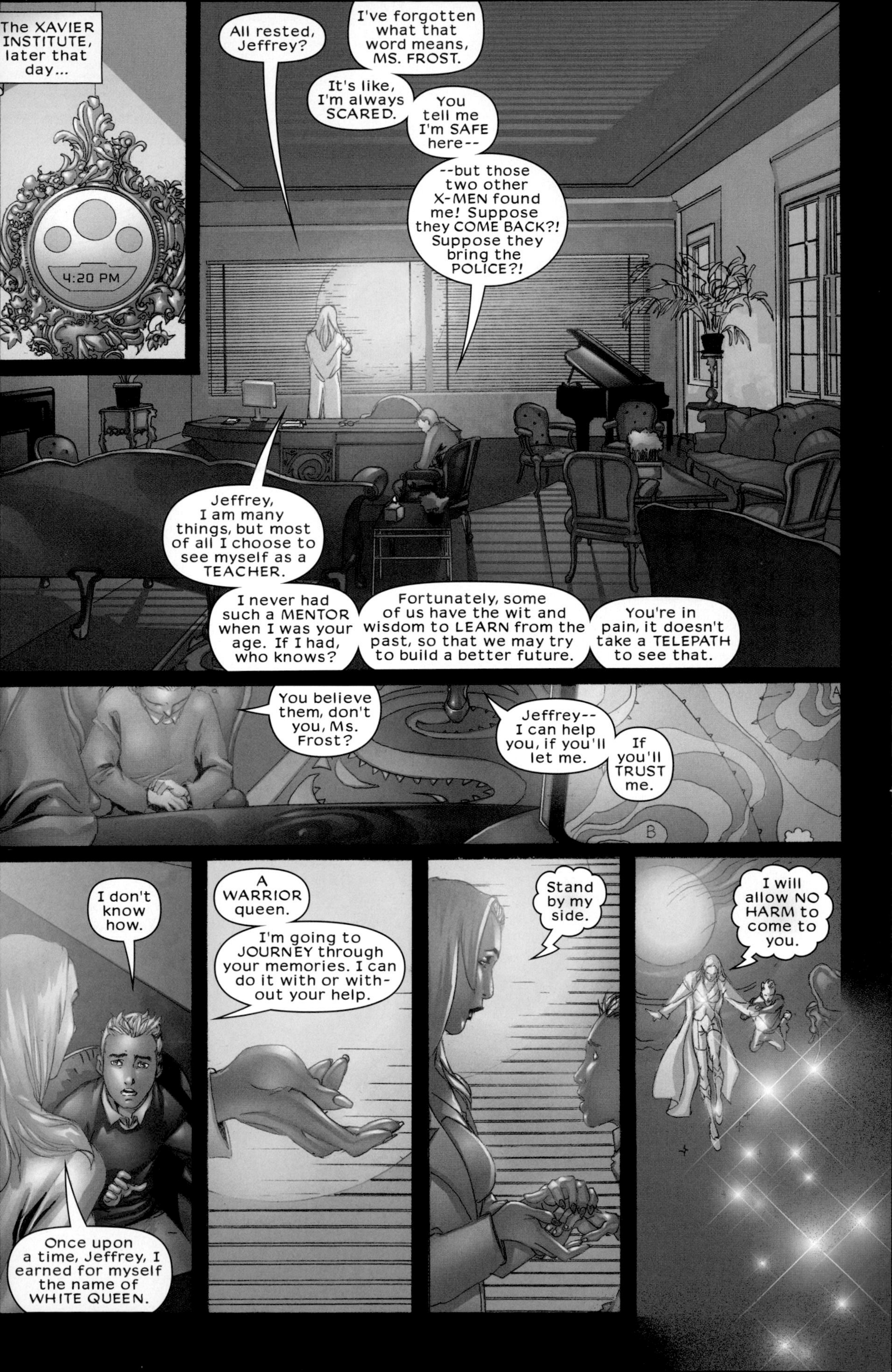
The XAVIER INSTITUTE, later that day...
4:20 PM
All rested, Jeffrey?
I've forgotten what that word means, MS. FROST.
It's like, I'm always SCARED.
You tell me I'm SAFE here--
--but those two other X-MEN found me! Suppose they COME BACK?! Suppose they bring the POLICE?!
Jeffrey, I am many things, but most of all I choose to see myself as a TEACHER.
I never had such a MENTOR when I was your age. If I had, who knows?
Fortunately, some of us have the wit and wisdom to LEARN from the past, so that we may try to build a better future.
You're in pain, it doesn't take a TELEPATH to see that.
You believe them, don't you, Ms. Frost?
Jeffrey-- I can help you, if you'll let me.
If you'll TRUST me.
I don't know how.
Once upon a time, Jeffrey, I earned for myself the name of WHITE QUEEN.
A WARRIOR queen.
I'm going to JOURNEY through your memories. I can do it with or with-out your help.
Stand by my side.
I will allow NO HARM to come to you.

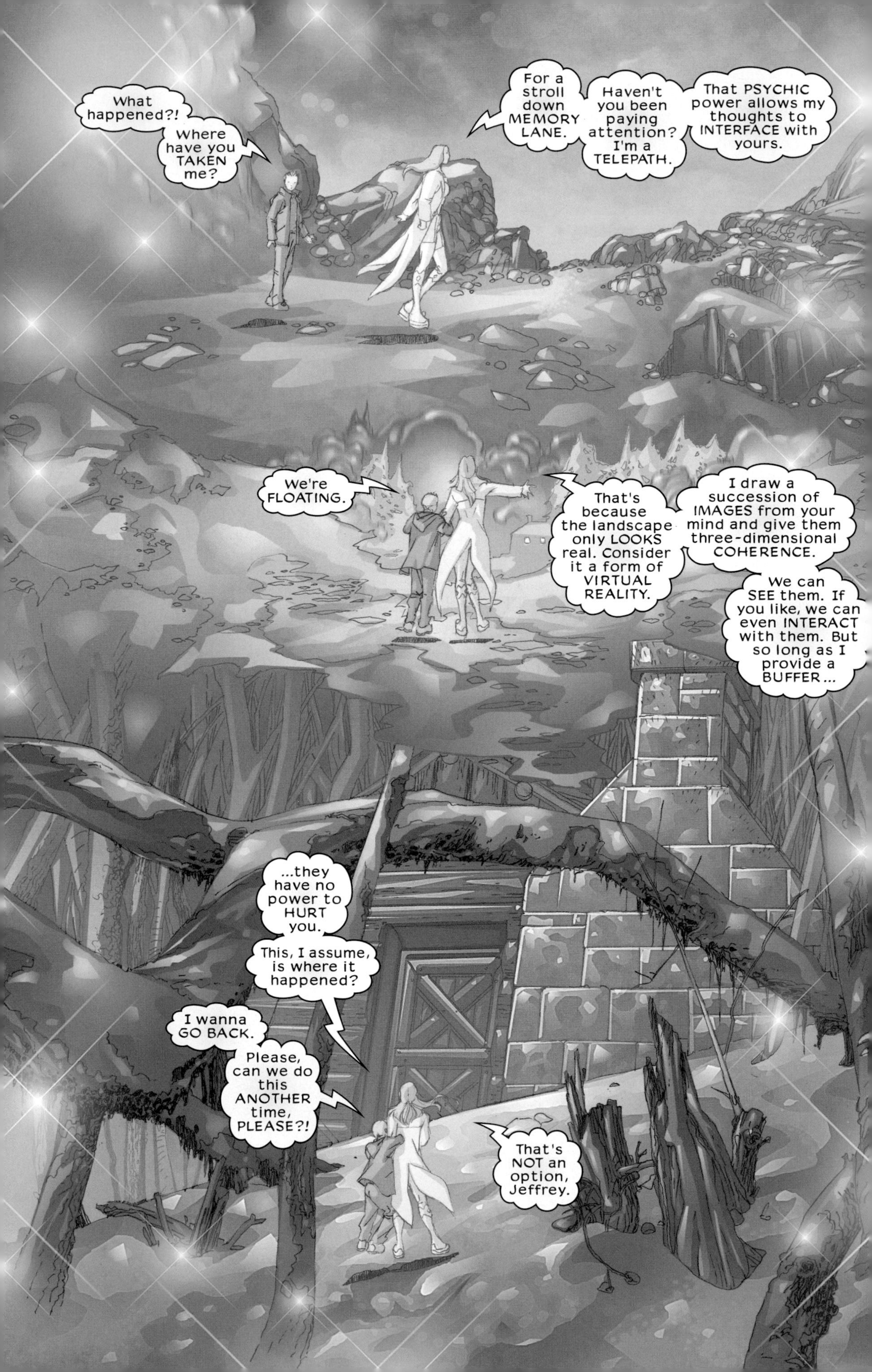
What happened?!
Where have you TAKEN me?
For a stroll down MEMORY LANE.
Haven't you been paying attention? I'm a TELEPATH.
That PSYCHIC power allows my thoughts to INTERFACE with yours.
We're FLOATING.
That's because the landscape only LOOKS real. Consider it a form of VIRTUAL REALITY.
I draw a succession of IMAGES from your mind and give them three-dimensional COHERENCE.
We can SEE them. If you like, we can even INTERACT with them. But so long as I provide a BUFFER...
...they have no power to HURT you.
This, I assume, is where it happened?
I wanna GO BACK.
Please, can we do this ANOTHER time, PLEASE?!
That's NOT an option, Jeffrey.

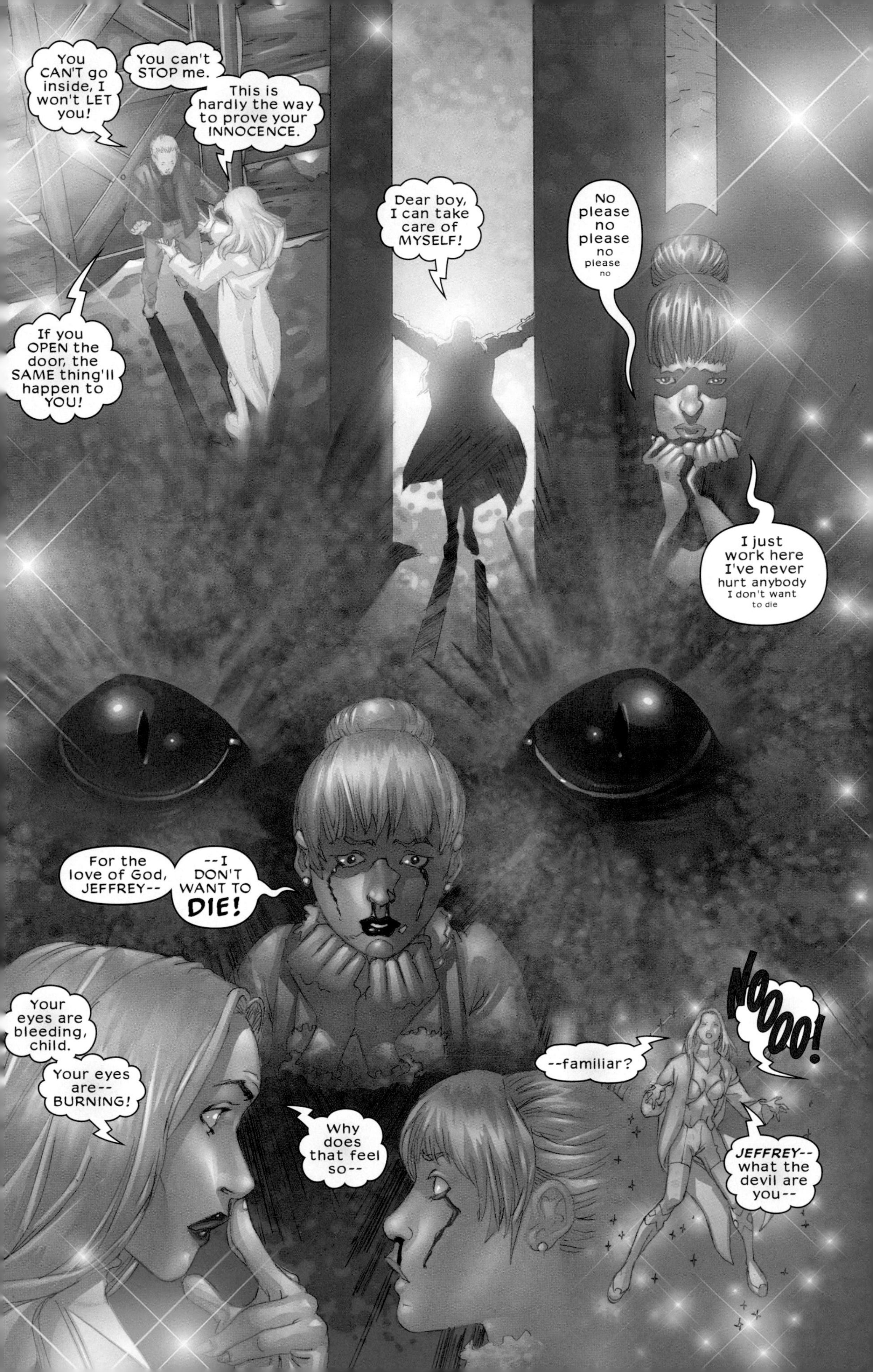
You CAN'T go inside, I won't LET you!
You can't STOP me.
This is hardly the way to prove your INNOCENCE.
If you OPEN the door, the SAME thing'll happen to YOU!
Dear boy, I can take care of MYSELF!
No please no please no please no
I just work here I've never hurt anybody I don't want to die
For the love of God, JEFFREY--
--I DON'T WANT TO DIE!
Your eyes are bleeding, child.
Your eyes are-- BURNING!
Why does that feel so--
--familiar?
NOOOO!
JEFFREY-- what the devil are you--

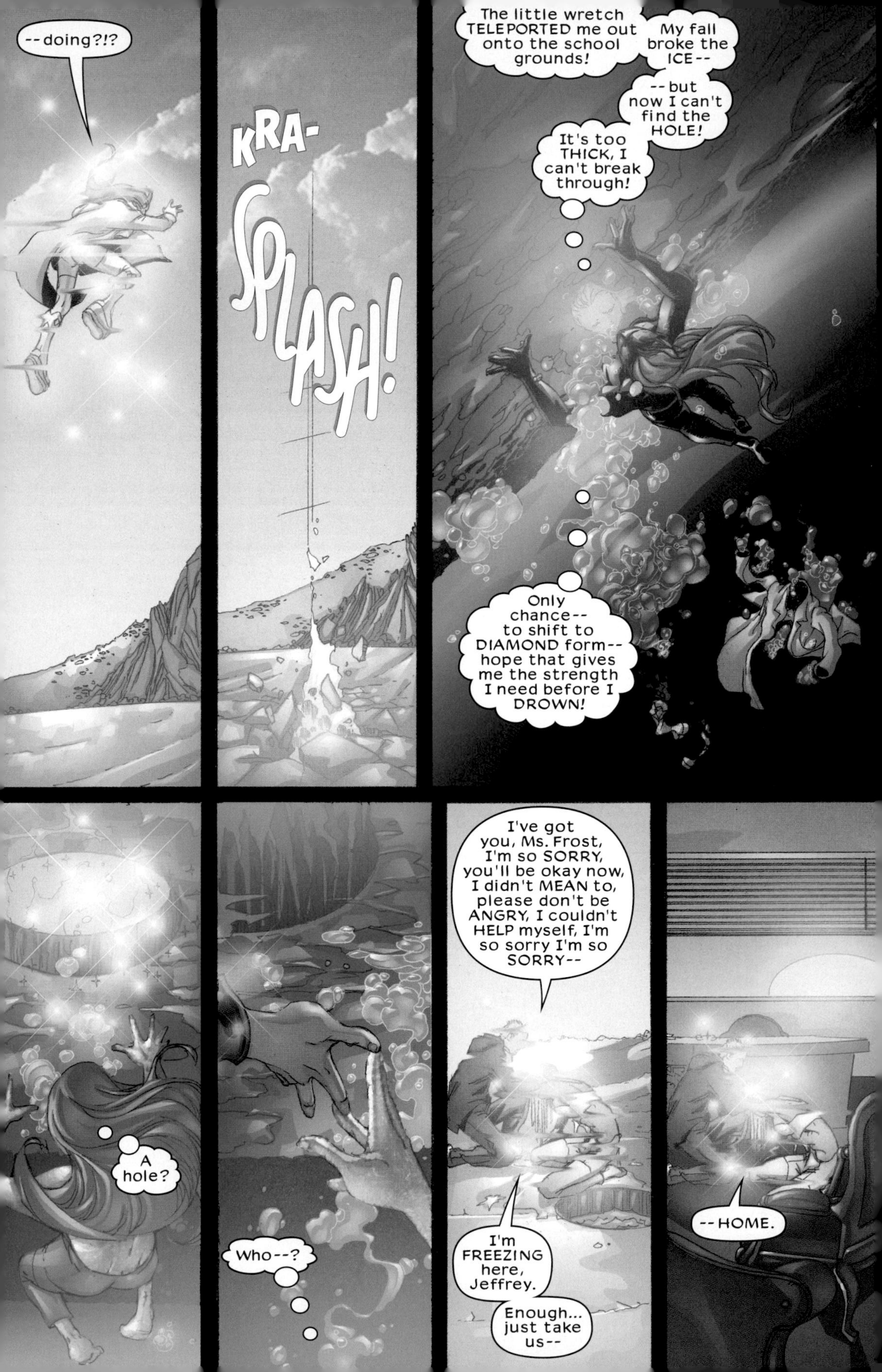
--doing?!?
KRA-
SPLASH!
The little wretch TELEPORTED me out onto the school grounds!
My fall broke the ICE--
--but now I can't find the HOLE!
It's too THICK, I can't break through!
Only chance-- to shift to DIAMOND form-- hope that gives me the strength I need before I DROWN!
A hole?
Who--?
I've got you, Ms. Frost, I'm so SORRY, you'll be okay now, I didn't MEAN to, please don't be ANGRY, I couldn't HELP myself, I'm so sorry I'm so SORRY--
I'm FREEZING here, Jeffrey.
Enough... just take us--
--HOME.

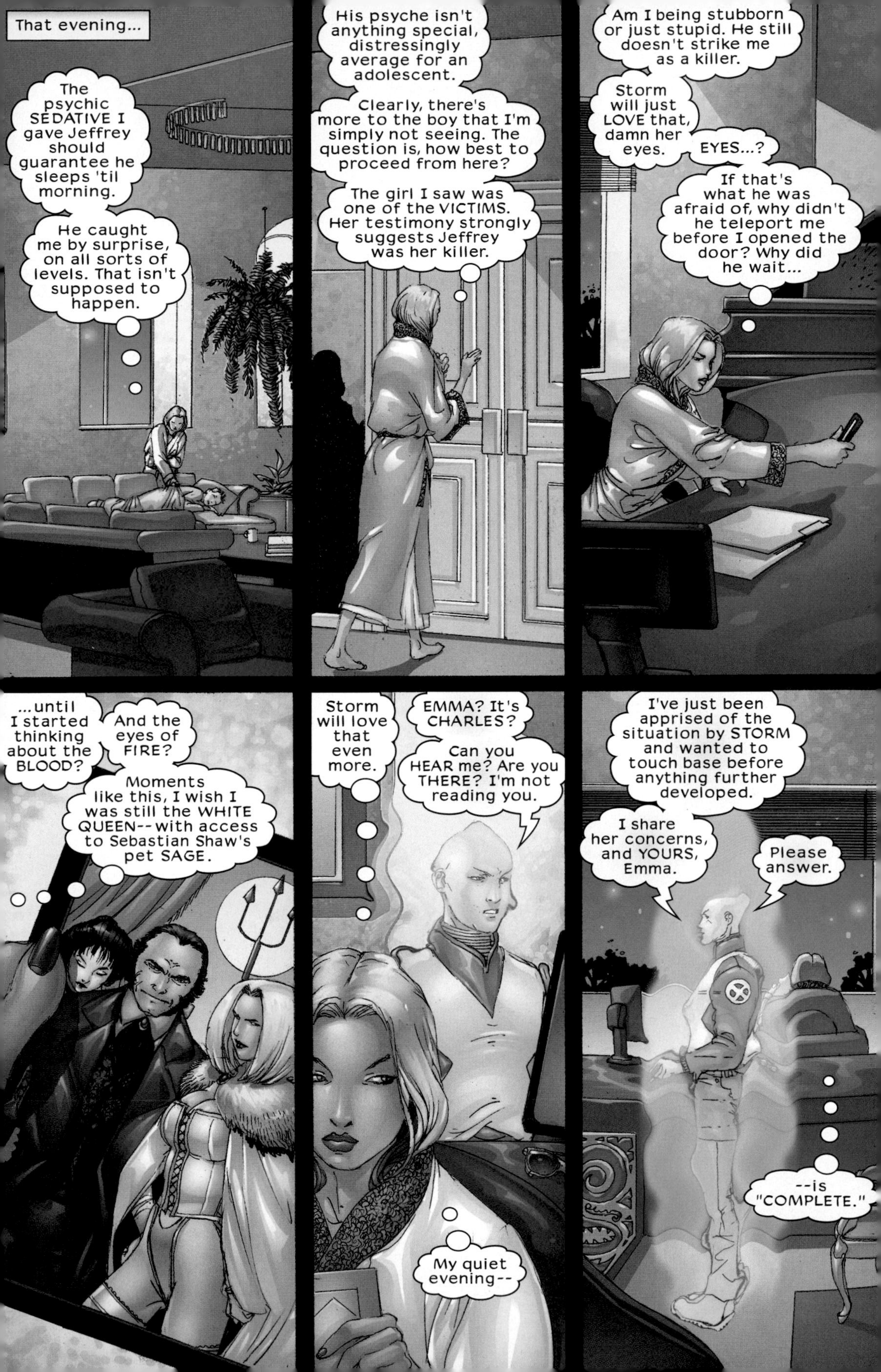

That evening...
The psychic SEDATIVE I gave Jeffrey should guarantee he sleeps 'til morning.
He caught me by surprise, on all sorts of levels. That isn't supposed to happen.
His psyche isn't anything special, distressingly average for an adolescent.
Clearly, there's more to the boy that I'm simply not seeing. The question is, how best to proceed from here?
The girl I saw was one of the VICTIMS. Her testimony strongly suggests Jeffrey was her killer.
Am I being stubborn or just stupid. He still doesn't strike me as a killer.
Storm will just LOVE that, damn her eyes.
EYES...?
If that's what he was afraid of, why didn't he teleport me before I opened the door? Why did he wait...
...until I started thinking about the BLOOD?
And the eyes of FIRE?
Moments like this, I wish I was still the WHITE QUEEN--with access to Sebastian Shaw's pet SAGE.
Storm will love that even more.
EMMA? It's CHARLES?
Can you HEAR me? Are you THERE? I'm not reading you.
My quiet evening--
I've just been apprised of the situation by STORM and wanted to touch base before anything further developed.
I share her concerns, and YOURS, Emma.
Please answer.
--is "COMPLETE."

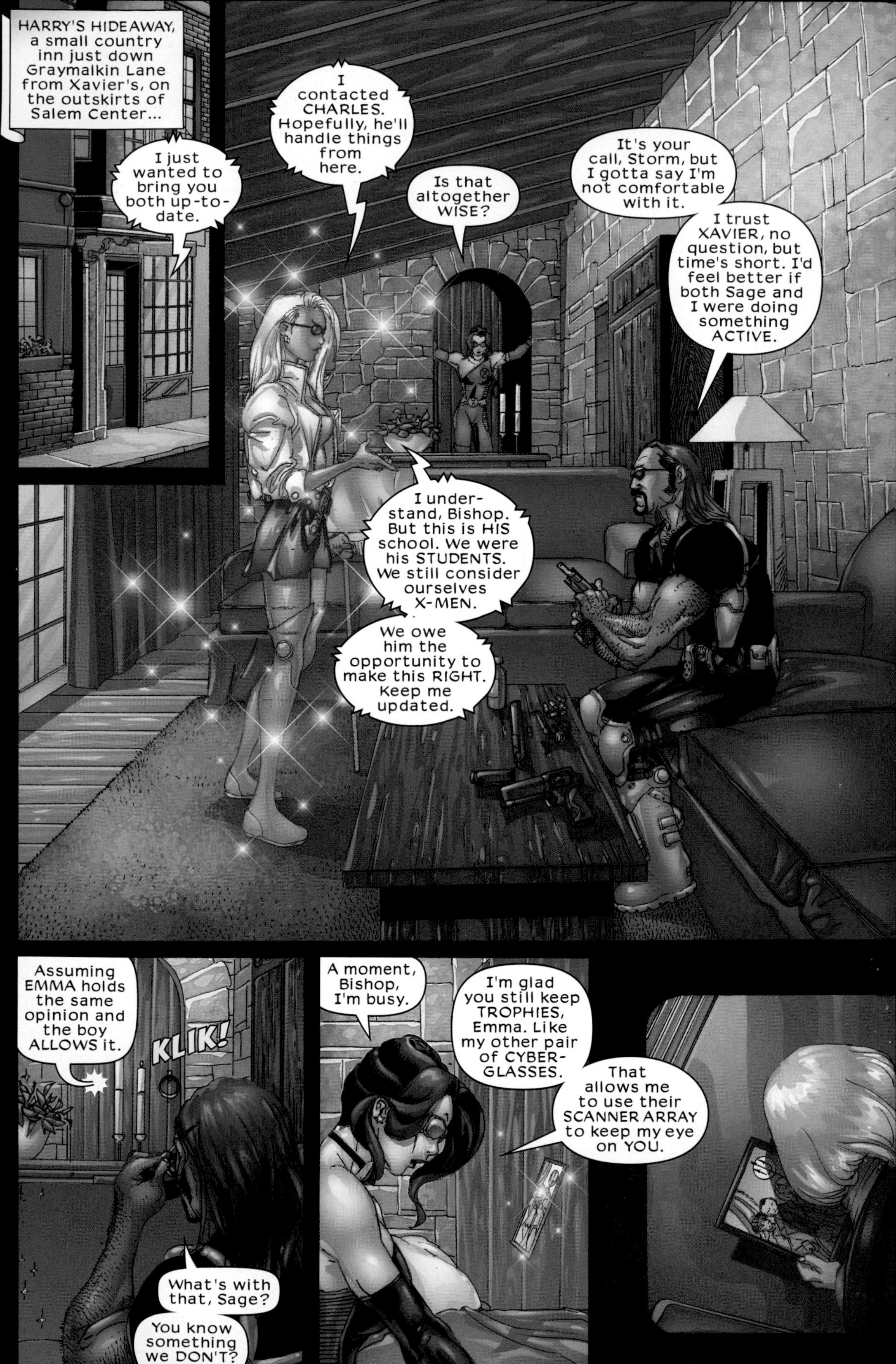

HARRY'S HIDEAWAY, a small country inn just down Graymalkin Lane from Xavier's, on the outskirts of Salem Center...
I just wanted to bring you both up-to-date.
I contacted CHARLES. Hopefully, he'll handle things from here.
Is that altogether WISE?
It's your call, Storm, but I gotta say I'm not comfortable with it.
I trust XAVIER, no question, but time's short. I'd feel better if both Sage and I were doing something ACTIVE.
I under-stand, Bishop. But this is HIS school. We were his STUDENTS. We still consider ourselves X-MEN.
We owe him the opportunity to make this RIGHT. Keep me updated.
Assuming EMMA holds the same opinion and the boy ALLOWS it.
KLIK!
What's with that, Sage?
You know something we DON'T?
A moment, Bishop, I'm busy.
I'm glad you still keep TROPHIES, Emma. Like my other pair of CYBER-GLASSES.
That allows me to use their SCANNER ARRAY to keep my eye on YOU.

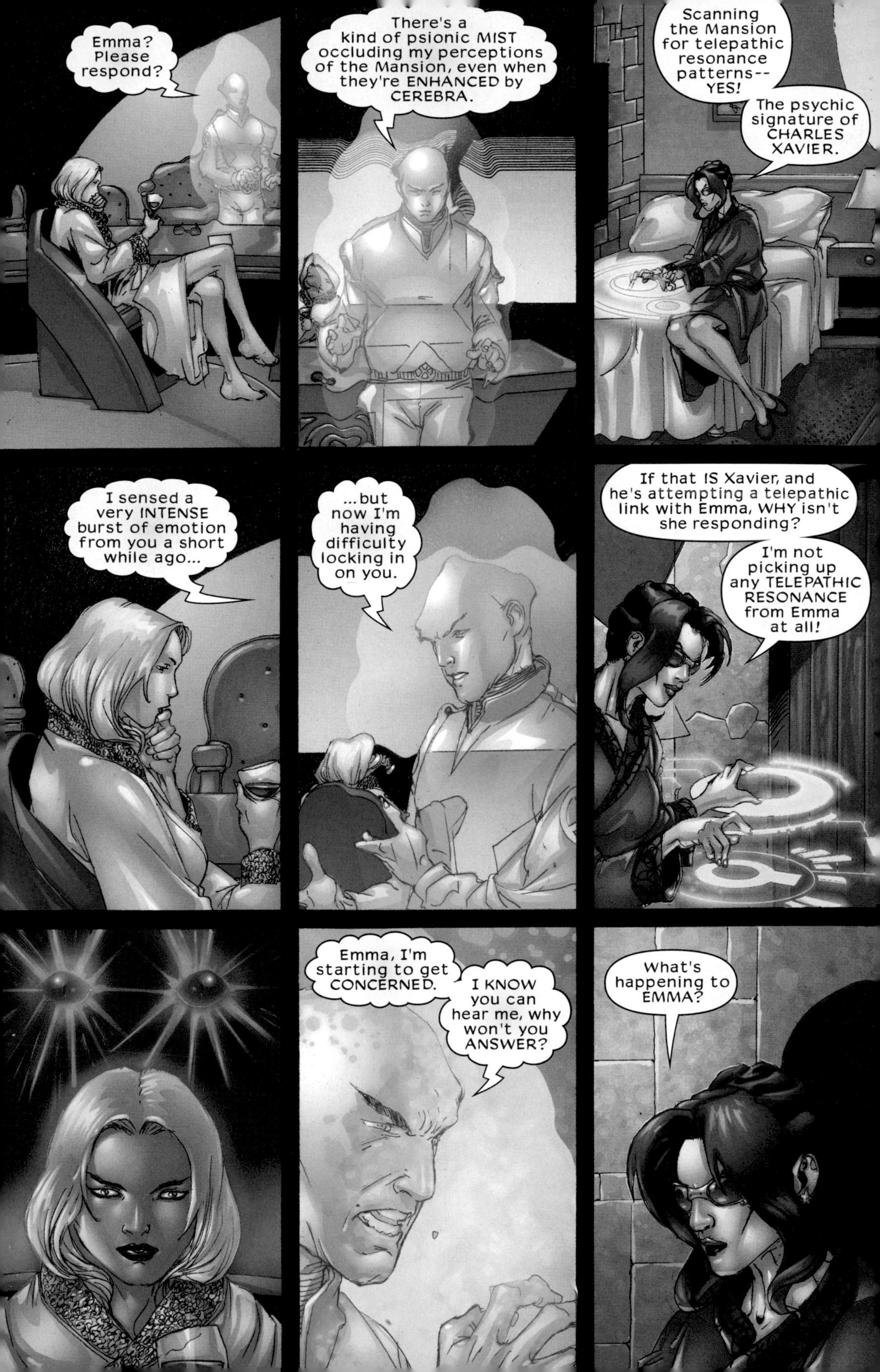
Emma? Please respond?
There's a kind of psionic MIST occluding my perceptions of the Mansion, even when they're ENHANCED by CEREBRA.
Scanning the Mansion for telepathic resonance patterns-- YES!
The psychic signature of CHARLES XAVIER.
I sensed a very INTENSE burst of emotion from you a short while ago...
...but now I'm having difficulty locking in on you.
If that IS Xavier, and he's attempting a telepathic link with Emma, WHY isn't she responding?
I'm not picking up any TELEPATHIC RESONANCE from Emma at all!
Emma, I'm starting to get CONCERNED.
I KNOW you can hear me, why won't you ANSWER?
What's happening to EMMA?

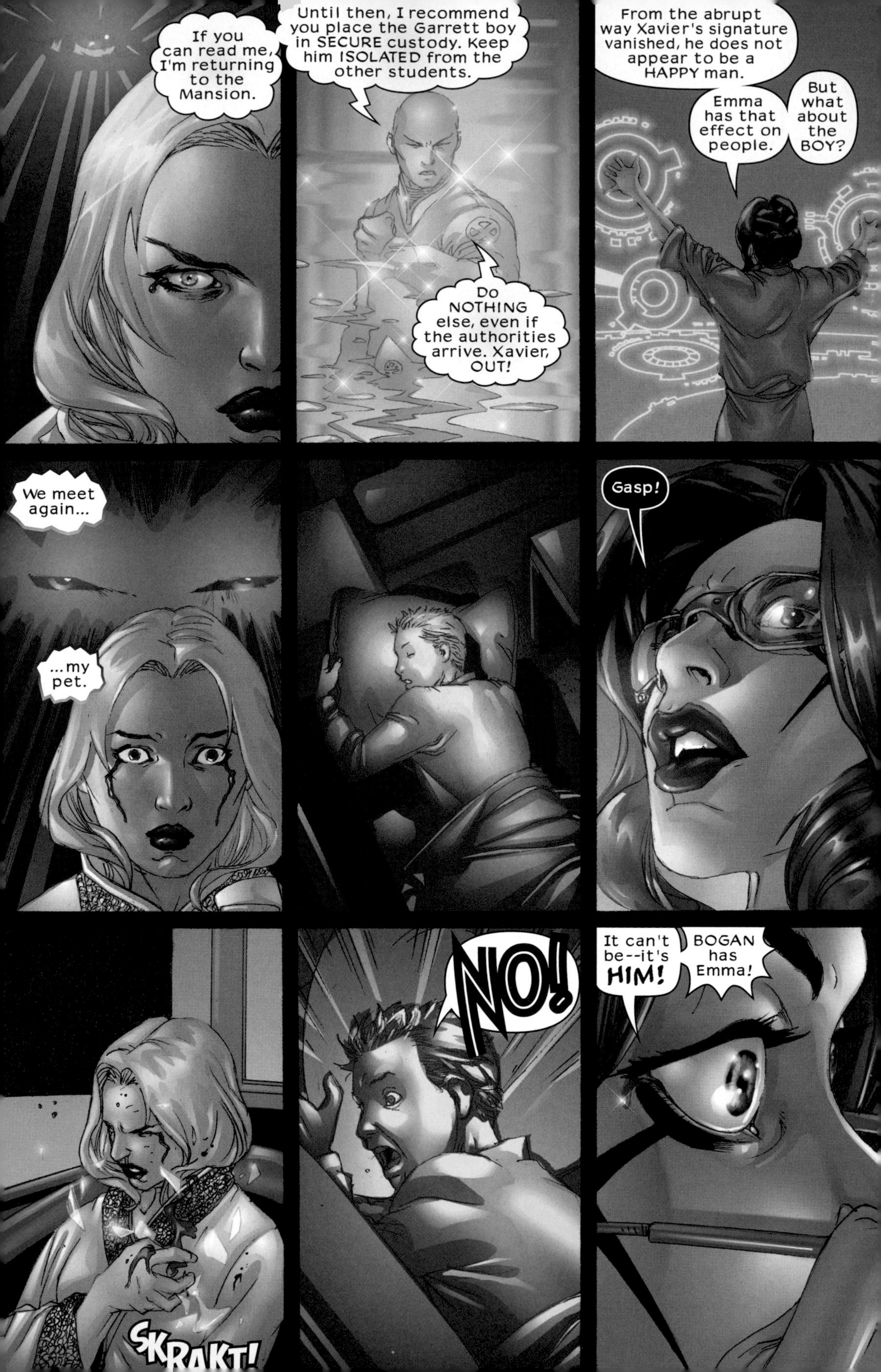
If you can read me, I'm returning to the Mansion.
Until then, I recommend you place the Garrett boy in SECURE custody. Keep him ISOLATED from the other students.
Do NOTHING else, even if the authorities arrive. Xavier, OUT!
From the abrupt way Xavier's signature vanished, he does not appear to be a HAPPY man.
Emma has that effect on people.
But what about the BOY?
We meet again...
...my pet.
Gasp!
SKRAKT!
NO!
It can't be--it's HIM!
BOGAN has Emma!

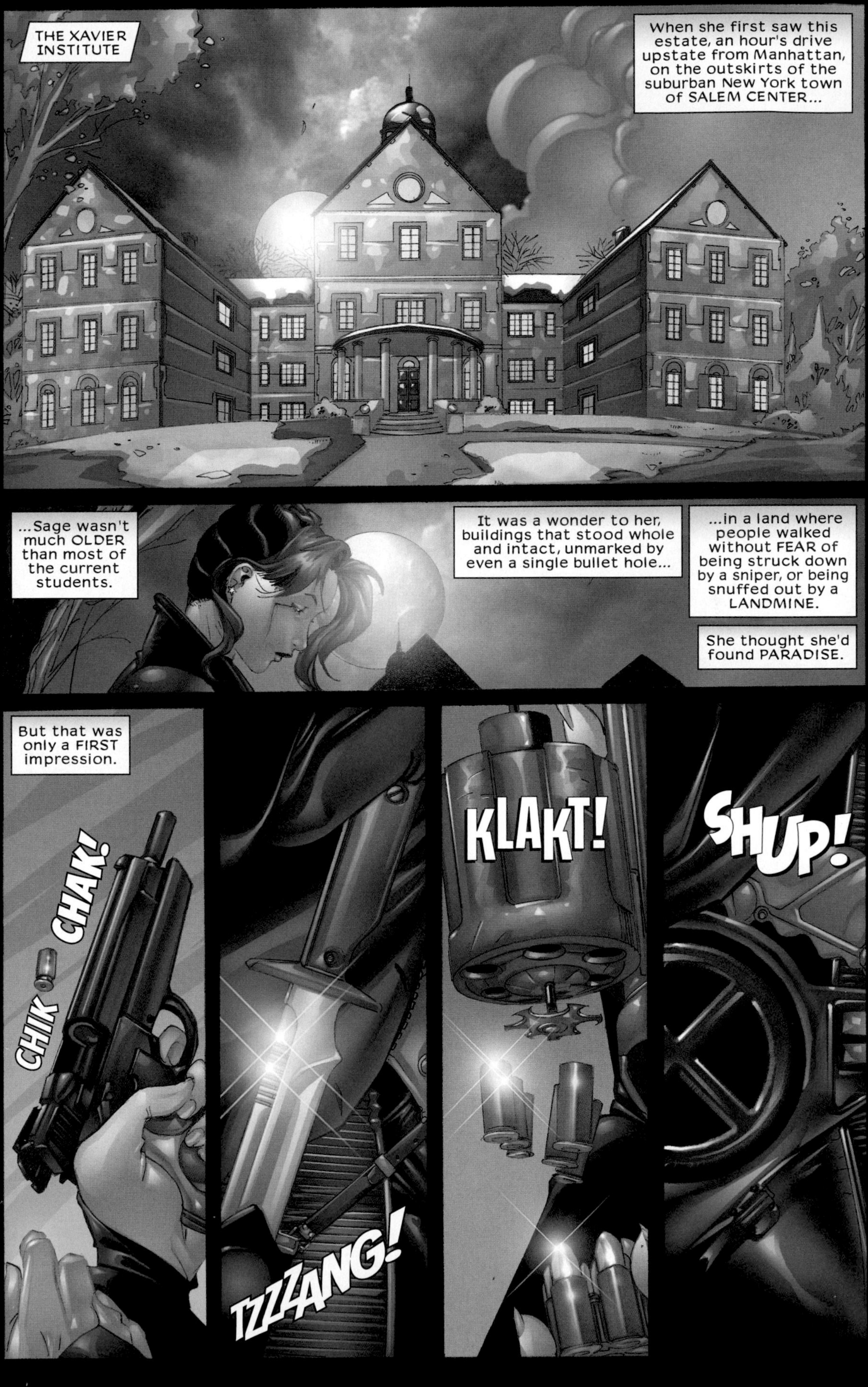
THE XAVIER INSTITUTE
When she first saw this estate, an hour's drive upstate from Manhattan, on the outskirts of the suburban New York town of SALEM CENTER...
...Sage wasn't much OLDER than most of the current students.
It was a wonder to her, buildings that stood whole and intact, unmarked by even a single bullet hole...
...in a land where people walked without FEAR of being struck down by a sniper, or being snuffed out by a LANDMINE.
She thought she'd found PARADISE.
But that was only a FIRST impression.
CHIK
CHAK!
TZZZANG!
KLAKT!
SHUP!

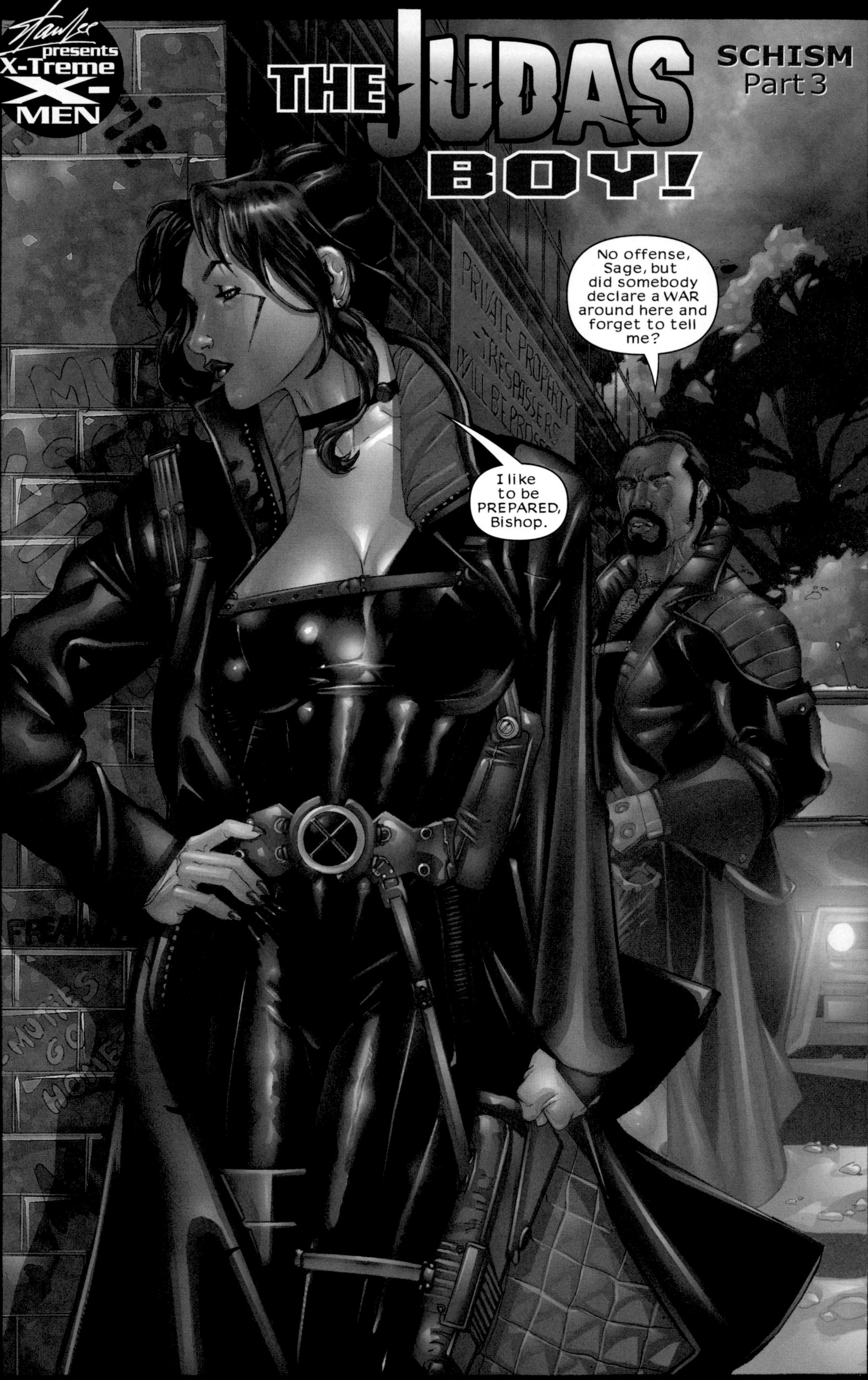
Stan Lee presents X-Treme X-MEN
THE JUDAS BOY!
SCHISM Part 3
No offense, Sage, but did somebody declare a WAR around here and forget to tell me?
I like to be PREPARED, Bishop.
PRIVATE PROPERTY TRESPASSERS WILL BE PROSE
FREAK
MUTIES GO HOME

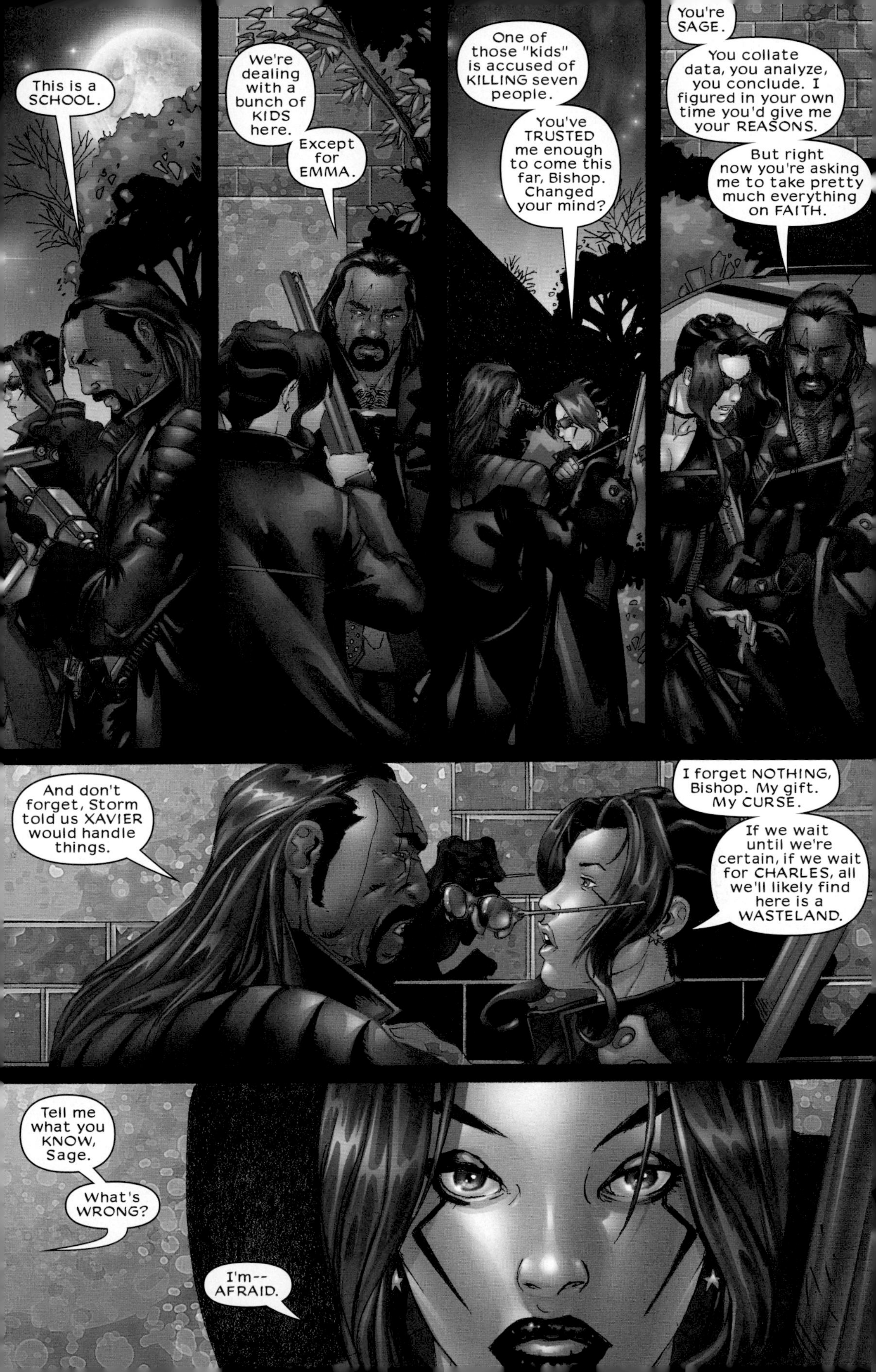
This is a SCHOOL.
We're dealing with a bunch of KIDS here.
Except for EMMA.
One of those "kids" is accused of KILLING seven people.
You've TRUSTED me enough to come this far, Bishop. Changed your mind?
You're SAGE.
You collate data, you analyze, you conclude. I figured in your own time you'd give me your REASONS.
But right now you're asking me to take pretty much everything on FAITH.
And don't forget, Storm told us XAVIER would handle things.
I forget NOTHING, Bishop. My gift. My CURSE.
If we wait until we're certain, if we wait for CHARLES, all we'll likely find here is a WASTELAND.
Tell me what you KNOW, Sage.
What's WRONG?
I'm-- AFRAID.

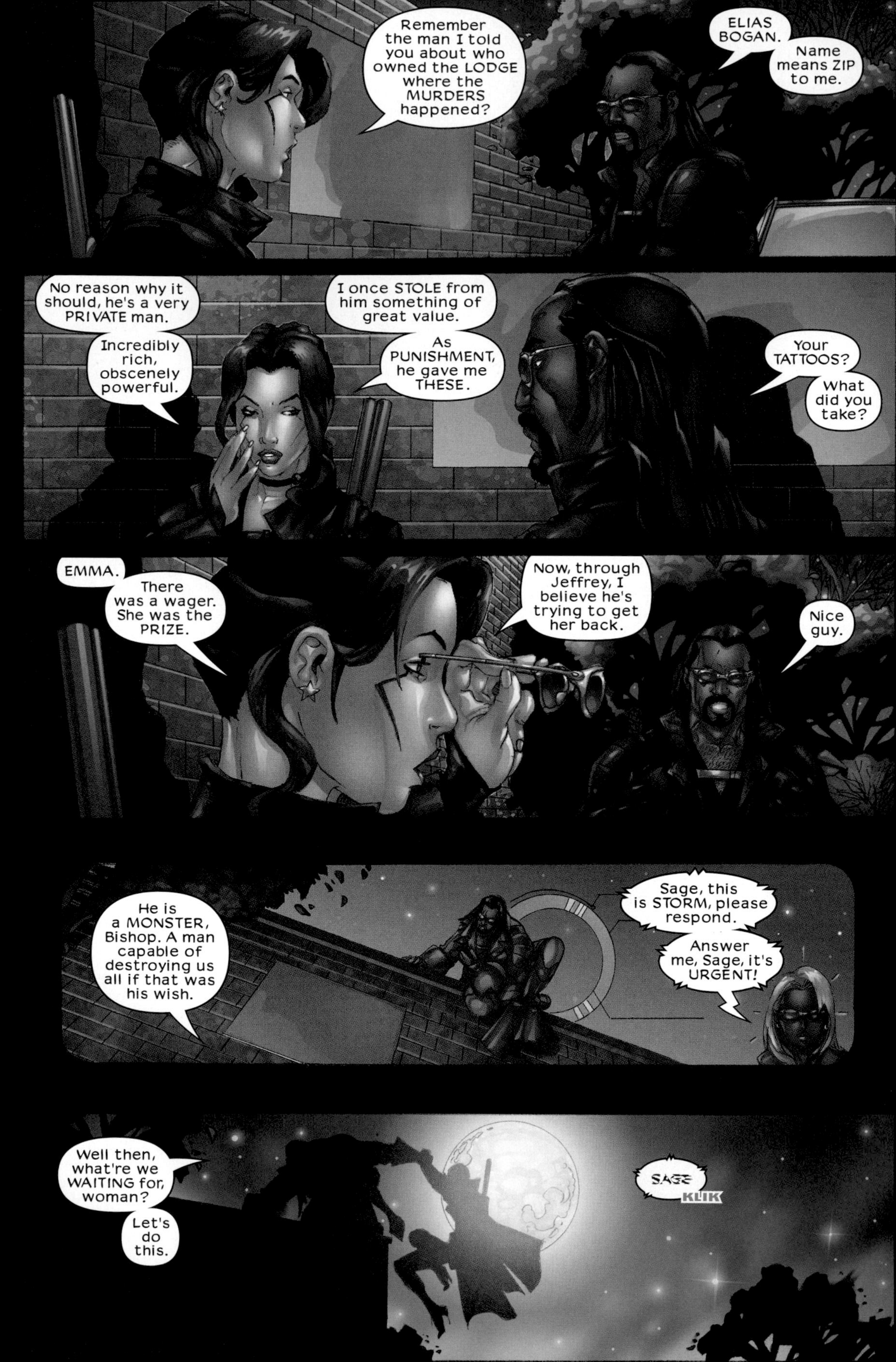

Remember the man I told you about who owned the LODGE where the MURDERS happened?
ELIAS BOGAN.
Name means ZIP to me.
No reason why it should, he's a very PRIVATE man.
Incredibly rich, obscenely powerful.
I once STOLE from him something of great value.
As PUNISHMENT, he gave me THESE.
Your TATTOOS?
What did you take?
EMMA.
There was a wager. She was the PRIZE.
Now, through Jeffrey, I believe he's trying to get her back.
Nice guy.
He is a MONSTER, Bishop. A man capable of destroying us all if that was his wish.
Sage, this is STORM, please respond.
Answer me, Sage, it's URGENT!
Well then, what're we WAITING for, woman?
Let's do this.
SAGE
KLIK

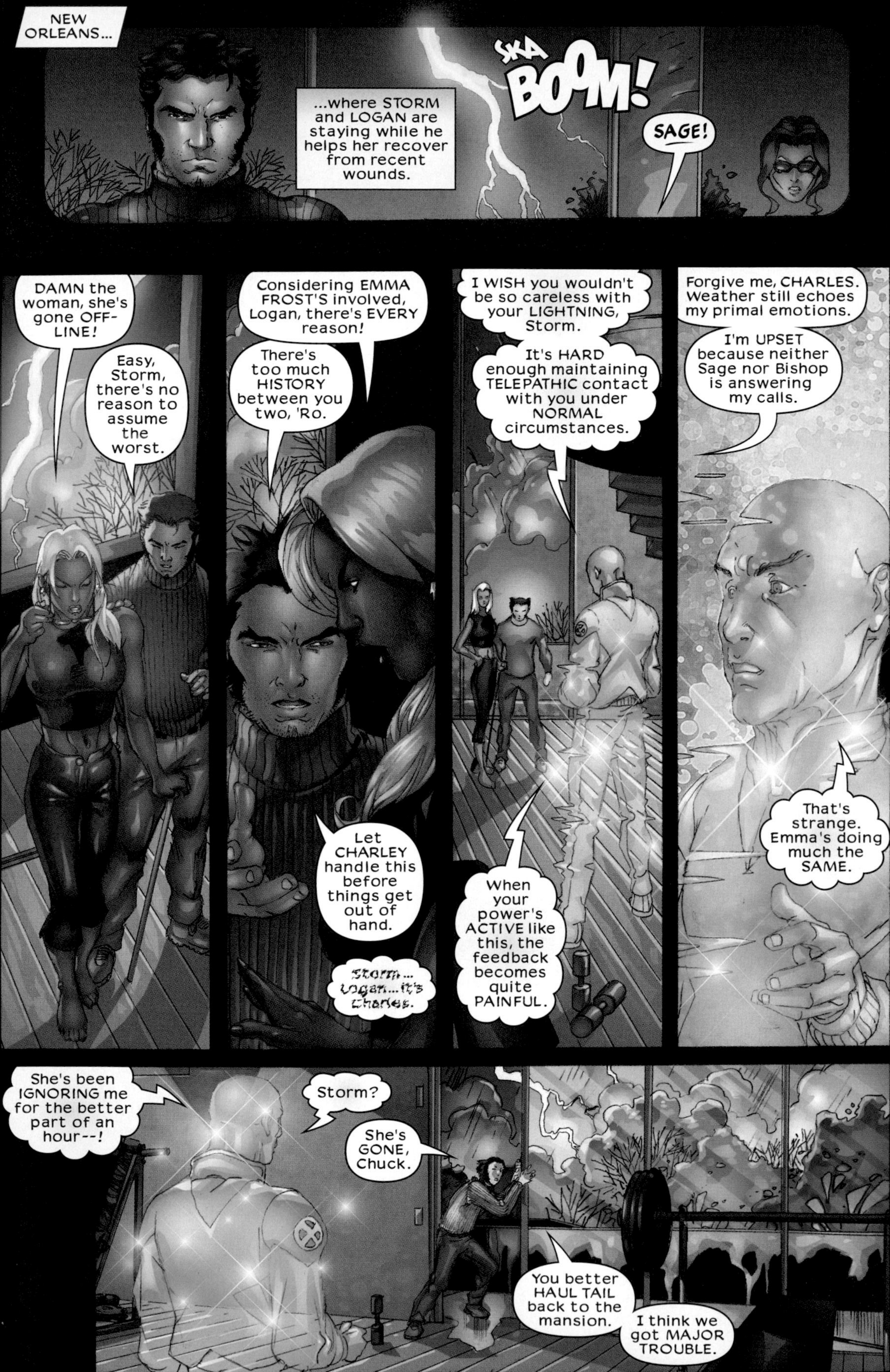
NEW ORLEANS...
...where STORM and LOGAN are staying while he helps her recover from recent wounds.
SKA BOOM!
SAGE!
DAMN the woman, she's gone OFF-LINE!
Easy, Storm, there's no reason to assume the worst.
Considering EMMA FROST'S involved, Logan, there's EVERY reason!
There's too much HISTORY between you two, 'Ro.
Let CHARLEY handle this before things get out of hand.
Storm... Logan... it's Charles.
I WISH you wouldn't be so careless with your LIGHTNING, Storm.
It's HARD enough maintaining TELEPATHIC contact with you under NORMAL circumstances.
When your power's ACTIVE like this, the feedback becomes quite PAINFUL.
Forgive me, CHARLES. Weather still echoes my primal emotions.
I'm UPSET because neither Sage nor Bishop is answering my calls.
That's strange. Emma's doing much the SAME.
She's been IGNORING me for the better part of an hour--!
Storm?
She's GONE, Chuck.
You better HAUL TAIL back to the mansion.
I think we got MAJOR TROUBLE.

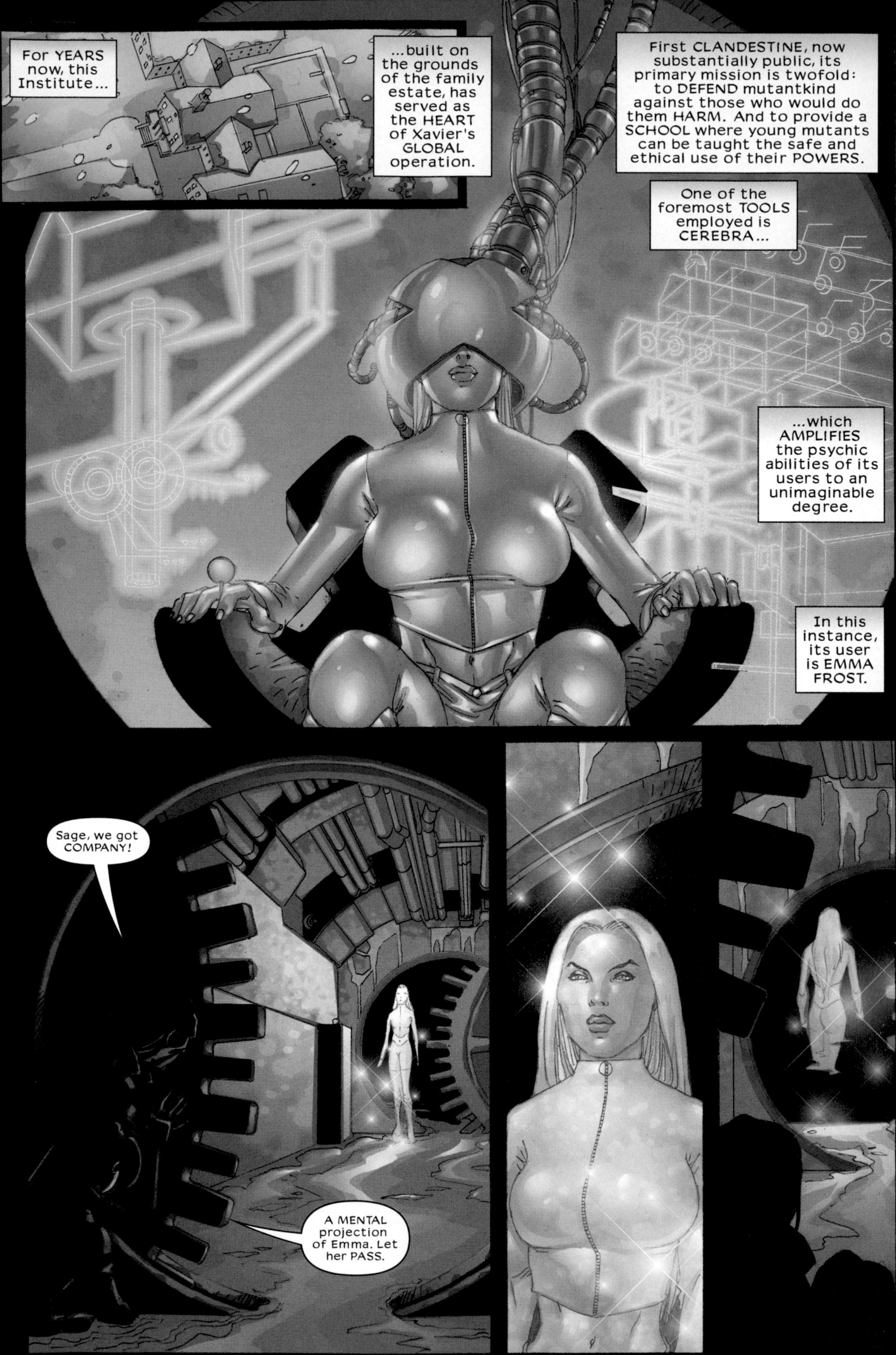
For YEARS now, this Institute...
...built on the grounds of the family estate, has served as the HEART of Xavier's GLOBAL operation.
First CLANDESTINE, now substantially public, its primary mission is twofold: to DEFEND mutantkind against those who would do them HARM. And to provide a SCHOOL where young mutants can be taught the safe and ethical use of their POWERS.
One of the foremost TOOLS employed is CEREBRA...
...which AMPLIFIES the psychic abilities of its users to an unimaginable degree.
In this instance, its user is EMMA FROST.
Sage, we got COMPANY!
A MENTAL projection of Emma. Let her PASS.

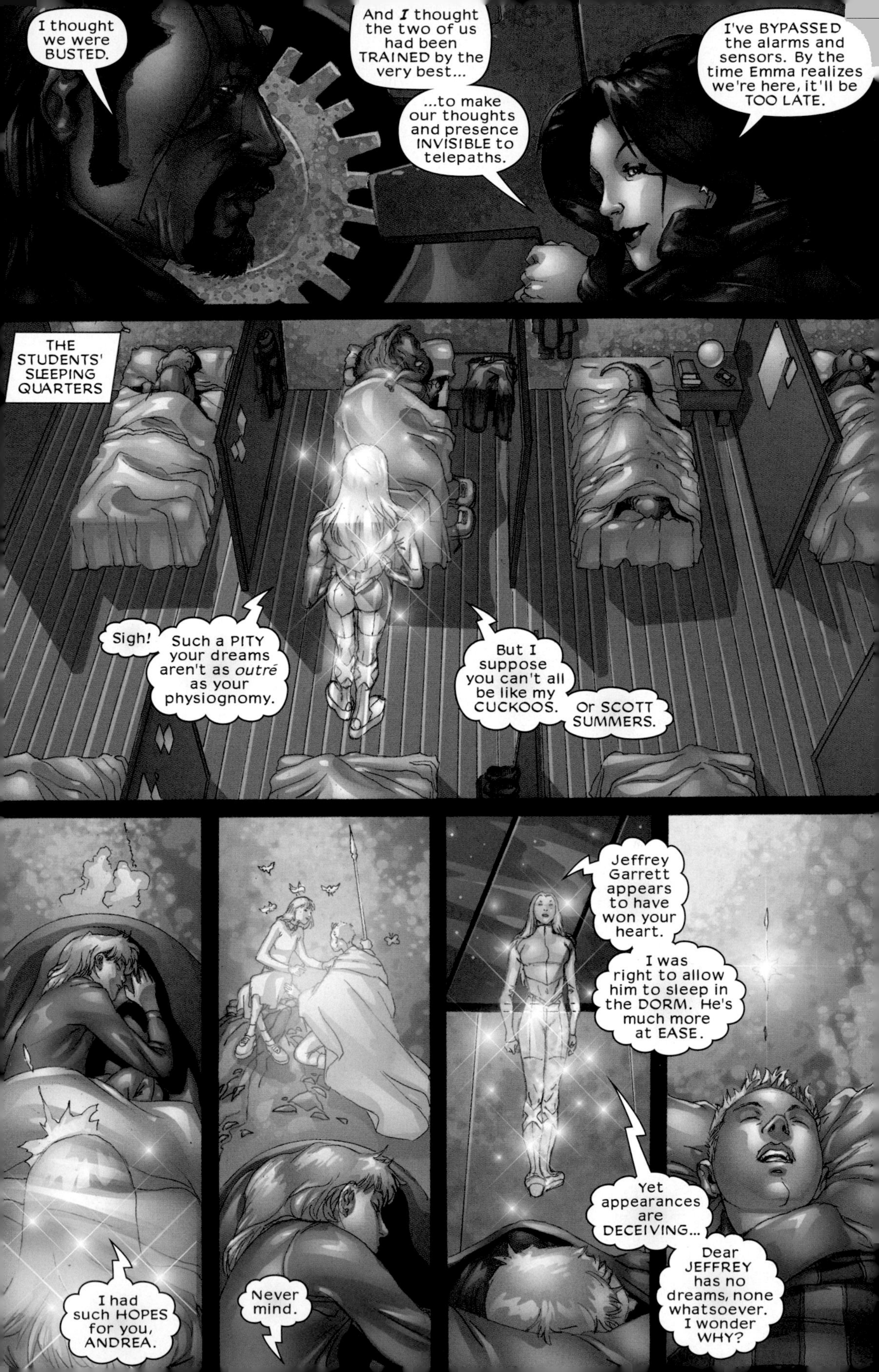
I thought we were BUSTED.
And *I* thought the two of us had been TRAINED by the very best...
...to make our thoughts and presence INVISIBLE to telepaths.
I've BYPASSED the alarms and sensors. By the time Emma realizes we're here, it'll be TOO LATE.
THE STUDENTS' SLEEPING QUARTERS
Sigh!
Such a PITY your dreams aren't as *outré* as your physiognomy.
But I suppose you can't all be like my CUCKOOS.
Or SCOTT SUMMERS.
I had such HOPES for you, ANDREA.
Never mind.
Jeffrey Garrett appears to have won your heart.
I was right to allow him to sleep in the DORM. He's much more at EASE.
Yet appearances are DECEIVING...
Dear JEFFREY has no dreams, none whatsoever. I wonder WHY?

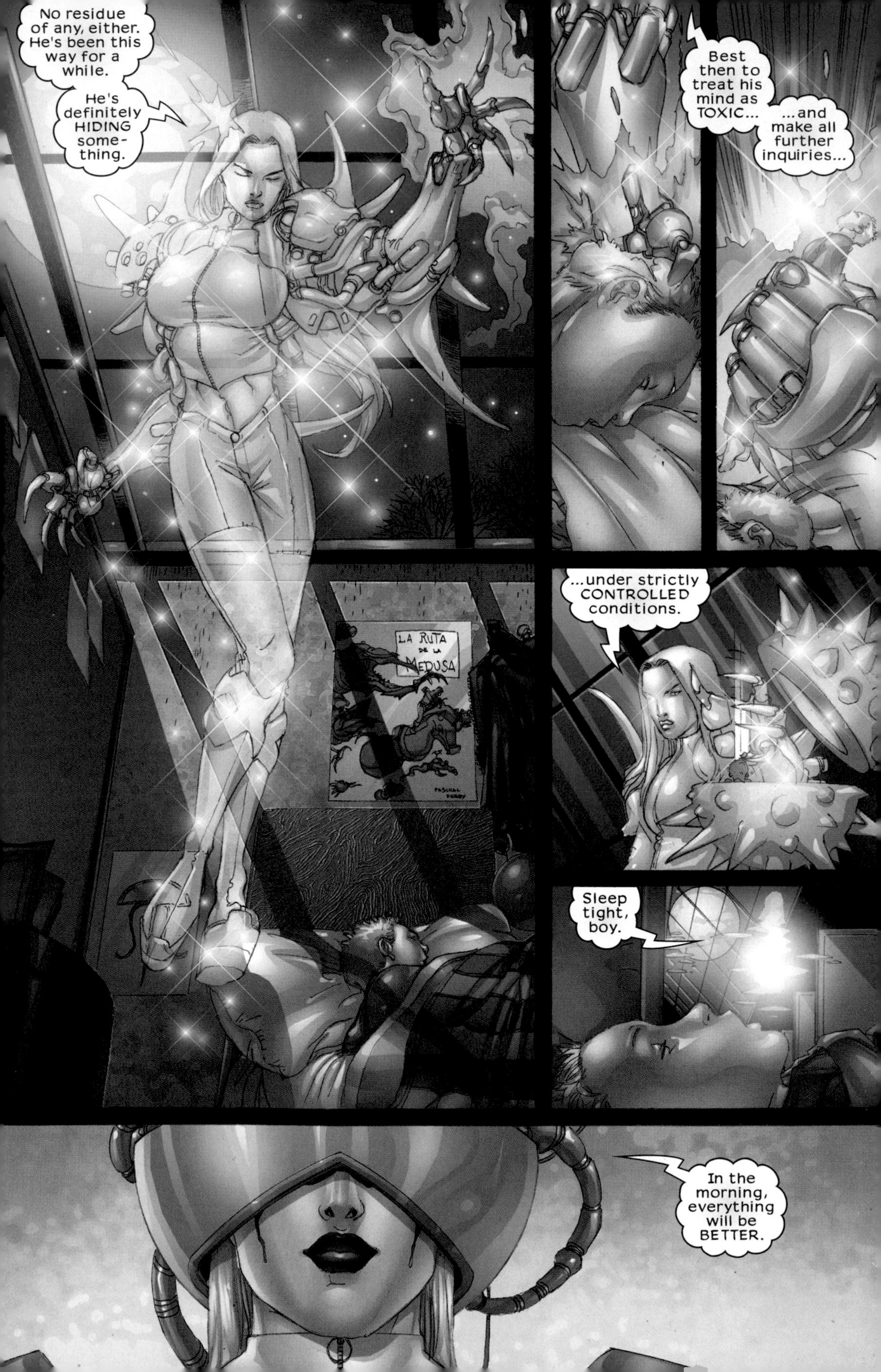
No residue of any, either. He's been this way for a while.
He's definitely HIDING some-thing.
Best then to treat his mind as TOXIC...
...and make all further inquiries...
LA RUTA DE LA MEDUSA
PASCUAL FERRY
...under strictly CONTROLLED conditions.
Sleep tight, boy.
In the morning, everything will be BETTER.

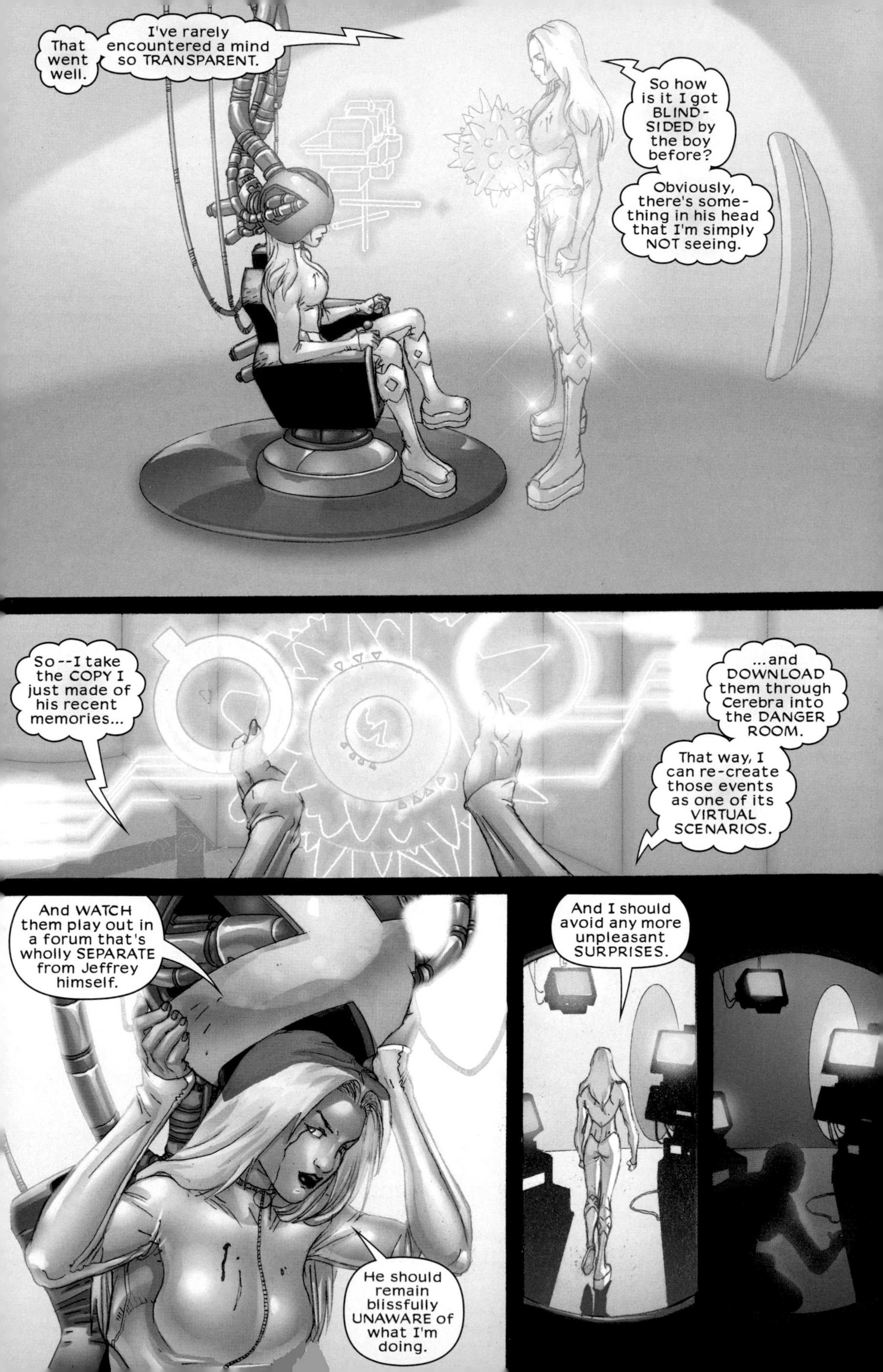

That went well.
I've rarely encountered a mind so TRANSPARENT.
So how is it I got BLIND-SIDED by the boy before?
Obviously, there's something in his head that I'm simply NOT seeing.
So--I take the COPY I just made of his recent memories...
...and DOWNLOAD them through Cerebra into the DANGER ROOM.
That way, I can re-create those events as one of its VIRTUAL SCENARIOS.
And WATCH them play out in a forum that's wholly SEPARATE from Jeffrey himself.
He should remain blissfully UNAWARE of what I'm doing.
And I should avoid any more unpleasant SURPRISES.

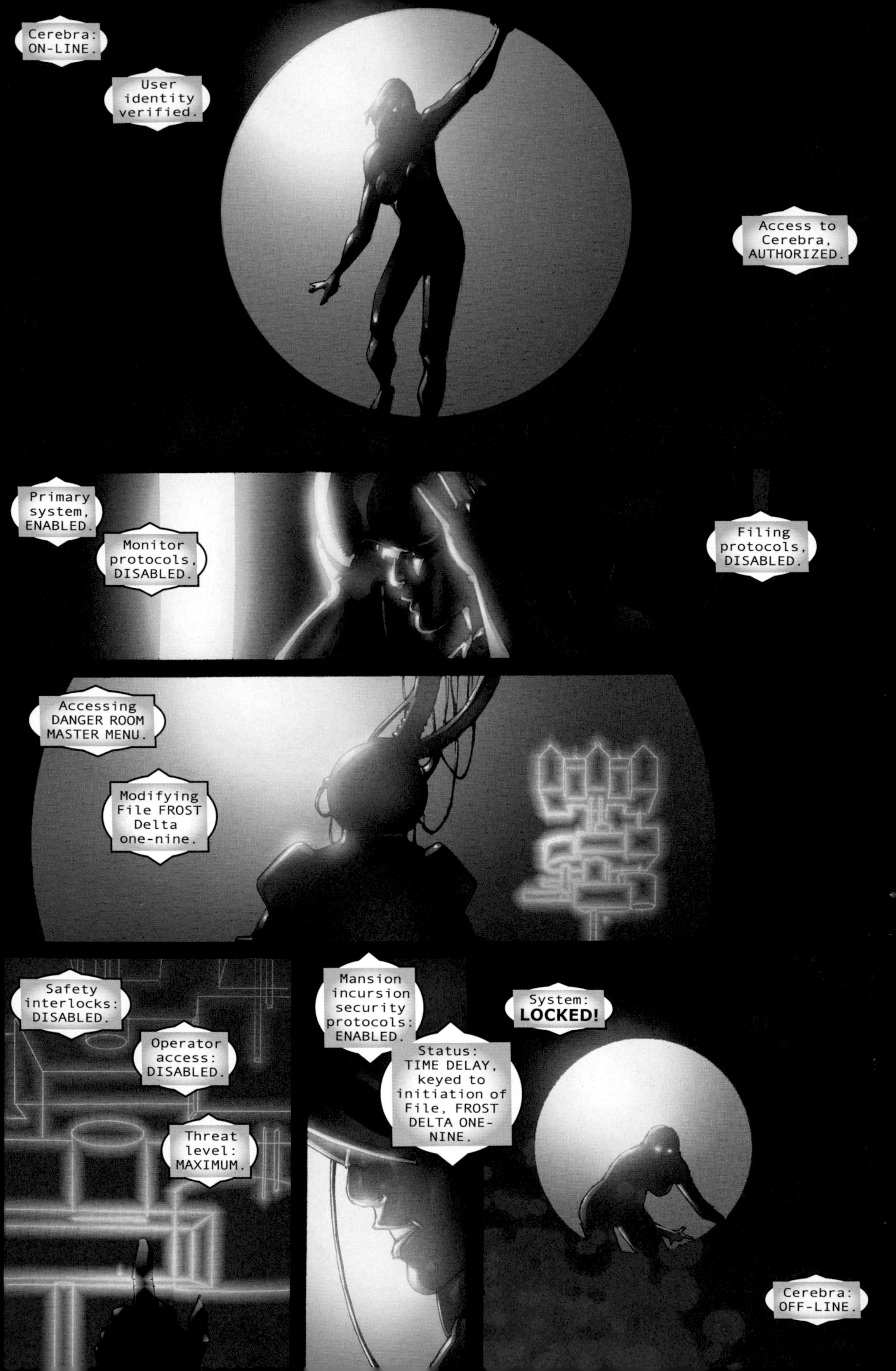

Cerebra: ON-LINE.
User identity verified.
Access to Cerebra, AUTHORIZED.
Primary system, ENABLED.
Monitor protocols, DISABLED.
Filing protocols, DISABLED.
Accessing DANGER ROOM MASTER MENU.
Modifying File FROST Delta one-nine.
Safety interlocks: DISABLED.
Operator access: DISABLED.
Threat level: MAXIMUM.
Mansion incursion security protocols: ENABLED.
Status: TIME DELAY, keyed to initiation of File, FROST DELTA ONE-NINE.
System: **LOCKED!**
Cerebra: OFF-LINE.

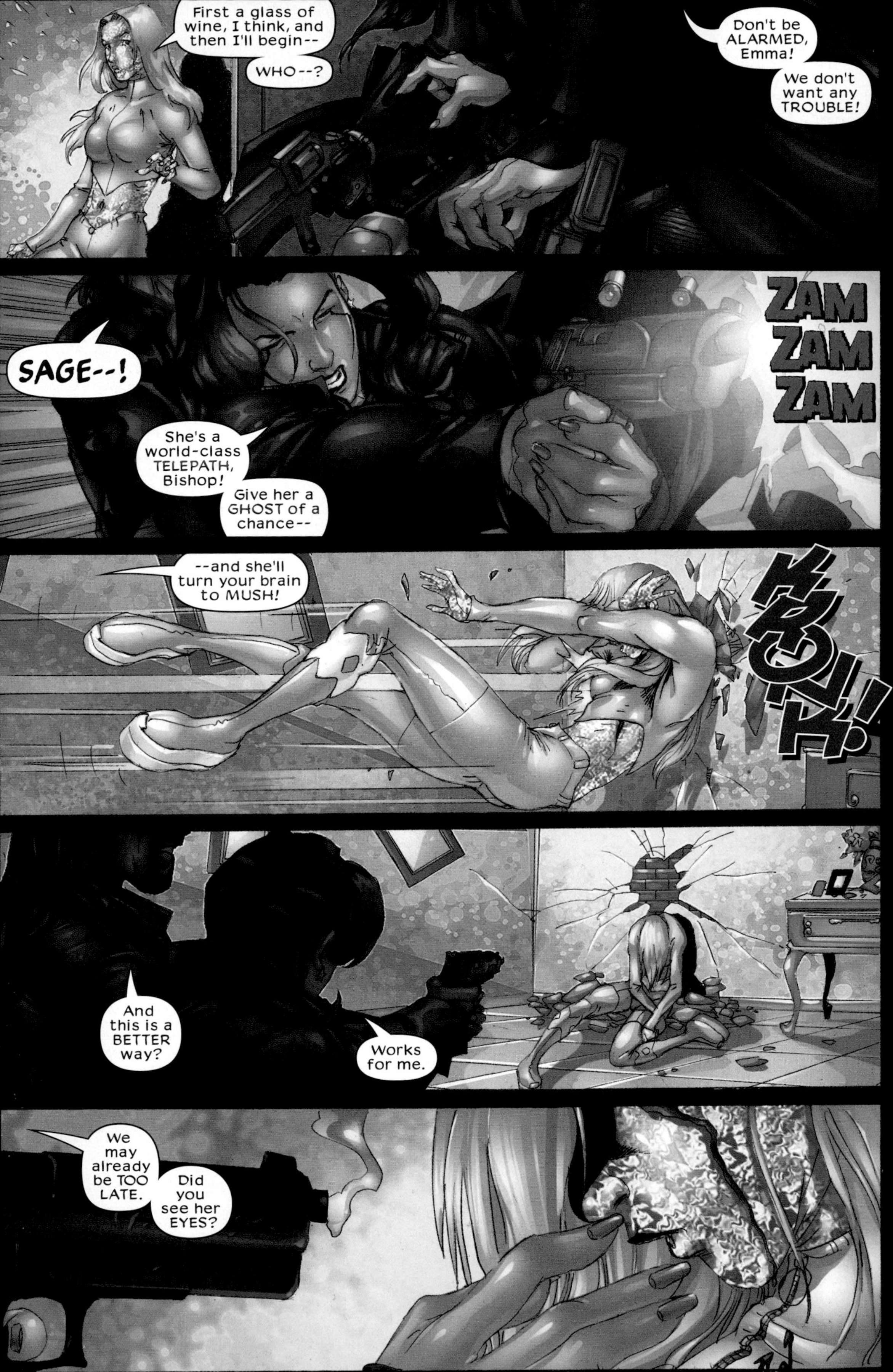
First a glass of wine, I think, and then I'll begin--
WHO--?
Don't be ALARMED, Emma!
We don't want any TROUBLE!
SAGE--!
ZAM ZAM ZAM
She's a world-class TELEPATH, Bishop!
Give her a GHOST of a chance--
--and she'll turn your brain to MUSH!
And this is a BETTER way?
Works for me.
We may already be TOO LATE.
Did you see her EYES?

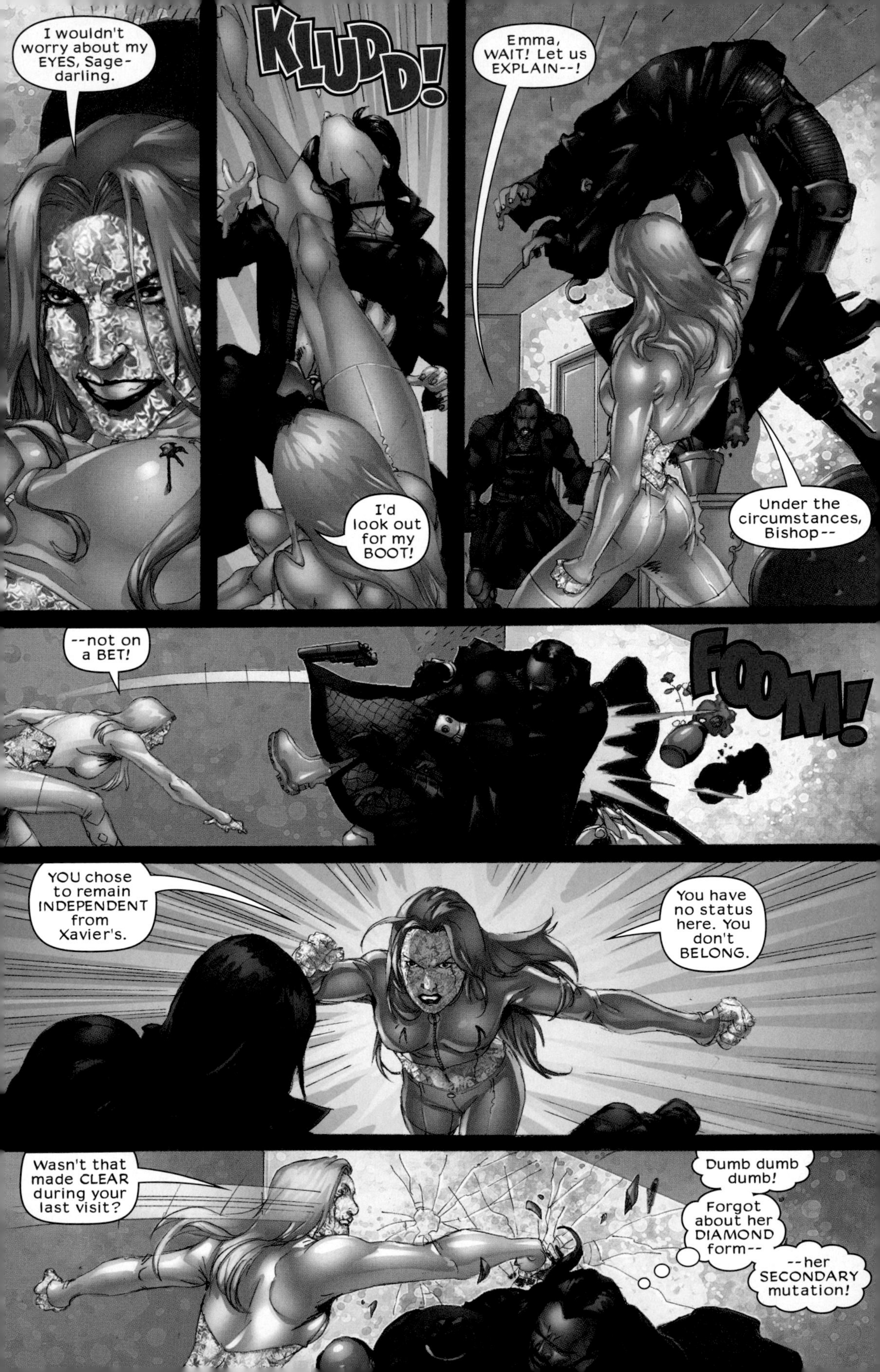
I wouldn't worry about my EYES, Sage-darling.
KLUDD!
I'd look out for my BOOT!
Emma, WAIT! Let us EXPLAIN--!
Under the circumstances, Bishop--
--not on a BET!
FOOM!
YOU chose to remain INDEPENDENT from Xavier's.
You have no status here. You don't BELONG.
Wasn't that made CLEAR during your last visit?
Dumb dumb dumb!
Forgot about her DIAMOND form--
--her SECONDARY mutation!

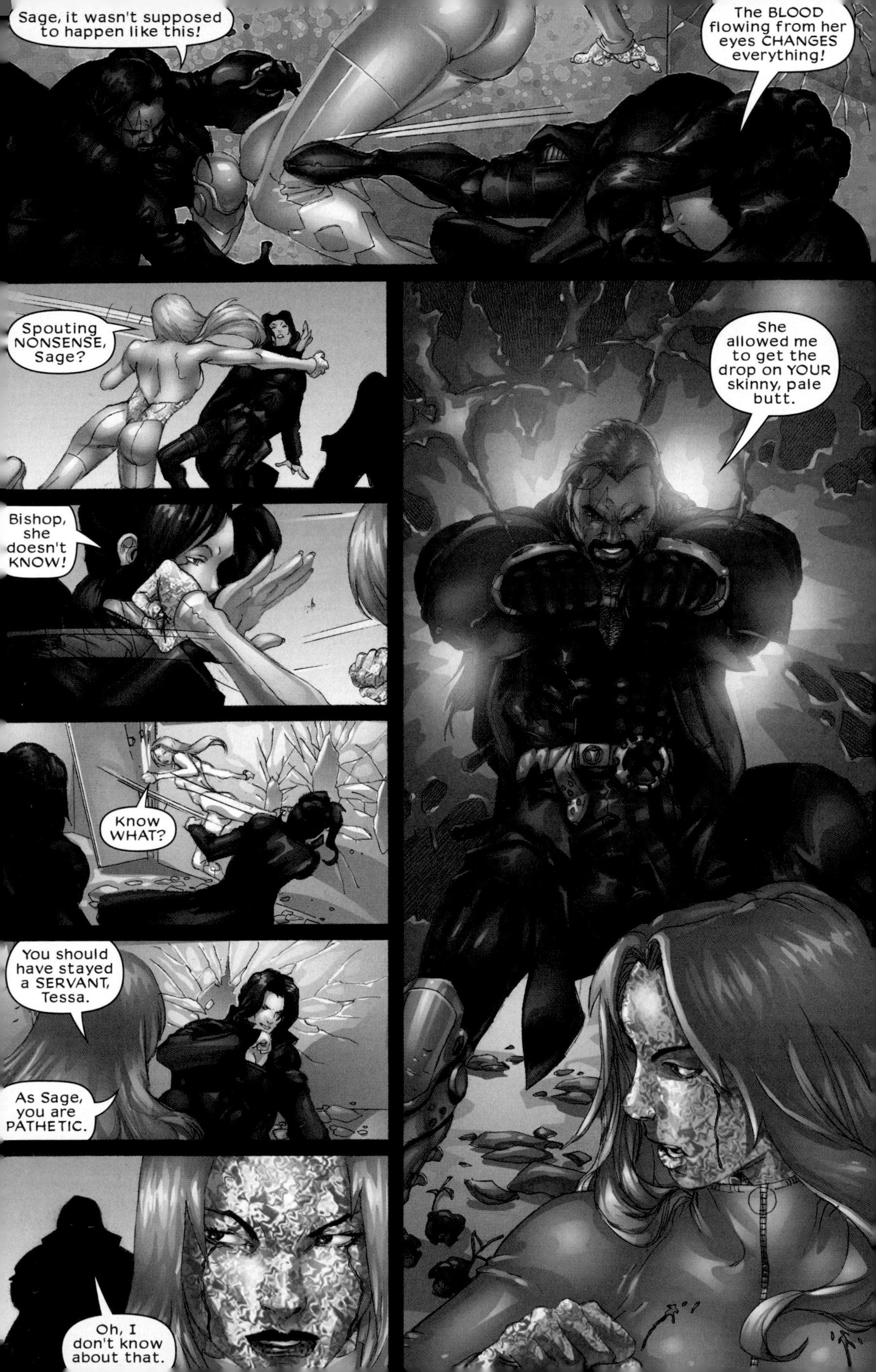
Sage, it wasn't supposed to happen like this!
The BLOOD flowing from her eyes CHANGES everything!
Spouting NONSENSE, Sage?
Bishop, she doesn't KNOW!
Know WHAT?
You should have stayed a SERVANT, Tessa.
As Sage, you are PATHETIC.
Oh, I don't know about that.
She allowed me to get the drop on YOUR skinny, pale butt.

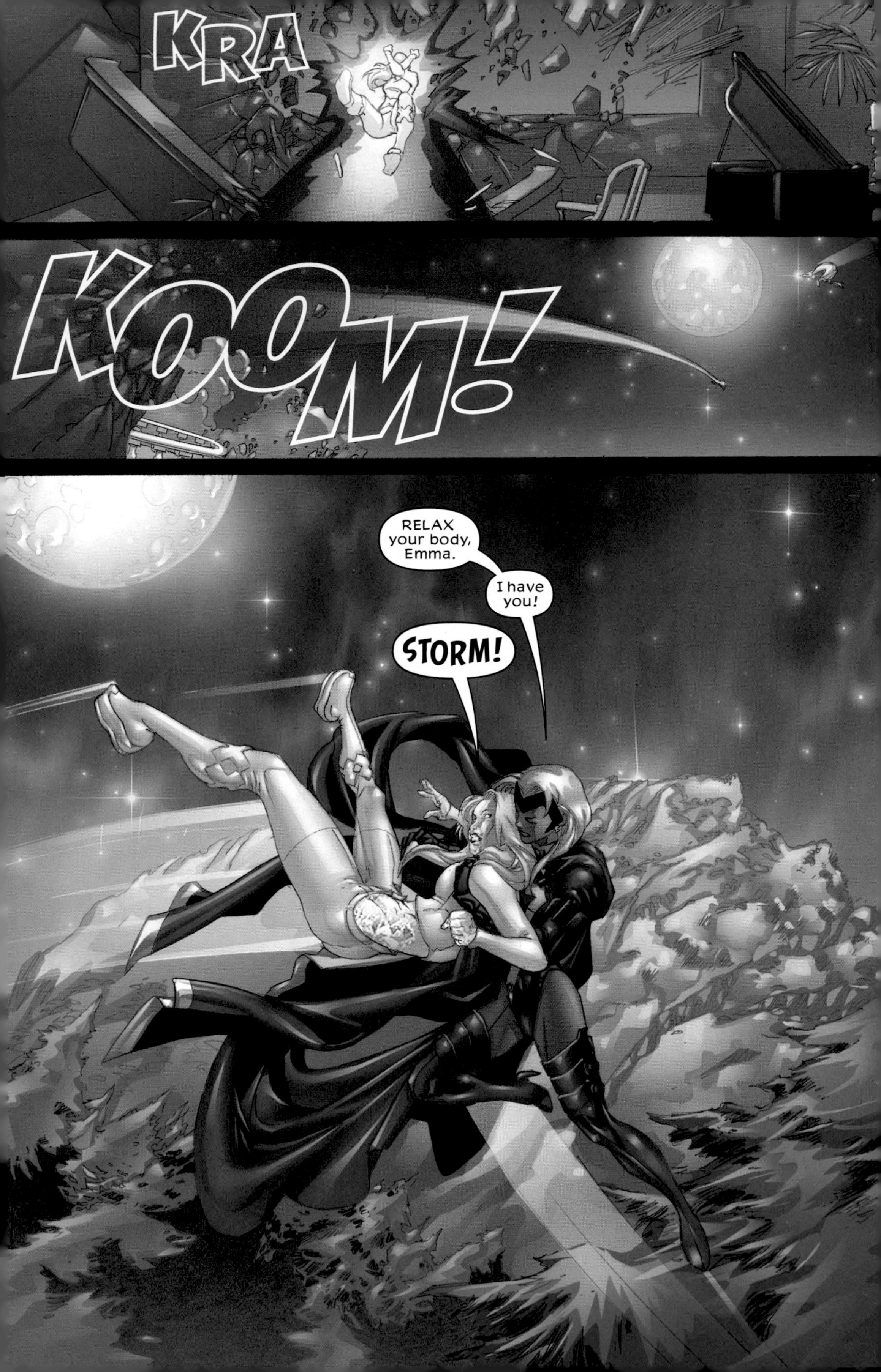
KRA
KOOM!
RELAX your body, Emma.
I have you!
STORM!

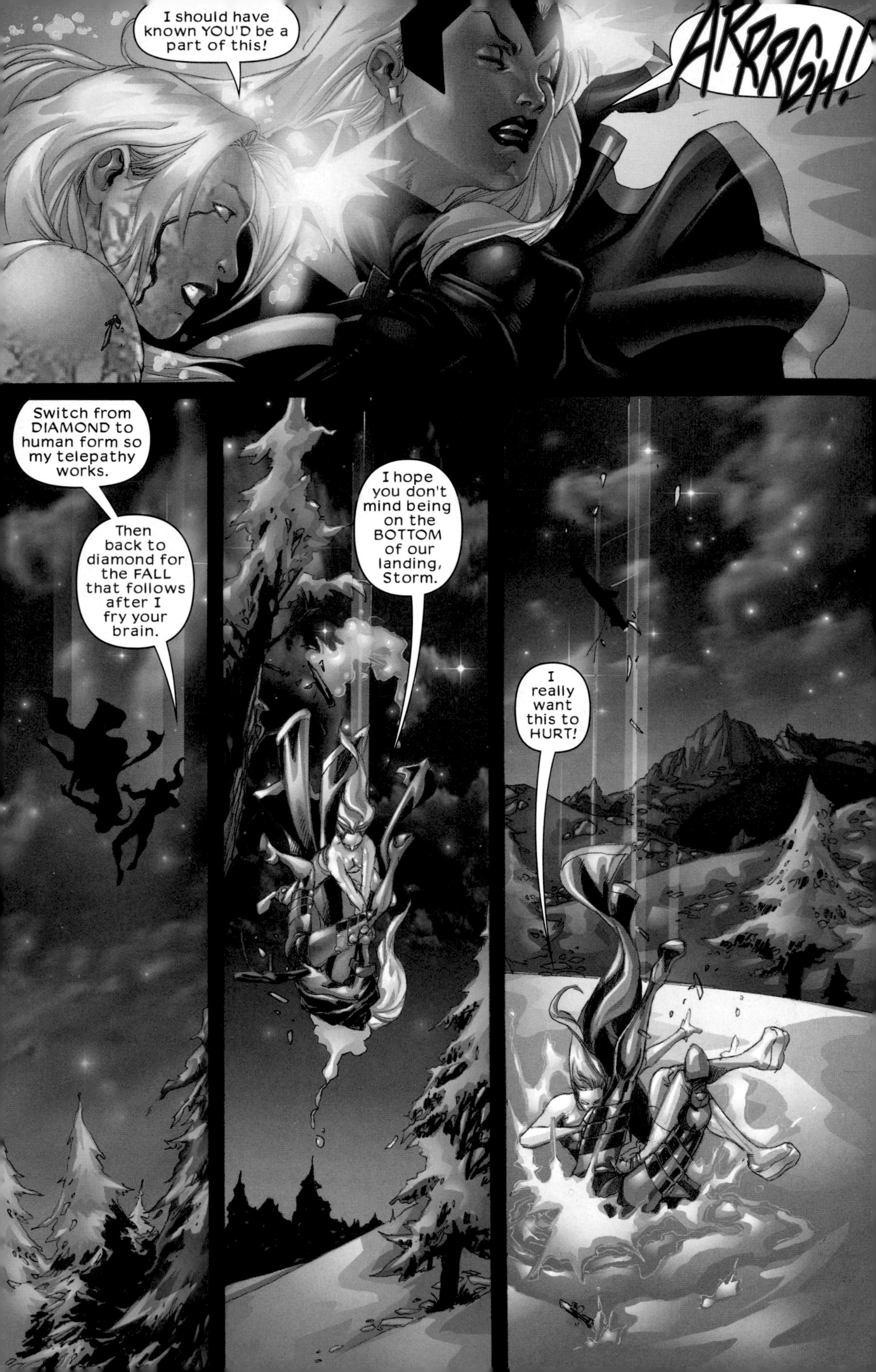

I should have known YOU'D be a part of this!
ARRRGH!!
Switch from DIAMOND to human form so my telepathy works.
Then back to diamond for the FALL that follows after I fry your brain.
I hope you don't mind being on the BOTTOM of our landing, Storm.
I really want this to HURT!

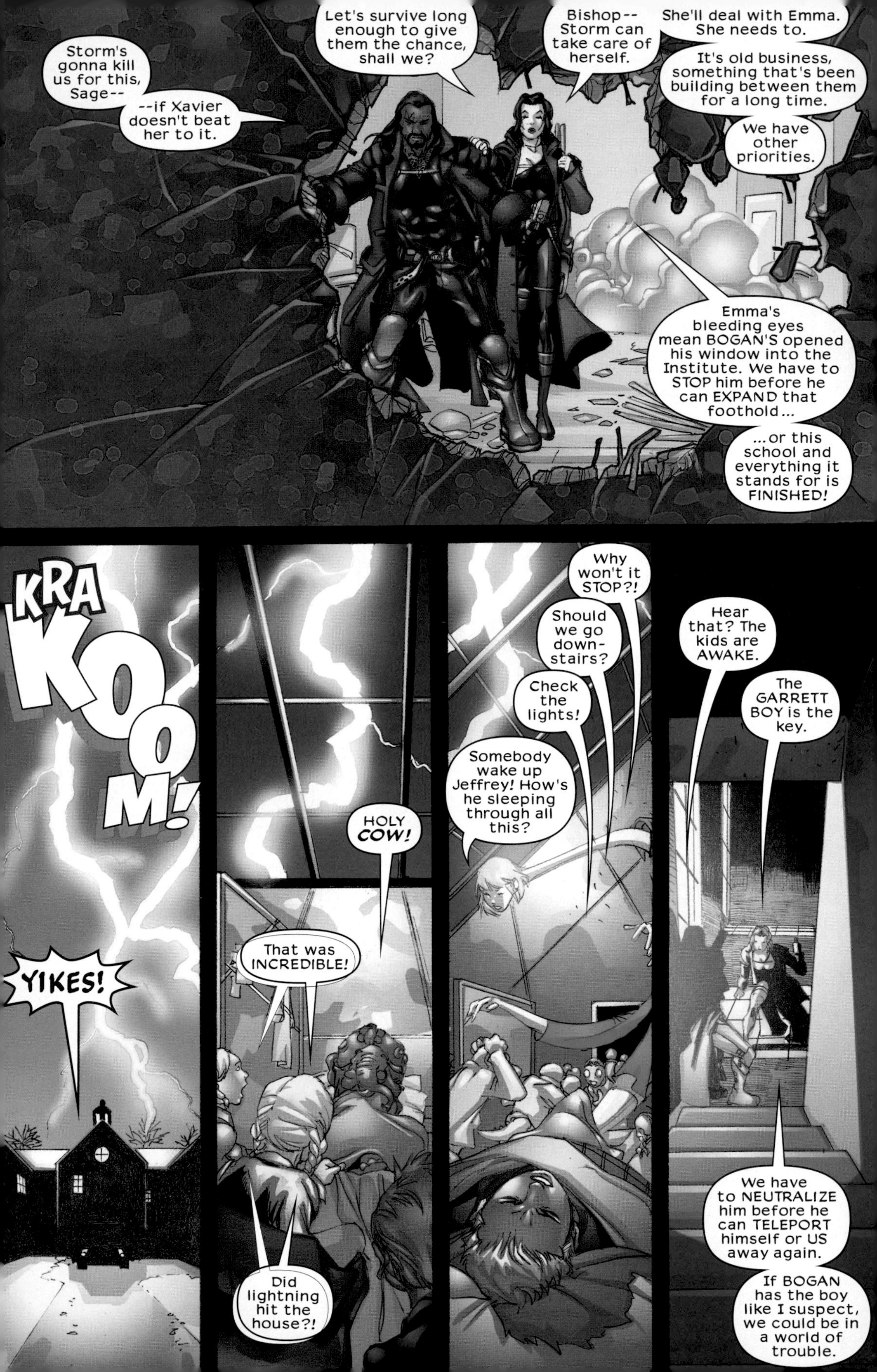
Storm's gonna kill us for this, Sage--
--if Xavier doesn't beat her to it.
Let's survive long enough to give them the chance, shall we?
Bishop-- Storm can take care of herself.
She'll deal with Emma. She needs to.
It's old business, something that's been building between them for a long time.
We have other priorities.
Emma's bleeding eyes mean BOGAN'S opened his window into the Institute. We have to STOP him before he can EXPAND that foothold...
...or this school and everything it stands for is FINISHED!
KRA KOOOM!
YIKES!
HOLY COW!
That was INCREDIBLE!
Did lightning hit the house?!
Why won't it STOP?!
Should we go down-stairs?
Check the lights!
Somebody wake up Jeffrey! How's he sleeping through all this?
Hear that? The kids are AWAKE.
The GARRETT BOY is the key.
We have to NEUTRALIZE him before he can TELEPORT himself or US away again.
If BOGAN has the boy like I suspect, we could be in a world of trouble.

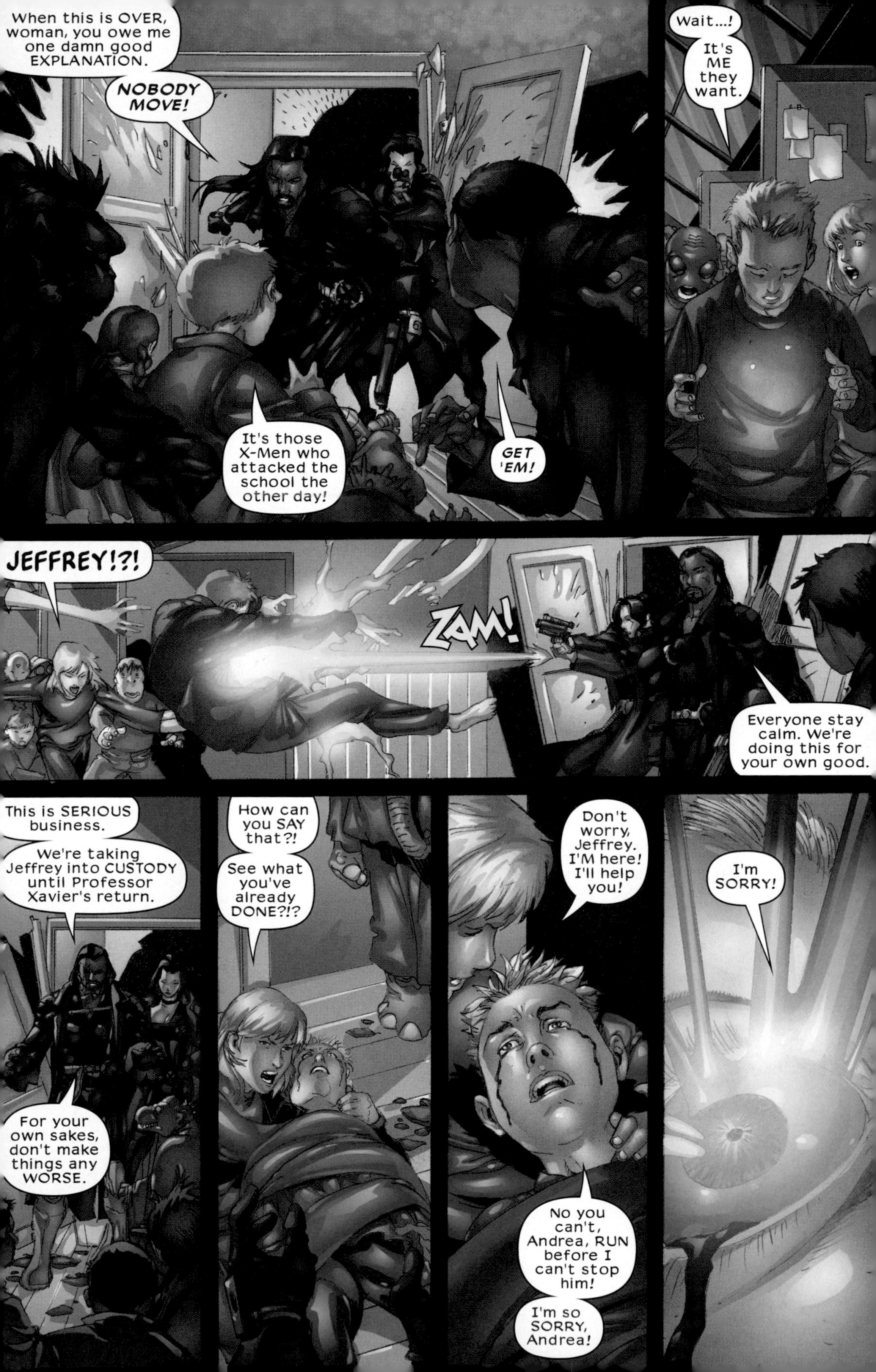
When this is OVER, woman, you owe me one damn good EXPLANATION.
NOBODY MOVE!
It's those X-Men who attacked the school the other day!
GET 'EM!
Wait...! It's ME they want.
JEFFREY!?!
ZAM!
Everyone stay calm. We're doing this for your own good.
This is SERIOUS business.
We're taking Jeffrey into CUSTODY until Professor Xavier's return.
For your own sakes, don't make things any WORSE.
How can you SAY that?!
See what you've already DONE?!?
Don't worry, Jeffrey. I'M here! I'll help you!
No you can't, Andrea, RUN before I can't stop him!
I'm so SORRY, Andrea!
I'm SORRY!

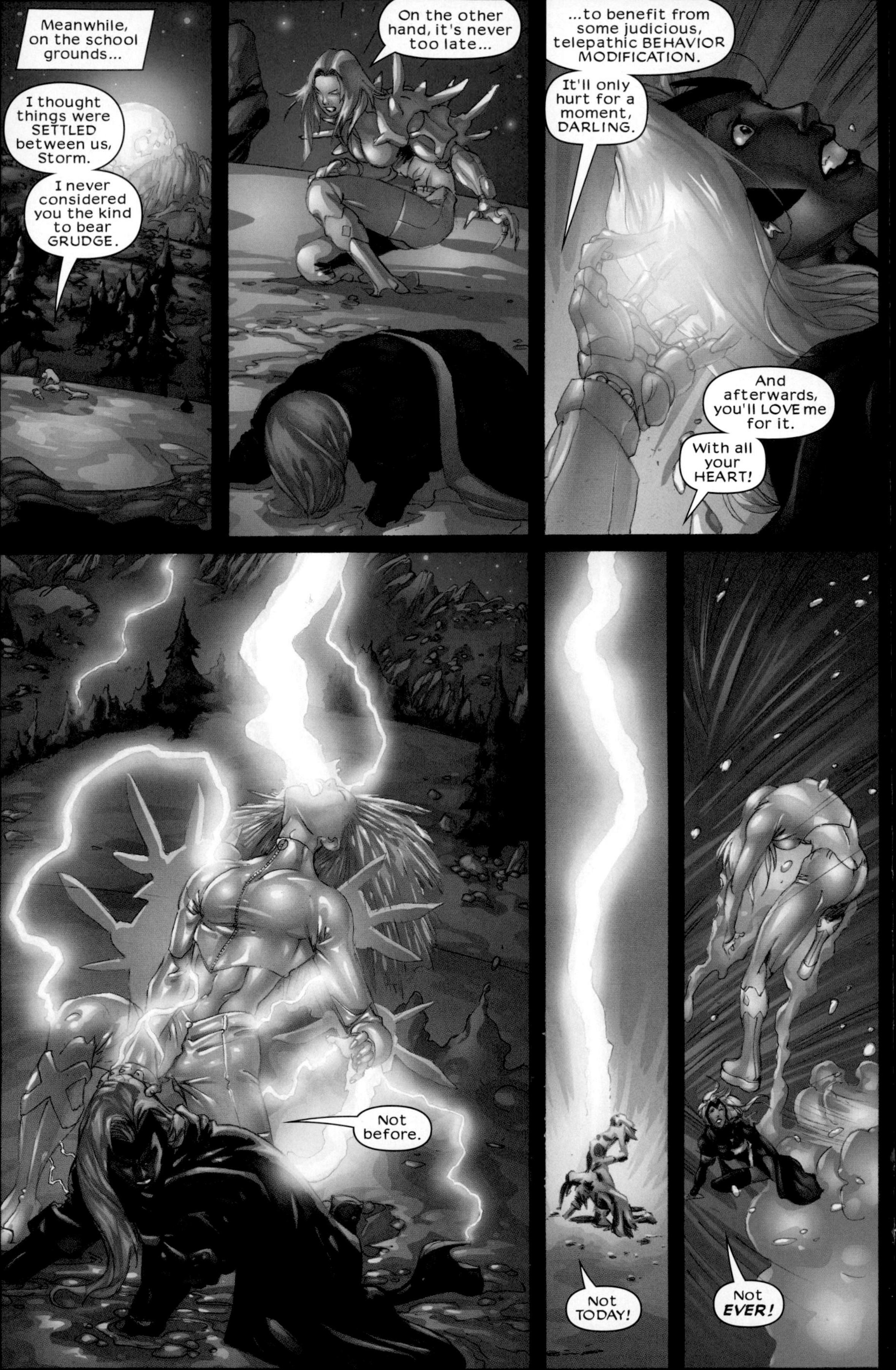
Meanwhile, on the school grounds...
I thought things were SETTLED between us, Storm.
I never considered you the kind to bear GRUDGE.
On the other hand, it's never too late...
...to benefit from some judicious, telepathic BEHAVIOR MODIFICATION.
It'll only hurt for a moment, DARLING.
And afterwards, you'll LOVE me for it.
With all your HEART!
Not before.
Not TODAY!
Not *EVER!*

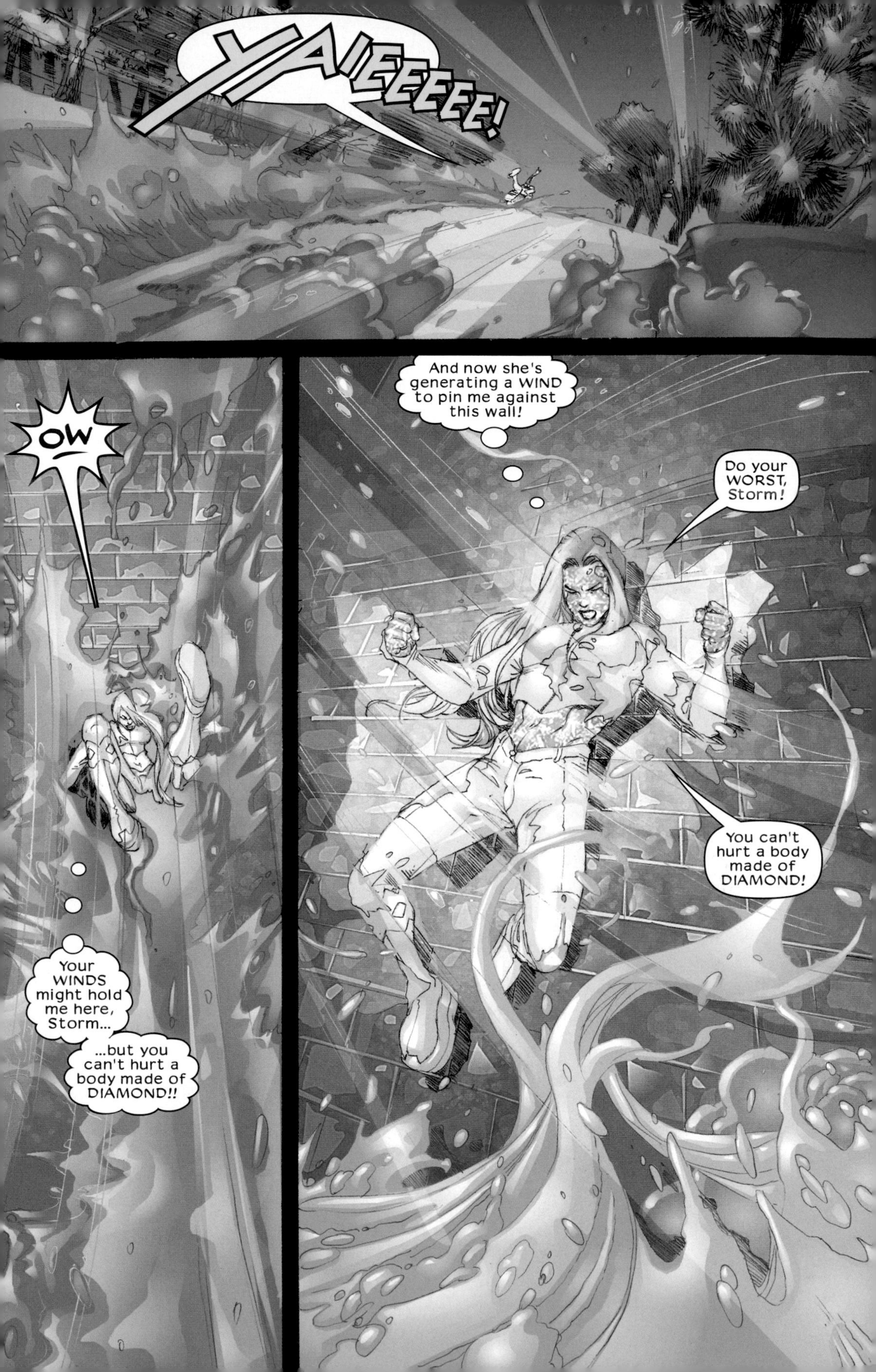
YAIEEEEEE!
OW
And now she's generating a WIND to pin me against this wall!
Do your WORST, Storm!
You can't hurt a body made of DIAMOND!
Your WINDS might hold me here, Storm...
...but you can't hurt a body made of DIAMOND!!

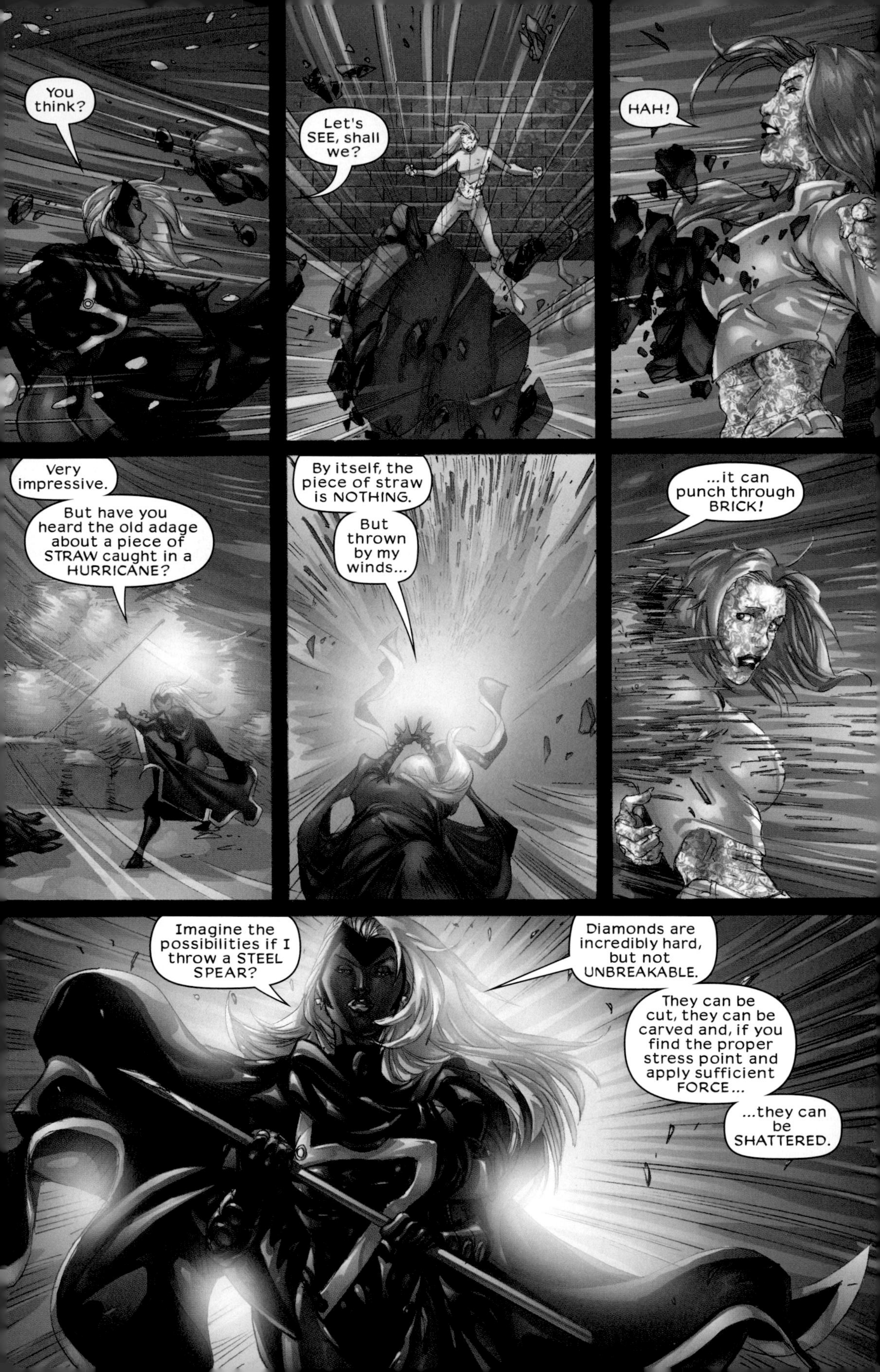
You think?
Let's SEE, shall we?
HAH!
Very impressive.
But have you heard the old adage about a piece of STRAW caught in a HURRICANE?
By itself, the piece of straw is NOTHING.
But thrown by my winds...
...it can punch through BRICK!
Imagine the possibilities if I throw a STEEL SPEAR?
Diamonds are incredibly hard, but not UNBREAKABLE.
They can be cut, they can be carved and, if you find the proper stress point and apply sufficient FORCE...
...they can be SHATTERED.

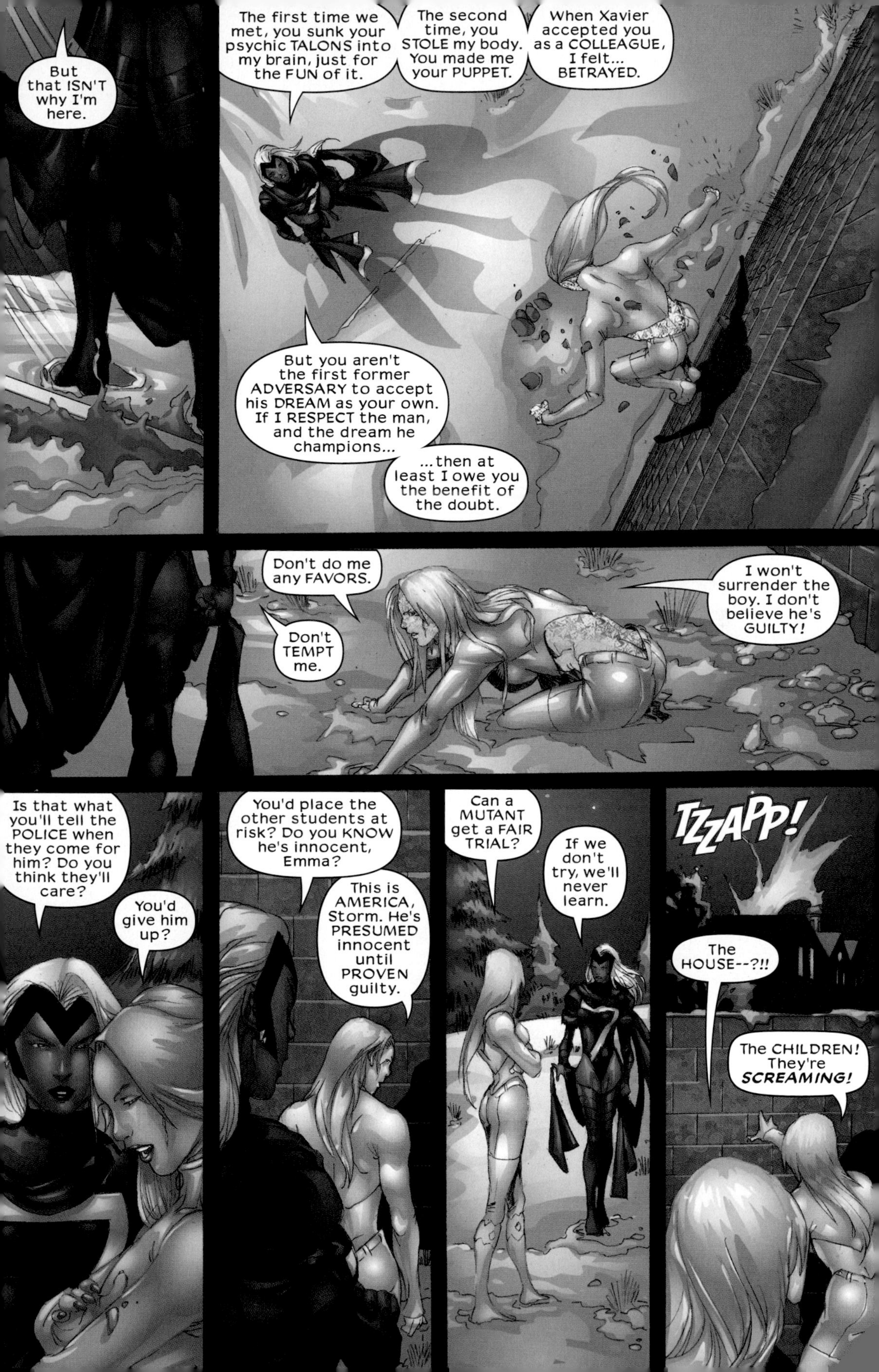
But that ISN'T why I'm here.
The first time we met, you sunk your psychic TALONS into my brain, just for the FUN of it.
The second time, you STOLE my body. You made me your PUPPET.
When Xavier accepted you as a COLLEAGUE, I felt... BETRAYED.
But you aren't the first former ADVERSARY to accept his DREAM as your own. If I RESPECT the man, and the dream he champions...
...then at least I owe you the benefit of the doubt.
Don't do me any FAVORS.
Don't TEMPT me.
I won't surrender the boy. I don't believe he's GUILTY!
Is that what you'll tell the POLICE when they come for him? Do you think they'll care?
You'd give him up?
You'd place the other students at risk? Do you KNOW he's innocent, Emma?
This is AMERICA, Storm. He's PRESUMED innocent until PROVEN guilty.
Can a MUTANT get a FAIR TRIAL?
If we don't try, we'll never learn.
TZZAPP!
The HOUSE--?!!
The CHILDREN! They're SCREAMING!

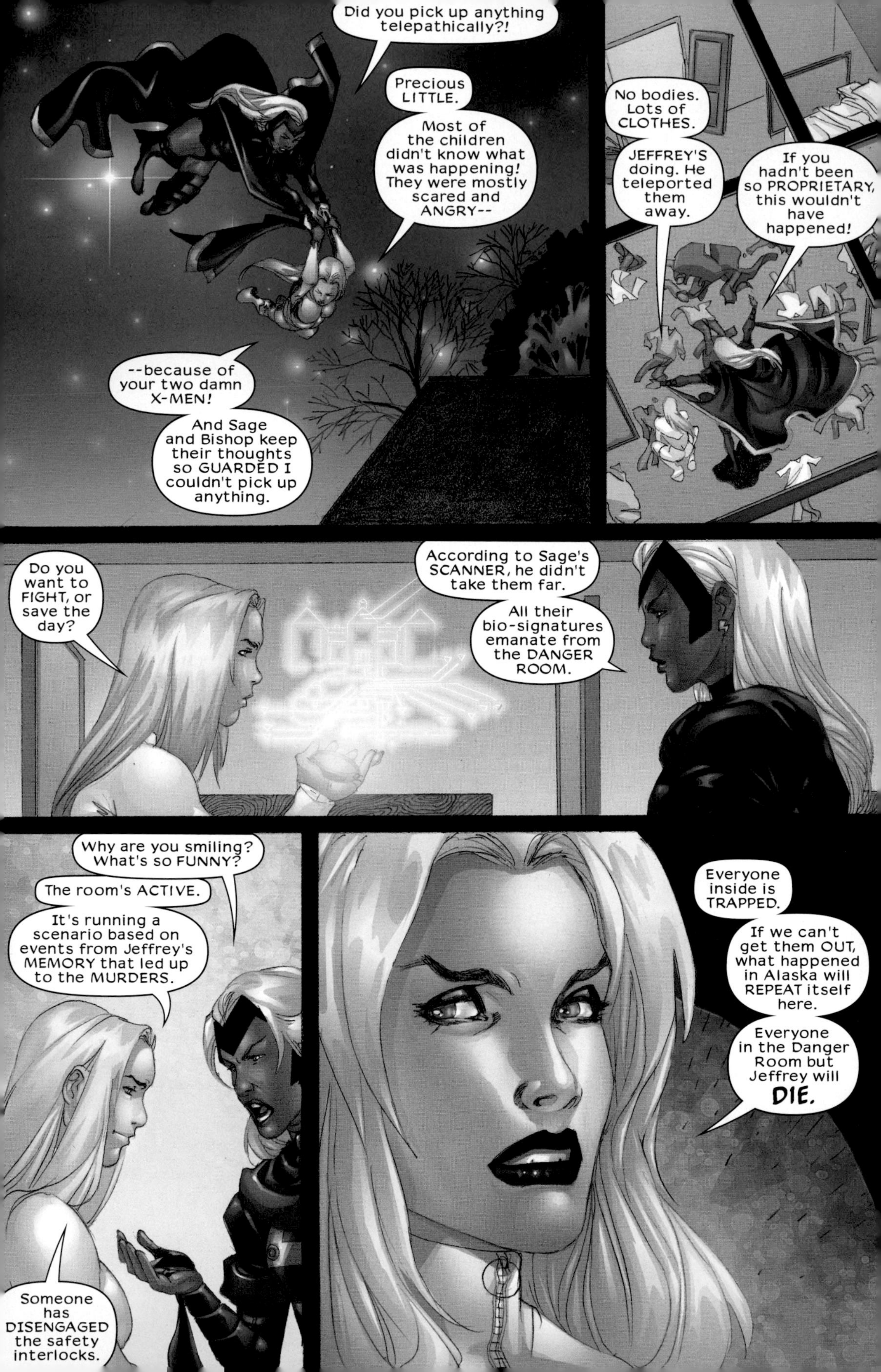

Did you pick up anything telepathically?!
Precious LITTLE.
Most of the children didn't know what was happening! They were mostly scared and ANGRY--
--because of your two damn X-MEN!
And Sage and Bishop keep their thoughts so GUARDED I couldn't pick up anything.
No bodies. Lots of CLOTHES.
JEFFREY'S doing. He teleported them away.
If you hadn't been so PROPRIETARY, this wouldn't have happened!
Do you want to FIGHT, or save the day?
According to Sage's SCANNER, he didn't take them far.
All their bio-signatures emanate from the DANGER ROOM.
Why are you smiling? What's so FUNNY?
The room's ACTIVE.
It's running a scenario based on events from Jeffrey's MEMORY that led up to the MURDERS.
Someone has DISENGAGED the safety interlocks.
Everyone inside is TRAPPED.
If we can't get them OUT, what happened in Alaska will REPEAT itself here.
Everyone in the Danger Room but Jeffrey will DIE.

COVER GALLERY

ISSUE #19

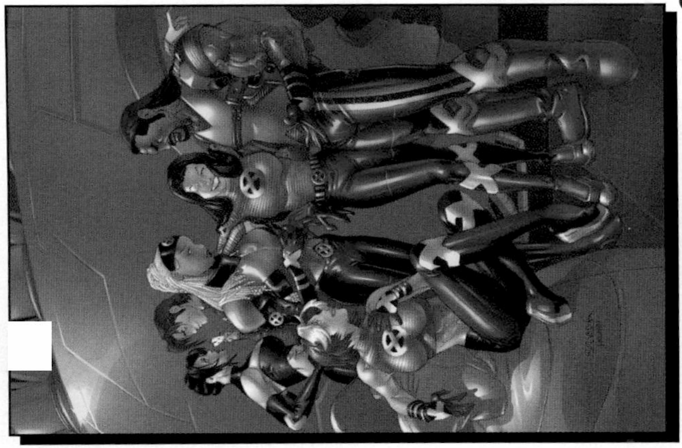

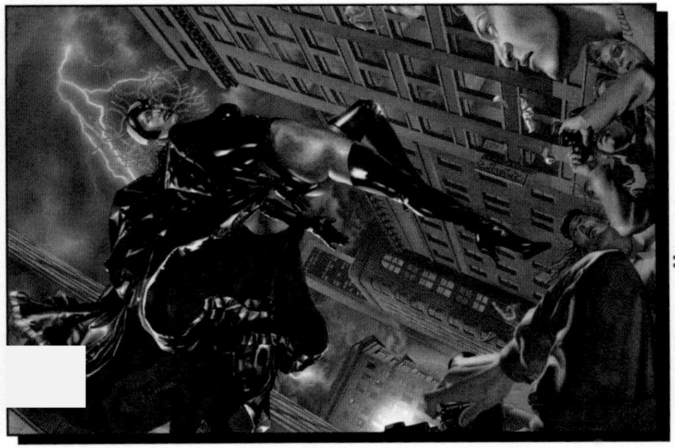

X-POSÉ #1

X-POSÉ #2

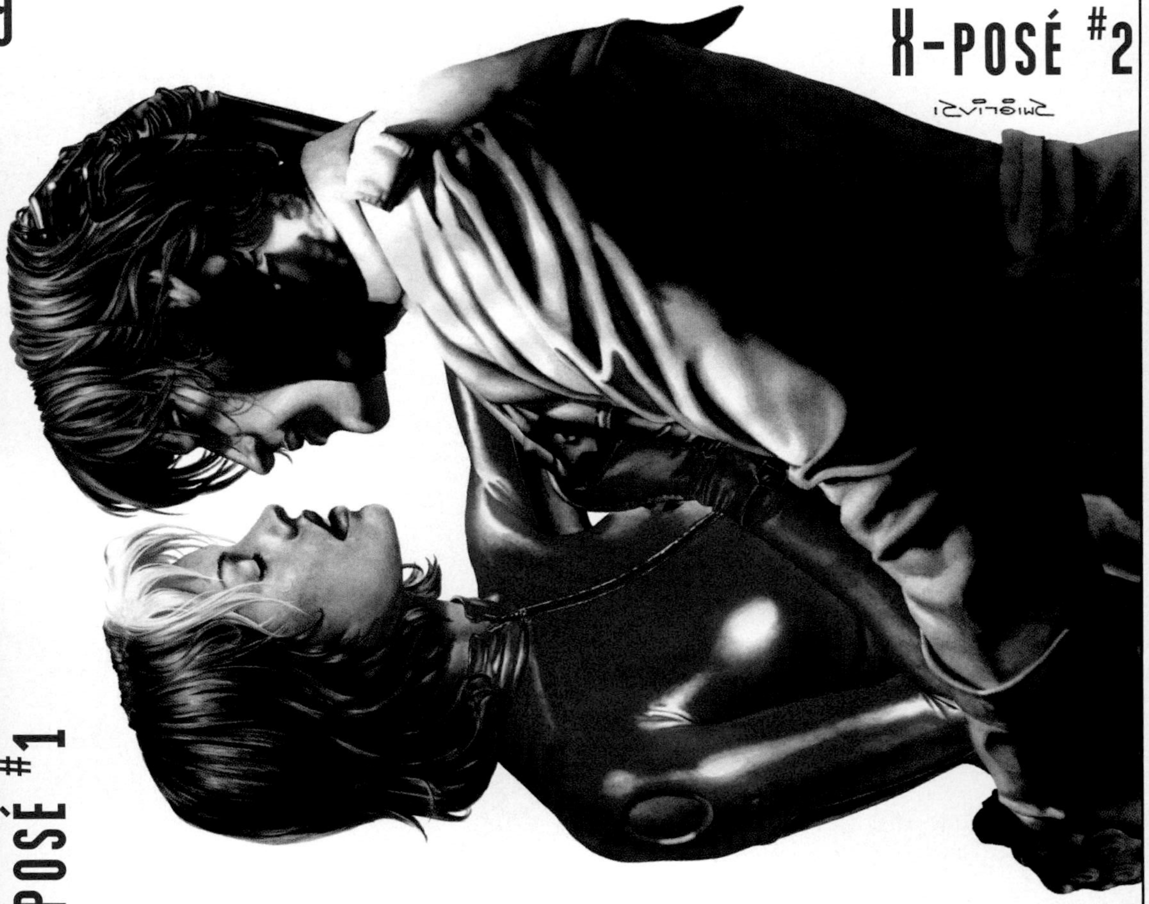

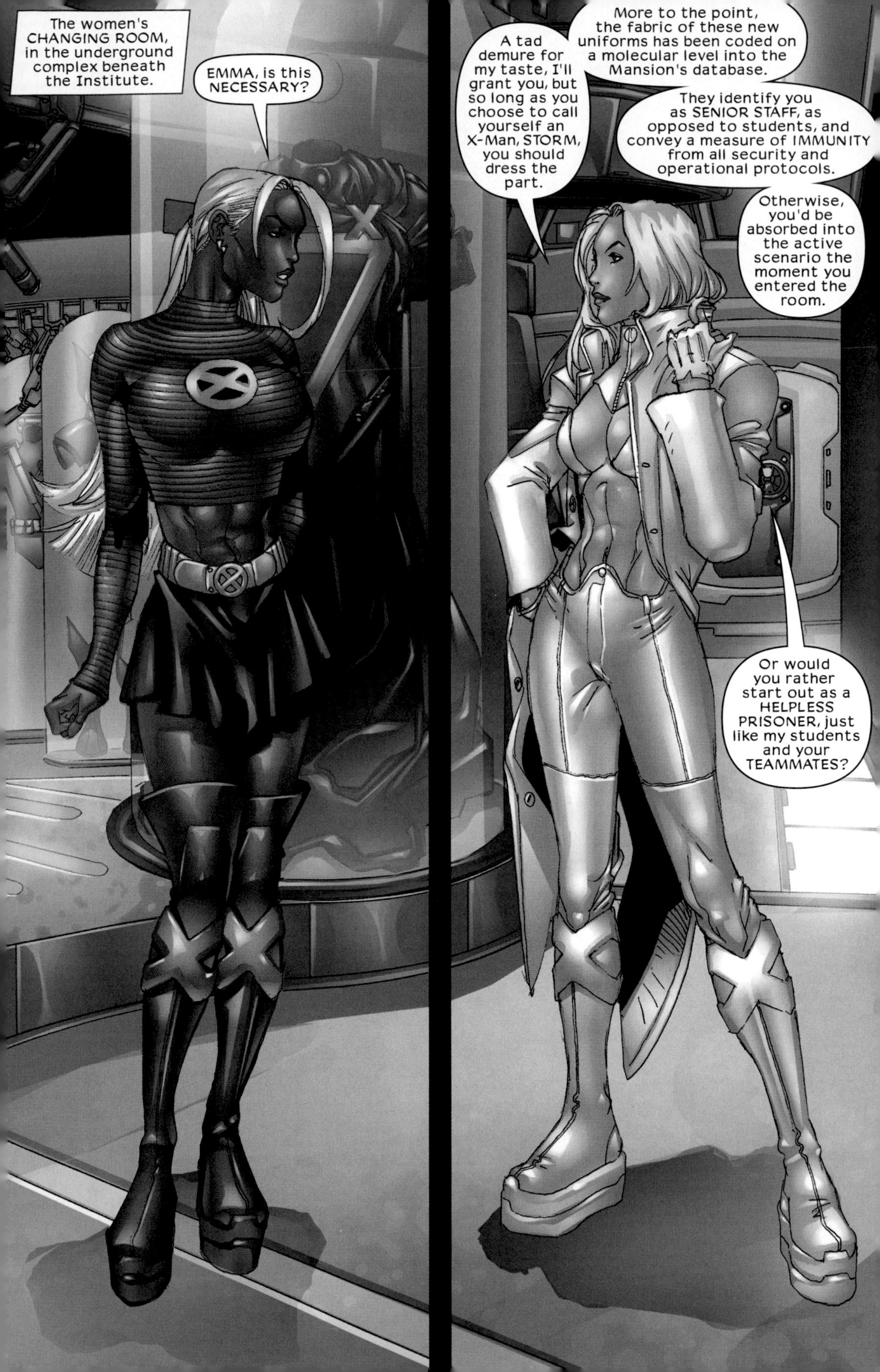

The women's CHANGING ROOM, in the underground complex beneath the Institute.
EMMA, is this NECESSARY?
A tad demure for my taste, I'll grant you, but so long as you choose to call yourself an X-Man, STORM, you should dress the part.
More to the point, the fabric of these new uniforms has been coded on a molecular level into the Mansion's database.
They identify you as SENIOR STAFF, as opposed to students, and convey a measure of IMMUNITY from all security and operational protocols.
Otherwise, you'd be absorbed into the active scenario the moment you entered the room.
Or would you rather start out as a HELPLESS PRISONER, just like my students and your TEAMMATES?

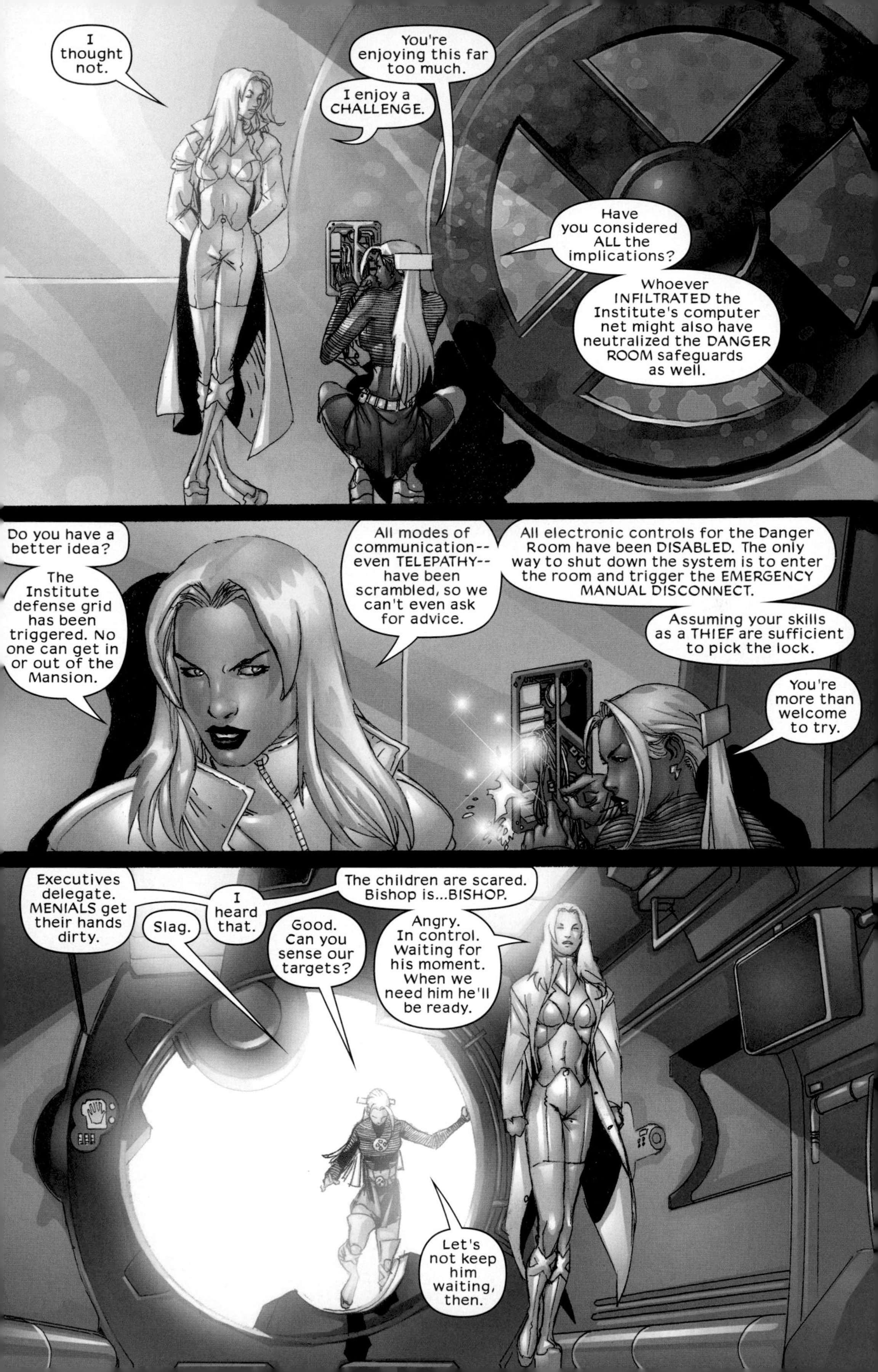
I thought not.
You're enjoying this far too much.
I enjoy a CHALLENGE.
Have you considered ALL the implications?
Whoever INFILTRATED the Institute's computer net might also have neutralized the DANGER ROOM safeguards as well.
Do you have a better idea?
The Institute defense grid has been triggered. No one can get in or out of the Mansion.
All modes of communication--even TELEPATHY--have been scrambled, so we can't even ask for advice.
All electronic controls for the Danger Room have been DISABLED. The only way to shut down the system is to enter the room and trigger the EMERGENCY MANUAL DISCONNECT.
Assuming your skills as a THIEF are sufficient to pick the lock.
You're more than welcome to try.
Executives delegate. MENIALS get their hands dirty.
I heard that.
Slag.
The children are scared. Bishop is...BISHOP.
Good. Can you sense our targets?
Angry. In control. Waiting for his moment. When we need him he'll be ready.
Let's not keep him waiting, then.

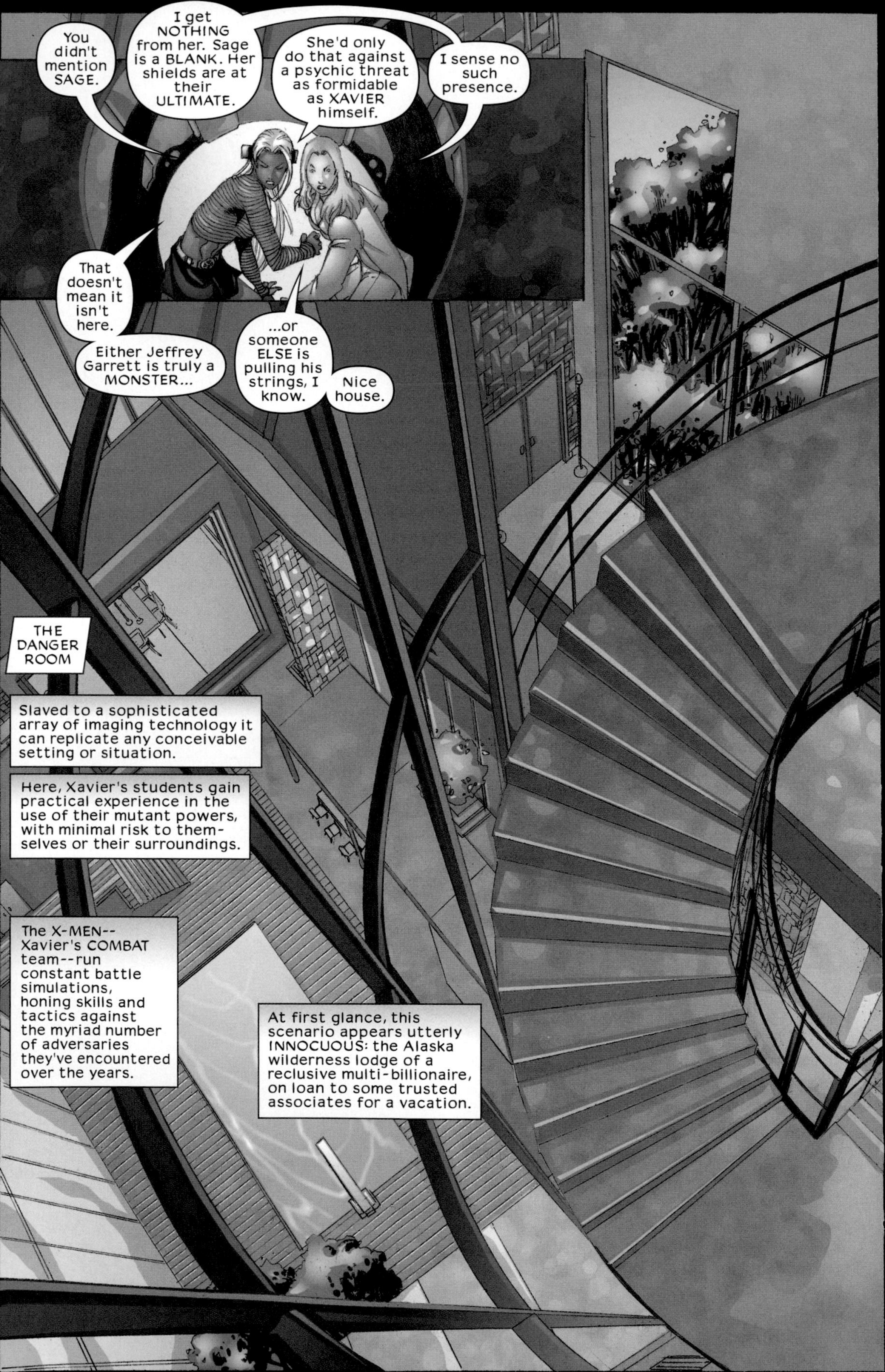
You didn't mention SAGE.
I get NOTHING from her. Sage is a BLANK. Her shields are at their ULTIMATE.
She'd only do that against a psychic threat as formidable as XAVIER himself.
I sense no such presence.
That doesn't mean it isn't here.
Either Jeffrey Garrett is truly a MONSTER...
...or someone ELSE is pulling his strings, I know.
Nice house.
THE DANGER ROOM
Slaved to a sophisticated array of imaging technology it can replicate any conceivable setting or situation.
Here, Xavier's students gain practical experience in the use of their mutant powers, with minimal risk to themselves or their surroundings.
The X-MEN--Xavier's COMBAT team--run constant battle simulations, honing skills and tactics against the myriad number of adversaries they've encountered over the years.
At first glance, this scenario appears utterly INNOCUOUS: the Alaska wilderness lodge of a reclusive multi-billionaire, on loan to some trusted associates for a vacation.

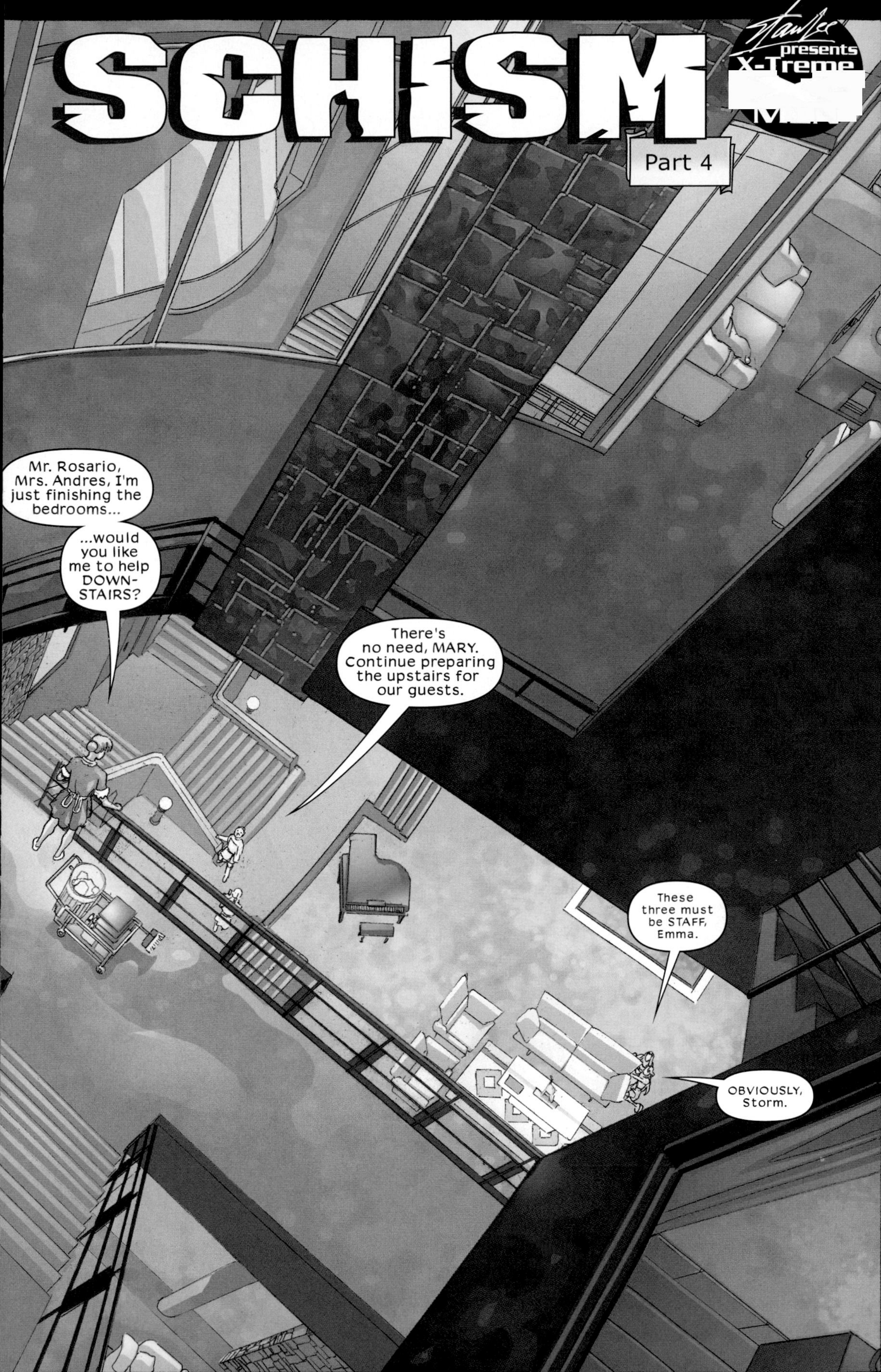

SCHISM
Part 4
Mr. Rosario, Mrs. Andres, I'm just finishing the bedrooms...
...would you like me to help DOWN-STAIRS?
There's no need, MARY. Continue preparing the upstairs for our guests.
These three must be STAFF, Emma.
OBVIOUSLY, Storm.

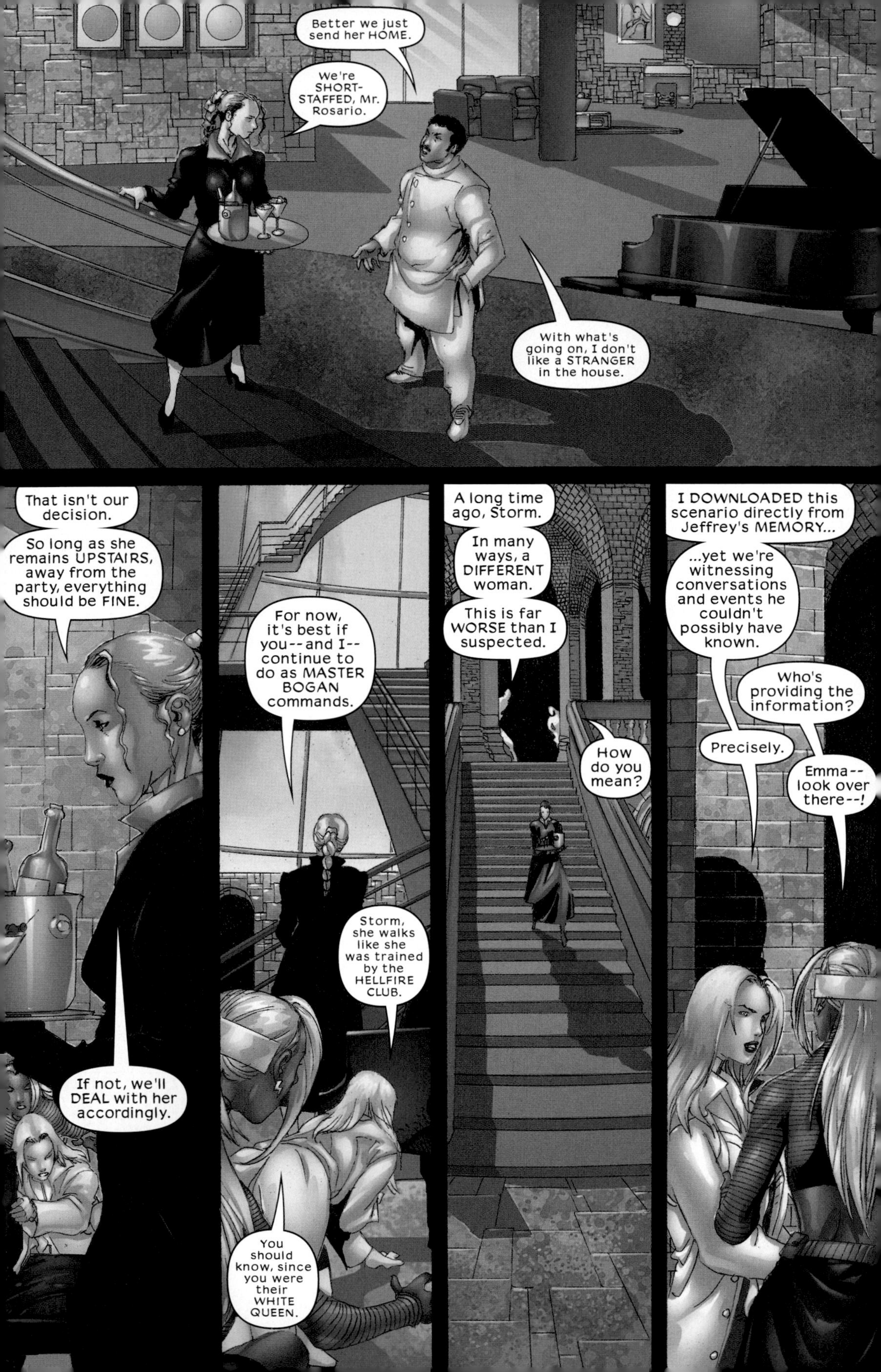

Better we just send her HOME.
We're SHORT-STAFFED, Mr. Rosario.
With what's going on, I don't like a STRANGER in the house.
That isn't our decision.
So long as she remains UPSTAIRS, away from the party, everything should be FINE.
If not, we'll DEAL with her accordingly.
For now, it's best if you--and I--continue to do as MASTER BOGAN commands.
Storm, she walks like she was trained by the HELLFIRE CLUB.
You should know, since you were their WHITE QUEEN.
A long time ago, Storm.
In many ways, a DIFFERENT woman.
This is far WORSE than I suspected.
How do you mean?
I DOWNLOADED this scenario directly from Jeffrey's MEMORY...
...yet we're witnessing conversations and events he couldn't possibly have known.
Who's providing the information?
Precisely.
Emma--look over there--!

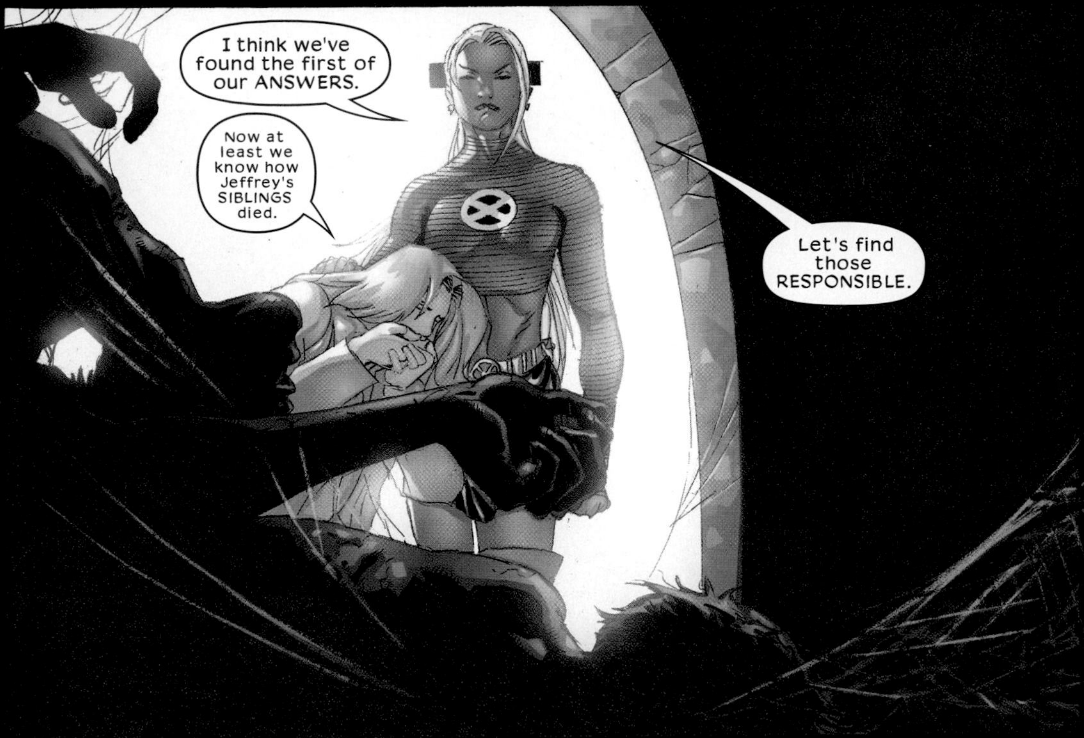
I think we've found the first of our ANSWERS.
Now at least we know how Jeffrey's SIBLINGS died.
Let's find those RESPONSIBLE.

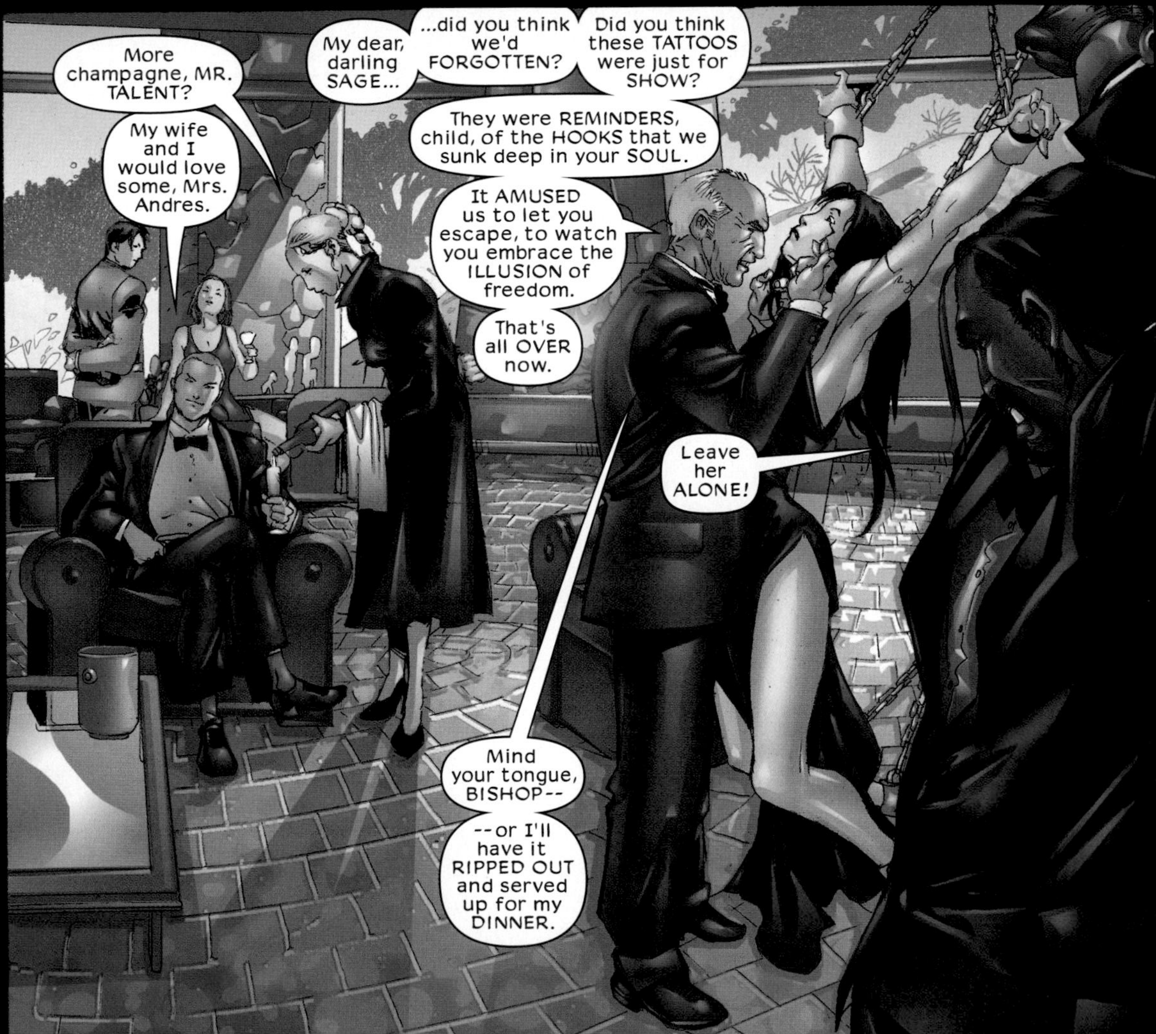
More champagne, MR. TALENT?
My wife and I would love some, Mrs. Andres.
My dear, darling SAGE...
...did you think we'd FORGOTTEN?
Did you think these TATTOOS were just for SHOW?
They were REMINDERS, child, of the HOOKS that we sunk deep in your SOUL.
It AMUSED us to let you escape, to watch you embrace the ILLUSION of freedom.
That's all OVER now.
Leave her ALONE!
Mind your tongue, BISHOP--
--or I'll have it RIPPED OUT and served up for my DINNER.

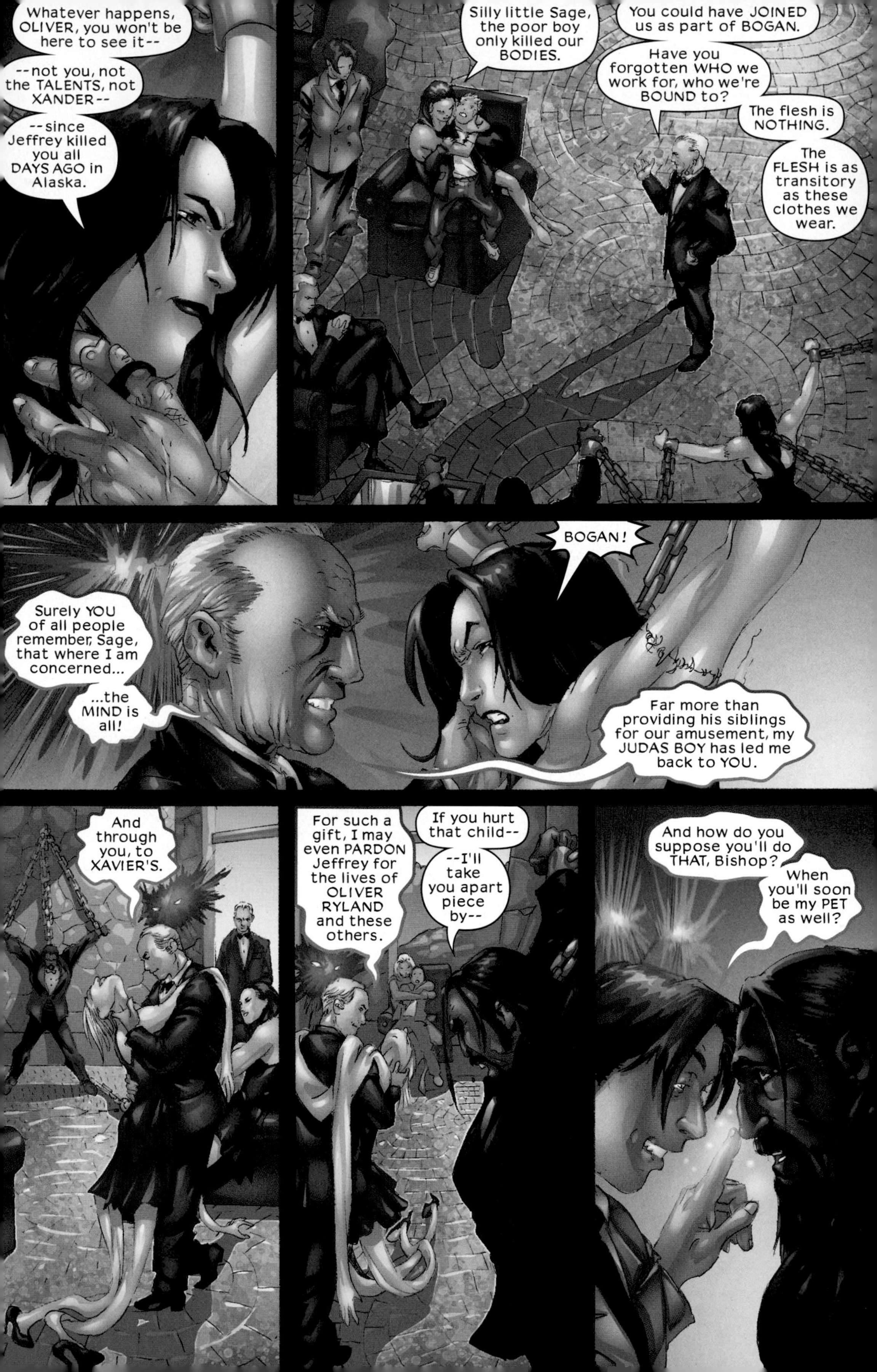
Whatever happens, OLIVER, you won't be here to see it--
--not you, not the TALENTS, not XANDER--
--since Jeffrey killed you all DAYS AGO in Alaska.
Silly little Sage, the poor boy only killed our BODIES.
You could have JOINED us as part of BOGAN.
Have you forgotten WHO we work for, who we're BOUND to?
The flesh is NOTHING.
The FLESH is as transitory as these clothes we wear.
BOGAN!
Surely YOU of all people remember, Sage, that where I am concerned...
...the MIND is all!
Far more than providing his siblings for our amusement, my JUDAS BOY has led me back to YOU.
And through you, to XAVIER'S.
For such a gift, I may even PARDON Jeffrey for the lives of OLIVER RYLAND and these others.
If you hurt that child--
--I'll take you apart piece by--
And how do you suppose you'll do THAT, Bishop?
When you'll soon be my PET as well?

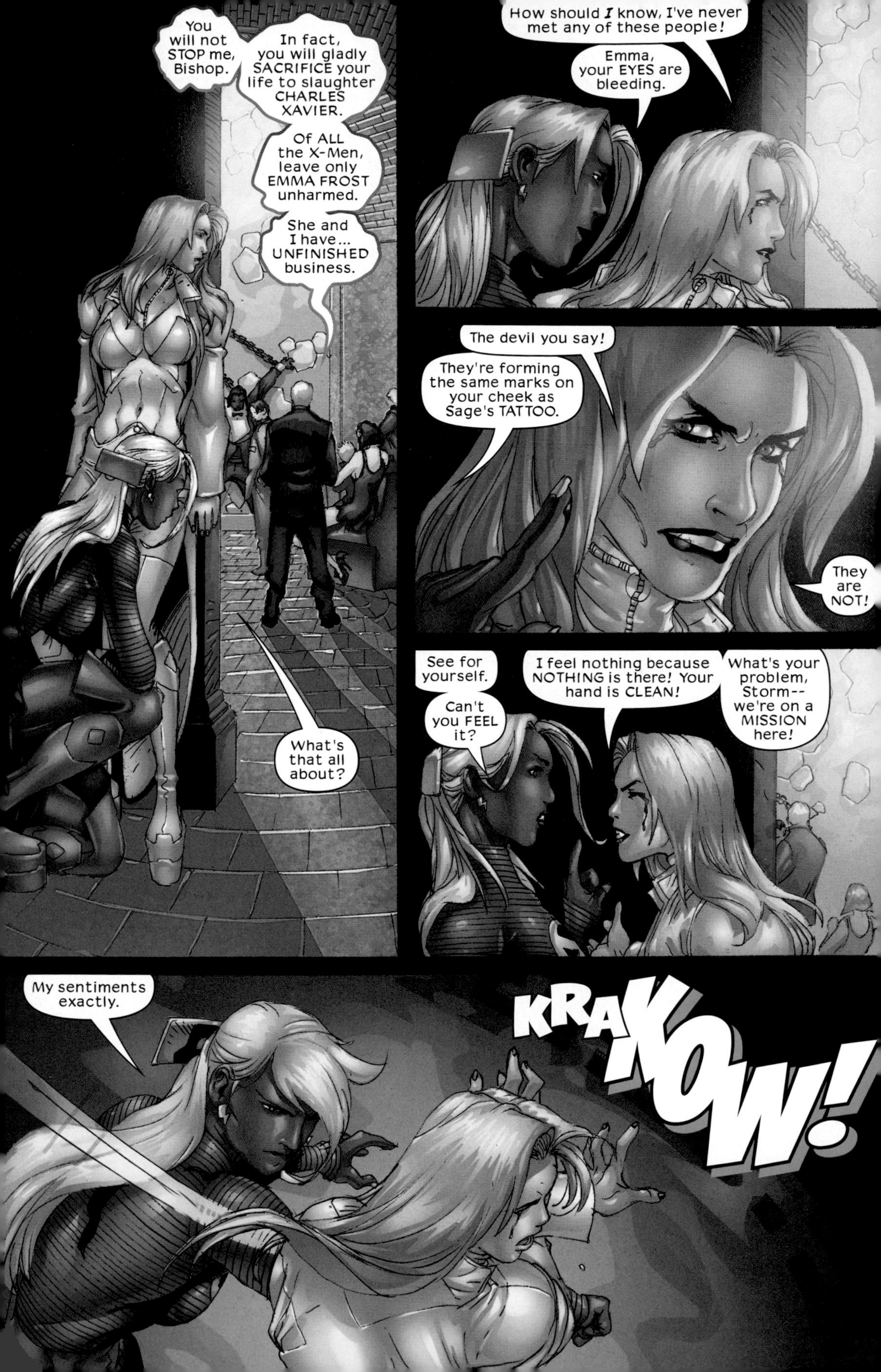
You will not STOP me, Bishop.
In fact, you will gladly SACRIFICE your life to slaughter CHARLES XAVIER.
Of ALL the X-Men, leave only EMMA FROST unharmed.
She and I have... UNFINISHED business.
What's that all about?
How should I know, I've never met any of these people!
Emma, your EYES are bleeding.
The devil you say!
They're forming the same marks on your cheek as Sage's TATTOO.
They are NOT!
See for yourself.
Can't you FEEL it?
I feel nothing because NOTHING is there! Your hand is CLEAN!
What's your problem, Storm--we're on a MISSION here!
My sentiments exactly.
KRAKOW!

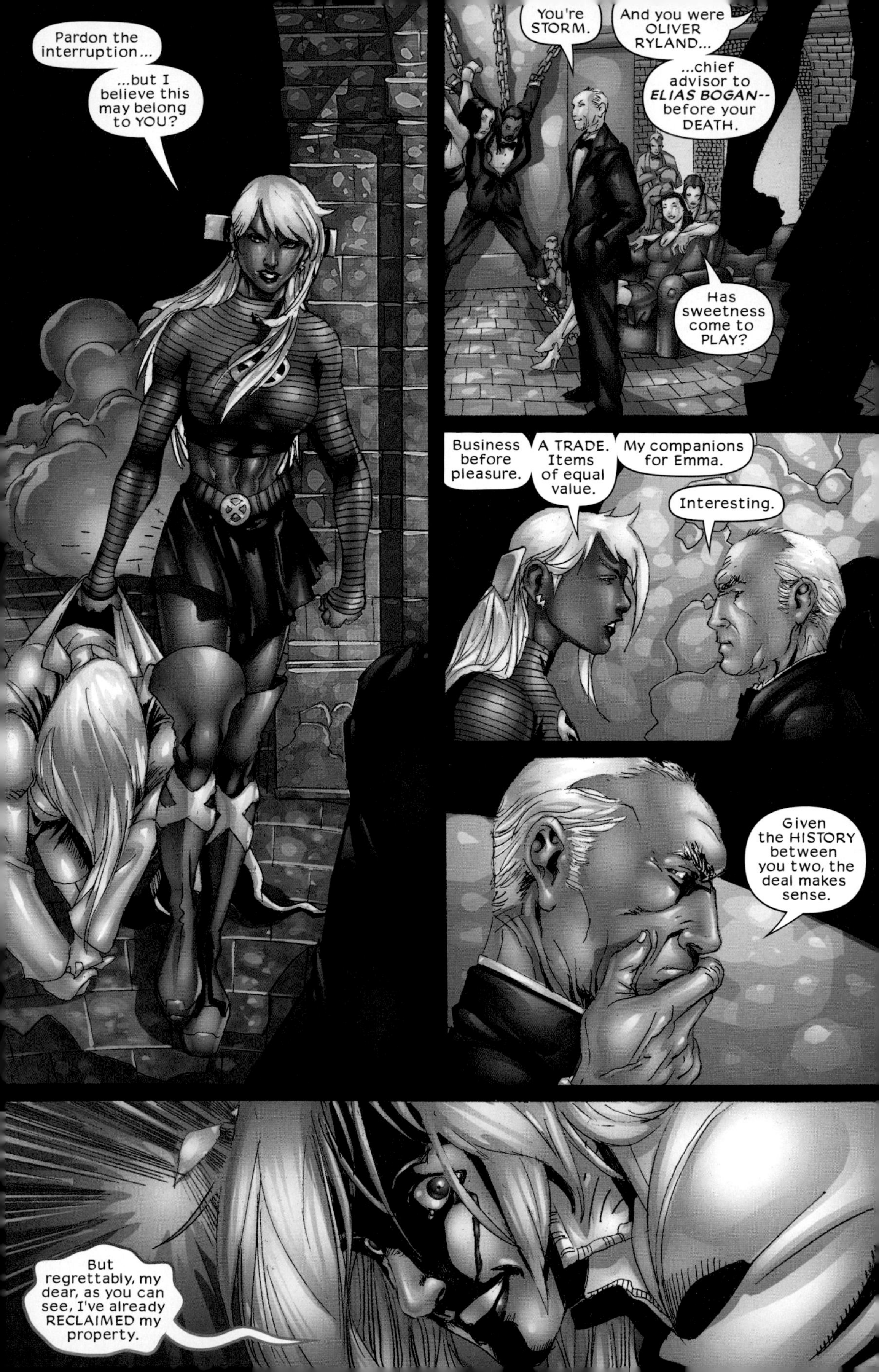
Pardon the interruption...
...but I believe this may belong to YOU?
You're STORM.
And you were OLIVER RYLAND...
...chief advisor to ELIAS BOGAN--before your DEATH.
Has sweetness come to PLAY?
Business before pleasure.
A TRADE. Items of equal value.
My companions for Emma.
Interesting.
Given the HISTORY between you two, the deal makes sense.
But regrettably, my dear, as you can see, I've already RECLAIMED my property.

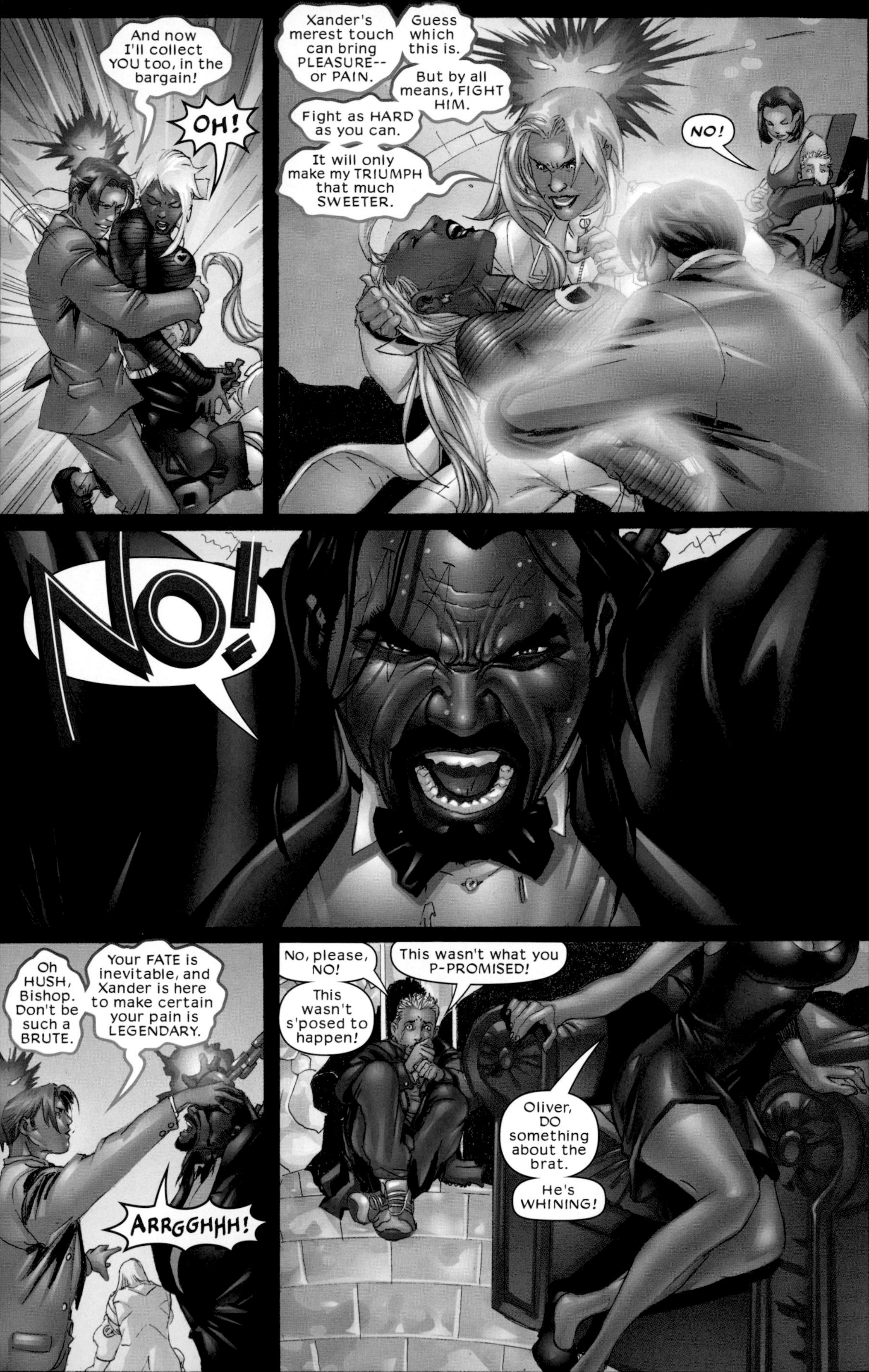

And now I'll collect YOU too, in the bargain!
OH!
Xander's merest touch can bring PLEASURE-- or PAIN.
Guess which this is.
But by all means, FIGHT HIM.
Fight as HARD as you can.
It will only make my TRIUMPH that much SWEETER.
NO!
NO!
Oh HUSH, Bishop. Don't be such a BRUTE.
Your FATE is inevitable, and Xander is here to make certain your pain is LEGENDARY.
ARRGGHHH!
No, please, NO!
This wasn't s'posed to happen!
This wasn't what you P-PROMISED!
Oliver, DO something about the brat.
He's WHINING!

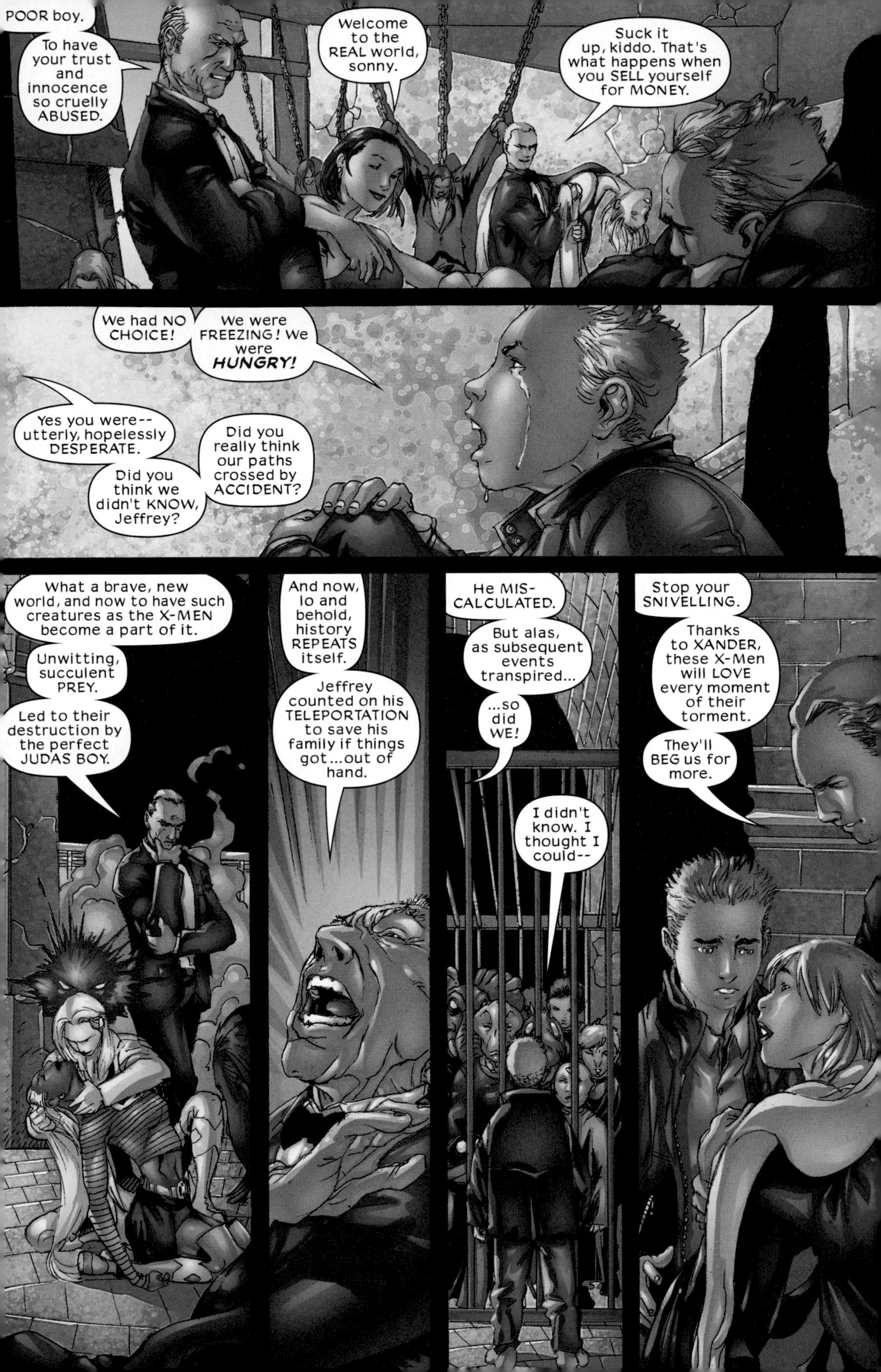
POOR boy.
To have your trust and innocence so cruelly ABUSED.
Welcome to the REAL world, sonny.
Suck it up, kiddo. That's what happens when you SELL yourself for MONEY.
We had NO CHOICE!
We were FREEZING! We were HUNGRY!
Yes you were--utterly, hopelessly DESPERATE.
Did you think we didn't KNOW, Jeffrey?
Did you really think our paths crossed by ACCIDENT?
What a brave, new world, and now to have such creatures as the X-MEN become a part of it.
Unwitting, succulent PREY.
Led to their destruction by the perfect JUDAS BOY.
And now, lo and behold, history REPEATS itself.
Jeffrey counted on his TELEPORTATION to save his family if things got...out of hand.
He MIS-CALCULATED.
But alas, as subsequent events transpired...
...so did WE!
I didn't know. I thought I could--
Stop your SNIVELLING.
Thanks to XANDER, these X-Men will LOVE every moment of their torment.
They'll BEG us for more.

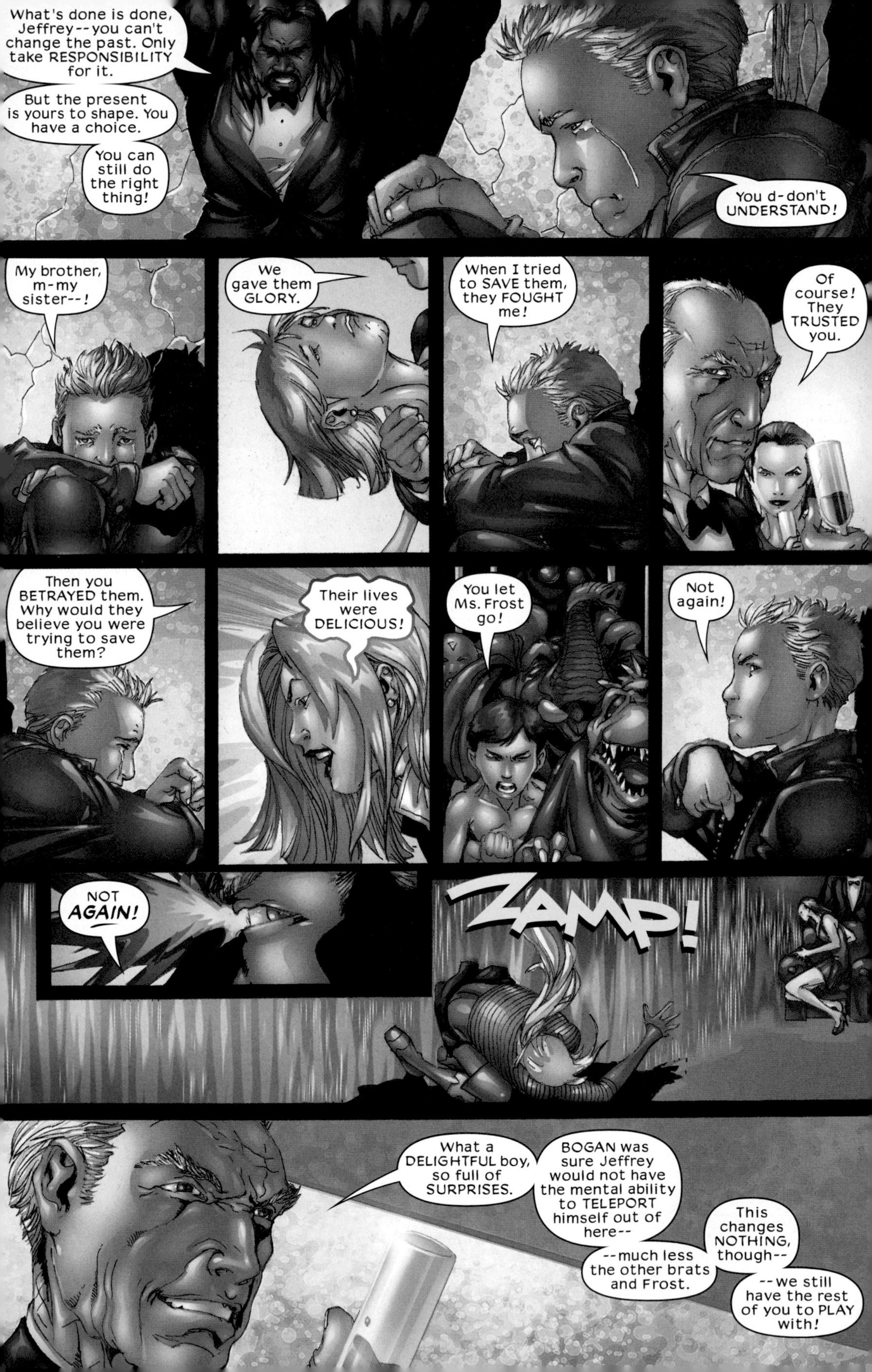

What's done is done, Jeffrey--you can't change the past. Only take RESPONSIBILITY for it.
But the present is yours to shape. You have a choice.
You can still do the right thing!
You d-don't UNDERSTAND!
My brother, m-my sister--!
We gave them GLORY.
When I tried to SAVE them, they FOUGHT me!
Of course! They TRUSTED you.
Then you BETRAYED them. Why would they believe you were trying to save them?
Their lives were DELICIOUS!
You let Ms. Frost go!
Not again!
NOT AGAIN!
ZAMP!
What a DELIGHTFUL boy, so full of SURPRISES.
BOGAN was sure Jeffrey would not have the mental ability to TELEPORT himself out of here--
--much less the other brats and Frost.
This changes NOTHING, though--
--we still have the rest of you to PLAY with!

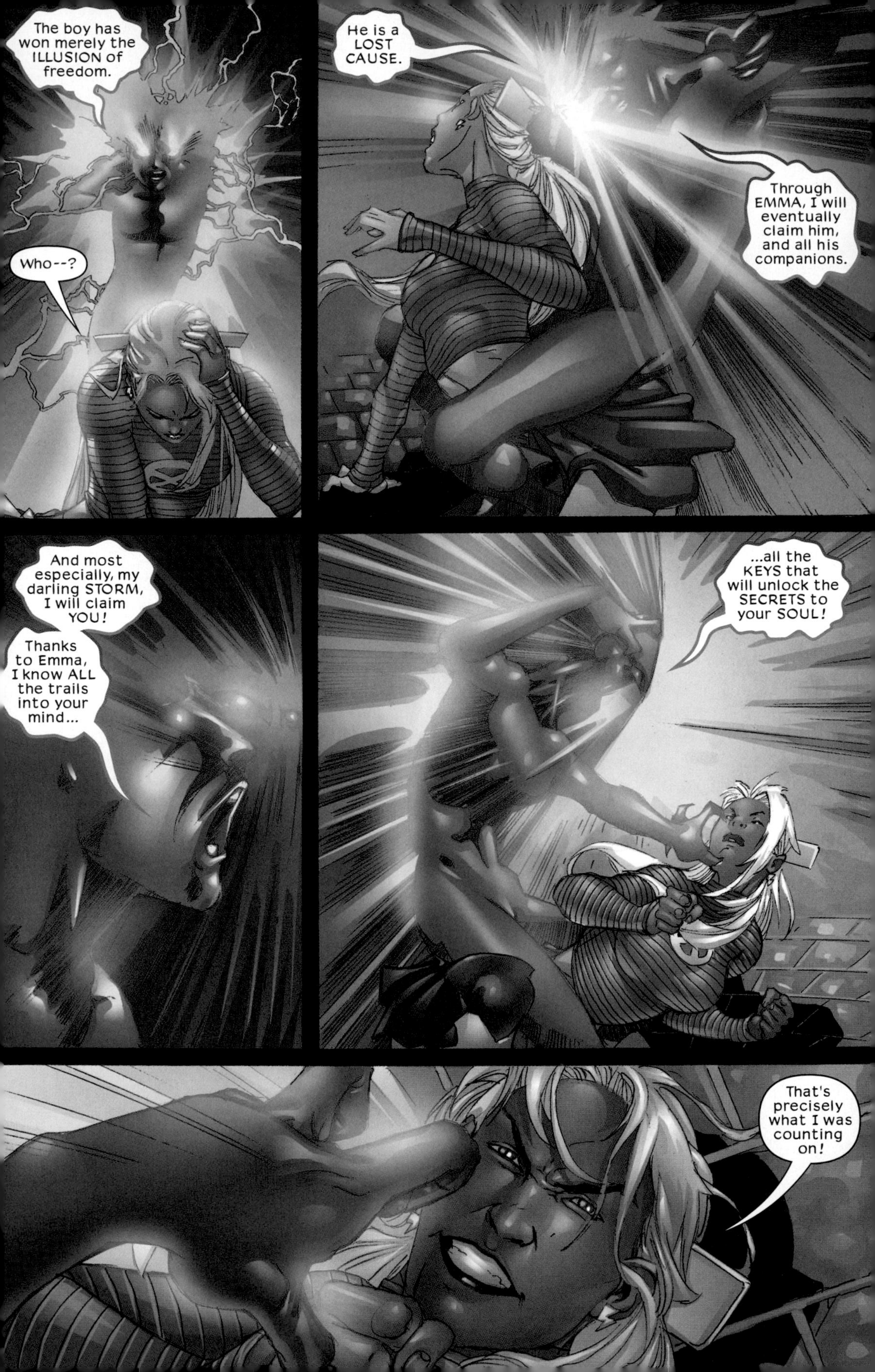
The boy has won merely the ILLUSION of freedom.
Who--?
He is a LOST CAUSE.
Through EMMA, I will eventually claim him, and all his companions.
And most especially, my darling STORM, I will claim YOU!
Thanks to Emma, I know ALL the trails into your mind...
...all the KEYS that will unlock the SECRETS to your SOUL!
That's precisely what I was counting on!

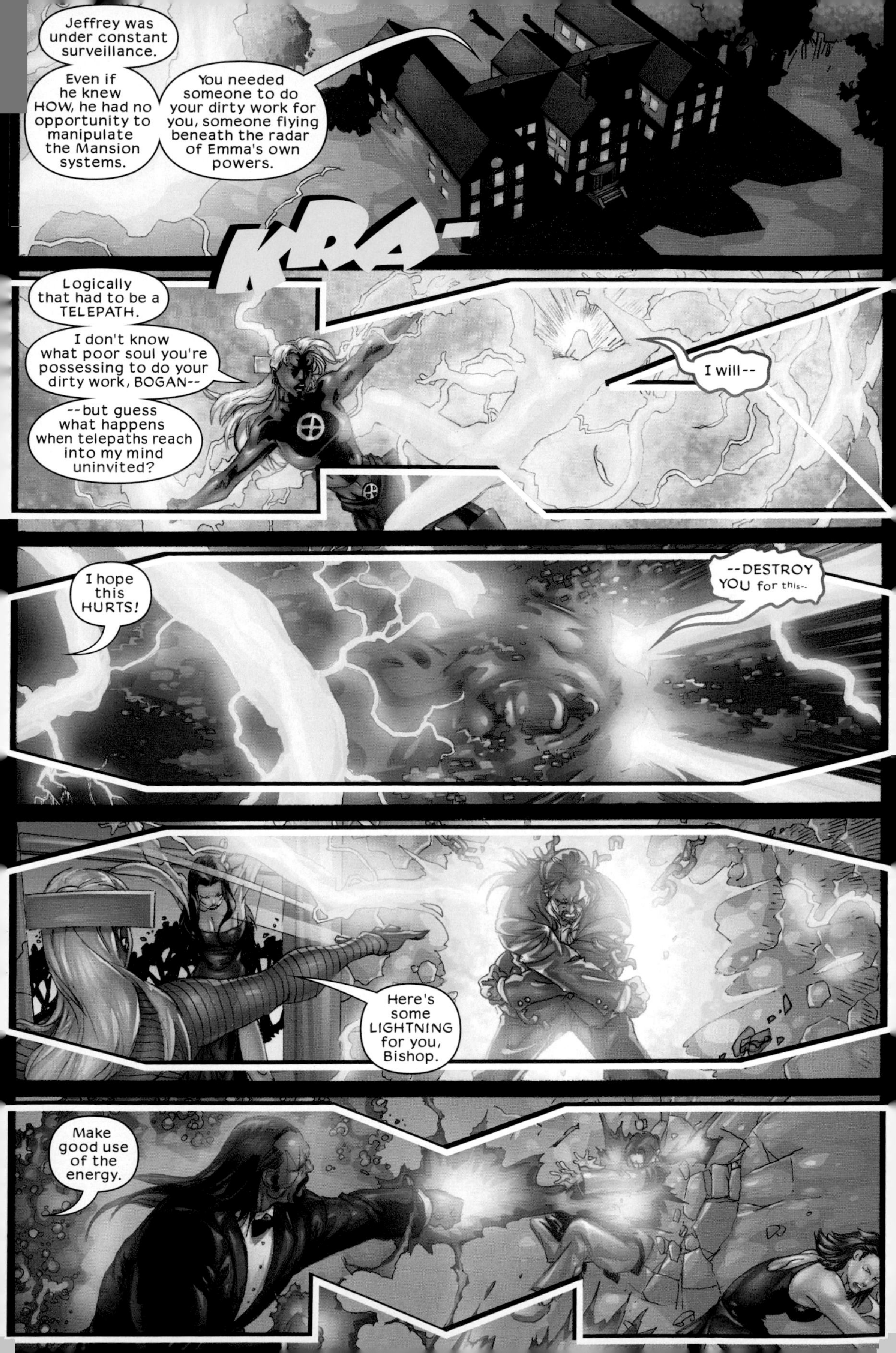
Jeffrey was under constant surveillance.
Even if he knew HOW, he had no opportunity to manipulate the Mansion systems.
You needed someone to do your dirty work for you, someone flying beneath the radar of Emma's own powers.
KRA-
Logically that had to be a TELEPATH.
I don't know what poor soul you're possessing to do your dirty work, BOGAN--
--but guess what happens when telepaths reach into my mind uninvited?
I will--
I hope this HURTS!
--DESTROY YOU for this--
Here's some LIGHTNING for you, Bishop.
Make good use of the energy.

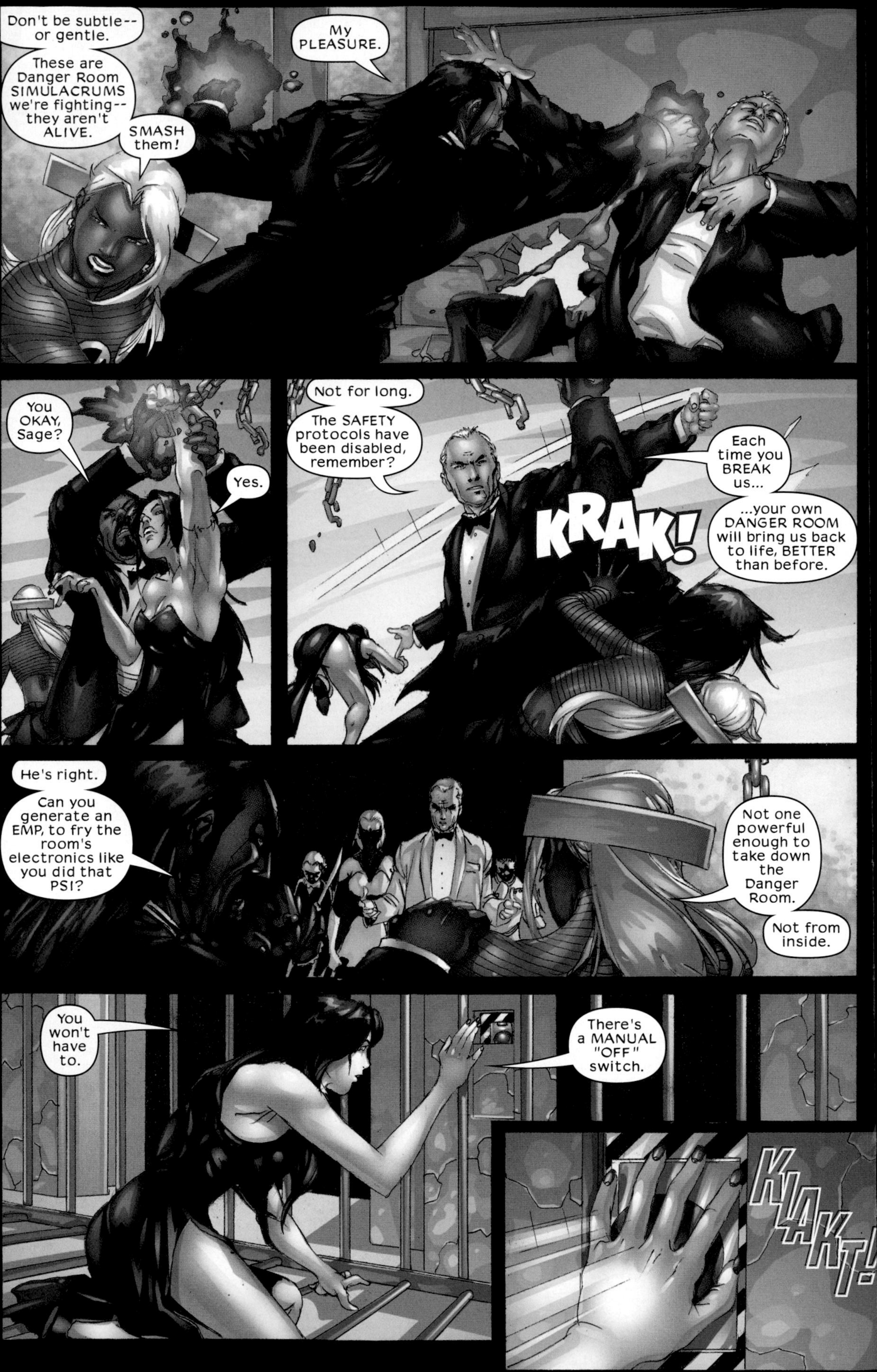
Don't be subtle-- or gentle.
These are Danger Room SIMULACRUMS we're fighting-- they aren't ALIVE.
SMASH them!
My PLEASURE.
You OKAY, Sage?
Yes.
Not for long.
The SAFETY protocols have been disabled, remember?
Each time you BREAK us...
...your own DANGER ROOM will bring us back to life, BETTER than before.
KRAK!
He's right.
Can you generate an EMP, to fry the room's electronics like you did that PSI?
Not one powerful enough to take down the Danger Room.
Not from inside.
You won't have to.
There's a MANUAL "OFF" switch.
KLAKT!

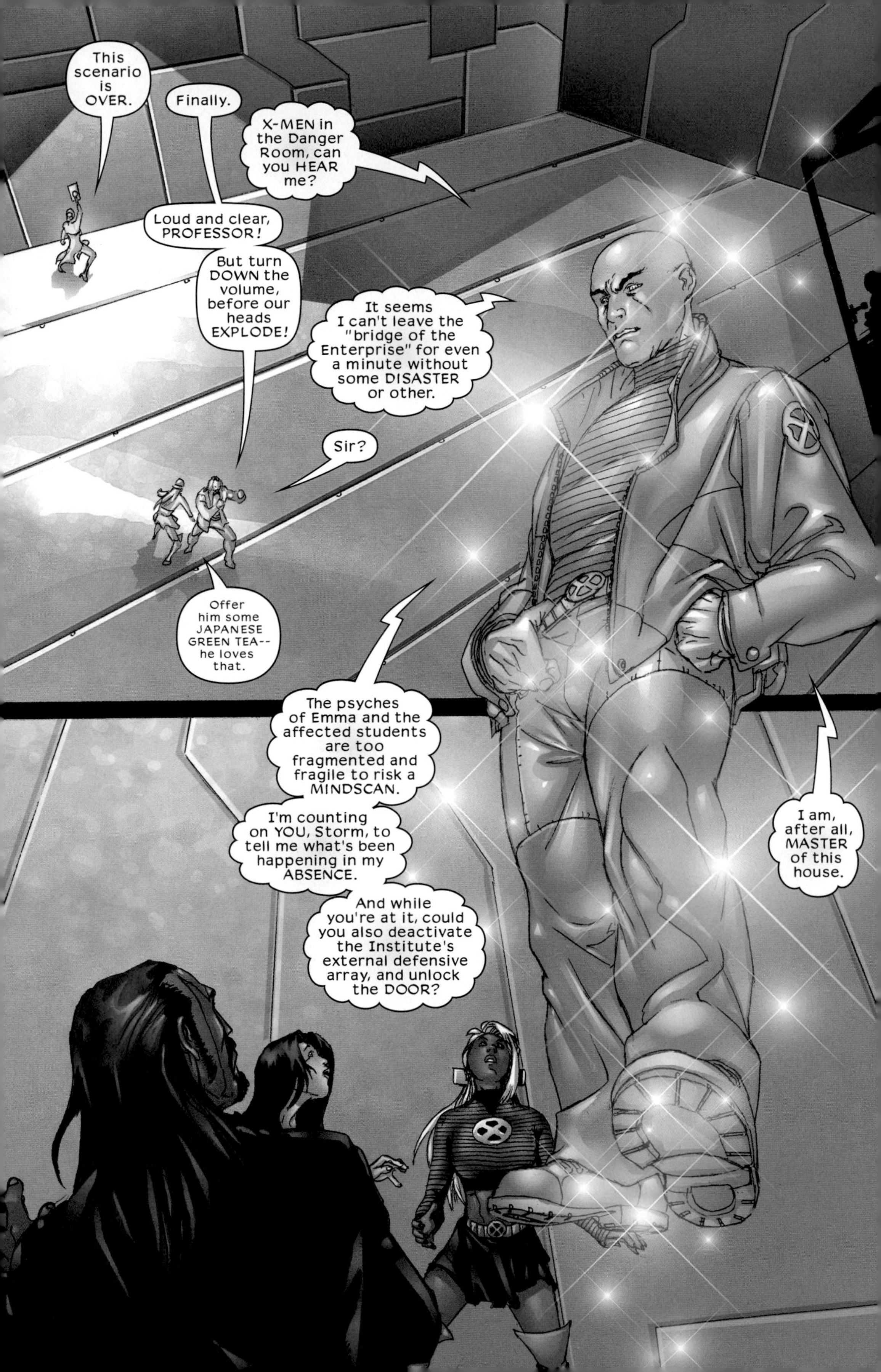
This scenario is OVER.
Finally.
X-MEN in the Danger Room, can you HEAR me?
Loud and clear, PROFESSOR!
But turn DOWN the volume, before our heads EXPLODE!
It seems I can't leave the "bridge of the Enterprise" for even a minute without some DISASTER or other.
Sir?
Offer him some JAPANESE GREEN TEA-- he loves that.
The psyches of Emma and the affected students are too fragmented and fragile to risk a MINDSCAN.
I'm counting on YOU, Storm, to tell me what's been happening in my ABSENCE.
And while you're at it, could you also deactivate the Institute's external defensive array, and unlock the DOOR?
I am, after all, MASTER of this house.

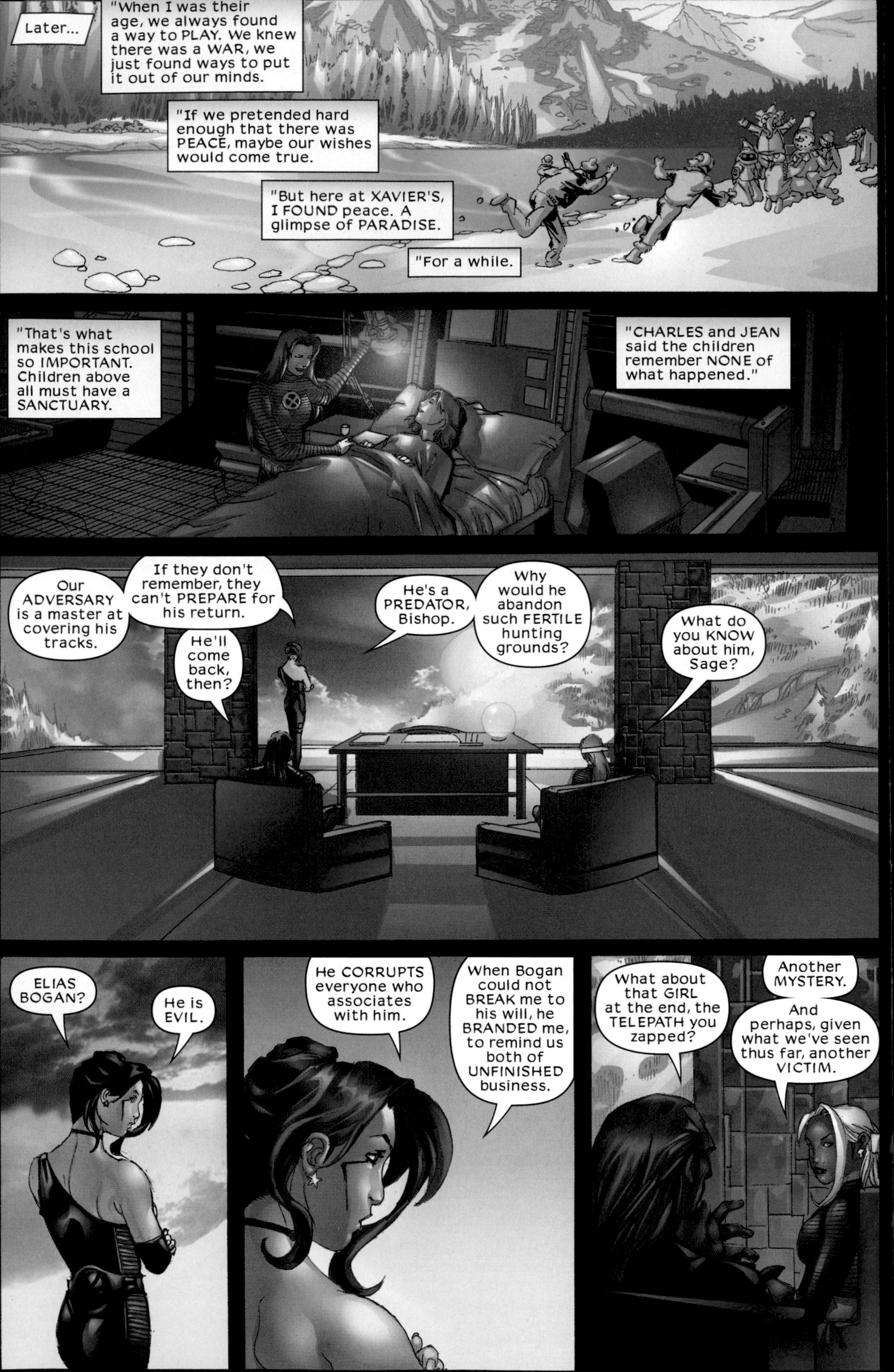
Later...
"When I was their age, we always found a way to PLAY. We knew there was a WAR, we just found ways to put it out of our minds.
"If we pretended hard enough that there was PEACE, maybe our wishes would come true.
"But here at XAVIER'S, I FOUND peace. A glimpse of PARADISE.
"For a while.
"That's what makes this school so IMPORTANT. Children above all must have a SANCTUARY.
"CHARLES and JEAN said the children remember NONE of what happened."
Our ADVERSARY is a master at covering his tracks.
If they don't remember, they can't PREPARE for his return.
He'll come back, then?
He's a PREDATOR, Bishop.
Why would he abandon such FERTILE hunting grounds?
What do you KNOW about him, Sage?
ELIAS BOGAN?
He is EVIL.
He CORRUPTS everyone who associates with him.
When Bogan could not BREAK me to his will, he BRANDED me, to remind us both of UNFINISHED business.
What about that GIRL at the end, the TELEPATH you zapped?
Another MYSTERY.
And perhaps, given what we've seen thus far, another VICTIM.

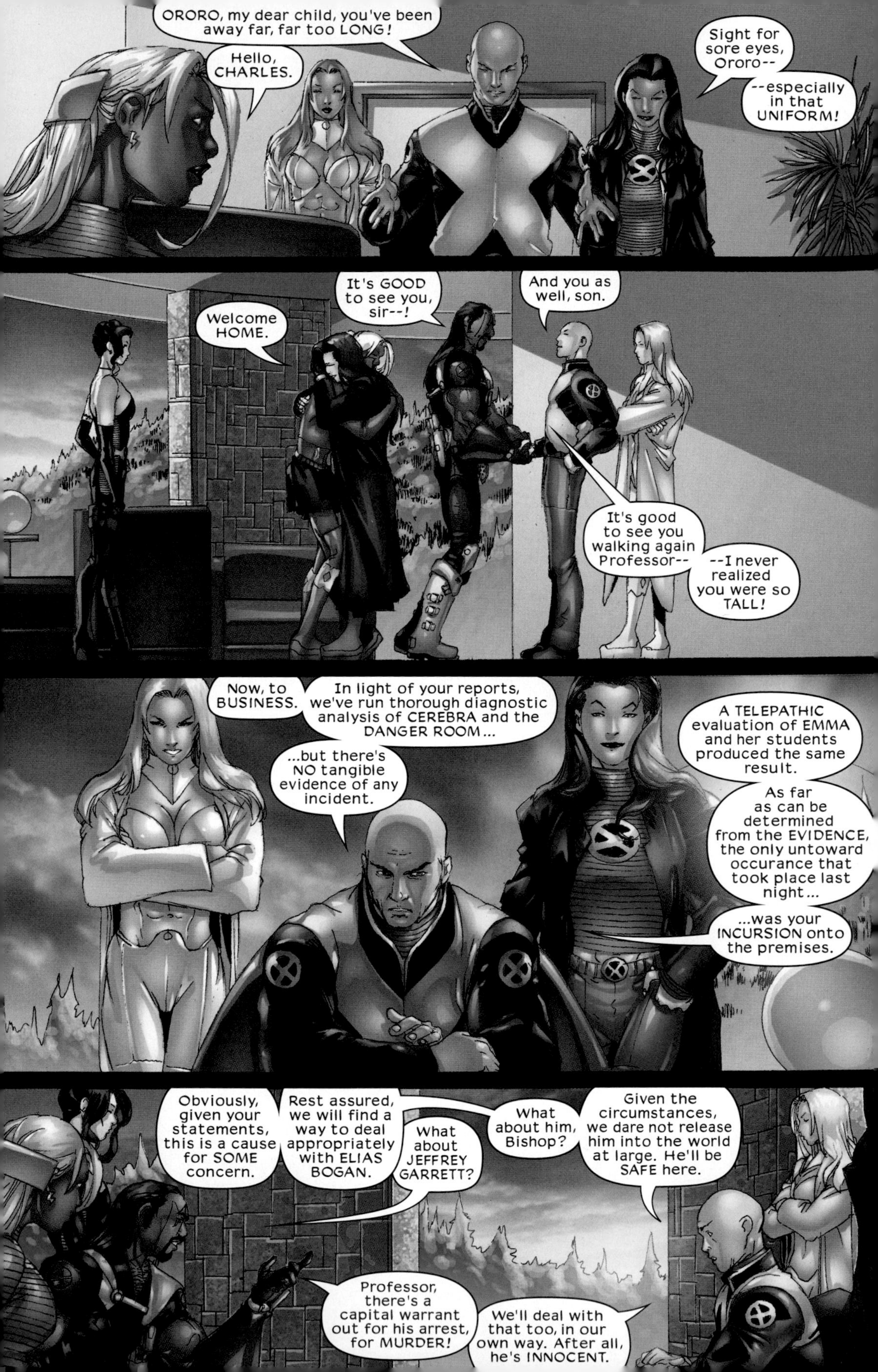
ORORO, my dear child, you've been away far, far too LONG!
Hello, CHARLES.
Sight for sore eyes, Ororo--
--especially in that UNIFORM!
Welcome HOME.
It's GOOD to see you, sir--!
And you as well, son.
It's good to see you walking again Professor--
--I never realized you were so TALL!
Now, to BUSINESS.
In light of your reports, we've run thorough diagnostic analysis of CEREBRA and the DANGER ROOM...
...but there's NO tangible evidence of any incident.
A TELEPATHIC evaluation of EMMA and her students produced the same result.
As far as can be determined from the EVIDENCE, the only untoward occurance that took place last night...
...was your INCURSION onto the premises.
Obviously, given your statements, this is a cause for SOME concern.
Rest assured, we will find a way to deal appropriately with ELIAS BOGAN.
What about JEFFREY GARRETT?
What about him, Bishop?
Given the circumstances, we dare not release him into the world at large. He'll be SAFE here.
Professor, there's a capital warrant out for his arrest, for MURDER!
We'll deal with that too, in our own way. After all, he's INNOCENT.

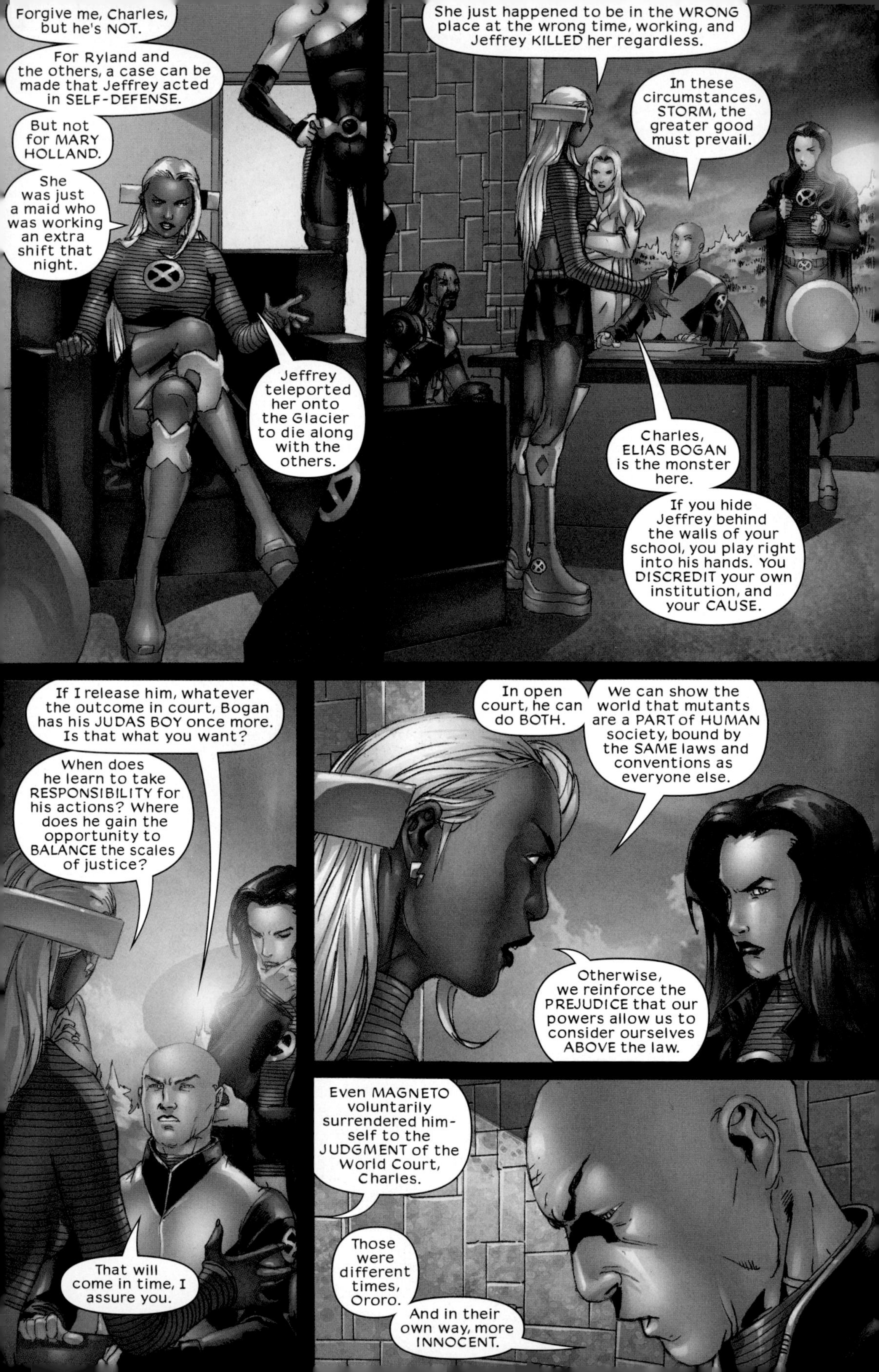
Forgive me, Charles, but he's NOT.
For Ryland and the others, a case can be made that Jeffrey acted in SELF-DEFENSE.
But not for MARY HOLLAND.
She was just a maid who was working an extra shift that night.
Jeffrey teleported her onto the Glacier to die along with the others.
She just happened to be in the WRONG place at the wrong time, working, and Jeffrey KILLED her regardless.
In these circumstances, STORM, the greater good must prevail.
Charles, ELIAS BOGAN is the monster here.
If you hide Jeffrey behind the walls of your school, you play right into his hands. You DISCREDIT your own institution, and your CAUSE.
If I release him, whatever the outcome in court, Bogan has his JUDAS BOY once more. Is that what you want?
When does he learn to take RESPONSIBILITY for his actions? Where does he gain the opportunity to BALANCE the scales of justice?
That will come in time, I assure you.
In open court, he can do BOTH.
We can show the world that mutants are a PART of HUMAN society, bound by the SAME laws and conventions as everyone else.
Otherwise, we reinforce the PREJUDICE that our powers allow us to consider ourselves ABOVE the law.
Even MAGNETO voluntarily surrendered him-self to the JUDGMENT of the World Court, Charles.
Those were different times, Ororo.
And in their own way, more INNOCENT.

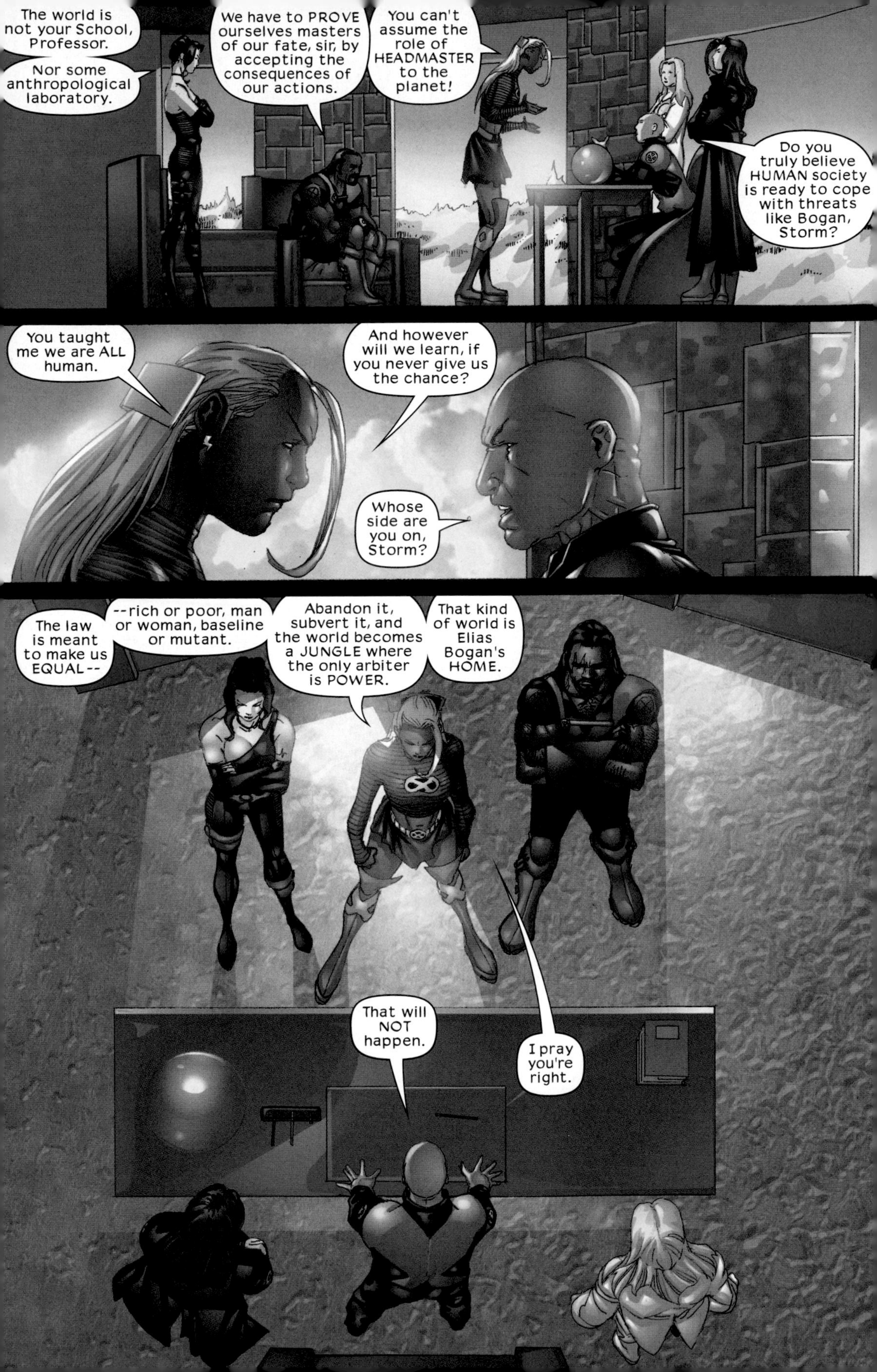
The world is not your School, Professor.
Nor some anthropological laboratory.
We have to PROVE ourselves masters of our fate, sir, by accepting the consequences of our actions.
You can't assume the role of HEADMASTER to the planet!
Do you truly believe HUMAN society is ready to cope with threats like Bogan, Storm?
You taught me we are ALL human.
And however will we learn, if you never give us the chance?
Whose side are you on, Storm?
The law is meant to make us EQUAL--
--rich or poor, man or woman, baseline or mutant.
Abandon it, subvert it, and the world becomes a JUNGLE where the only arbiter is POWER.
That kind of world is Elias Bogan's HOME.
That will NOT happen.
I pray you're right.

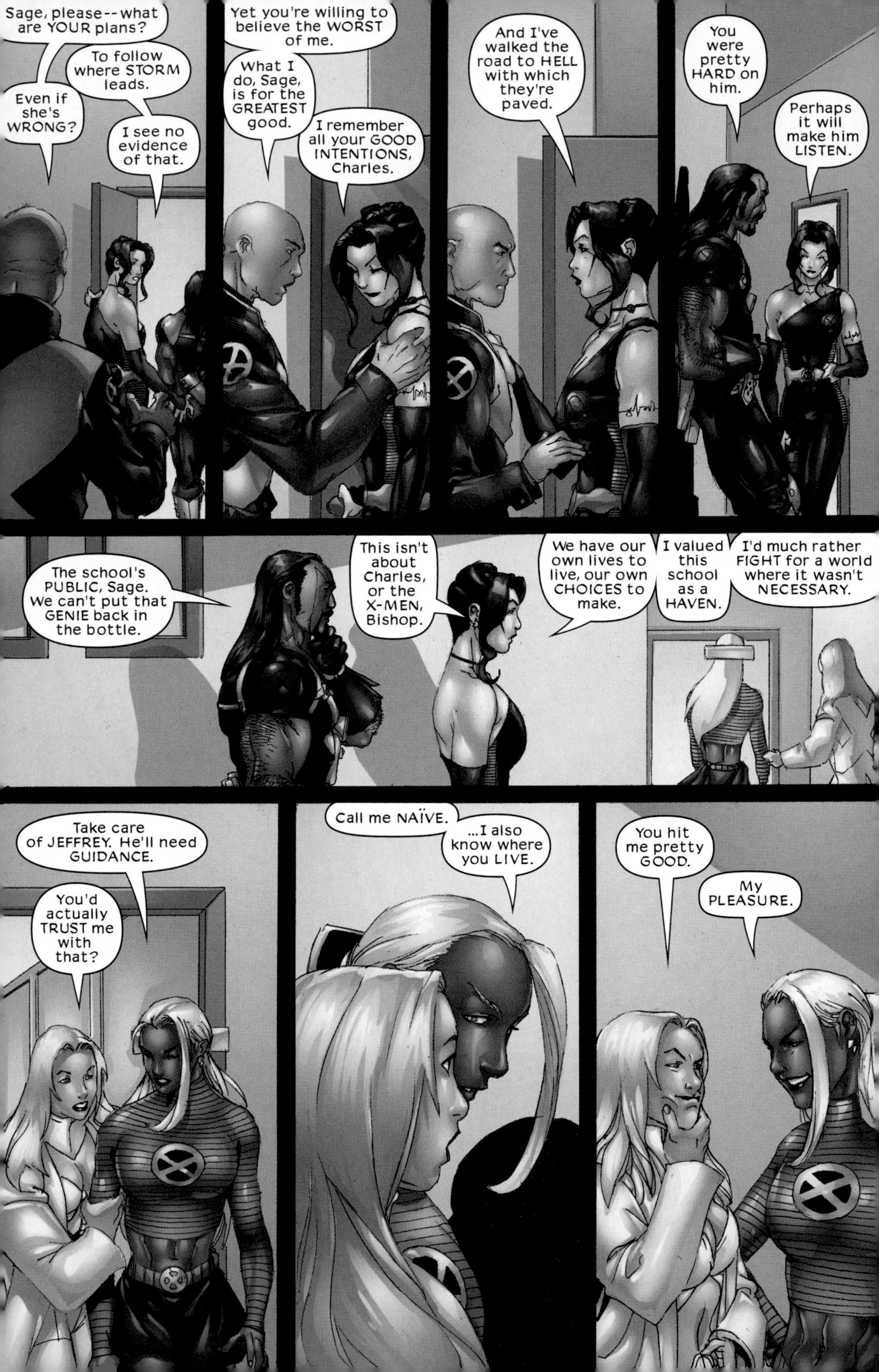
Sage, please--what are YOUR plans?
To follow where STORM leads.
Even if she's WRONG?
I see no evidence of that.
Yet you're willing to believe the WORST of me.
What I do, Sage, is for the GREATEST good.
I remember all your GOOD INTENTIONS, Charles.
And I've walked the road to HELL with which they're paved.
You were pretty HARD on him.
Perhaps it will make him LISTEN.
The school's PUBLIC, Sage. We can't put that GENIE back in the bottle.
This isn't about Charles, or the X-MEN, Bishop.
We have our own lives to live, our own CHOICES to make.
I valued this school as a HAVEN.
I'd much rather FIGHT for a world where it wasn't NECESSARY.
Take care of JEFFREY. He'll need GUIDANCE.
You'd actually TRUST me with that?
Call me NAÏVE.
...I also know where you LIVE.
You hit me pretty GOOD.
My PLEASURE.

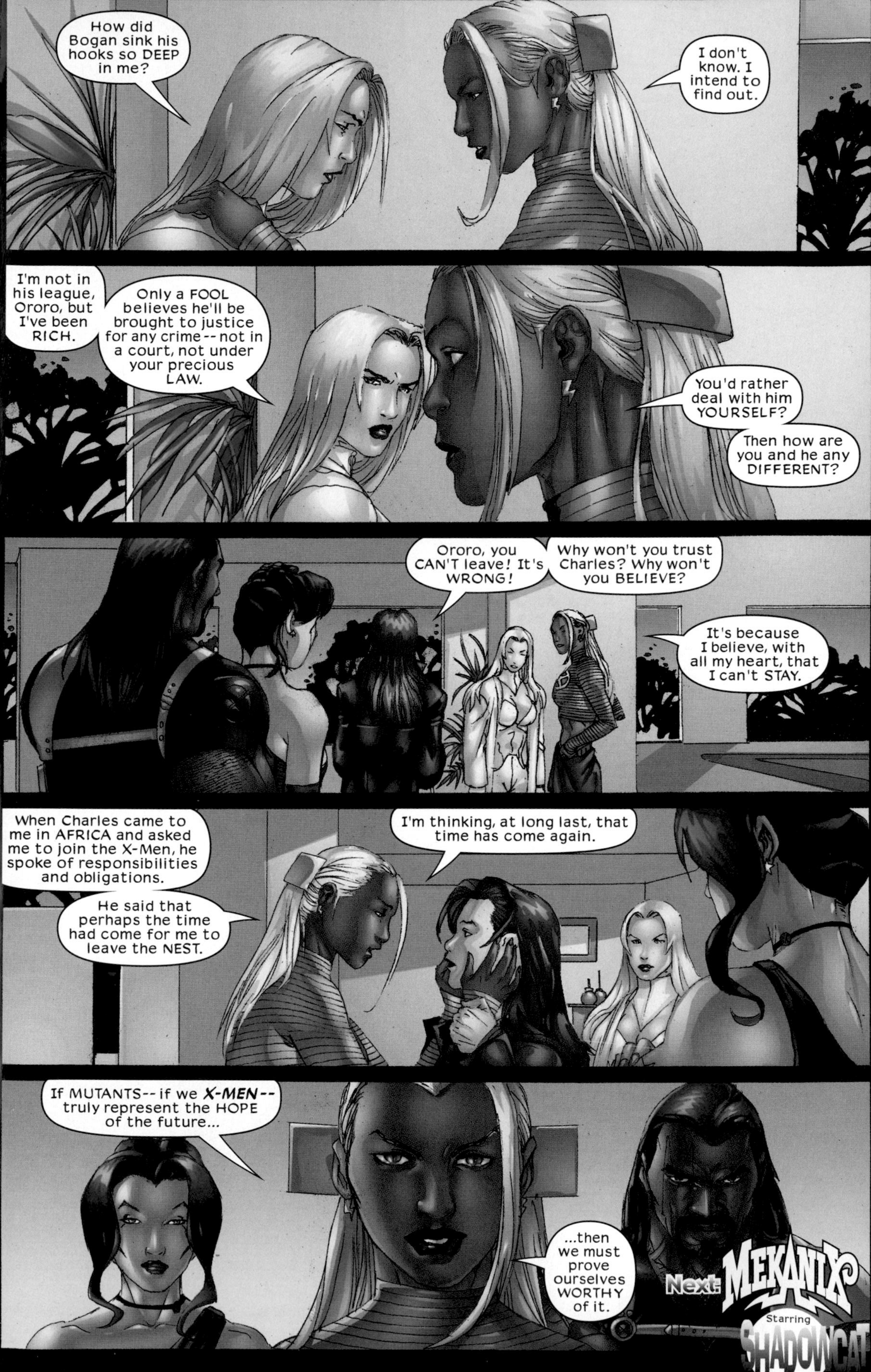
How did Bogan sink his hooks so DEEP in me?
I don't know. I intend to find out.
I'm not in his league, Ororo, but I've been RICH.
Only a FOOL believes he'll be brought to justice for any crime -- not in a court, not under your precious LAW.
You'd rather deal with him YOURSELF?
Then how are you and he any DIFFERENT?
Ororo, you CAN'T leave! It's WRONG!
Why won't you trust Charles? Why won't you BELIEVE?
It's because I believe, with all my heart, that I can't STAY.
When Charles came to me in AFRICA and asked me to join the X-Men, he spoke of responsibilities and obligations.
He said that perhaps the time had come for me to leave the NEST.
I'm thinking, at long last, that time has come again.
If MUTANTS-- if we X-MEN-- truly represent the HOPE of the future...
...then we must prove ourselves WORTHY of it.
Next: MEKANIX
Starring
SHADOWCAT

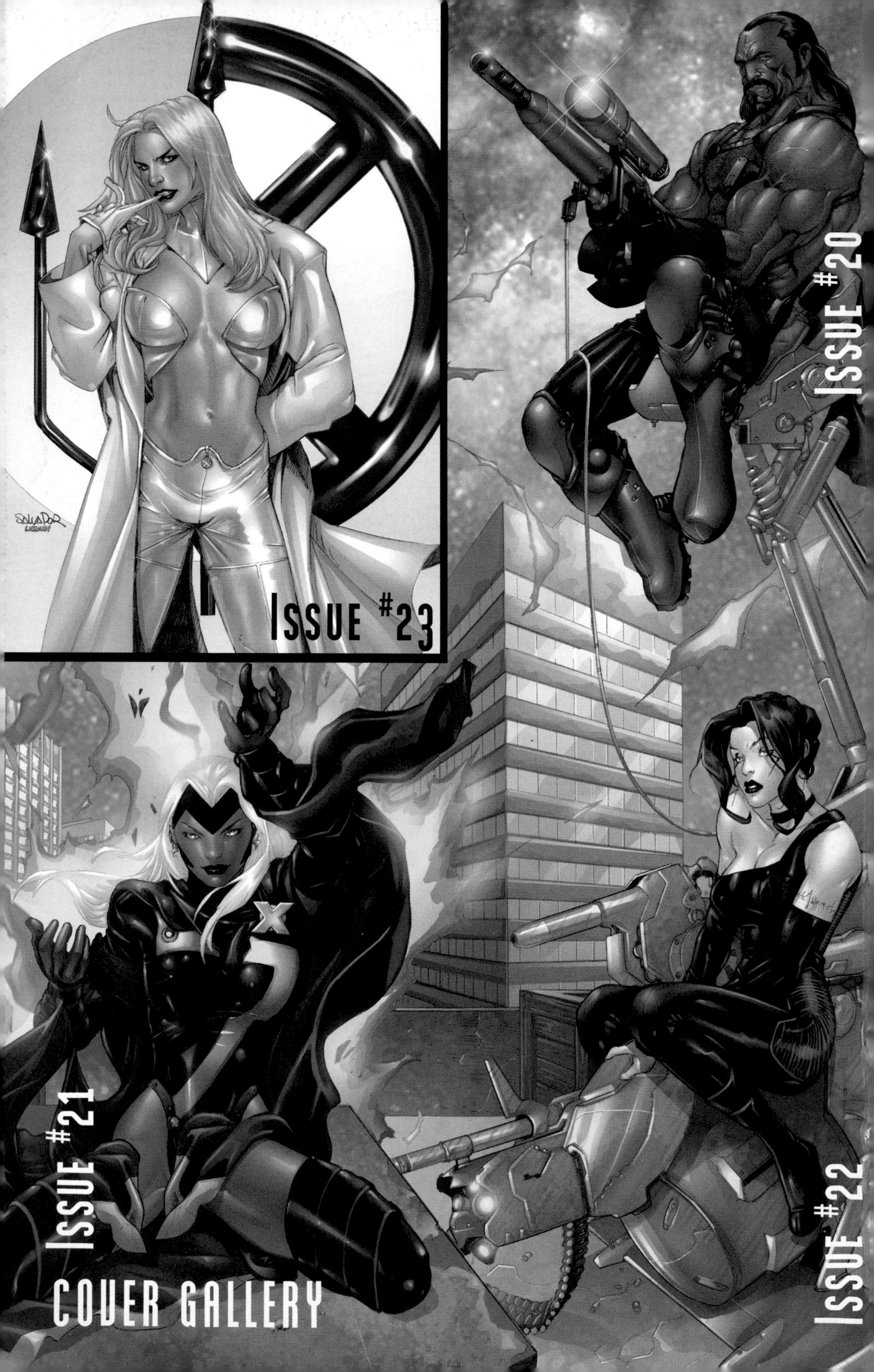
Issue #23
Issue #20
Issue #21
Issue #22
COVER GALLERY
SALVADOR LIQUIDI